Literature, Criticism, and Style

Revised Edition

Steven Croft and Helen Cross

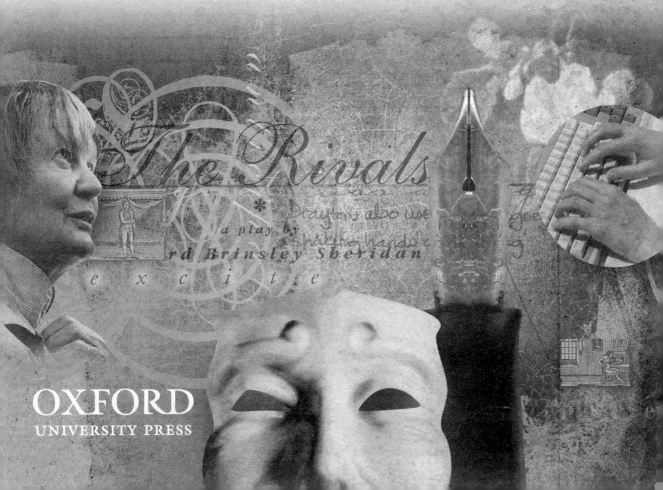

OXFORD
UNIVERSITY PRESS

OXFORD
UNIVERSITY PRESS

Great Clarendon Street, Oxford OX2 6DP
Oxford University Press is a department of the University of Oxford.
It furthers the University's objective of excellence in research, scholarship, and
education by publishing worldwide in

Oxford New York
Auckland Bangkok Buenos Aires Cape Town Chennai
Dar es Salaam Delhi Hong Kong Istanbul Karachi Kolkata
Kuala Lumpur Madrid Melbourne Mexico City Mumbai Nairobi
São Paulo Shanghai Taipei Tokyo Toronto

Oxford is a registered trade mark of Oxford University Press
in the UK and in certain other countries

© Steven Croft and Helen Cross 2000
First published 1997
Revised Edition published 2000
10 9 8 7 6

A CIP catalogue record for this book is available from the British Library

ISBN 0 19831473 6

Cover image by Gary Thompson
Illustrative montages by Gary Thompson pp. 1, 6, 47, 85, 109, 150, 171, 179,
187, 193, 217, 239, 265, 297, 309, 317, 322; line work heads by John Dunne pp.
6, 34, 47, 79, 85, 98, 140, 150, 165, 171, 187, 193, 239, 249, 283, 322
Handwriting by Kathy Baxendale pp. 176, 177, 314, 315

Orders and enquiries to Customer Services:
Tel: 01536 741068   Fax 01536 454519

Designed and Typeset by Mike Brain Graphic Design Limited, Oxford
Printed in Great Britain by The Bath Press, Bath

Contents

Acknowledgements

• •

The authors and publisher are grateful for permission to reprint the following copyright material:

Margaret Atwood: extracts from *The Handmaid's Tale* (Cape, 1986, Virago, 1997), copyright © O. W. Toad Ltd 1985, reprinted by permission of Curtis Brown Ltd, London, and written permission of McClelland and Stewart, Inc, the Canadian Publishers.

Iain Banks: extract from *The Crow Road* (Abacus, 1995), reprinted by permission of Little Brown, London.

Laurence Binyon: 'For the Fallen (September 1914)' from *Collected Poems 1869–1943*, 2 vols. (Macmillan), reprinted by permission of The Society of Authors on behalf of the Laurence Binyon Estate.

Alison Brackenbury: 'School Dinners' from *Christmas Roses and Other Poems* (1988) reprinted by permission of the publishers, Carcanet Press Ltd.

Vera Brittain: extract from *Testament of Youth*, (first published by Victor Gollancz Ltd 1933), © Literary Executors of Vera Brittain 1970, reprinted by permission of her literary executor, Mark Bostridge, and Victor Gollancz Ltd.

Rupert Brooke: letter to Katharine Cox from *The Letters of Rupert Brooke* edited by Geoffrey Keynes (1968), reprinted by permission of the publisher, Faber & Faber Ltd.

Angela Carter: extract from 'The Snow Pavilion' first published in *New Stories 4* (Hutchinson, 1979), copyright © Angela Carter 1979, reprinted by permission of the Estate of Angela Carter c/o Rogers, Coleridge & White, 20 Powis Mews, London W11 1JN.

Wendy Cope: 'Engineers' Corner' from *Making Cocoa for Kingsley Amis* by Wendy Cope (1986), reprinted by permission of the publishers, Faber & Faber Ltd.

Richard Curtis: 'Sons and Aztecs' from *The Faber Book of Parodies* edited by Simon Brett, reprinted by permission of PFD on behalf of Richard Curtis.

Elizabeth Daryush: 'Anger lay by me all night long' from *Collected Poems* edited by D. Davie (1976), reprinted by permission of the publishers, Carcanet Press Ltd.

Margaret Drabble: extract from 'Hassan's Tower' in *Winter's Tales* (Macmillan, 1966), copyright © Margaret Drabble 1966, reprinted by permission of PFD on behalf of Margaret Drabble.

Carol Ann Duffy: 'Mean Time', 'Havisham', 'Confession', 'First Love', and 'Stuffed' from *Mean Time* by Carol Ann Duffy (Anvil Press Poetry, 1993), reprinted by permission of the publisher.

Gavin Ewart: 'Ending' from *No Fool Like an Old Fool* (Victor Gollancz, 1976), reprinted by permission of Margo Ewart.

E. M. Forster: extract from *A Passage to India* (1924) reprinted by permission of The Provost and Scholars of King's College, Cambridge, and The Society of Authors as the literary representatives of the E. M. Forster Estate.

Brian Friel: extract from *Making History* (1989), reprinted by permission of the publishers, Faber & Faber Ltd.

Paul Fussell: extract from introduction to *The Bloody Game: An Anthology of Modern War*, edited by Paul Fussell (Scribners, London 1991), reprinted by permission of Little, Brown and Company (UK).

John Galsworthy: extract from *Strife* (Duckworth, 1964), reprinted by permission of C. Sinclair Stevenson.

Jane Gardam: 'Stone Trees' from *Pangs of Love* by Jane Gardam (Hamish Hamilton), reprinted by permission of David Higham Associates.

Grahame Greene: 'I Spy' from *Twenty-One Stories* by Grahame Greene (Heinemann, 1954), reprinted by permission of David Higham Associates.

Seamus Heaney: 'Mother of the Groom' from *Wintering Out* by Seamus Heaney and 'Digging' from *Death of a Naturalist* reprinted by permission of the publishers, Faber & Faber Ltd.

John Hersey: extract from *Hiroshima* (Hamish Hamilton, 1966, Penguin revised edition, 1968), copyright © 1946 by John Hersey, copyright © renewed 1973 by John Hersey, copyright © John Hersey 1985, reprinted by permission of Penguin Books Ltd.

Susan Hill: extracts from 'Missy' and 'Halloran's Child' taken from *A Bit of Singing and Dancing* by Susan Hill, (Hamish Hamilton), copyright © Susan Hill, 1971, 1972, 1973, reprinted by permission of Sheil Land Associates Ltd.

A. E. Housman: 'Eight O'Clock' from *Last Poems* reprinted by permission of The Society of Authors as the literary representative of the Estate of A. E. Housman.

Ted Hughes: 'Wind', 'Swifts', and 'Second Glance at a Jaguar', all from *New Selected Poems 1957-1994*, reprinted by permission of the publishers, Faber & Faber Ltd.

Ruth Prawer Jhabvala: extract from *Heat and Dust* (1975) reprinted by permission of the publisher, John Murray (Publishers) Ltd.

James Joyce: extract from 'The Boarding House' from *Dubliners*, copyright © Estate of James Joyce, reprinted by permission of the Estate of James Joyce.

Brian Keenan: extract from *An Evil Cradling* (Hutchinson, 1992), reprinted by permission of The Random House Group on behalf of Brian Keenan.

Philip Larkin: 'Naturally the Foundation Will Pay Your Expenses' from *Collected Poems* (1988), reprinted by permission of the publishers, Faber & Faber Ltd.

D. H. Lawrence: extract from *The Rainbow* (Penguin, 1949), reprinted by permission of Laurence Pollinger Ltd and the Estate of Frieda Lawrence Ravagli.

Felicia Hardison Londre: extract from 'A Streetcar Running Fifty Years' in *The Cambridge Companion to Tennessee Williams* edited by Matthew C. Roundane (Cambridge University Press, 1997), reprinted by permission of the publisher.

Ian McEwan: extracts from *Enduring Love* (Jonathan Cape, 1997), copyright © Ian McEwan 1997, reprinted by permission of the Random House Group Ltd, Alfred A. Knopf, Inc., and the author, c/o Rogers Coleridge & White; extract from an Interview with Ian McEwan by Professor Christopher Ricks on *The Book Programme*, BBC 2, 7th March 1979, reprinted by permission of the BBC and the author, c/o Rogers Coleridge & White; and extract from an interview with Ian McEwan by Eric Schoek of the Capitola Book Cafe, © 1995 Capitola Book Cafe, reprinted by permission of the author, c/o Rogers Coleridge & White.

Iris Murdoch: extracts from *The Bell* (Chatto & Windus), reprinted by permission of The Random House Group Ltd.

Grace Nichols: 'The Fat Black Woman Goes Shopping' from *The Fat Black Woman's Poems* (Virago, 1984), copyright © Grace Nichols 1984, reprinted by permission of Curtis Brown Ltd, London, on behalf of Grace Nichols.

Wilfred Owen: letter to Susan Owen from *Wilfred Owen: Collected Letters* edited by Harold Owen and John Bell (1967), copyright © Oxford University Press 1967, reprinted by permission of Oxford University Press.

John Pilger: extract from 'Video Nasties' in *Distant Voices* by John Pilger (Vintage, 1992), reprinted by permission of David Higham Associates.

Sylvia Plath: 'Frog Autumn' from *Collected Poems* (1981), reprinted by permission of the publishers, Faber & Faber Ltd.

Willy Russell: extract from *Educating Rita* (Methuen, 1985), copyright © 1985 by Willy Russell, reprinted by permission of the publisher.

Siegfried Sassoon: 'Base Details' from *Collected Poems 1908–1956* (Faber, 1984), Copyright Siegfried Sassoon, reprinted by permission of George Sassoon, c/o Barbara Levy Literary Agency.

Iain Crichton Smith: 'To My Mother' from *Selected Poems* (1985), reprinted by permission of the publishers, Carcanet Press Ltd.

Alice Walker: extract from *The Color Purple* (The Women's Press Ltd, 1983), reprinted by permission of David Higham Associates.

Elizabeth Walter: extract from 'Dual Control' from *Dead Women and Other Haunting Experiences* by Elizabeth Walter (Collins Harvill, 1975), copyright © Elizabeth Walter 1975, reprinted by permission of A. M. Heath & Company Ltd.

Fay Weldon: extract from *Praxis* (Hodder & Stoughton, 1980) copyright © Fay Weldon 1980, reprinted by permission of the publisher and Curtis Brown Group Ltd on behalf of the author.

Tennessee Williams: extracts from *A Streetcar Named Desire* (New Directions), copyright © 1947,1953 by Tennessee Williams, renewed 1975, 1981 The University of the South, reprinted by permission of Casarotto Ramsay Ltd on behalf of The University of the South, Sewanee, Tennessee and New Directions Publishing Corp. All Rights whatsoever in this play are strictly reserved and application for performance etc. must be made before rehearsal to Casarotto Ramsay Ltd., National House, 60-66 Wardour Street, London W1V 4ND. No performance may be given unless a licence has been obtained.

Oscar Wilde: extract from letter to Lord Alfred Douglas from *The Letters of Oscar Wilde* edited by Merlin Holland and Sir Rupert Hart-Davis, letters copyright © the Estate of Oscar Wilde 1962, 1985, 2000, editorial matter © Sir Rupert Hart-Davis 1962, 1985, 2000, Merlin Holland 2000, reprinted by permission of Fourth Estate Ltd.

Jeanette Winterson: extract from *Oranges Are Not the Only Fruit* (Pandora Press, 1985), reprinted by permission of the author.

Virginia Woolf: extract from *Orlando* (Hogarth Press, 1928), reprinted by permission of The Society of Authors as the Literary Representative of the Estate of Virginia Woolf.

We are also grateful to the following students for allowing us to use their responses as examples: Julia Landon, Louise Marshall, James Parkinson, Richard J Smith and Ian Swainson; and to the following for permission to reproduce material from examination papers and specimen papers: The Associated Examining Board (AEB), Northern Examinations and Assessment Board (NEAB). Any example answers to examination questions or hints on answers used in this book are the sole responsibility of the authors and have not been provided or approved by the examining boards.

We have tried to trace and contact all copyright holders before publication. If notified the publishers will be pleased to rectify any errors or omissions at the earliest opportunity.

Section I
Encountering Literature

1 An Introduction to AS- and A-level Literature Study

Reasons for choosing to study English Literature at A-level or AS-level can vary tremendously. Some sixth-form students choose the subject because they have always loved English and want to go on to study it at Higher Education level. Others choose it simply because they enjoyed English at GCSE level and achieved a reasonable result.

However, English is also a popular choice with 'mature' students. Very often the circumstances under which these students study are rather different from those of the school-based student. They might be studying the course over one year by attending an evening class at the local college or they might be attending workshop sessions at a college, or studying at home on a distance learning or correspondence basis.

Whatever your individual circumstances, though, the work that you will need to complete and the demands of assessment will be exactly the same. Obviously, everyone is an individual and one of the great strengths of English is that it encourages and requires the development of that individuality through studies that are stimulating, challenging, and enjoyable. This 'enjoyment' factor should not be dismissed lightly. Of course it does not mean that you will 'like' every text that you read. After all, it is possible to enjoy studying a text purely because of the academic challenges it presents. Enjoyment is important for another reason – students who enjoy their studies tend to be the ones whose motivation is highest and who ultimately achieve the best results.

Your past experience of studying English will probably have shown that it differs from other subjects. Unlike most other subjects, English Literature does not consist of a body of knowledge that you can 'learn' in the conventional sense. Instead, you need to develop your own ideas and responses to the texts that you study and to base these responses firmly on evidence that you have gathered from your own readings of these. The development of these informed, independent opinions and judgements will underpin everything that you do in your study of literature at A-level or AS-level.

This text is specifically linked to the AQA Specification A (5741 and 6741). The specification is designed to encourage students to develop an interest in and enjoyment of English Literature through reading widely, critically and independently, across centuries, genre and gender and through experience of an extensive range of views about texts and how to read them.

The general aims of the specification at AS- and A-level are to:

- encourage students to develop interest and enjoyment in literary studies through reading widely, critically and independently
- introduce students to the tradition of English Literature

More specifically, at AS-level the specification aims to:

1 develop confident, independent and reflective readers of a range of texts
2 encourage candidates to express their responses effectively
3 encourage the use of critical concepts and terminology with understanding and discrimination
4 encourage candidates to reflect on their own responses to texts, to consider other readers' interpretations, and to develop some awareness of the contexts in which texts are written

At A-level, the specification aims to:

1 broaden and deepen the knowledge, skills and understanding developed in the AS, enabling candidates to gain a wider sense of the scope of literary study
2 encourage candidates to use detailed knowledge and understanding of individual texts to explore comparisons between them
3 encourage candidates to appreciate the significance of cultural and historical influences upon readers and writers

It is worth considering these aims carefully because the Assessment Objectives, which are at the heart of your studies, stem directly from them.

The Assessment Objectives are set out below. Study them carefully because everything you do in your study of English Literature will relate directly to these objectives. (They are exactly the same for all Examination Boards' specifications.)

Assessment objectives

The differences between AS- and A-level Assessment Objectives reflect the differences in the depth and breadth of the requirements for the specification.

Assessment Objectives AO2 and AO5 apply to both AS- and A-level, but at A-level the scope and level of demand have been extended. Assessment Objectives 1, 3 and 4 are common to both AS- and A-level.

The assessment will assess a candidate's ability to:

At AS-level

1   communicate clearly the knowledge, understanding and insight appropriate to literary study, using appropriate terminology and accurate and coherent written expression;

2i respond with knowledge and understanding to literary texts of different types and periods;

3   show detailed understanding of the ways in which writers' choices of form, structure and language shape meanings;

4   articulate independent opinions and judgements, informed by different interpretations of literary texts by other readers;

5i show understanding of the contexts in which literary texts are written and understood

At A-level

1   communicate clearly the knowledge, understanding and insight appropriate to literary study, using appropriate terminology and accurate and coherent written expression;

2ii respond with knowledge and understanding to literary texts of different types and periods, exploring and commenting on relationships and comparisons between literary texts;

3   show detailed understanding of the ways in which writers' choices of form, structure and language shape meanings;

4   articulate independent opinions and judgements, informed by different interpretations of literary texts by other readers;

5ii evaluate the significance of cultural, historical and other contextual influences on literary texts and study.

It is worth noting that although these objectives are common to all Exam Boards, individual Boards may have created specifications which test them in different ways from the approach used in AQA Specification A. Do consult the specification for the course you are studying to ensure that you are clear about how these objectives will be tested.

Reading, talking, and writing

Your studies will involve a good deal of reading with your set texts forming the heart of this. However, the most successful students are those whose reading takes them beyond the texts that they must study. Such students read widely around the texts and the subject, building up a knowledge and understanding of literature that is not restricted simply to set texts. This background reading is the key element in developing an appreciation of literature and often is the difference between those students who achieve the higher grades and those who do not.

Discussion is also an important way in which to develop and test out your ideas about literature. Although your teachers or lecturers will give you guidance, they will not tell you what to think. They will encourage you to weigh various views and interpretations against each other and to formulate your own ideas. Talking to others about your ideas is an important (and enjoyable) way of doing this, so you will probably find yourself involved in a good deal of discussion work, in class, small groups, or with a partner.

If you are studying literature through a distance learning or correspondence course you are at a disadvantage here in not having the same opportunity to exchange ideas with others on a regular basis. It may be a good idea to find yourself a 'mentor' who can help you by talking through the work with you.

As far as 'writing' goes the course will involve writing about a whole variety of texts in many different forms. There will be essays on the set texts, 'unseen' pieces to be tackled, coursework pieces to complete, and notes of different kinds to be made.

Certainly this book will provide a full complement of spoken and written activities and will introduce you to a wide range of texts to help prepare you for your final assessment.

Summary   The work that you do will require you to:
- analyse texts
- explore and express your views on them
- work independently
- take a major responsibility for your learning
- develop and articulate independent opinions and judgements on the material you study
- be aware of different interpretations of the literary texts you study

Aims of the book

With the Assessment Objectives in mind, *Literature, Criticism, and Style* has been devised to guide you through your AS- and A-level courses.

Section I introduces the main types of writing that you are likely to study during your course. It offers approaches and strategies for tackling each genre and each unit culminates in a Special Feature, looking at the work of an important writer in that genre.

Section II looks particularly at the skills required in writing about texts. Its aim is to help you write confidently and effectively about set texts and unseens. It also gives insights into how to write about context, how to compare texts and how to study themes.

Section III addresses the skills you will need towards the end of your course as you approach the exam. It looks at individual papers as well as how to tackle coursework and revision. The Chronology and Glossary should help to put your study of literature into perspective and to sum up the terms of literary criticism.

Throughout the text you will find a range of activities which are designed to help you consolidate your knowledge and understanding of English Literature at AS- and A-level. Some of these activities may be based on texts that you are studying as part of your course. Others may be on texts that you have not read or studied. The completion of these activities will help you to develop your ideas and skills in a variety of ways and may introduce you to new ways of looking at the texts that you are studying.

Above all we hope that you will enjoy your study of Literature at AS- or A-level and that this book will add to that enjoyment and contribute to your success.

2 The Novel

Objectives
- To find ways of gaining an overview when studying a novel
- To analyse more specific aspects of a novel, such as characterisation and narrative viewpoint
- To develop your own responses to novels
- To prepare for studying a set text

What is a novel?

The word 'novel' usually means something new – a novelty. Some of the earliest novels, written in the Seventeenth and Eighteenth Centuries, would have been just that. One dictionary definition describes a novel as:

" a fictitious prose narrative or tale presenting a picture of real life, especially of the emotional crises in the life-history of the men and women portrayed. **"**

Jane Austen's view was that a novel was:

" ...only some work in which the greatest powers of the mind are displayed, in which the most thorough knowledge of human nature, the happiest delineation of its varieties, the liveliest effusions of wit and humour, are conveyed to the world in the best chosen language. **"**

A 'novelty' suggests something fairly lightweight, entertaining, and perhaps not of lasting significance. Early novels such as those of Samuel Richardson were sometimes serious and carried strong moral messages, but could often be rather sentimental. Nowadays we tend to make a distinction between 'literary' novels and popular fiction – but this dividing line can be blurred. As part of your A-level Literature course, you will be expected to study novels which are 'literary' and to develop the ability to recognize the differences. However, it can also be interesting to study popular, mass market novels and to consider how the conventions of writing fiction are applied in them.

Activity

In a small group, imagine that one of you has never read or encountered a novel before. Other members of the group should try to explain what a novel is. Bear in mind the definitions given on page 6 but also use your own experience of reading novels. Feed back the most useful points in your explanation to the whole group.

Studying the novel

Every AS- or A-level Literature specification will require that you study at least one novel as a set text for examination. Usually this will be chosen for you from a short list issued by the Exam Board. If your specification has a coursework option or an additional set text examination paper where you are asked to study and compare two or more texts, you may also have the opportunity to study and write about novels you have chosen yourself.

At the outset, studying a set text novel can seem a daunting prospect. If yours happens to be Dickens's *Bleak House*, or Eliot's *Middlemarch*, it may well be the longest book you have ever read. If it is a Twentieth-Century novel which does not follow realistic conventions or a novel from an earlier period where the language is unfamiliar, you may feel that you will struggle to master it. Some novels are difficult, but usually they are rewarding and a 'good read' too, once you become engaged with the plot and characters and more familiar with the author's language and ideas. In this unit we will develop strategies for approaching them and identify the most important things to pay attention to.

One concept we need to keep in mind is that there are two main attitudes or positions we can take when we study a novel. The first attitude we can hold is that what is important is the content or the 'world' which the author has created. This is a world we can enter into, full of people, places, things, and events, to which we respond with liking or hatred, pity or criticism, as we do to the real world. Studying from this position, we will discuss the characters almost as if they were beings with the ability to choose their actions.

The second position we can take, is to see the novel as a 'text', as a created work of art, and to look at it in a much more detached and analytical way. Characters are devices which the author uses and manipulates to create a particular effect. Their only existence is in the precise words on the page. Studying with this attitude, we will be more likely to consider what a character's role is in the construction of a plot, or the effect of using particular language to describe a place or person.

As you study a novel for AS- or A-level, you will most likely begin by responding from the first position, but you will also develop your understanding of the more analytical viewpoint. You will always need to know how the text is written as well as what it says.

When studying a set text novel, there are several aspects of the novel which you will need to know well. Most examination questions, though they may be worded in different ways, will focus on one of these.

- **An overview**   You need to have a clear understanding of the plot and central ideas, how events follow on and are related, and how the novel is structured. Questions might ask you to show how the novel's structure affects the reader's response, particularly if it is not a straightforward chronological narrative.
- **Narrative viewpoint**   Who tells the story? Why has the writer chosen this viewpoint? How does this affect the reader's response?
- **Characters**   Questions often focus on one or more characters, their development or their relationships.
- **The society, setting, or world in which the novel takes place**   Questions may centre on this, or may ask about the relationship between a character and the society in which he or she lives.
- **Language and style**   There may be distinctive qualities in the writer's choice of language, for example, in the use of imagery or comic exaggeration. Questions may ask you to consider why the writer has made these choices. What is their purpose and effect?
- **Extracts**   Questions may ask you to write in detail about a key passage and to place it in context by relating it to the whole text.

If you are studying novels for coursework, you may not need to explore all of these aspects in detail. You may decide to concentrate on one feature, particularly if you are going to compare two or more texts (see Units 11 and 16).

Approaching the text

With a large text like a novel, we need to become familiar enough with it to 'find our way around' easily. We need to be able to locate incidents and important passages quickly. Here are some strategies that will help you to gain this familiarity.

- If you have time, read through the novel fairly quickly before you begin to study it. This gives you the opportunity to gain an overall impression of the novel and to read it, as it was intended, for entertainment. It will also help you to see how different aspects of the novel fit together when you begin to study it in depth. You will see how the plot is constructed and have an idea of what form of novel it is.
- Do some research. Find out what you can about the author and what was going on when the novel was written. Knowing something about the

historical and social background and about the conventions and beliefs of the time can help you to understand things which may otherwise seem strange or incomprehensible.

- Keep a separate notebook or 'log' for your work on each text. Try dividing a notebook into sections, one for each important aspect of the novel. You will need pages for each of the main characters, the setting, the narrator, themes and ideas, and language and style. As you work through the novel, jot down your observations about each aspect in the appropriate places. Include important quotations and page references. Then, when you need the information for a discussion or an essay on one of these topics, it will be easy to locate.

- You may find it helpful to annotate your copy of the text, marking important passages so that you can find them again easily. It is important, however, to be aware of the regulations for the specification and paper for which you are studying. In some examinations, you are permitted to take your copy of the text with you on condition that it is a 'clean copy' and has no notes or markings written on it. In others, you are not allowed to have access to the text and must work from memory. These two situations require rather different revision strategies, and there is some advice on this in Unit 15. If yours is a syllabus which does not permit access to the text, then annotation can be a great help when you are revising. It is also useful if you are preparing for a coursework assignment. Some guidance on effective annotation and an example appear in Unit 7.

Let us turn now to exploring some texts. As we examine different aspects of novels in this unit, we will look at examples from these three very different novels by writers often set at AS- or A-level.

- *Emma* by Jane Austen
- *Hard Times* by Charles Dickens
- *The Handmaid's Tale* by Margaret Atwood

Activity

> Use reference books and/or information provided in editions of these novels to find out what you can about each of these authors and their eras.

An overview

Novels come in many shapes and sizes, from short novellas (more like long short stories) with a few characters and fairly simple plots, to enormously large and complex works, with numerous characters, plots, and subplots and with many different strands which may or may not be interconnected.

There are also different genres or forms of novel. For example:

- **Fictional biography or autobiography** focuses on the life and development of one character.

- **Picaresque novels** follow a central character on a journey through life in which he or she encounters a series of 'adventures' which form separate episodes.
- **Social or 'Protest' novels** use the characters and the world they inhabit as a way of criticizing or protesting about social or political issues.

Novelists sometimes choose to combine more than one of these types.

The plot, or storyline, of a novel can also be constructed in different ways. The simplest plots relate events in straightforward chronological order, from the point of view of a single narrator, but there have been many variations on this. For example:

- In *Hard Times*, Dickens moves from one group of people in Coketown to another. The connections between them all are not completely clear until the end, when we realize he has constructed a network of threads which link them.
- In *The Handmaid's Tale*, the narrative alternates between chapters which tell the story in the 'present' of the novel and others which are flashbacks. Entitled *Night* or *Nap*, these are times when the narrator has a chance to reminisce, dream or daydream about the past.
- Emily Brontë, in *Wuthering Heights*, uses two narrators and departs from chronological order by plunging us into the middle of a mysterious situation and then going back in time to explain how it has come about. She then repeats this process to show how the situation is resolved.

Activity

> 1 Discuss the structure of your set text novel. Is it simply chronological or does it operate in some other way? What do you think is the effect of this structure?
> 2 Widen your discussion to cover any other novels you have read with interesting structures.

Opening pages

Usually, we can learn quite a lot about a novel by looking closely at the first few pages. The writer will be trying to engage our attention so that we want to read on. So it is quite likely that some of the important situations, characters, and themes will be presented right from the start.

Activity

> 1 Here are the opening pages of the three novels. Read them carefully.
> 2 Working with a partner, choose one of these and discuss it in detail, making notes on the following points.
> - Who is the narrator and what, if anything, can you find out about him or her? Is the narrative in the third person or the first person?
> - What characters (including the narrators) are introduced? What do you learn about them?
> - What situation is presented? Does the story begin in a particular place? If so, how is it described? What atmosphere is generated?

- Does the writer begin by explaining clearly who is who and what is what? Or are you plunged into the middle of a situation and left to work out what is going on from hints the writer gives you?
- Can you get a sense of the author's tone? Is the writing straightforward? Might there be hidden messages or other levels of meaning?
- What do you notice about the writer's style? What sort of imagery, vocabulary, and sentence structures are used?
- What do you think this novel is going to be 'about'? Can you get a sense of any important ideas or themes that may be central to it?
- In what ways does the writer arouse your curiosity? Do you want to read further? Why?

3 Present and compare your notes with the whole group. What similarities and differences are there between the three passages?

4 Try working on the opening pages of any other novel which you are studying in the same way.

Emma

Chapter 1

Emma Woodhouse, handsome, clever, and rich, with a comfortable home and happy disposition, seemed to unite some of the best blessings of existence; and had lived nearly twenty-one years in the world with very little to distress or vex her.

She was the youngest of the two daughters of a most affectionate, indulgent father, and had, in consequence of her sister's marriage, been mistress of his house from a very early period. Her mother had died too long ago for her to have more than an indistinct remembrance of her caresses; and her place had been supplied by an excellent woman as governess, who had fallen little short of a mother in affection.

Sixteen years had Miss Taylor been in Mr Woodhouse's family, less as a governess than as a friend, very fond of both daughters, but particularly of Emma. Between *them* it was more the intimacy of sisters. Even before Miss Taylor had ceased to hold the nominal office of governess, the mildness of her temper had hardly allowed her to impose any restraint; and the shadow of authority being now long passed away, they had been living together as friend and friend very mutually attached, and Emma doing just what she liked; highly esteeming Miss Taylor's judgement, but directed chiefly by her own.

The real evils, indeed, of Emma's situation were the power of having rather too much her own way, and a disposition to think a little too well of herself; these were the disadvantages which threatened alloy to her many enjoyments. The danger, however, was at present so unperceived, that they did not by any means rank as misfortunes with her.

Sorrow came – a gentle sorrow – but not at all in the shape of any disagreeable consciousness. Miss Taylor married. It was Miss Taylor's loss which first brought grief. It was on the wedding-day of this beloved friend that Emma first sat in mournful thought of any continuance. The wedding over, and the bride-people gone, her father and herself were left to dine together, with no prospect of a third to cheer a long evening. Her father composed himself to sleep after dinner, as usual, and she had then only to sit and think of what she had lost.

Jane Austen

Hard Times

Chapter 1
The One Thing Needful
'Now, what I want is, Facts. Teach these boys and girls nothing but Facts. Facts alone are wanted in life. Plant nothing else, and root out everything else. You can only form the minds of reasoning animals upon Facts: nothing else will ever be of any service to them. This is the principle on which I bring up these children. Stick to Facts, sir!'
The scene was a plain, bare, monotonous vault of a schoolroom, and the speaker's square forefinger emphasized his observations by underscoring every sentence with a line on the schoolmaster's sleeve. The emphasis was helped by the speaker's square wall of a forehead, which had his eyebrows for its base, while his eyes found commodious cellarage in two dark caves, overshadowed by the wall. The emphasis was helped by the speaker's mouth, which was wide, thin, and hard set. The emphasis was helped by the speaker's voice, which was inflexible, dry, and dictatorial. The emphasis was helped by the speaker's hair, which bristled on the skirts of his bald head, a plantation of firs to keep the wind from its shining surface, all covered with knobs, like the crust of a plum pie, as if the head had scarcely warehouse-room for the hard facts stored inside. The speaker's obstinate carriage, square coat, square legs, square shoulders – nay, his very neckcloth, trained to take him by the throat with an unaccommodating grasp, like a stubborn fact, as it was – all helped the emphasis.
'In this life, we want nothing but Facts, sir; nothing but Facts!'
The speaker, and the schoolmaster, and the third grown person present, all backed a little, and swept with their eyes the inclined plane of little vessels then and there arranged in order, ready to have imperial gallons of facts poured into them until they were full to the brim.

Charles Dickens

The Handmaid's Tale

Chapter 1
We slept in what had once been the gymnasium. The floor was of varnished wood, with stripes and circles painted on it, for the games that were formerly played there; the hoops for the basketball nets were still in place, though the nets were gone. A balcony ran around the room, for the spectators, and I thought I could smell, faintly like an after image, the pungent scent of sweat, shot through with the sweet taste of chewing gum and perfume from the watching girls, felt-skirted as I knew from pictures, later in mini-skirts, then pants, then in one ear-ring, spiky green-streaked hair. Dances would have been held there; the music

lingered, a palimpsest of unheard sound, style upon style, an undercurrent of drums, a forlorn wail, garlands made of tissue-paper flowers, cardboard devils, a revolving ball of mirrors, powdering the dancers with a snow of light.

There was old sex in the room and loneliness, and expectation, of something without a shape or name. I remember that yearning, for something that was always about to happen and was never the same as the hands that were on us there and then, in the small of the back, or out back, in the parking lot, or in the television room with the sound turned down and only the pictures flickering over lifting flesh.

We yearned for the future. How did we learn it, that talent for insatiability? It was in the air; and it was still in the air, an afterthought, as we tried to sleep, in the army cots that had been set up in rows, with spaces between so we could not talk. We had flannelette sheets, like children's, and army-issue blankets, old ones that still said U.S. We folded our clothes neatly and laid them on the stools at the ends of the beds. The lights were turned down but not out. Aunt Sara and Aunt Elizabeth patrolled; they had electric cattle prods slung on thongs from their leather belts.

Margaret Atwood

Narrative viewpoint

You will have noticed that in *Emma* and *Hard Times* the authors have chosen to use third-person narrative, while Margaret Atwood uses a first-person narrator for *The Handmaid's Tale*. There are advantages and disadvantages, and different possibilities in each.

Writing in the first person, the author takes on the role of a character (or characters) and tells the story 'from the inside'. This can strengthen the illusion that the novel is 'real', by making us, the readers, feel involved and able to empathize with the character. However, this usually also limits our perspective to this one character's perceptions: we only see other characters through his or her eyes. We cannot know of events the narrator does not witness unless they are reported by another character, for example in conversation.

As we have only this narrator's words to go on, we need to ask how far we can trust the narrator. He or she might be biased, deluded, blind to the true significance of events, or even deliberately deceiving the reader. Often, this very question adds interest to a first-person narrative.

The narrator in *The Handmaid's Tale* is Offred, a woman living in a future society in which people are restricted to very narrow, specific roles. Offred is a handmaid. Her job is to 'breed' to ensure the survival of her nation, while other women are responsible for domestic chores and some carry out the formal duties of a wife. Much of her narrative is in **stream of consciousness**, a form in which the writer aims to give a sense of how a character's mind works by tracking her thoughts as they flow from one topic to another. We have to piece together our impressions of Offred from what she reveals of her thoughts and feelings, her actions, and her attitudes to other characters.

Activity

Here, early in the novel, Offred describes her living quarters and ponders her situation. Read the extract and make a note of everything that you learn about her as a person and as a storyteller. Consider also how far she engages your interest and sympathy.

The Handmaid's Tale

Chapter 2

A window, two white curtains. Under the window, a window seat with a little cushion. When the window is partly open – it only opens partly – the air can come in and make the curtains move. I can sit in the chair, or on the window seat, hands folded, and watch this. Sunlight comes in through the window too, and falls on the floor, which is made of wood, in narrow strips, highly polished. I can smell the polish. There's a rug on the floor, oval, of braided rags. This is the kind of touch they like: folk art, archaic, made by women, in their spare time, from things that have no further use. A return to traditional values. Waste not want not. I am not being wasted. Why do I want?

A bed. Single, mattress medium-hard, covered with a flocked white spread. Nothing takes place in the bed but sleep; or no sleep. I try not to think too much. Like other things now, thought must be rationed. There's a lot that doesn't bear thinking about. Thinking can hurt your chances, and I intend to last. I know why there is no glass, in front of the water-colour picture of blue irises, and why the window only opens partly and why the glass in it is shatterproof. It isn't running away they're afraid of. We wouldn't get far. It's those other escapes, the ones you can open in yourself, given a cutting edge.

So. Apart from these details, this could be a college guest room, for the less distinguished visitors; or a room in a rooming-house, of former times, for ladies in reduced circumstances. That is what we are now. The circumstances have been reduced; for those of us who still have circumstances.

But a chair, sunlight, flowers: these are not to be dismissed. I am alive, I live, I breathe, I put my hand out, unfolded, into the sunlight. Where I am is not a prison but a privilege, as Aunt Lydia said, who was in love with either/or.

Margaret Atwood

....

Summary

Probably you will have noted the following points.

- She notices and describes her surroundings in detail and specific details spark off trains of thought about her life in an interior monologue. She pays attention to these things because there is plenty of time to do so and nothing else to occupy her.
- She separates herself from the people in authority by referring rather anonymously to 'they' and 'them'.

- She feels limited by her life and is not satisfied living by the maxims she has been taught. She longs for something more -'Waste not want not. I am not being wasted. Why do I want?'
- She is determined to survive, even if this means denying the truth sometimes – 'Thinking can hurt your chances, and I intend to last.'
- She is optimistic enough to recognize what is good in her surroundings – 'But a chair, sunlight, flowers: these are not to be dismissed.'
- Her language is usually simple and she does not use specific imagery. Many of her sentences are short or incomplete. Their confiding quality suggests we already know what she is talking about and who 'they' are, when in fact we know nothing about the regime in which she lives. She likes to play with words and double meanings in a wry, humorous way – 'The circumstances have been reduced; for those of us who still have circumstances.'

••

Third-person narrative offers different possibilities. The author or narrator adopts a position which is 'godlike', or becomes a 'fly on the wall' reporting everything to us, the readers. This omniscient (all-knowing) narrator, from a vantage point outside the action, can relate events which may occur in different places, at different times, or even simultaneously. Often we are told how different characters feel so we see things from more than one perspective. Sometimes the author might tell the story dispassionately, without commenting or judging. Usually, however, authors make their presence felt. This might be through obvious authorial intrusion, where the writer butts into the narrative to express an opinion or comment on a situation, or it might be more subtle. For example, a character may be described in language we recognize as sarcastic, 'tongue-in-cheek', or ironic, making it clear that the author is critical or mocking; or positive or negative judgements may simply be revealed by the writer's choice of vocabulary.

We can easily detect Dickens's opinion of 'the speaker' in the opening page of *Hard Times*: describing his forehead as a 'square wall' and his voice as 'inflexible, dry, and dictatorial' is only the beginning of his portrait of the rigid Mr Gradgrind. A few pages later, he is concluding his description of Stone Lodge, Mr Gradgrind's 'matter of fact home' and his fact-ridden 'model' children. His bitter sarcasm is clear:

'... Iron clamps and girders ... mechanical lifts ... everything that heart could wish for.'

A moment later Dickens 'intrudes' in his own voice to express his doubts:

'Everything? Well I suppose so.'

Jane Austen does something similar, but rather more gently. Primarily, her opening paragraphs in *Emma* introduce her central character. Little in the way of judgement can be detected except where she informs us that:

'The real evils indeed of Emma's situation were the power of having rather too much her own way, and a disposition to think a little too well of herself.'

She does create characters who are 'types', such as Emma's father Mr Woodhouse, the anxious hypochondriac and Miss Bates, the non-stop talker. Their traits are exaggerated, but her mockery of them tends to be affectionate, without the ferocity of Dickens. Often, she comments ironically with the voice of 'society', when it is clear that her own intention is to question or poke fun at the conventional view as she does in the famous opening lines of *Pride and Prejudice*:

'It is a truth universally acknowledged, that a single man in possession of a good fortune must be in want of a wife.'

This question of the writer's stance towards characters or situations can be quite complex. Even in third-person narrative, things are often filtered through the perceptions of one particular character. We may need to consider carefully whether the author's views match those of this character or not. Alternatively, the author may choose to write with a 'voice' which is neither his or her own nor that of one of the characters in the novel.

Most of *Emma* is told from Emma's point of view, with her values and prejudices, but it is also possible to detect that Jane Austen shares some of her views and not others. Emma disapproves of two characters whose social status is inferior to her own. First, the self-satisfied Mrs Elton, who fails to recognize her position in Hartfield society and is much too familiar with Emma and her friends. She is:

'a vain woman, extremely well satisfied with herself, and thinking much of her own importance; that she meant to shine and be very superior, but with manners which had been formed in a bad school, pert and familiar; that all her notions were drawn from one set of people, and one style of living; that if not foolish she was ignorant, and that her society would certainly do Mr Elton no good ...
... Happily it was now time to be gone. They were off; and Emma could breathe.'

On the other hand, she also disapproves of respectable young farmer Robert Martin, whom she considers a bad match for her young protégé, Harriet Smith:

'His appearance was very neat, and he looked like a sensible young man, but his person had no other advantage; and when he came to be contrasted with gentlemen, she thought he must lose all the ground he had gained in Harriet's inclination ...
..."He is very plain, undoubtedly – remarkably plain: – but that is nothing, compared with his entire want of gentility. I had no right to expect much, and I did not expect much; but I had no idea that he could be so very clownish, so totally without air. I had imagined him, I confess, a degree or two nearer gentility."'

In the novel, it is clear that we are expected to agree with Emma about Mrs Elton. She is indeed an awful woman. However, where Robert Martin is concerned, we come to see that Emma is snobbish and misguided and that Jane Austen intends us to question her opinion.

Activity

> 1 Look once more at the openings of *Emma* and *The Handmaid's Tale*.
> Working with a partner, rewrite the first paragraph of *The Handmaid's Tale* in the third person and the first two paragraphs of *Emma* in the first person (with Emma as the narrator). Discuss the results. What is lost and what gained from changing the narrative viewpoint?
> 2 Think carefully about the narrative viewpoint in the novel you are studying. Who is the narrator? Can you trust their narrative? How aware are you of the author's presence? Look for examples of authorial intrusion.

Characters

Much of the interest in a novel lies in the characters whose world we enter and in whose lives we share. We usually respond to them first as people. We can analyse their personalities, trace how they are affected by events and empathize or disapprove of them. However, we do need to remember that they do not have lives outside the pages of the novel and so it is rarely useful to speculate about their past or future experiences. More importantly, we need to pay attention to how they are presented.

It has already been suggested that it is useful to keep a 'log' to record key passages and quotations for each important character which can be built up as you work through the text.

Summary

Characters are revealed to us in various ways.
- **Description**   The author often provides an introductory 'pen-portrait' and then builds up our knowledge with details as the narrative proceeds. Key passages describe main characters or make us aware of how they change and develop.
- **Dialogue**   Other characters often give important clues when they discuss the character concerned. We may also find out a lot about someone from his or her own speech.
- **Thoughts and feelings**   The 'inner life' of a character can be revealed directly, particularly in a first-person narrative.
- **Actions and reactions**   How characters behave in various situations will inform our view of them.
- **Imagery and symbols**   Characters may be described using simile and metaphor, or may be associated symbolically with, for example, a colour or an element. In Emily Brontë's *Wuthering Heights*, Heathcliff is frequently linked with fire and with the colour black. Similarly, in Thomas Hardy's *Tess of the D'Urbervilles*, Tess is associated with the colour red which suggests danger or marks her out as a 'fallen woman' from the beginning.

Activity

> Here are some introductory character sketches from *Emma*, *Hard Times*, and *The Handmaid's Tale*. Working in a small group, make notes on these points.
> - What kind of information does each author provide about the character in question?
> - Do you learn anything of the character's inner life or just factual or superficial information?
> - How does each writer use language in each case? Consider sentence structure, vocabulary, use of imagery, and other effects.
> - What can you detect of the author's attitude to the character?

1

Mr John Knightley was a tall, gentleman-like, and very clever man; rising in his profession, domestic, and respectable in his private character; but with reserved manners which prevented his being generally pleasing; and capable of being sometimes out of humour. He was not an ill-tempered man, not so often unreasonably cross as to deserve such a reproach; but his temper was not his great perfection; and indeed, with such a worshipping wife, it was hardly possible that any natural defects in it would not be increased.

2

The Commander has on his black uniform, in which he looks like a museum guard. A semi-retired man, genial but wary, killing time. But only at first glance. After that he looks like a midwestern bank president, with his straight neatly brushed silver hair, his sober posture, shoulders a little stooped. And after that there is his moustache, silver also, and after that his chin, which really you can't miss. When you get down as far as the chin he looks like a vodka ad, in a glossy magazine, of times gone by.
His manner is mild, his hands large, with thick fingers and acquisitive thumbs, his blue eyes uncommunicative, falsely innocuous.

3

[Mr Bounderby] was a rich man: banker, merchant, manufacturer, and what not. A big, loud man, with a stare and a metallic laugh. A man made out of a coarse material, which seemed to have been stretched to make so much of him. A man with a great puffed head and forehead, swelled veins in his temples, and such a strained skin to his face that it seemed to hold his eyes open and lift his eyebrows up. A man with a pervading appearance on him of being inflated like a balloon, and ready to start. A man who could never sufficiently vaunt himself a self-made man. A man who was always proclaiming, through that brassy speaking-trumpet of a voice of his, his old ignorance and his old poverty. A man who was the Bully of humility.

4

Moira, sitting on the edge of my bed, legs crossed, ankle on knee, in her purple overalls, one dangly earring, the gold fingernail she wore to be eccentric, a cigarette between her stubby yellow-ended fingers. Let's go for a beer.

5

Harriet certainly was not clever, but she had a sweet, docile, grateful disposition; was totally free from conceit; and only desiring to be guided by any one she looked up to. Her early attachment to [Emma] herself was very amiable; and her inclination for good company, and power of appreciating what was elegant and clever shewed that there was no want of taste, though strength of understanding must not be expected.

Development of a character and a relationship

Now let us look at a character in more detail. If you are asked to explore the way a character is presented and how he or she changes and develops in the course of a novel, it is a good idea to choose a few passages or episodes from different parts of the novel, which feature the character, to examine in detail. These may be descriptive passages, moments of dramatic action, episodes where the character contrasts or is in conflict with others, or where he or she faces a decision.

Louisa Gradgrind

Dickens created the bleak world of Coketown, the setting of *Hard Times*, to expose and mock the philosophy of Utilitarianism. This set of beliefs saw people only in terms of their usefulness as workers or tools for industry and wealth-creation. No allowances were made for people having imaginations or emotional lives.

Many of Dickens's characters, such as Mr Bounderby, are caricatures whose traits are exaggerated in the extreme. The effect is comic, but they also allow Dickens to make serious points and express his anger. Sometimes, he is accused of creating only caricatures, unrealistic people without depth, but this is by no means always the case. In *Hard Times*, the caricatures are usually recognizable by their comical names, while the central characters who develop as 'real' people are allowed to have ordinary names. Louisa Gradgrind, a victim of her father's belief that facts are 'The one thing needful', is one of these. The account of how her life and development are distorted, and of how her father learns to regret his rigid methods, is moving.

Activity

We first meet Louisa when her father is appalled to have discovered her with her brother Tom, spying on the local circus, a forbidden entertainment. Study the passage closely, and make notes on how Dickens presents her and her relationship with her father. Consider in particular:
- the imagery used to describe Louisa's manner
- what is revealed about each of them by the dialogue

Hard Times

Chapter 3
A Loophole

'In the name of wonder, idleness, and folly!' said Mr Gradgrind, leading each away by a hand; 'what do you do here?'

'Wanted to see what it was like,' returned Louisa shortly.

'What it was like?'

'Yes, father.'

There was an air of jaded sullenness in them both, and particularly in the girl: yet, struggling through the dissatisfaction of her face, there was a light with nothing to rest upon, a fire with nothing to burn, a starved imagination keeping life in itself somehow, which brightened its expression. Not with the brightness natural to cheerful youth, but with uncertain, eager, doubtful flashes, which had something painful in them, analogous to the changes on a blind face groping its way.

She was a child now, of fifteen or sixteen; but at no distant day would seem to become a woman all at once. Her father thought so as he looked at her. She was pretty. Would have been self-willed (he thought in his eminently practical way), but for her bringing-up.

'Thomas, though I have the fact before me, I find it difficult to believe that you, with your education and resources, should have brought your sister to a scene like this.'

'I brought him, father,' said Louisa quickly. 'I asked him to come.'

'I am sorry to hear it. I am very sorry indeed to hear it. It makes Thomas no better, and it makes you worse, Louisa.'

She looked at her father again, but no tear fell down her cheek.

'You! Thomas and you, to whom the circle of the sciences is open; Thomas and you, who may be said to be replete with facts; Thomas and you, who have been trained to mathematical exactness; Thomas and you here!' cried Mr Gradgrind. 'In this degraded position! I am amazed.'

'I was tired. I have been tired a long time, ' said Louisa.

'Tired? Of what?' asked the astonished father.

'I don't know of what – of everything I think.'

'Say not another word,' returned Mr Gradgrind. 'You are childish. I will hear no more.'

Charles Dickens

Louisa is presented in opposition to her father and his world of facts, but as yet the conflict is mostly within her, as her thwarted imagination fights for life. The images of light and an inward 'fire with nothing to burn' will recur frequently. She often gazes at the smoking chimneys of the Coketown factories which she knows must contain flames which have been suppressed, like her own imagination, and which burst out when darkness falls.

The dialogue reveals just how little capacity Gradgrind has for understanding his children. Notice the contrast between Louisa's short answers and her father's pompous, wordy style. She seems sullen, but also honest and very self-controlled. Her dry education has rendered her incapable of tears or emotional displays. His final accusation, that she is childish, is ironic. She has never been allowed to be a child. The passage does mark the first time Gradgrind is surprised by his children. Later it will be Louisa's tragedy which jolts him out of his complacency.

Now let us examine two further passages which reveal something of how their characters and their relationship alter.

Activity

> **1** Study the extracts carefully, together with the one on the previous page. Discuss how the characters and their relationship are presented in each case.
> **2** Write a detailed comparison of the three passages. In what ways does Dickens convey the changes in Louisa's and Gradgrind's characters and in their relationship? Remember to consider:
> - the imagery used in the setting
> - characters dialogue, actions, and reactions

Hard Times

Chapter 15
Father and Daughter
[Mr Gradgrind has just proposed that in the name of reason, Louisa should undertake a loveless marriage to the appalling Mr Bounderby, a rich banker and merchant.]
'I now leave you to judge for yourself,' said Mr Gradgrind. 'I have stated the case, as such cases are usually stated among practical minds; I have stated it, as the case of your mother and myself was stated in its time. The rest, my dear Louisa, is for you to decide.'
From the beginning, she had sat looking at him fixedly. As he now leaned back in his chair, and bent his deep-set eyes upon her in his turn, perhaps he might have seen one wavering moment in her, when she was impelled to throw herself upon his breast, and give him the pent-up confidences of her heart. But, to see it, he must have overleaped at a bound the artificial barriers he had for many years been erecting, between himself and all those subtle essences of humanity which will elude the utmost cunning of algebra until the last trumpet ever to be sounded shall blow even algebra to wreck. The barriers were too many and too high for such a leap. With his unbending, utilitarian, matter of fact face, he hardened her again; and the moment shot away into the plumbless depths of the past, to mingle with all the lost opportunities that are drowned there.
Removing her eyes from him, she sat so long looking silently towards the town, that he said, at length: 'Are you consulting the chimneys of the Coketown works, Louisa?'
'There seems to be nothing there, but languid and monotonous smoke. Yet when the night comes, fire bursts out, Father!' she answered, turning quickly.
'Of course I know that, Louisa. I do not see the application of the remark.' To do him justice, he did not, at all.

Charles Dickens

Hard Times

Chapter 28
Down

[Long since married to Bounderby, Louisa has discovered and is tempted by the possibility of real love with another man. She returns to her father in great distress.]

When it thundered very loudly, [Mr Gradgrind] glanced towards Coketown, having it in his mind that some of the tall chimneys might be struck by lightning. The thunder was rolling into the distance, and the rain was pouring down like a deluge, when the door of his room opened. He looked round the lamp upon his table, and saw, with amazement, his eldest daughter.

'Louisa!'

'Father, I want to speak to you.'

'What is the matter? How strange you look! And good Heaven,' said Mr Gradgrind, wondering more and more, 'have you come here exposed to this storm?'

She put her hands to her dress, as if she hardly knew. 'Yes.' Then she uncovered her head, and letting her cloak and hood fall where they might, stood looking at him: so colourless, so dishevelled, so defiant and despairing, that he was afraid of her.

'What is it? I conjure you, Louisa, tell me what is the matter?'

She dropped into a chair before him, and put her cold hand on his arm.

'Father, you have trained me from my cradle.'

'Yes Louisa.'

'I curse the hour in which I was born to such a destiny.'

He looked at her in doubt and dread, vacantly repeating, 'Curse the hour? Curse the hour?'

'How could you give me life, and take from me all the inappreciable things that raise it from the state of conscious death? Where are the graces of my soul? Where are the sentiments of my heart? What have you done, O father, what have you done, with the garden that should have bloomed once, in this great wilderness here!'

She struck herself with both hands upon her bosom.

'If it had ever been here, its ashes alone would save me from the void in which my whole life sinks.'

Charles Dickens

Activity

1 Choose a character from a novel you are studying. Then select three or four passages from different parts of the novel which show 'key' moments for that character.

2 Analyse the passages carefully, paying close attention to how language and imagery are used to present the character at different times.

3 Using examples from these passages, write a short essay about the development of your chosen character.

4 Alternatively, choose an important relationship from a novel you are working on and follow steps 1 to 3.

The setting

The imaginary 'world' of a novel, into which the reader is invited, is often more than simply 'the place where the story happens'. The physical environment may be important in itself or as a backdrop to the action but it can also be used to reflect the characters and their experiences. It can also be symbolic of the ideas the writer wishes to convey. However, the 'world' of a novel will also portray a society with its own culture, politics, and values. Characters may exist comfortably in their worlds, but often, the whole thrust of a novel depends on the central character being a misfit, or being in conflict with some aspect of their 'society', whether this is their family, their social class, a religious group, or a state.

The world of a novel can be as small as a household or as large as a nation. Jane Austen set herself tight limits, saying that 'Three or four families in a country village is the very thing to work on.' *Emma* is set in Highbury, a 'large and populous village almost amounting to a town'. London is only sixteen miles distant, but far enough in those days to seem out of easy reach. The action concerns only a few of the 'best' families in the village – those with whom the Woodhouses, at the top of their social ladder, can associate, and one or two others of lower status who provide material for comedy.

Although Jane Austen is quick to make fun of hypocrisy and snobbery, she does not challenge the rigid class boundaries of Highbury; in fact in this novel she endorses them. Emma's attempts to disregard them are definitely seen as misguided. Her matchmaking with Mr Elton on behalf of her 'friend' Harriet Smith, pretty, but illegitimate and penniless, causes only pain and embarrassment.

In *Hard Times*, the world Dickens creates is that of a northern English industrial town, a larger world than Jane Austen's Highbury. Like some of his characters, the setting is a caricature. It is based on a real town, but has exaggerated features. His intention of protesting against the deadening effects of Utilitarianism is never clearer than when he introduces us to Coketown. He presents us with an environment where the physical surroundings reflect the social conditions. Read his description and then consider it through the activity which follows.

Hard Times

Chapter 5
The Key-note
Coketown, to which Messrs Bounderby and Gradgrind now walked, was a triumph of fact; it had no greater taint of fancy in it than Mrs Gradgrind herself. Let us strike the key-note, Coketown, before pursuing our tune.
It was a town of red brick, or of brick that would have been red if the smoke and ashes had allowed it; but, as matters stood it was a town of unnatural red and black like the painted face of a savage. It was a town of machinery and tall chimneys, out of which interminable serpents of smoke trailed themselves for ever and ever, and never got uncoiled. It had a black canal in it, and a river that

ran purple with ill-smelling dye, and vast piles of building full of windows where there was a rattling and a trembling all day long, and where the piston of the steam-engine worked monotonously up and down, like the head of an elephant in a state of melancholy madness. It contained several large streets all very like one another, and many small streets still more like one another, inhabited by people equally like one another, who all went in and out at the same hours, with the same sound upon the same pavements, to do the same work, and to whom every day was the same as yesterday and tomorrow, and every year the counterpart of the last and the next.

Charles Dickens

Activity

How does Dickens present Coketown? Make notes on his use of:
• simile and metaphor
• colour and the senses
• the rhythm of the passage
• sentence construction

The world of *The Handmaid's Tale* is wider again. It is set in the future, in an imaginary state in America, The Republic of Gilead. Fearful about declining population, due to man-made environmental disaster, a dictatorship has assigned roles to all people, but particularly to women. Wives are idealized, non-sexual beings. They wear virginal blue, while those women capable of the all-important child-bearing are assigned to them as handmaids or breeders, dressed in red. This symbolizes blood, sex, and childbirth. It marks them out as 'fallen women'. Gilead is a state ruled by terror, in which it is highly dangerous to ask questions or to assert one's individuality in any way. We do not even discover the narrator's real name: she is merely the handmaid 'Of-Fred'.

None of this is made clear to us at the start of the novel. Only gradually as we read Offred's stream of consciousness narrative do we piece together enough information to understand what is going on. It is quite a way into the text before we are provided with some 'historical background'. Here, Offred, waiting to assist at a birth, remembers some of the teaching she received at the Red Centre, where the handmaids are trained.

The Handmaid's Tale

Chapter 19

The siren goes on and on. That used to be the sound of death, for ambulances or fires. Possibly it will be the sound of death today also. We will soon know. What will Ofwarren give birth to? A baby, as we all hope? Or something else, an Unbaby, with a pinhead or a snout like a dog's, or two bodies, or a hole in its heart or no arms, or webbed hands and feet? There's no telling. They could tell once, with machines, but that is now outlawed. What would be the point of knowing, anyway? You can't have them taken out; whatever it is must be carried to term.

The chances are one in four, we learned that at the Centre. The air got too full, once, of chemicals, rays, radiation, the water swarmed with toxic molecules, all of that takes years to clean up, and meanwhile they creep into your body, camp out in your fatty cells. Who knows, your very flesh may be polluted, dirty as an oily beach, sure death to shore birds and unborn babies. Maybe a vulture would die of eating you. Maybe you light up in the dark, like an old-fashioned watch. Death-watch. That's a kind of beetle, it buries carrion.

I can't think of myself, my body, sometimes, without seeing the skeleton: how I must appear to an electron. A cradle of life, made of bones; and within, hazards, warped proteins, bad crystals, jagged as glass. Women took medicines, pills, men sprayed trees, cows ate grass, all that souped-up piss flowed into the rivers. Not to mention the exploding atomic power plants, along the San Andreas fault, nobody's fault, during the earthquakes, and the mutant strain of syphilis no mould could touch. Some did it themselves, had themselves tied shut with catgut or scarred with chemicals. How could they, said Aunt Lydia, O how could they have done such a thing? Jezebels! Scorning God's gifts! Wringing her hands.

It's a risk you're taking, said Aunt Lydia, but you are the shock troops, you will march out in advance, into dangerous territory. The greater the risk, the greater the glory. She clasped her hands, radiant with our phony courage. We looked down at the tops of our desks. To go through all that and give birth to a shredder: it wasn't a fine thought. We didn't know exactly what would happen to the babies that didn't get passed, that were declared Unbabies. But we knew they were put somewhere, quickly, away.

Margaret Atwood

Activity

> Read the passage carefully and discuss in a small group what you learn about the following points.
> • What has happened in Gilead in the past.
> • What conditions are like in Gilead now.
> • The laws and customs of Gilead in respect of pregnancy and childbirth.
> • How propaganda and religion are used to ensure the women fit in with the needs of the regime.

In *Hard Times* and *The Handmaid's Tale*, the settings are very important. In both cases the writers have presented aspects they dislike about their own societies in an exaggerated form. This enables them to draw attention to these and to protest in an indirect way whilst being thought-provoking and entertaining. While Dickens demonstrates in Coketown the terrible results of extreme Utilitarianism, Margaret Atwood writes as a feminist, concerned about the environment and about women being defined and limited by their traditional roles. Both writers create worlds where people are reduced to particular functions. However, both have a hopeful note in that the 'human spirit' is not entirely crushed despite such repressive regimes. 'Fancy' and imagination may be buried and distorted in *Hard Times*, but they do not die completely. Similarly, through the very telling of her story we know that Offred is far more than just her 'viable ovaries'.

Activity

> Study and make notes on the setting of the novel you are studying.
> - What sort of 'world' is it? How large or small, open or restrictive? What are its rules, values, beliefs, and customs?
> - Locate passages where the author describes the physical surroundings, comments on the social order, or where characters act or speak in a way which represents their society.
> - Do the characters fit comfortably in their world or are they in opposition to it? Is this shown to be a good or bad thing?

Language and style

Unless we are studying linguistics, we do not usually discuss a writer's use of language in isolation from its content. What we are concerned with is how effectively language is used to create worlds or present characters, situations, and ideas. So you probably will have noticed that as we have looked at each of these aspects of the novel, we have always examined the writer's language and style at the same time.

Summary

Here are some of the features of language we have considered.
- **Narrative voice:** the choice of first-person or third-person narrative.
- **Imagery:** the use of simile and metaphor. Look particularly for recurring images or patterns of imagery.
- **Sentence/paragraph structure:** the use of sentences which are long or short, complete or incomplete, complex or simple.
- **Vocabulary:** the selection of one word or group of words rather than another.

For some examples, look again at the extracts from *Hard Times* which present Louisa Gradgrind and Coketown.

The modern novel

Novels by Twentieth-Century authors, particularly contemporary writers, are regularly set for A-level study. They are also popular choices for coursework or comparative studies. Writers of our own time may engage our interest by exploring situations or aspects of life or society which are familiar to us, and we are less likely to find their language archaic or old-fashioned, so they can seem more accessible than those of the Eighteenth or Nineteenth Centuries.

On the other hand, since around the second decade of the Twentieth Century, when 'modernist' artists, writers and musicians tried deliberately to break away from conventions and rules, writers have tended to experiment with the form of the novel in many ways. For example, Virginia Woolf, a key modernist writer, challenged the 'rules' of novel writing in several ways. In one of her novels, *Jacob's Room*, the central character never appears or speaks, and an impression of him has to be pieced together from the comments and reactions of other characters. In *The Waves*, each paragraph represents the thoughts of one of six narrators who take it in turns to 'speak' their interior monologues.

More recent modern novels set for AS- or A-level, written since 1950, are rarely straightforward, third-person chronological narratives. We have already considered Margaret Atwood's *The Handmaid's Tale*; here are some further examples of how modern novelists experiment with the genre:

- *Waterland*, by Graham Swift, is built up like the construction of a mosaic with each chapter contributing an event, or some aspect of the setting or the historical background, until the last 'piece' falls into place. As a historian, Swift is interested in showing us that what becomes of people is the result or culmination of many things that have occurred in the past, of which the significance may not have been obvious at the time.
- In *Enduring Love*, Ian McEwan bases his plot on a fictional psychiatric case study, which he presents in an appendix to the novel as if it were a genuine article from a scientific journal. The novel's 'ending' is hidden there. He also shifts the narrative viewpoint away from the protagonist at times by inserting several letters received from other characters.
- French author Georges Perec wrote one novel, translated into English as *A Void*, in which the narrator never uses the letter 'e' – which happens to be the initial of a woman he loved. In another of his works, *W or the Memory of Childhood*, the first person narrator alternates childhood memories with chapters describing a strange island where life is entirely focused on sport, but which comes gradually to bear an uncanny resemblance to the concentration camp in which his parents died.

Such deliberate choices of structure, narrative technique or language can sometimes, though not always, be overt in modern novels and provide plenty of ideas to discuss and analyse. On the other hand, their plots and themes may be obscure. They are less likely to fit into patterns or have predictable – especially happy – endings, and may leave us with more questions than answers.

The Victorian novelist Anthony Trollope once wrote that novels should be written because writers 'have a story to tell', not because they 'have to tell a story', but literary novelists have almost always set out to do something more. From the strong moralistic messages of the earliest novels, like those of Samuel Richardson, through the Nineteenth-Century concern with exposing social injustice as we saw in *Hard Times*, to present-day questioning of almost every previously accepted belief, novelists have set out not just to tell stories, but to convey messages or explore ideas.

In the modern world, few of the religious beliefs, political systems or moral codes which ordered life in earlier times have remained unchallenged. Events like the World Wars, the Holocaust and nuclear bombings have forced people to think about human life in different ways. Assumptions which would have been standard a hundred years ago no longer seem viable. While philosophers have always asked questions about the nature of reality and the meaning of life, some Twentieth-Century thinking tends towards denying 'meaning' altogether. It is suggested, for example, that

- human life is not controlled or shaped by a greater power: 'God is dead'
- there is no such thing as 'fate' or 'destiny'; what happens to us and even the fact that we exist at all is random – a matter of pure chance
- if human life is to have any meaning, we have to create that meaning ourselves
- deciding what is 'good' and what is 'evil' is no longer just a matter of following codes like the Old Testament commandments or Islamic Law. Ethical questions are far more open to debate and individuals are confronted with complex moral choices

So, in many ways, life has become less clear-cut. Our age is a melting-pot of ideas, exciting, perhaps, for its openness, but also bewildering and disturbing.

Not surprisingly, this is reflected in modern literature. If the 'story' of human life no longer has a coherent 'shape' or obvious meaning, neither do the stories of many modern novels. Sometimes it seems that they do not 'have a story to tell' at all. Writers may use their novels to explore their own personal views about life or morality. In the first half of the Twentieth Century, novels – some of which, like the work of D. H. Lawrence or James Joyce, went on to become literary classics – were suppressed or banned for condoning homosexuality or for being sexually explicit in ways which are very mild by today's standards. These days, you can expect novels to air almost any issue: incest, sexual 'deviance', euthanasia and religious fanaticism all feature in novels currently set for AS- or A-level.

The most successful modern novels are like the best novels of any age. They combine the exploration of ideas which concern or interest us with stories which engage and hold the attention of the reader. However, while the older novels we study are likely to have remained popular and become 'classics', we have no way of knowing whether modern novels will stand the test of time and continue to appeal to future generations of readers. With older novels, we have access to critical writings and other people's opinions. Studying a modern text can force us to create opinions of our own. All this being said, we can approach a modern novel just as we would any other.

We have already considered one modern novel, *The Handmaid's Tale*, and will go on to look more closely at the work of another contemporary novelist, Ian McEwan, in the Special Feature which follows. To see something of the variety to be found in modern novels, we can introduce an example by Iris Murdoch, a writer who was also a philosopher and particularly interested in moral questions.

Iris Murdoch's *The Bell*

In *The Bell*, a rather unlikely collection of people come together to live in a lay community attached to Imber Abbey, which houses an enclosed order of nuns. Led by Michael Meade, an ex-schoolmaster, their aim is to live a simple, religious life, but with the arrival of several guests – including Paul Greenfield, an art historian who is studying ancient manuscripts in the convent, his estranged wife Dora, and Toby Gashe, who has just left school and is 'greatly attracted by the idea of living and working ... with a group of holy people who have given up the world' – this is disrupted completely. Toby expects the community will be 'clean, simple and vigorous', but all sorts of complex motives and sexual undercurrents lie beneath the surface.

Michael Meade has suppressed his homosexuality and kept secret the fact that he had a relationship with one of his ex-pupils, Nick Fawley. Nick, an unpredictable character, is now a guest of the community through the influence of his sister Catherine, who is shortly to take her vows and enter the abbey. Michael becomes attracted to Toby and allows his feelings to show. Nick is jealous, while Toby's disillusionment and fear of homosexuality lead him to become sexually involved with Dora. At the same time, Catherine harbours a secret love for Michael.

The 'bell' of the title is the ancient bell of Imber Abbey, lost for centuries and associated with the legend of a nun who betrayed her vows and was cursed. The bell is said to have leaped from the tower into the lake in response to this. A new bell is about to be installed when Toby unearths the old one at the bottom of the lake. He and Dora wildly plan to surprise everyone with a 'miracle' by replacing the new bell with the old one. At the climax of the novel there is a ceremony to admit both the bell and Catherine – who is also, in a sense, betraying her vows – to the abbey. Sabotaged by Nick, the ceremony goes horribly (and rather comically) wrong. Like the submerged bell, underlying passions come to the surface, and the community erupts in madness and suicide.

The symbol of the bell, with its legend, draws together the themes of religious belief and sexuality. When Toby and Dora succeed in dragging it from the lake, they are overcome by desire for each other, and their sexual union, inside the bell itself, is announced by its sound, which is said to portend death. The bell, and Catherine on her way to a 'pure' life in the convent, are both toppled by the sexual drives which cannot be suppressed by religion and which eventually destroy the community.

Iris Murdoch writes rather differently here from the other modern novelists we have mentioned so far. Her style can seem deceptively straightforward in comparison. She tells a good story with great precision, and we are sometimes almost unaware of the complexity of its ideas and symbolism.

Activity

> Read the following extract from the beginning of _The Bell_ and ask yourself the questions we used earlier to explore 'Opening pages', on page 10.

Dora Greenfield left her husband because she was afraid of him. She decided six months later to return to him for the same reason. The absent Paul, haunting her with letters and telephone bells and imagined footsteps on the stairs had begun to be the greater torment. Dora suffered from guilt, and with guilt came fear. She decided at last that the persecution of his presence was to be preferred to the persecution of his absence.

Dora was still very young, though she vaguely thought of herself as past her prime. She came of a lower middle-class London family. Her father had died when she was nine years old, and her mother, with whom she had never got on very well, had married again. When Dora was eighteen she entered the Slade school of art with a scholarship, and had been there two years when she encountered Paul. The role of an art student suited Dora. It was indeed the only role she had ever been able whole-heartedly to play. She had been an ugly and wretched schoolgirl. As a student she grew plump and peach-like and had a little pocket money of her own, which she spent on big multi-coloured skirts and jazz records and sandals. At that time, which although it was only three years ago now seemed unimaginably remote, she had been happy. Dora, who had so lately discovered in herself a talent for happiness, was the more dismayed to find that she could be happy neither with her husband nor without him.

Paul Greenfield, who was thirteen years older than his wife, was an art historian connected with the Courtauld Institute. He came of an old family of German Bankers and had money of his own. He had been born in England and attended an English public school, and preferred not to remember the distinction of his ancestors. Although his assets were never idle, he did not speak of stocks and shares. He first met Dora when he came to lecture on medieval wood-carving at the Slade.

Dora had accepted his proposal of marriage without hesitation and for a great many reasons. She married him for his good taste and his flat in Knightsbridge. She married him for a certain integrity and nobility of character which she saw in him. She married him because he was so wonderfully more grown-up than her thin neurotic art-student friends. She married him a little for his money. She admired him and was extremely flattered by his attentions. She hoped, by making what her mother (who was bursting with envy) called a 'good marriage', to be able to get inside society and learn how to behave; although this was something she did not put clearly to herself at the time. She married, finally, because of the demonic intensity of Paul's desire for her. He was a passionate and poetic suitor, and something exotic in him touched Dora's imagination, starved throughout her meagre education, and unsatisfied still amid the rather childish and provincial gaieties of her student life. Dora, though insufficiently reflective to suffer from strong inferiority feelings, had never valued herself highly. She was amazed that Paul should notice her at all, and she passed quickly from this amazement to the luxurious pleasure of being able so easily to delight this subtle and sophisticated person. She never doubted that she was in love.

Iris Murdoch

- You probably noticed immediately that this is a third-person narrative. Murdoch adopts an 'omniscient' position, which allows her not only to describe characters from the outside, but to give us access to their thoughts, feelings and motives. She provides precise, explicit information about them, and seems very much in control of what we know and how we respond. She begins with a statement that arouses curiosity, but does not leave us to work much out for ourselves. (Compare this with the opening of *The Handmaid's Tale*.)

- The focus is very much on aquainting us with the character, background and life history of one character, Dora Greenfield. Although she is presented in the third person, because we are told so much about her inner world the narrative viewpoint is partly hers. We are also introduced to her husband, Paul, but more from Dora's perspective than his own, so that he seems a secondary character. Dora is not the novel's only important character, however. Later, the perspective shifts so that at different times Toby Gashe or Michael Meade is at the centre of the narrative. In a sense, Murdoch goes beyond the limits of what is 'realistic' by doing this: only God or an omniscient being can see into the minds of more than one person!
- There is little here to suggest what the novel's 'situation' or setting is going to be. Like us, Dora has yet to become aquainted with the Community.
- Though the perspective is partly Dora's, we also get a sense of what Murdoch's attitude to her character might be. She seems detached, or even ruthless, about Dora's lack of depth – she is 'insufficiently reflective to suffer from strong inferiority feelings' – and Murdoch exposes Dora's motives for marrying Paul, and yet she doesn't judge Dora. (Later in the novel we find that she presents all her important characters in this way: she is honest about their qualities and failings, but invites us to understand them and to feel compassion for them.)
- The style is quite factual and precise. The sentences tend to be short, even clipped, but are sometimes paired and balanced. Look closely again at how the opening paragraph is constructed. There is plenty of detail and a few telling images, for example, where Dora is suggested by 'plump and peachlike'. We get a sense that Murdoch is carefully controlling her use of language.

Now that you know a little more about the novel look at this extract from later in the text. Toby and Dora are about to put into action their ambitious plan to raise the bell from the bottom of the lake.

Activity

> 1 Read the following passage carefully. Focus on the characters of Toby and Dora and make notes on how they are presented here.
> 2 Use your notes to write a response to the following question:
> Write as fully as you can about how Toby and Dora and the relationship between them are presented in the following extract, which is taken from Chapter 17 of *The Bell*.

The mechanical details of the plan aroused in Toby a sort of ecstasy. It was all so difficult and yet so exquisitely possible and he brooded over it as over a work of art. It was also his homage to Dora and his proof to himself that he was in love. Ever since the moment in the chapel when Dora's image had so obligingly filled out that blank form of femininity towards which Toby interrogatively turned his inclinations he had been, he felt, under her domination, indeed as he almost precisely put it, under her orders. The fact that Dora was married troubled Toby very little. He had no intention of making any declaration to Dora or revealing by any word or gesture what was his state of mind. He took a proud satisfaction in this reticence, and felt rather like a medieval knight who sighs and suffers for a lady whom he has scarcely seen and will never possess. This conception of her remoteness made the vitality of her presence and the easy friendliness with which, in their curious enterprise, she treated him, all the more delightful. She had for him a radiance and an authority, and the freshness of the emotion which she aroused gave him a sense almost of the renewal of innocence.

[Toby] made his way cautiously along the path beside the lake. The moon had not failed them and was high in the sky and almost full and the wide glimmering scene of trees and water was attentive, significant as if aware of a great deed which was to be done. The lake, so soon to yield up its treasure, was serene, almost inviting, and the air was warm. He walked faster now, watching out for the figure of Dora ahead of him, almost breathless with anticipation and excitement. They had agreed to meet at the barn. He knew very well that there were a hundred things which could go wrong; but he burned with a confidence and with the hope of delighting Dora and with a sheer feverish desire to get at the bell.

He reached the open space by the ramp and stopped. After the soft swishing sound of his footsteps there was an eerie silence. Then Dora emerged, taking shape in the moonlight, from the path leading to the barn. He spoke her name. 'Thank God,' said Dora in a low voice. 'I've been absolutely scared stiff in this place. There were such funny noises, I kept thinking the drowned nun was after me.'

A clear sound arose quite near them suddenly in the reeds and they both jumped. It was a harsh yet sweet trilling cry which rose several notes and then died bubbling away.

'Whatever was that?' said Dora.

'The poor man's nightingale, Peter Topglass calls him. He won't bother us. Now, Dora, quickly to work.'

'I think we're perfectly mad,' said Dora. 'Why did we ever have this insane idea? Why did you encourage me?' She was half serious.

'Everything will be all right,' said Toby. Dora's flutter made him calm and decisive. He paused, breathing deeply. The sedge warbler sang again, a little farther off. The lake was brittle and motionless, the reeds and grasses moving very slightly in the warm breeze, the moon as bright as it could be. It seemed then to Toby fantastic that in a moment there would be the roar of a tractor, the breaking into the lake. He felt as an army commander might feel just before launching a surprise attack.

He took a few steps into the wood. The tractor was there where he had left it, just outside the barn on the lake side. It was lucky that the barn had large doors opening both ways so that it had been possible to drive the tractor straight through. He had not dared to bring it any nearer to the water for fear its polished red radiator might be visible during daylight from the causeway. He quickly took off his clothes, and dressed only in his bathing trunks approached the tractor, shining his torch on it and checking the hawser and the winch. The winch had not been in use lately, but Toby had given it a good oiling and it seemed to be perfectly sound. He unwound a good length of hawser and looped it loosely round the drum. All this while Dora was hovering about behind him. At such a moment, attached as he was to her, he envied his medieval prototype who at least did not have to deal with both his lady and his adventure at the same time. For most of the operation Dora was useless.

'Just stand by near the water, would you,' said Toby, ' and do what I tell you.' He took a deep breath. He felt himself magnificent. He started the engine of the tractor.

Iris Murdoch

Set text examination questions

Novels are long and complex, and you will have devoted a substantial amount of time on your course to studying your text. As with any other set text, the time you are given to write about your set text novel in AS- or A-level Literature examinations is very short – perhaps as little as 45 minutes. This means you will only be able use a very small part of your knowledge about the text. In your answer, you must be relevant and selective.

Examination questions will focus your attention on one aspect of the text, such as a character. You need to keep this idea in your mind throughout and make sure every point you make is relevant to the question.

It is vital in questions on the novel that you are selective, i.e that you have the ability to home in quickly on episodes in the text which are most useful in answering the question and choose quotations which best illustrate your ideas. Examiners frequently complain that students are not sufficiently selective about what they include.

However little time you have, it is a good idea to give a small part of that to planning your answer. Even two or three minutes can be enough to help you work out what it is essential to mention and to find a sense of direction in your writing.

For detailed guidance on all aspects of revising set texts and developing exam-writing skills see Unit 15.

Coursework with novels

In coursework, you can explore a topic in more detail and in a more leisurely way than you can under the pressure of examination time limits. If you are concentrating on one novel text for coursework, any of the aspects covered in this unit will provide the basis for a coursework essay question.

Many students also choose to study novels for the comparative element of the course. Reading two or more novels which have something in common, and working out the connections and contrasts between them, can be very satisfying. There is more on this in Unit 11; for more on writing coursework essays and framing suitable questions see Unit 16.

Special Feature: Ian McEwan

Ian McEwan was born into an Army family in 1948. He spent much of his early childhood abroad, living in Germany, Singapore and North Africa, where he enjoyed the outdoor life and read widely, before being sent to boarding school, which he describes as a 'dark time'. He studied English at Sussex University, initially aiming for an academic career, but felt his student life had 'no sparkle'. Later, at the University of East Anglia, he specialized in modern fiction, had what he calls a 'second adolescence', and was 'on the edge of hippydom' and the student politics of the early 1970s. He also became more interested in creative writing than academic work, and published his first short stories. Since then, he has written eight novels and several film scripts.

In many of his earlier stories, and his first novel, *The Cement Garden*, published in 1978, the focus is on adolescence, while the characters in his recent works, *Enduring Love* (1997) and *Amsterdam* (1998) are highly educated, financially comfortable adults. His novels address a range of themes and situations, but at the heart of most of his work there is a concern with people and relationships and with how these are affected by internal, psychological forces and external pressures.

His work also reveals a fascination with the macabre and he is often accused of deliberately writing to 'shock', or of creating a 'nasty world...of horrible imaginings – and sometimes deeds'. In a television interview for BBC2's *The Book Programme* in 1979, he responded to such a challenge:

'If I'm sitting down facing an empty sheet of paper – what is going to compel me into writing fiction is not what is nice and easy and pleasant and somehow affirming, but somehow what is bad and difficult and unsettling. That's the kind of tension I need to start me writing. Beyond that, I suppose, I've always been trying to assert some kind of slender optimism in my stories, and I don't think I can really do that unless I can do it in a world that seems to me to be fundamentally threatening, so what I really worry about is gratuitous optimism, not gratuitous violence ...

'If we're talking about shock, I'm slightly shocked at all this shock, I haven't really met anybody who has told me that they were shocked by my stories. I've met plenty of people who didn't like them; I've yet to meet somebody who said: 'Your stories are so revolting I couldn't read them.'

If his stories do often involve cruelty, violence or humiliation, they also tackle ethical issues: *The Cement Garden* has been described as a 'fable' and

Amsterdam as a 'morality tale', but he does not necessarily spell out his moral messages. His aim is to do something more subtle:

'I try to keep that sense of the story that is moral in some kind of abeyance, and hope that through restraint, one will generate a degree of compassion for the right people, even if the right people are in some other sense, the wrong people.'

His writing also tends to be very precise, revealing his preference for clarity and the care he takes with choices of language and detail.

These qualities make him a writer who provokes strong feelings. As interviewer Christopher Ricks put it, there is

'a hard sheen to everything he does, a combination of fire and ice which chills some people and scorches others'.

Several novels by Ian McEwan, each rather different, have been chosen as set texts on A-level syllabuses, including *The Cement Garden*, *The Child in Time*, *Enduring Love* and *Amsterdam*. In this special feature we will look in more detail at *Enduring Love*.

Starting points

McEwan often chooses real situations, genuine unusual 'cases' and live issues as the starting points of his novels.

- *The Cement Garden* was based on a real case in which some orphaned children concealed the death of their mother and buried the body so that they would not be separated or taken into care.
- In *Amsterdam*, McEwan explores issues like political 'sleaze'. The sexual antics of politicians have regularly hit the headlines in the last two decades. The novel illustrates the opposition between the individual's right to privacy and the public's 'right to know', if the person involved is a public figure. The recent legalisation of euthanasia in The Netherlands and cases where people have tried to capitalize on this also provide crucial material for the plot.
- *Enduring Love* is constructed around two such notions. First, the opening is based on a real incident involving an accident with a helium-filled balloon. McEwan uses this to introduce a moral question about how far human beings can be expected to be *altruistic*, in other words to put themselves in danger in order to help others. In McEwan's own words:

'It's actually based on a real event. There's a helium balloon, in a high wind, there's a man in his fifties with a young boy and they're trying to tether this balloon. The man is rather inexperienced and panic-stricken and they're having a great deal of difficulty. The boy is in the basket, the man half out of the basket, the wind is blowing hard and he's being dragged along the ground. The narrator, plus three or four other people, converge on this wide, high field and come running over to help. At some point the wind lifts all of them – they've all got ropes – and they're faced with an immediate dilemma.

They know that if they can all hang on, their combined weight will bring the thing to the ground. If one lets go, it's crazy for anyone else to hang on. In this I saw a parable, a microcosm, of one of those great conflicts in our lives between altruism and that other primary necessity of looking after yourself.'

The book's other starting point is a rare psychological disorder known as de Clerambault's Syndrome, which causes the sufferer to fall violently and obsessively in love with someone who does not reciprocate, and also to have delusions that the love is returned. McEwan read case studies and an account by a man whose life had been ruined by a stalker suffering from the syndrome.

The best way into the novel, though, is to go straight to the text itself. The first chapter of *Enduring Love* has been called 'near perfect'. It is indeed very striking. It illustrates clearly some of the 'tactics' McEwan uses in the novel as a whole and provides plenty of ideas for discussion, so we will look at a substantial extract from the novel's opening pages.

Activity

> **1** Read the extract carefully, making notes on the following points and any other features that capture your attention.
> - the effect and implications of the very first sentence
> - the type of narrative and the 'voice' of the narrator
> - what you learn about the characters
> - any narrative 'techniques' you notice
> - how much you learn about what actually happened
>
> **2** Discuss your ideas with a partner and/or with the rest of the group.

Enduring Love

The beginning is simple to mark. We were in sunlight under a turkey oak, partly protected from a strong, gusty wind. I was kneeling on the grass with a corkscrew in my hand, and Clarissa was passing me the bottle – a 1987 Daumas Gassac. This was the moment, this was the pinprick on the time map: I was stretching out my hand, and as the cool neck and the black foil touched my palm, we heard a man's shout. We turned to look across the field and saw the danger. Next thing, I was running towards it. The transformation was absolute: I don't recall dropping the corkscrew, or getting to my feet, or making a decision, or hearing the caution Clarissa called after me. What idiocy, to be racing into this story and its labyrinths, sprinting away from our happiness among the fresh spring grasses by the oak. There was the shout again, and a child's cry, enfeebled by the wind that roared in the tall trees along the hedgerows. I ran faster. And there, suddenly, from different points around the field, four other men were converging on the scene, running like me.

I see us from three hundred feet up, through the eyes of the buzzard we had watched earlier, soaring, circling and dipping in the tumult of currents: five men running silently towards the centre of a hundred-acre field. I approached from the south-east, with the wind at my back. About two hundred yards to my left two men ran side by side. They were farm labourers who had been repairing the fence along the field's southern edge where it skirts the road. The same distance beyond them was the motorist, John Logan, whose car was banked on the grass verge with its door, or doors, wide open. Knowing what I know now, it's odd to evoke the figure of Jed Parry directly ahead of me, emerging from a line of beeches on the far side of the field a quarter of a mile away, running into the wind. To the buzzard Parry and I were tiny forms, our white shirts brilliant against the green, rushing towards each other like lovers, innocent of the grief this entanglement would bring. The encounter that would unhinge us was minutes away, its enormity disguised from us not only by the barrier of time but by the colossus in the centre of the field that drew us in with the power of a terrible ratio that set fabulous magnitude against the puny human distress at its base. What was Clarissa doing? She said she walked quickly towards the centre of the field. I don't know how she resisted the urge to run. By the time it happened – the event I am about to describe, the fall – she had almost caught us up and was well placed as an observer, unencumbered by participation, by the ropes and the shouting, and by our fatal lack of co-operation. What I describe is shaped by what Clarissa saw too, by what we told each other in the time of obsessive re-examination that followed: the aftermath, an appropriate term for what happened in a field waiting for its early summer mowing. The aftermath, the second crop, the growth promoted by that first cut in May.

I'm holding back, delaying the information. I'm lingering in the prior moment because it was a time when other outcomes were still possible; the convergence of six figures in a flat green space has a comforting geometry from the buzzard's perspective, the knowable, limited plane of the snooker table. The initial conditions, the force and the direction of the force, define all the consequent pathways, all the angles of collision and return, and the glow of the overhead light bathes the field, the baize and all its moving bodies, in reassuring clarity. I think that while we were still converging, before we made contact, we were in a state of mathematical grace. I linger on our dispositions, the relative distances and the compass point – because as far as these occurrences were concerned, this was the last time I understood anything clearly at all.

What were we running towards? I don't think any of us would ever know fully. But superficially the answer was a balloon. Not the nominal space that encloses a cartoon character's speech or thought, or by analogy, the kind that's driven by mere hot air. It was an enormous balloon filled with helium, that elemental gas forged from hydrogen in the nuclear furnace of the stars, first step along the way in the generation of multiplicity and variety of matter in the universe, including ourselves and all our thoughts.

We were running towards a catastrophe, which itself was a kind of furnace in whose heat identities and fates would buckle into new shapes. At the base of the balloon was a basket in which there was a boy, and by the basket, clinging to a rope, was a man in need of help.

Even without the balloon the day would have been marked for memory, though in the most pleasurable of ways, for this was a reunion after a separaton of six weeks, the longest Clarissa and I had spent apart in our seven years. On the way out to Heathrow I had made a detour to Covent Garden and found a semi legal place to park, close to Carluccio's. I went in and put together a picnic whose centre-piece was a great ball of mozzarella which the assistant fished out of an earthenware vat with a wooden claw. I also bought black olives, mixed salad and focaccia. Then I hurried up Long Acre to Bertram Rota's to take delivery of Clarissa's birthday present. Apart from the flat and our car, it was the most expensive single item I had ever bought. The rarity of this little book seemed to give off a heat I could feel through the thick brown paper wrapping as I walked back up the street.

Summary

You will probably have noticed some of the following points:

- The opening sentence can be read as a straightforward statement, but it also carries the implication that although the 'beginning is simple to mark', the rest of the story may not be. It also leads you straight into the story at the point he has chosen to be the start of his narrative.
- This is a first-person narrative. The narrator describes the scene in detail, using precise, rather scientific language. He is exact about the species of the tree, the make and year of the bottle of wine, the size of the field, the distances between people and the directions from which they approach. His imagined aerial view, 'from the buzzard's perspective', implies that he wants to see the incident in a detached or objective way and analyse it as a scientist would, using mathematical vocabulary like 'plane' and 'force'. Not content with telling us merely that the balloon is filled with helium, he goes on to expound rather pretentiously on the importance of helium in the creation of the universe.
- Apart from what the narrator reveals about himself through his 'style', we learn little about the characters until the end of the extract. There are hints, in Clarissa's name and the vintage wine, which are reinforced by the information in the last paragraph, that these people are rather affluent and well-educated. Their picnic comes from an exclusive-sounding London delicatessen and the narrator has spent a large sum of money buying a rare book for his partner Clarissa's birthday. Their relationship seems to be a close one: they have spent little time apart in seven years, their reunion is described as 'pleasurable' and the expensive gift has been chosen with care.
- The narrative technique could be described as one of avoidance: this narrator tantalizes the reader by doing everything he can to avoid telling us what actually happened. Though he seems to begin directly enough, he
  - takes time filling in details of the scene with mathematical precision
  - veers off to tell us how the scene might look through the eyes of a buzzard
  - pauses in his own narrative to wonder what Clarissa was doing
  - admits that he is 'holding back, delaying the information' with the excuse that he wants to hold on to 'the prior moment because it was a time when other outcomes were still possible'
  - tells us that the event he is about to describe was a catastrophe
  - and when he finally tells us what he saw, he still doesn't tell us what happened, but instead embarks on a flashback to earlier in the day which delays his account of the incident for a further five pages

Later in the chapter, he at last begins to report the incident itself, but continues to use delaying tactics. Look at what he does even at the very climax of the story. By this time, the running men have reached the balloon and have hold of it by a rope, but haven't managed to rescue the small boy, who is in danger of being blown away:

I heard what was coming two seconds before it reached us. It was as though an express train were traversing the treetops, hurtling towards us. An airy, whining, whooshing sound grew to full volume in half a second. At the inquest the Met office figures for wind speeds that day were part of the evidence, and there were some gusts, it was said, of seventy miles an hour. This must have been one, but before I let it reach us, let me freeze the frame – there's a security in stillness – to describe our circle.

To my right the ground dropped away. Immediately to my left was John Logan, a family doctor from Oxford, forty-two years old, married to a historian, with two children. He was not the youngest of our group, but he was the fittest. He played tennis and belonged to a mountaineering club ...

This method of creating suspense is a feature of the novel which we will consider again later.

The plot

The word 'plot' is particularly appropriate in the case of *Enduring Love*, as it has many of the features of a psychological thriller or a detective story. The balloon incident of the opening chapter, which results in the death of John Logan, turns out to be a catalyst which links together the fates of several characters who would not otherwise have met and sets off a complex series of inter-related events. The idea that much of what happens to us is purely a matter of chance fascinates Ian McEwan.

'I often think that when people talk of coincidences that they're almost bound to occur because we're like so many atoms in a turbulent sustem or a gas under pressure. If you lead an averagely busy life, the number of people that you collide with, so to speak, is extraordinary. One could become your husband, or your wife, or for that matter, your murderer. That random element in life is a gift to a novelist to make a pattern of it, to make some sense of it, to contest its meaning or even ask whether there's any meaning to it at all. That's part of the pleasure and unpredictability of writing a novel.'

It is their involvement in the accident which brings the narrator, Joe Rose, face to face with Jed Parry. This triggers the syndrome which turns Parry into a threatening stalker and provides the material for the main plot, which reaches a climax when Joe is driven to visit an 'underworld' of drug dealers to acquire a gun to defend himself, and Clarissa becomes Parry's hostage. This is mirrored by a sub-plot, in which Joe attempts to help Logan's widow, who wrongly suspects her husband of infidelity. Parry is deluded about an unreal love, while Mrs Logan is deluded about a love which was genuine.

Themes

In outline, this plot sounds rather sensational, but under the surface, the novel explores several themes and ideas.

- **Love**   As the title suggests, love is a central theme here, but it takes several forms. The title is ambiguous: Parry's irrational 'love' for Joe *endures*, and Joe has to *endure* it, to put up with it. Joe's relationship with Clarissa, which seems stable and loving at the start, is threatened by Joe's desperate attempts to deal with Parry's obsession, and we are left to wonder whether their love will *endure*. We also see Parry's love for his God, Joe's love for science and Clarissa's for literature.

- **Science, romance and religion**   'Rational' science is set against 'irrational' romantic love and religion. Joe, the scientist, who has an explanation for everything but is not very emotionally self-aware, contrasts with Clarissa, who is devoted to the study of the romantic poet Keats. Here is an example of them differing. Joe has just read her a scientific paper on babies' smiles.

A

Everything was being stripped down, she said, and in the process some larger meaning was lost. What a zoologist had to say about a baby's smile could be of no real interest. The truth of that smile was in the eye and heart of the parent, and in the unfolding love which only had meaning through time.
We were having one of our late-night kitchen table sessions. I told her I thought she had spent too much time lately in the company of John Keats. A genius no doubt, but an obscurantist too who had thought science was robbing the world of wonder, when the opposite was the case. If we value a baby's smile, why not contemplate its source? Are we to say that all infants enjoy a secret joke? Or that God reaches down and tickles them? Or, least implausibly, because they learn smiling from their mothers? But then, deaf-blind babies smile too. That smile must be hard-wired, and for good evolutionary reasons. Clarissa said that I had not understood her. There was nothing wrong with analysing the bits, but it was easy to lose sight of the whole. I agreed. The work of synthesis was crucial. Clarissa said I still did not understand her, she was talking about love. I said I was too, and how babies who could not yet speak got more of it for themselves. She said no, I still didn't understand. There we had left it. No hard feelings. We had had this conversation in different forms on many occasions.

Joe also finds himself up against Parry, who is fanatically religious as well as deluded. Joe's research reveals an explanation for Parry's behaviour, but it can't help him to deal with powerful emotions, whether they are his own or other people's. However, we do see that Joe's science enables him to appreciate and wonder at the world around him: it is as inspiring as poetry is to Clarissa and religion to Parry.

- **Moral choices**   As we saw earlier, McEwan sees the balloon incident as a parable, a tale which makes a moral point. Here is Joe's version – in scientific terms, of course – of the choice which faces all five men in the moment when the balloon is lifted from the ground.

B

I didn't know, nor have I ever discovered, who let go first. I'm not prepared to accept that it was me. But everyone claims not to have been first. What is certain is that if we had not broken ranks, our collective weight would have brought the balloon to earth a quarter of the way down the slope a few seconds later as the gust subsided. But as I've said, there was no team, there was no plan, no agreement to be broken. No failure. So can we accept that it was right, every man for himself? Were we all happy afterwards that this was a reasonable course? We never had that comfort, for there was a deeper covenant, ancient and automatic, written in our nature. Co-operation – the basis of our earliest hunting successes, the force behind our evolving capacity for language, the glue of our social cohesion. Our misery in the aftermath was proof that we knew we had failed ourselves. But letting go was in our nature too. Selfishness is also written on our hearts. This is our mammalian conflict – what to give to the others, and what to keep for yourself. Treading that line, keeping the others in check, and being kept in check by them, is what we call morality. Hanging a few feet above the Chilterns escarpment, our crew enacted morality's ancient, irresolvable dilemma: us, or me.

> There are other moments of moral choice. Joe raids Clarissa's desk for signs of infidelity, again explaining his behaviour in terms of human evolutionary instincts. Later, though, when he decides to get hold of a gun and when he shoots Parry, he no longer stops to consider the biological reasons for his actions.

Activity

> With a partner, or in a small group, discuss the two short extracts above, making sure that you understand the ideas and issues involved.
> 1 In extract A, do you have more sympathy with Joe's scientific viewpoint or Clarissa's 'romantic' ideals? Why?
> 2 Of the two 'human instincts' which operate in extract B, which do you think is the stronger? Would you hold on or would you let go? Can you think of any real life cases which illustrate a similar dilemma?
> 3 Comment on the narrator's use of language in each extract.

Characters

This is a novel where characters, themes and narrative style are closely interlinked. We have already seen how Joe's character is bound up with his being a scientist and that this affects the way he tells his story. McEwan made this choice very deliberately:

'I've always wanted prose that has about it a great clarity. Having a scientist narrate this novel I was able to indulge my own taste for precision in what's happening.'

At the same time, though, McEwan causes us to have doubts about whether we can entirely trust Joe's account by undermining him in various ways. As we see the reactions of others around him, we may gradually begin to doubt his perceptions and even his sanity. This has a double edge: we can simultaneously empathize with Joe's experience of the nightmare of not being believed, and we can also see exactly why Clarissa and the police have their doubts about him. Joe himself regularly reminds us of the unreliability, in scientific terms, of human perception, memory and motivation.

Activity

> With a partner, remind yourself of the extracts you have already read and look closely at the following passages. Discuss your responses to Joe, the narrator.
> **1** How far do you trust his version of events, how much sympathy do you feel for him, and why?
> **2** If you have doubts about him, how does McEwan bring this about?

A

Here, Joe first confides in Clarissa his fears about Parry, who has been following him.

... I had to tell her. 'Do you remember, the day it happened, just as we were falling asleep the phone rang?'
'Mmm. Wrong number.'
'It was that guy with the pony tail. You know, the one who wanted me to pray. Jed Parry.'
She frowned. 'Why didn't you say? What did he want?'
I didn't pause. 'He said he loved me...'
For a fraction of time the world froze as she took this in. Then she laughed. Easily, merrily.
'Joe! You didn't tell me. You were embarrassed? You clot!'
'It was just one more thing. And then, I felt bad about not telling you, so it got harder. And then I didn't want to interrupt last night.'
'What did he say? Just, I love you, like that?'
'Yeah. He said, I feel it too. I love you...'
Clarissa put her hand over her mouth, little-girl-style. I hadn't expected delight. 'A secret gay love affair with a Jesus freak! I can't wait to tell your science friends.'
'All right, all right.' But I felt lightened to have her teasing me. 'There's more though.'
'You're getting married.'
'Listen. Yesterday he was following me.'
'My God. He's got it bad.'
I knew I had to prise her from this levity, for all the comfort it gave. 'Clarissa, it's scary.' I told her about the presence in the library, and how I had run out into the square. She interrupted me.
'But you didn't actually see him in the library.'
'I saw his shoe as he went out the door. White trainers, with red laces. It had to be him.'
'But you didn't see his face.'
'Clarissa, it was him!'
'Don't get angry with me, Joe. You didn't see his face, and he wasn't in the square.'
'No. He'd gone.'

She was looking at me in a new way now and was moving through the conversation with the caution of a bomb disposal expert. 'Let me get this straight. You had this idea you were being followed even before you saw his shoe?'

'It was just a feeling, a bad feeling. It wasn't until I was in the library with time to think about it that I realised how it was getting to me.'

'And then you saw him.'

'Yeah. His shoe.'

She glanced at her watch and took a pull from her mug. She was going to be late for work.

'You should go,' I said. 'We can talk this evening.'

She nodded but she did not rise. 'I don't really understand what's upsetting you. Some poor fellow has a crush on you and is trailing you about. Come on, it's a joke, Joe! It's a funny story you'll be telling your friends. At worst it's a nuisance. You mustn't let it get to you.'

I felt a childish pang of sorrow when she got to her feet. I liked what she was saying. I wanted to hear it again in different ways. She came round to my side of the table and kissed me on the head. 'You're working too hard. Go easy on yourself. And remember that I love you. I *love* you.' We kissed again, deeply.

I followed her downstairs, and watched as she prepared to leave. Perhaps it was the worried smile she gave me as she bustled past to pack her briefcase, perhaps it was the solicitous way she told me she would be back at seven and would phone me during the day, but standing there on the polished dance floor parquet I felt like a mental patient at the end of visiting hours. *Don't leave me here with my mind,* I thought. *Get them to let me out.*

B

Much later, Joe struggles to convince anyone that a shooting incident to which he and Clarissa are witnesses was in fact a bungled attempt on his own life organized by Parry. These are his thoughts as he waits to give his statement to the sceptical police.

I had decided while I was sitting with Clarissa not to press the police too hard. The disposition of events would do the work. My complaint earlier was on file, the scene in the restaurant was confirmation of an absolute kind. Parry had to be charged with attempted murder, and until he was I needed protection. Now that I was the only one left from the restaurant, now the excitement was fading, I felt my isolation and vulnerability. Parry was all around me. I took care to sit facing the door, well away from the only window. Each time someone came in I felt a cold drop in my stomach. Paranoia constructed an image of him for me, standing across the street from the police station, flanked by the men in coats. I went and stood in the station entrance and looked. I felt neither surprise nor relief that he wasn't there. Taxis and chauffered cars were bringing the crowds in for the evening's opera. It was nearly seven fifteen. Time had folded in on itself. The happy people who passed by me on their way home or to bars and cafes were blessed with a freedom they did not feel and I did not have: they were unencumbered, they had no one who wanted to kill them.

In the end, Joe is proved right, but by this time, his own extreme reactions have caused him to appear almost as obsessed and deluded as Parry, so we may no longer have faith in him as the 'rational scientist.' Clarissa expresses this in a letter in which she apologizes for having doubted Joe but makes it clear that she can no longer see him in quite the same way.

… I thought Parry was a pathetic and harmless crank. At worst, I thought of him as a creature of your imagining. I never guessed he would become so violent. I was completely wrong and I'm sorry, really sorry.
But what I was trying to say last night was this: your being right is not a simple matter. I can't quite get rid of the idea that there might have been a less frightening outcome if you had behaved differently … you became so intense and strange and worked up about him. … You became more and more agitated and obsessed. You didn't want to talk to me about anything else. … As the Parry thing grew I watched you go deeper into yourself and further and further away from me. You were manic, and driven, and very lonely. You were on a case, a mission. Perhaps it became a substitute for the science you wanted to be doing. You did the research, you made the logical inferences and you got a lot of things right, but in the process you forgot to take me along with you, you forgot how to confide.

Inevitably, the other characters are also mainly presented through Joe's eyes, including Clarissa, whom he loves, and Parry, who fills him with revulsion and fear. However, McEwan uses several devices to shift the narrative viewpoint away from him at times.

- Some chapters are in the form of letters, like the one above, from either Clarissa or Parry, which enables him to reveal something of their inner worlds.
- One episode – the first major disagreement between Joe and Clarissa – is related in Joe's 'voice' but from Clarissa's point of view. He writes after the event, when she has told him what she thought and felt at the time:

  It would make more sense of Clarissa's return to tell it from her point of view. Or at least, from that point as I later construed it.

- The 'scientific paper' and case study which end the novel shift our perspective again, this time to view Jed, Clarissa and Joe himself 'objectively'. They become merely 'P', 'M' and 'R'.

  This case confirms the reports of some commentators (Trethowan 1967; Seeman 1978; Mullen & Pathe) on the relevance of absent or missing fathers. It must remain a matter for conjecture at this stage whether R, aged 47, represented a father figure to P, or whether, as a successful, socially integrated individual, he represented an ideal to which P aspired.

Writing about *Enduring Love*

Questions on examination papers at AS level are most likely to ask you to focus on one of the following:

- the presentation of one of the three main characters
- the relationships between the characters

- the development of one of the novel's themes
- narrative techniques, such as methods of creating suspense, in the novel as a whole or in particular episodes

At A2 level you may be asked to explore themes, methods and use of language in more depth and detail. You might study McEwan's novels for coursework or to compare them with texts by other authors. For example, it would be interesting to compare *Enduring Love* with another novel about love, obsession and madness, Colin Thubron's *A Cruel Madness*. Both have narrators whose trustworthiness we doubt, but where Joe Rose is vindicated, the narrator of *A Cruel Madness* turns out to be deluded.

To put into practice some of what you have learned, try this written task.

Activity

In this extract, the narrator first becomes fully aware of Jed Parry. Just after the balloon accident, Joe goes, in a state of shock, to investigate the shattered corpse of John Logan and Parry follows him. Read the passage carefully and write a short essay in response to the following question:

Write as fully as you can about how Jed Parry is presented in this scene, his first appearance in the novel. Comment also on anything that the narrator reveals about himself in the course of his account.

I turned away and saw Parry coming towards me across the field. He must have been following me down closely for he was already within talking distance. He must have seen when I paused in the shelter of the trees.
I watched him over Logan's head as he slowed and called out to me, 'Don't touch him, please don't touch him'.
I hadn't intended to, but I said nothing. I was looking at Parry as though for the first time. He stood with his hands resting on his hips staring not at Logan, but at me. Even then, he was more interested in me. He had come to tell me something. He was tall and lean, all bone and sinew, and he looked fit. He wore jeans and box-fresh trainers tied with red laces. His bones fairly burst out of him the way they hadn't with Logan. His knuckles brushing against his leather belt were big and tight-knobbed under the skin which was white and stretched tight. The cheek bones were also tight and high-ridged and together with the pony-tail gave him the look of a pale Indian brave. His appearance was striking, even faintly threatening, but the voice gave it all away. It was feebly hesitant, neutral as to region, but carrying a trace, or acknowledgement, of Cockney – a discarded past or an affectation. Parry had his generation's habit of making a statement on the rising inflection of a question – in humble imitation of Americans, or Australians, or as I heard one linguist explain, too mired in relative judgments, too hesitant and apologetic to say how things were in the world.
Of course, I didn't think of any of this at the time. All I heard was a whine of powerlessness, and I relaxed. What he said was, 'Clarissa's really worried about you? I said I'd come down and see if you're all right?

My silence was hostile. I was old enough to dislike his presumption of first names, or for that matter, of claiming to know Clarissa's state of mind. I didn't even know Parry's name at this point. Even with a dead man sitting between us, the rules of social engagement prevailed. As I heard it later from Clarissa, Parry had come over to her to introduce himself, then turned away to follow me down the hill. She had said nothing to him about me.

'Are you all right?'

I said, 'There's nothing we can do but wait,' and I gestured in the direction of the road, one field away.

Parry took a couple of steps closer and looked down at Logan, then back to me. The grey-blue eyes gleamed. He was excited, but no one could ever have guessed to what extent.

'Actually, I think there is something we can do.'

I looked at my watch. It was fifteen minutes since I had phoned the emergency services. 'You go ahead,' I said. 'Do what you like.'

'It's something we can do together?' he said as he looked about for a suitable place on the ground. The wild thought came to me that he was proposing some form of gross indecency with a corpse. He was lowering himself, and with a look was inviting me to join him. Then I got it. He was on his knees.

'What we could do,' he said with a seriousness which warned against mockery, 'is to pray together?' Before I could object, which for the moment was impossible because I was speechless, Parry added, 'I know it's difficult. But you'll find it helps. At times like this, you know, it really does help.'

I took a step away from both Logan and Parry. I was embarrassed, and my first thought was not to offend a true believer. But I got a grip on myself. He wasn't concerned about offending me.

'I'm sorry,' I said pleasantly. 'It's not my thing at all.'

Parry tried to speak reasonably from his diminished height. 'Look, we don't know each other and there's no reason why you should trust me. Except that God has brought us together in this tragedy and we have to, you know, make whatever sense of it we can?' Then seeing me make no move, he added, 'I think you have a special need for prayer?'

I shrugged and said, 'Sorry. But you go right on ahead.' I Americanised my tone to suggest a lightheartedness I did not feel.

Parry wasn't giving up. He was still on his knees. 'I don't think you understand. You shouldn't, you know, think of this as some kind of duty. It's like, your own needs are being answered? It's got nothing to do with me, really, I'm just the messenger. It's a gift.'

As he pressed harder, so the last traces of my embarrassment disappeared. 'Thanks, but no.'

3 Poetry

Objectives
- To identify ways in which you can approach the reading of poetry
- To explore ways of writing about poetry
- To consider some of the features to look for in analysing poems
- To prepare for studying set poetry texts
- To prepare for encountering 'unseen' poetry texts

What is poetry?

The question of what exactly poetry is – what marks it out as being different from prose, is a question that poets, writers, philosophers, and critics have, over the centuries, tried to answer. In fact, there are almost as many 'definitions' of poetry as there are poets. Here are some of them:

❝ Poetry is the spontaneous overflow of powerful feelings: it takes its origin from emotion recollected in tranquillity. ❞ *(William Wordsworth)*

❝ Poetry is the sound of human speech at those times when it comes closest to the speech of angels and the speech of animals. ❞ *(John Wain)*

❝ Poetry: the best words in the best order. ❞ *(Samuel Taylor Coleridge)*

❝ Poetry is not a turning loose of emotion, but an escape from emotion; it is not the expression of personality, but an escape from personality. ❞ *(T. S. Eliot)*

You will have noticed how these 'definitions' present quite different views of what poetry actually is. Think about each of these views and what these writers, drawn from different centuries, are saying about the nature of poetry. Through your study of English you will have come into contact with a variety of poetry, perhaps ranging from the works of Chaucer and Shakespeare to those of twentieth-century writers. Are these views borne out by your experiences of poetry so far?

Activity

> **1** Think about your own view of poetry for a moment. Without discussing it with others, write a short paragraph describing what you think poetry is.
> **2** Now compare your view with a partner and discuss how similar, or different, your views are.

Reading poetry

The study of poetry is a central element in all AS- or A-level English Literature specifications. Whether you are studying a poetry set text, looking at the poetry of a Shakespeare play, writing on poetry for coursework or preparing for examinations involving 'unseen' texts, you will engage in detailed study of various poems. Even though the outcome of your work might be presented in different forms, the skills, techniques, and approaches that you need to use are essentially the same.

It is true that the poetry elements of AS- and A-level English Literature present particular challenges. For a number of reasons, some poetry is only fully accessible to us today if we carry out a certain amount of research such as looking up difficult words, phrases, and references. However, 'responding to poetry' cannot be 'taught' (or learned, for that matter) in the same way that some subjects can. It is no good looking for some kind of 'secret formula' that you can apply to any poem. Although most poetry is written to be read by others, and in that sense carries a 'public' voice, it can also be an intensely individual medium of communication and the responses it can evoke can be equally intense and individual. Much poetry works in a very personal way and your response to a particular poem might not be the same as another person's. Words and images carry with them connotations that might trigger different responses in the minds of different people. So while it is often possible to say what a poem 'is about' in general terms, the only really genuine response is that 'personal response' that an individual reader feels.

This does not mean that 'anything goes', of course. For example, comments like 'I haven't a clue about this' or 'This means nothing to me' may be personal responses but they are not much good in terms of a 'literary' response. At AS- or A-level you will be required to give what the objectives describe as 'independent opinions and judgements, informed by different interpretations by other readers' and to 'respond with knowledge and understanding to literary texts of different types and periods'.

In this section we will look at some of the things that you can do to find your way into and through a poem. Here are some general strategies for improving your understanding of poetry.

- Read voraciously – become as familiar as possible with as wide a range of poetry as possible.
- Think about how language is used and make a note of any interesting features, lines, images, etc. that you come across in your reading of poetry.
- Think about the ideas contained in the poems you read.
- Read other people's responses to poetry – not as a substitute for forming your own views but as a 'broadening' influence. (These responses could be found in various study guides, articles in literary journals, or reviews in newspapers or critical works.) They might suggest things that had not occurred to you or they might stimulate your own thoughts if you disagree with their view.
- Read poems aloud – either in company or alone. Very often reading a poem aloud helps deepen understanding and it certainly gives you a greater insight into features such as tone and rhythm.
- Adopt a questioning attitude. Whenever you read a poem ask yourself questions about it. The three key questions to ask are: 'What is this poem about?'; 'How is it written?'; 'Why has the poet chosen to write the poem in this particular way?'
- If you are studying the work of an individual poet, reading beyond the set poems will help you to understand the particular poems you are working on.

Activity   Think of other strategies that you could use to help make your study of poetry more effective. It might be helpful to discuss your ideas with a partner and make a list of them.

Having said that there is no set formula that can be applied to poetry to produce the required response, there are certain features of poetry that you will need to be aware of in order to begin to appreciate how a poem 'works', i.e. what the poet does to achieve the desired effect on the reader. Different critical books may refer to them in slightly different terms but basically these are the key elements that combine to create the overall effect of a poem. You will, no doubt, be familiar with some or all of these already.

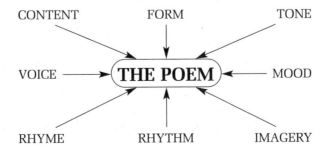

Activity

> Consider each of these aspects of poetry. Discuss your ideas in a small group and write brief notes explaining what each means.

Using these aspects of poetry to answer questions on the poems you study is really just a more detailed way of asking those three basic questions that we have already mentioned: 'What is this poem about?'; 'How is it written?'; 'Why has the poet chosen to write it in this particular way?' Answering these three questions will take you to the heart of almost any poem.

However, although we may look at elements such as content, form, and imagery in order to study their particular contributions to a poem, in reality they are completely interrelated and interdependent. The overall effect (and effectiveness) of a poem is dependent on all the individual elements within it working in unity (or acting in discord with one another if that produces the effect that the poet wants).

Content and poetic voice

In simple terms the **content** of a poem is what it is all about – the ideas, themes, and storyline that it contains.

It is useful to begin a consideration of a poem by getting a general outline of what it is about. This is sometimes referred to as the **surface meaning** of the poem. Establishing this surface meaning will give you a framework on which to build the more detailed and complex ideas that form as your analysis of the poem develops. Sometimes it is possible to respond to a poem without fully understanding every word or phrase and sometimes meaning 'evolves' as you continue to study a poem. However, having an initial idea or impression of what a poem is about, can be an important first step towards a fuller and more assured understanding.

When considering the content of a poem it is also important to identify the **poetic voice** of the poem. In other words decide who the 'speaker' of the poem is. In many cases the poetic voice may well be the poet's, but it may be that the words of the poem are 'spoken' through a character that the poet has created or a narrator figure other than the poet. This happens in *The Canterbury Tales*, where usually a particular character is telling the tale. Chaucer (the writer) often then interrupts his character (his fictitious narrator) to address the reader.

Identifying the 'speaker' also helps to determine a number of other aspects of the poem such as tone, mood, and the overall intention behind the poem. The poetic voice could be the poet's genuine voice expressing a heartfelt emotion or it could be the voice of a narrator expressing a view or feeling that the poet may or may not share.

Activity
> Now have a look at this poem by Philip Larkin. How does an awareness of the poetic voice here help you form an impression of what the poet is saying?

Naturally the Foundation Will Pay Your Expenses

Hurrying to catch my Comet
   One dark November day,
Which soon would snatch me from it
   To the sunshine of Bombay,
I pondered pages Berkeley
   Not three weeks since had heard,
Perceiving Chatto darkly
   Through the mirror of the Third.

Crowds, colourless and careworn,
   Had made my taxi late,
Yet not till I was airborne
   Did I recall the date –
That day when Queen and Minister
   And Band of Guards and all
Still act their solemn-sinister
   Wreath-rubbish in Whitehall.

It used to make me throw up,
   These mawkish nursery games:
O when will England grow up?
   – But I outsoar the Thames,
And dwindle off down Auster
   To greet Professor Lal
(He once met Morgan Forster),
   My contact and my pal.

Philip Larkin

Naturally the Foundation Will Pay Your Expenses is written in the first person and so the 'voice' could be that of the poet himself speaking. However, to appreciate Larkin's intentions here it is necessary to recognize that the 'speaker' of the poem is a narrator figure. The views that he expresses are not necessarily those of Larkin himself. In fact, the 'speaker' here is an English academic who jets around the world giving his paper to major universities. Larkin is present here too but his attitudes and ideas lie behind the words spoken by his character. He satirizes his character in order to cast a critical light on the persona he has created and the views that are expressed through him.

Activity

> **1** Now read the following poems through carefully.
> **2** Before you discuss your ideas with anyone write down your first thoughts on what each poem is about and on the poetic voice which each presents. Spend about ten minutes setting your ideas down.
> **3** Now join two or three other students in a small group. Each read their notes out to the others as a starting point for discussion on the content and poetic voice of the poems.
> **4** Review your notes and make any changes or additions that you wish in the light of the discussion. Do you find any aspect of these poems difficult to explain? If so, can you say why?

Mother of the Groom

What she remembers
Is his glistening back
In the bath, his small boots
In the ring of boots at her feet.

Hands in her voided lap,
She hears a daughter welcomed.
It's as if he kicked when lifted
And slipped her soapy hold.

Once soap would ease off
The wedding ring
That's bedded forever now
In her clapping hand.

Seamus Heaney

School Dinners

Why do I dream now, of people from school?
I am not old. They are not dead.
Yet warm before waking they surface, thin,
or in Janice's case, still fat.
                          She dyed her hair
in red rat's tails; thought brash. She hitched her skirt,
her wide thighs wobbled. She was kind as silk.
One day, chattering, tipped salad cream
over her favourite pudding;
                          did remember
to ask the boy's address, but found it false.
They left the seaside camp. She had a daughter,

who now, I think, must be the age
of Janice in my dream; when giggling still
she reached out for the cheap gold-coloured jug.

Eight people made that table. Who do I still know?
No one who could tell me how she lives,
cooking great Sunday dinners? married? happy?
My ignorance stays perfect as the moon
dropped, like a coin through a barley field,
drowned, in all the blue waste of the sky.

Sitting by my daughter in a car
borne smooth and cool, through tunnelled trees
it strikes me, quick as shivering, that when
they must end, yet I will see them there
small and clear, in the battered jug,
their mistakes; their tails of red hair.

Alison Brackenbury

Tone and mood

The effect that a poem has on the reader is very closely determined by the tone and mood that it creates. As we have already discussed, a poem contains a 'voice' and like any voice it can project a certain **tone** that gives the listener (or reader) certain messages. Obviously there are many different kinds of tone. The tone might be angry or reflective, melancholy or joyful, bitter or ironic. Just as the tone of voice in which someone speaks tells us a great deal about the way they feel, so the tone of the 'poetic voice' tells us a great deal about how the poet or the narrator of the poem feels.

The **mood**, on the other hand, although very closely connected with the tone, is not quite the same thing. When we refer to the mood of a poem we are really talking about the **atmosphere** that the poem creates. Very often tone and mood in a poem are closely linked and a certain tone produces a certain mood. For example, if the poet uses a melancholy tone it is unlikely that the mood of the poem will be bright and lively. Sometimes, though, the poet may quite deliberately use a tone that does not match the mood the poem creates in order to achieve a particular effect – underlining a certain irony, for example. The overall impact of a poem stems not only from the literal meaning of the words but from the tone and mood that they create. One of the most effective ways of recognizing the tone of a poem is to hear the poem read aloud.

Try reading poems out loud for yourself, experimenting with different ways of reading each particular poem. The more practice you get at reading poems aloud and the more you are able to hear others read them, the better able you will be 'hear' poems in your mind when you read them to yourself. The tone of a poem can be communicated to the reader or listener in many ways and it is through being sensitive to the poet's tone that we can begin to understand the intention that lies behind the words.

Here are three well-known poems for you to consider.

Upon Westminster Bridge,

Sept. 3, 1802
Earth has not anything to show more fair:
Dull would he be of soul who could pass by
A sight so touching in its majesty:
This City now doth, like a garment, wear
The beauty of the morning: silent, bare,
Ships, towers, domes, theatres, and temples lie
Open unto the fields, and to the sky;
All bright and glittering in the smokeless air.
Never did sun more beautifully steep
In his first splendour, valley, rock or hill;
Ne'er saw I, never felt, a calm so deep!
The river glideth at his own sweet will:
Dear God! the very houses seem asleep;
And all that mighty heart is lying still!

William Wordsworth

Engineers' Corner

Why isn't there an Engineers' Corner in Westminster
Abbey? In Britain we've always made more fuss of a
ballad than a blueprint... How many schoolchildren
dream of becoming great engineers?
Advertisement placed in *The Times* by the Engineering Council.

We make more fuss of ballads than of blueprints –
That's why so many poets end up rich,
While engineers scrape by in cheerless garrets.
Who needs a bridge or dam? Who needs a ditch?

Whereas the person who can write a sonnet
Has got it made. It's always been the way,
For everybody knows that we need poems
And everybody reads them every day.

Yes, life is hard if you choose engineering –
You're sure to need another job as well;
You'll have to plan your projects in the evenings
Instead of going out. It must be hell.

While well-heeled poets ride around in Daimlers,
You'll burn the midnight oil to earn a crust,
With no hope of a statue in the Abbey,
With no hope, even, of a modest bust.

No wonder small boys dream of writing couplets
And spurn the bike, the lorry and the train.
There's far too much encouragement for poets –
That's why this country's going down the drain.

Wendy Cope

Frog Autumn

Summer grows old, cold-blooded mother.
The insects are scant, skinny.
In these palustral homes we only
Croak and wither.

Mornings dissipate in somnolence.
The sun brightens tardily
Among the pithless reeds. Flies fail us.
The fen sickens.

Frost drops even the spider. Clearly
The genius of plenitude
Houses himself elsewhere. Our folk thin
Lamentably.

Sylvia Plath

Activity

1 Read each of the poems through to yourself, deciding what sort of tone of voice you would use for each.
2 In a small group, take turns to read each poem out loud. If possible, use a cassette recorder to tape these readings.
3 Discuss the readings and make brief notes on the kind of tone that you think is most appropriate for each poem. Describe the kind of mood that is created in each.
4 Discuss the methods used by these poets to create a specific tone and mood.

Summary

Here are some ideas of how tone and mood can be created:
- through the loudness or softness of the voice speaking the poem
- through the rhythm that is created
- through the poet's choice of words
- through the emphasis placed on particular words or phrases
- through the breaks and pauses that the poet places in the poem (often the things which go unsaid can tell you a great deal)

Imagery

Essentially the true 'meaning' of a poem lies in the total effect that it has upon the reader. Very often that effect will stimulate a response which is not just a reaction to what the poet has to say, but which draws on the reader's own intellectual and emotional experience. Imagery can be of central importance in creating this response within the reader.

The concept of imagery is a very simple one and although it is used a good deal in poetic writing it is of course found in other kinds of writing too. An **image** is language used in such a way as to help us to see, hear, taste, feel, think about or generally understand more clearly or vividly what is being said or the impression that the writer wishes to convey.

Images can work in several ways in the mind of the reader. On a simple level an image can be used literally to describe something. For example, in *Upon Westminster Bridge* (see page 54) the lines '... silent, bare/Ships, towers, domes, theatres, and temples lie/Open unto the fields, and to the sky;/All bright and glittering in the smokeless air' create a **literal image** in our minds of the scene that Wordsworth wishes to convey.

Often, though, images are **non-literal** or **figurative**: the thing being described is compared to something else with which it has something in common to make the description more vivid to the reader. You will, no doubt, already be familiar with images, such as similes and metaphors, which work in this way. However, just in case you need it, here is a reminder of the difference between the two, along with a definition of personification.

The simile

Similes are easy to spot because they make the comparison quite clear often by using the words 'as' or 'like'. For example, looking back at *Upon Westminster Bridge* once more the lines 'This City now doth, like a garment, wear/The beauty of the morning ...' simply but effectively convey a sense of the beauty of the scene which 'clothes' the city but which also serves to conceal the less attractive aspects of the city which lie beneath the 'garment'.

The metaphor

In some ways a metaphor is like a simile in that it too creates a comparison. However, it is less direct than the simile in that it does not use 'as' or 'like' to create the comparison. Often the metaphor actually describes the subject as *being* the thing to which it is compared. For example, Wordsworth concludes *Upon Westminster Bridge* with the line, 'And all that mighty heart is lying still!'. Literally, of course, the city is not a heart, but metaphorically-speaking it can be seen as the 'heart' of the country, the capital city, and the centre of government.

Personification

Personification occurs when poets attribute an inanimate object or abstract idea with human qualities or actions. For example, in *Upon Westminster Bridge*, Wordsworth speaks of the river as if it were alive – 'The river glideth at his own sweet will'.

Aural imagery

Some kinds of images rely not upon the 'pictures' that they create in the mind of the reader but on the effect that they have on the ear, or a combination of both.

Alliteration involves the repetition of the same consonant sound, usually at the beginning of each word, over several words together. Larkin uses this technique in *Naturally the Foundation Will Pay Your Expenses* (see page 51), for example. It can be seen in phrases such as 'I pondered pages ... Crowds, colourless and careworn ... Still act their solemn-sinister ...' and much of its impact lies in the effect that the repetition of the sounds creates on the reader's ear as well as the mind's eye.

Another kind of aural device is **assonance**. This involves the repetition of a vowel sound to achieve a particular kind of effect. The long, drawn out 'o' sounds created in the first line of *Frog Autumn* (see page 55), 'Summer grows old, cold-blooded mother' creates an impression of lethargy and lack of vitality as summer passes and winter approaches.

A third aural device is that of **onomatopoeia**. This refers to words that by their sound reflect their meaning. On a simple level words like 'bang' or 'thud' actually sound like the noises they describe.

It must be stressed, however, that the important thing is not so much to be able to spot the different kinds of images that might be present in a poem but to understand why the poet has used a particular image and be able to see how it works in the mind of the reader. Being able to say 'the poet uses alliteration in stanza three' is of no value in terms of the critical appreciation of a poem, but being able to show what the alliteration contributes to the overall effect of the poem is valuable.

For more on these individual forms of imagery see the Glossary, page 328.

Activity

> 1 Read the poem on page 58 and list five or six images that Hughes uses. Make brief notes on what these images mean to you, what they make you think about or anything that you find striking about them.
> 2 Join with two or three other students and compare your ideas. Decide together the meaning of the key images and their effects in the poem.
> 3 Write a short essay (about two pages in length) outlining your own thoughts and responses to the poet's use of imagery here.

Wind

This house has been far out at sea all night,
The woods crashing through darkness, the booming hills,
Winds stampeding the fields under the window
Floundering black astride and blinding wet

Till day rose; then under an orange sky
The hills had new places, and wind wielded
Blade-light, luminous black and emerald,
Flexing like the lens of a mad eye.

At noon I scaled along the house-side as far as
The coal-house door. Once I looked up –
Through the brunt wind that dented the balls of my eyes
The tent of the hills drummed and strained its guyrope,

The fields quivering, the skyline a grimace,
At any second to bang and vanish with a flap:
The wind flung a magpie away and a black-
Back gull bent like an iron bar slowly. The house

Rang like some fine green goblet in the note
That any second would shatter it. Now deep
In chairs, in front of the great fire, we grip
Our hearts and cannot entertain book, thought,

Or each other. We watch the fire blazing,
And feel the roots of the house move, but sit on,
Seeing the window tremble to come in,
Hearing the stones cry out under the horizons.

Ted Hughes

Rhyme

Rhyme can make an important contribution to the 'musical quality' of a poem and like rhythm it affects the sound and the overall impact of the piece. The system of rhyme within a poem, or **rhyme scheme**, can influence this effect in a variety of ways. It might act as a unifying influence and draw a poem together, or it could give a poem an incantatory quality or add emphasis to particular elements of the vocabulary (or diction). There are various kinds of rhymes and rhyme schemes and although most rhymes work on the basis of the rhyme occurring at the end of a line, some occur within the line. These are called **internal rhymes**.

In the same way that rhythm in a poem often follows a recognized pattern, so does rhyme. Working out the rhyme scheme is quite a straightforward business and is done by indicating lines that rhyme together through giving them the same letter of the alphabet. As an example, read the short poem that follows on page 59.

Eight O'Clock

He stood, and heard the steeple	a
Sprinkle the quarters on the morning town.	b
One, two, three, four, to market-place and people	a
It tossed them down.	b
Strapped, noosed, nighing his hour,	c
He stood and counted them and cursed his luck;	d
And then the clock collected in the tower	c
Its strength, and struck.	d

A. E. Housman

Housman uses an abab, cdcd rhyme scheme, i.e. alternate lines rhyme within stanzas. Let us now consider some examples of traditional forms and patterns. Pairs of lines that rhyme are called **couplets** or **rhyming couplets**. Two lines that rhyme together and that are written in iambic pentameter (see page 62) are known as **heroic couplets**. Sometimes a whole poem can consist entirely of rhyming couplets or the couplet can be used as part of a larger rhyme scheme. A Shakespearean sonnet uses the couplet to draw the poem to an end, as in Shakespeare's *Sonnet XVIII*, for example:

So long as man can breathe or eyes can see,
So long lives this, and this gives life to thee.

Rhyming couplets tend to create a bold, assertive effect and strongly convey a point or message. They can also be used for comic effect, to deflate an argument or character.

The **quatrain** is a set of four rhyming lines. Usual rhyme schemes are abab, abcb, aaaa, or abba. In *Jerusalem*, Blake uses the abcb scheme –

And did those feet in ancient time
Walk upon England's mountains green?
And was the holy Lamb of God
On England's pleasant pastures seen?

The quatrain is a flexible form that is used to create many effects but often, as here, it produces a sense of unity within compact and regular stanzas.

A **sestet** is a six-line stanza that can be arranged in a number of ways. The last six lines of an Italian sonnet (see page 67) are also called the sestet. In '*The lowest trees have tops, the ant her gall*', Dyer uses a regular ababcc rhyme scheme:

The lowest trees have tops, the ant her gall,
The fly her spleen, the little spark his heat;
The slender hairs cast shadows, though but small,
And bees have stings, although they be not great;
Seas have their source, and so have shallow springs:
And love is love, in beggars and in kings.

The **octave** is an eight-line stanza and can be constructed in a number of ways. It can be formed by linking two quatrains together or it can have a rhyme scheme that integrates all eight lines. It is also the name given to the first eight lines of an Italian sonnet.

As with all the elements of a poem though, the important thing is not to be able to spot the use of rhymes or even to work out the rhyme scheme but to ask yourself: 'Why has the poet used rhyme in this way and what does it contribute, together with all the other features, to the overall impact of the poem?'. The answer to this question is what really matters.

Summary

Here are some effects that rhyme might have on a poem.
- It can make a poem sound pleasing to the ear and perhaps add a musical quality. Conversely, it can create a jarring effect.
- It could serve to emphasize certain words – very often the words that rhyme are given a certain prominence.
- It can act as a kind of unifying influence on the poem, drawing lines and stanzas together through the pattern it imposes on them.
- It can give a poem an incantatory or 'ritualistic' feel.
- It can influence the rhythm of the verse.
- It can give a sense of finality – the rhyming couplet is often used to give a sense of 'ending'.
- It can exert a subconscious effect on the reader, drawing together certain words or images, affecting the sound, or adding emphasis in some way.

Activity

> 1 Read this poem carefully to yourself and write down your initial ideas on how the poet uses rhyme and with what effect.
> 2 In a small group, compare your ideas. Discuss how you think the use of rhyme affects the poem and what it contributes to its overall impact.

Ending

The love we thought would never stop
now cools like a congealing chop.
The kisses that were hot as curry
are bird-pecks taken in a hurry.
The hands that held electric charges
now lie inert as four moored barges.
The feet that ran to meet a date
are running slow and running late.
The eyes that shone and seldom shut
are victims of a power cut.
The parts that then transmitted joy
are now reserved and cold and coy.
Romance, expected once to stay,
has left a note saying GONE AWAY.

Gavin Ewart

Rhythm

When you were thinking about definitions of poetry at the beginning of this unit you might well have thought about rhythm as being one of the features that can set poetry apart from other kinds of writing. Although it is by no means true of all poems, one of the basic differences between a poem and a piece of prose is that a poem can contain some form of regular beat or rhythm.

Often this sense of rhythm can exert a profound influence on the overall effect of the poem giving it its feeling of 'movement' and life. The poet can use rhythm to create many different effects or to emphasize a certain aspect or idea in the poem. Very often it is also an important contributing factor to the mood or atmosphere and to what is sometimes referred to as the 'musical quality' of a poem. Music can be gentle and flowing, harsh or discordant, stilted and uneven in phrasing, or regular in tempo. It can have a rhythm that reflects a serious or solemn mood or a rhythm that suggests the comic or absurd. Just the same is true about the rhythms of poetry.

Here are some examples of the ways in which poets use language to create varying rhythms.

Syllable stress   Language possesses natural rhythms which are built into it and which we use automatically every time we pronounce words. For example, if we think of a word like 'delicately' it comes quite naturally to us to stress the first syllable and not the second. Not to do so would be to mispronounce the word. Poets often use these natural rhythms within words to help contribute to the overall rhythmic effect.

Emphatic stress   Poets sometimes choose to place emphasis on a particular word or phrase in order to achieve a particular result. The stress might be shifted to reinforce a particular tone or sometimes to affect the meaning. For example, think about Wordsworth's famous line 'I wandered lonely as a cloud' and how different emphases can change the overall effect:

'*I* wandered lonely as a cloud' ,   'I *wandered* lonely as a cloud',
'I wandered *lonely* as a cloud',   'I wandered lonely as a *cloud*'
and so on. The natural rhythm will often tell you what is right.

Phrasing and punctuation   The rhythm of a poem (or any other piece of writing) can be influenced by factors such as word order and length of phrases or sentences and these in turn can be influenced by the choice of punctuation marks, line and stanza breaks, and use of repetitions.

Metre   Technically speaking the whole notion of rhythm in poetry is closely tied up with the idea of metre. This concept originated from the principles of Classical Greek and Latin verse and was adopted by English poets from early times. Such principles stated that a line of verse should follow a precise and regular pattern in terms of the number of syllables it contained and the stress pattern that it used. This pattern was then repeated throughout the poem. Regular patterns of these stressed and unstressed syllables are called **metres** (see also syllable stress, above).

On a basic level the pattern created by a regular metre can be seen in nursery rhymes and limericks. For example, each stanza of *Mary Had a Little Lamb* follows this pattern:

Mary had a little lamb,
Its fleece was white as snow.
And everywhere that Mary went
The lamb was sure to go.

In identifying the metre of a poem the first thing to do is to establish how the rhythm pattern is made up. To help do this the syllables are divided up into groups of two or three (depending on the particular pattern) and each of these groups is called a **foot**. The number of **feet** in a line can vary. Here are the main patterns:

one foot – monometer	five feet – pentameter
two feet – dimeter	six feet – hexameter
three feet – trimeter	seven feet – heptameter
four feet – tetrameter	eight feet – octameter

The process of identifying the metre is called **scansion**. In scansion a $'$ or a — above a word indicates a stressed syllable while a $\breve{}$ is used to denote an unstressed syllable and feet are divided up using vertical lines |. (A double vertical line ‖ indicates **caesura** which simply means a brief pause in the middle of a line of poetry.) For example, look at these lines by Keats:

When I | have fears | that I | may cease | to be
Before | my pen | hath gleaned | my teem | ing brain,

Each line consists of five metrical feet. Each foot consists of an unstressed and a stressed syllable. A foot that is made up in this way ($\breve{}\,'$) is called an **iambic foot (iamb)** and a line that is made up of five feet is called a **pentameter**. These lines, therefore are written using a metrical form called **iambic pentameter**.

If you were to look at the whole of this poem you would find that Keats also uses a rhyme scheme. Verse which is written in iambic pentameter and which does not use a rhyme scheme is called **blank verse**. This is one of the most frequently used forms in English poetry and it has been estimated that three-quarters of all English verse is written in blank verse. One of its attractions is that it is a metrical form that very closely follows the patterns of natural speech and for this reason was used as the staple form by dramatists such as Shakespeare as well as by poets such as Milton and Wordsworth. It also can capture a reflective, thoughtful mood. The following example (on page 63) shows Wordsworth's use of the form as he describes skating on the frozen lake as a boy.

The Prelude

Book 1 (1850)
And in the frosty season, when the sun
Was set, and visible for many a mile
The cottage windows blazed through twilight gloom,
I heeded not their summons: happy time
It was indeed for all of us – for me
It was a time of rapture! Clear and loud
The village clock tolled six, – I wheeled about,
Proud and exulting like an untired horse
That cares not for his home. All shod with steel,
We hissed along the polished ice in games
Confederate, imitative of the chase
And woodland pleasures, – the resounding horn,
The pack loud chiming, and the hunted hare.
So through the darkness and the cold we flew,
And not a voice was idle; with the din,
Smitten, the precipices rang aloud;
The leafless trees and every icy crag
Tinkled like iron; while far distant hills
Into the tumult sent an alien sound
Of melancholy not unnoticed, while the stars
Eastward were sparkling clear, and in the west
The orange sky of evening died away.

William Wordsworth

Although the iambic foot is the most common form there are other syllable patterns which poets use to create different effects. For example, the **trochaic foot (trochee)** consists of a stressed syllable followed by an unstressed one ($/\,\smile$). A well-known poem which makes use of the trochaic foot (trochee) is Blake's *The Tyger*.

Tyger! | Tyger! | burning | bright
In the | forests | of the | night.

One of the effects of the trochaic metre is that the stressed first syllable adds emphasis and power to the words.

The **dactylic foot (dactyl)** consists of a stressed syllable followed by two unstressed ones ($/\,\smile\,\smile$) as in Tennyson's *The Charge of the Light Brigade*.

Half a league, | half a league,
Half a league | onward

The dactylic metre reflects the rhythm of the horse at gallop giving a kind of 'drumming of hooves' feel to the poem. With its two unstressed syllables following the stressed one, this metre can also be used to create a sad, reflective, sometimes heavy mood.

The **anapaestic foot** (**anapaest**) consists of two unstressed syllables followed by a stressed one ($\breve{}\breve{}/$) while the **spondaic foot** (**spondee**) simply has two stressed syllables ($//$). Hardy uses both in his poem *A Wife Waits*.

Will's | at the dance | in the Club | -room below,

Where | the tall liqu | or cups foam;

I | on the pave | ment up here | by the Bow,

Wait, wait, | to | steady | him home.

The anapaests here create a sense of movement, and perhaps underlying tension, reflecting the wayward husband's revelry whereas the spondee, at the beginning of the final line, gives a sense of the wife's patience and resignation as she waits to help her drunken husband home. Note how the reversal of the rhythm pattern at the end reflects the husband's return.

Twentieth-Century poets have tended to move away from strict metrical forms but metre can still be an important element in modern poetry. By its nature though, metre is a mechanical and repetitive device which often is at variance with the natural rhythms that a poem may contain. Few poets stick religiously to the metrical pattern that they adopt and poetry should always be read according to the natural rhythms of the language rather than its metrical plan.

Remember when you are writing about a poem that identifying its metrical pattern is of little value in itself. You will gain little reward in an exam for simply mentioning the metre of a poem. The key thing is that you are able to say what it contributes to the effect of the poem overall. Do not worry if you cannot remember the technical terms – the main thing is that you are able to describe what is happening. Technical terms are a kind of shorthand way of doing this but they are by no means essential. What matters is your understanding of how the poem works as a piece of writing.

Activity

> Read through this poem by Hardy several times. Try to get a feel of the rhythm pattern. You could try tapping it out if it helps. Attempt to describe the kind of rhythm pattern that Hardy uses. What kind of 'feel' do you think it gives to the poem? Write a short description of the effect that both rhyme and rhythm create in *The Voice*.

The Voice

Woman much missed, how you call to me, call to me,
Saying that now you are not as you were
When you had changed from the one who was all to me,
But as at first, when our day was fair.

Can it be you that I hear? Let me view you, then,
Standing as when I drew near to the town
Where you would wait for me: yes, as I knew you then,
Even to the original air-blue gown!

Or is it only the breeze, in its listlessness
Travelling across the wet mead to me here,
You being ever dissolved to wan wistlessness,
Heard no more again far or near?

   Thus I; faltering forward,
   Leaves around me falling,
Wind oozing thin through the thorn from the norward
   And the woman calling.

Thomas Hardy

The Voice is one of a number of poems that Hardy wrote soon after the death of his wife, Emma. His feelings of loss were intensified by the fact that in the later years of their marriage they had grown apart. Here he remembers the love that they shared in their younger days. The poem begins with a regular rhythm created through a repetition of dactyls:

/ ˘ ˘ | / ˘ ˘ | / ˘ ˘ | / ˘ ˘
Woman much | missed, how you | call to me, | call to me,
/ ˘ ˘ | / ˘ ˘ | / ˘ ˘ | /
Saying that | now you are | not as you | were
/ ˘ ˘ | / ˘ ˘ | / ˘ ˘ | / ˘ ˘
When you had | changed from the | one who was | all to me,

The dactyls help to create a mood of sad reflection and the repetition of:

/ ˘ ˘ | / ˘ ˘
call to me, | call to me

introduces a slightly haunting feel, suggestive of a calling voice being carried on the wind. The rhyming of 'call to me' with 'all to me' creates a link between the imagined caller and the poet and emphasizes how much he misses her now. Similarly, the rhyme of the second and fourth lines of the stanza emphasizes the contrast between the poet's present pain and the happiness the couple enjoyed in years past – 'you are not as you were/when our day was fair'.

The second stanza echoes the rhythm of the first in its repetition of dactyls:

/ ˘ ˘ | / ˘ ˘ | / ‖ ˘ ˘ | / ˘ ˘
Can it be | you that I | hear? ‖ Let me | view you, then,

and the sense of the poet's uncertainty is increased through his questioning and the caesura in the line. In stanza three again we have the repetition of the dactyls and the questioning continues as the poet wonders whether he really hears the voice of his loved one or if it is simply a trick of the wind:

/ ˘ ˘ | / ˘ ˘ | / ˘ ˘ | / ˘ ˘
Or is it | only the | breeze, in its | listlessness
/ ˘ ˘ | / ˘ ˘
Again we have the echoing rhyme, this time of 'listlessness'/'wistlessness'.

In the final stanza, however, the regular pattern the poet has established is broken. The caesura of 'Thus I; ‖ faltering forward' creates a halting, stumbling feel to the line reflecting the breakdown in the poet as his grief overwhelms him. The trochees of 'faltering forward' and 'falling' dominate the stanza and underline the sense of pain and despair that the poet feels – a pain that is made almost tangible through the image:

Wind oōzing | thin thr̆ough t̆he | thorn from t̆he | norward

There is a partial return of the dactyls here but, as the final dactyl trails away unfinished, they are dominated by the emphatic stress of the trochees in the last words of each line of this stanza. The final line itself echoes the opening line of the poem but now the dactyls have been replaced by the more emphatic trochees as the poet is left with the haunting voice in his mind:

And t̆he | womăn | calling.

We are left with the two words 'falling/calling' which create a striking effect through a combination of the rhyme and the trochaic metre and encapsulate the poet's experience here.

This poem clearly illustrates the contribution that rhythm can make to the overall effect of the poem but its importance, as here, cannot be appreciated in isolation. Its use is inextricably bound up with the language of the poem and the ideas that the poet wants to express.

Form

There are many different ways in which poems can be structured. One thing is certain though. A poet does not simply choose a certain form at random. It will have been carefully chosen and will have a direct bearing on what the poet hopes to achieve through the poem. In considering the form of a particular poem, therefore, we are back to that central question – why? In this case 'Why has the poet chosen to use this particular form?'

Form can refer to the way that the poem is actually written down on the page or to the way that the lines are organized, grouped, or structured. (This is sometimes called **poetic form**.) In terms of its structure, poetry can be divided into two categories. First, there is the kind of poetry where the lines follow on one from another continuously without breaks, such as in Wordsworth's *The Prelude*, Milton's *Paradise Lost* or Keats' *Endymion*. The technical term for this is **stichic poetry**, but do not worry too much about the technical terms; the important thing is to be able to recognize that poems differ in the way that they are put together.

Secondly, there is the kind of poetry where the lines are arranged in groups which are sometimes called verses but are more correctly referred to as **stanzas**. This is called **strophic poetry**. Keats uses this form in *The Eve of St. Agnes* (see pages 259–264), as does Blake in *The Tyger*, Heaney in *Mid-Term Break*, and Hughes in *Crow*, for example.

There are many different kinds of stanza, with variations depending on the number of lines they contain. (See section on Rhyme, page 58 and Glossary, page 328 for further descriptions.)

The Sonnet

The Sonnet is a very popular form in English poetry and it is one that you are likely to come across in your studies. In basic terms a sonnet is a fourteen-line poem and the lines are usually arranged in one of two ways. First, there is the **Petrarchan** or **Italian Sonnet** (so called simply because it is named after the Medieval Italian writer, Petrarch). This kind of sonnet is arranged with a first part that consists of eight lines (the octave) and a second and concluding part of six lines (the sestet). There can be variations in the rhyme scheme but generally it follows the pattern *abbaabba cdecde*. If you look back at Wordsworth's *Upon Westminster Bridge* (see page 54) you will see that it follows this pattern.

The other form is the **Shakespearean** or **English Sonnet**. The rhyme scheme of this divides up into three quatrains and a concluding couplet. The rhyme scheme in this kind of sonnet usually follows the *abab cdcd efef gg* pattern.

Free Verse

Although forms which adhere to a strict pattern are still frequently used by poets in the Twentieth Century, there has been a trend towards poetry that does not have the constraints of metre or rhyme upon it and Free Verse has become predominant. This form of verse often does not have lines that are equal in length or that have a regular metre and often it does not rhyme. To a large extent this flexibility allows poets the freedom to create forms to suit their own purposes and create the effects that they want in their writing.

Certain forms of poetry have been used to express themes which can be broadly grouped together. (This is sometimes called **thematic form**.) For example, the Ode, the Ballad, the Elegy, the Aubade, the Pastoral, the Lyric, the Epic, and the Song all refer to particular kinds of poetry that have a broad thematic link in common. (See Glossary for more information on specific forms, page 328.)

Obviously the 'form' of a poem in terms of its physical structure is inseparably linked to the idea of its thematic 'form'. In turn, the whole concept of form is interlinked with other features such as rhyme, rhythm, and the poet's overall intention. What is important is that you are able to suggest reasons why a poet has chosen a particular form and comment on how it contributes, along with all these other features, in creating the poem's overall effect.

Handling 'difficult' poetry

It is, of course, far too simplistic to think in terms of 'easy' poetry and 'hard' poetry. Like some of the poems in this unit, poetry can often be 'easy to read' but, in fact, deal with complex themes and ideas that need careful thought. However, in the course of your AS- or A-level study, you might come across poetry that presents you with rather different problems.

These problems can arise for a number of reasons but here are some of the most common.

- You could encounter a problem of vocabulary – it may be that the poet uses difficult words that you do not understand or that the poem was written in a different age and so aspects of the language have changed.
- The poem could be concerned with concepts, ideas, or themes completely outside your sphere of experience.
- The poem might contain references that are difficult or obscure in some way, e.g. references based on classical mythology.
- It might use imagery that is difficult to decipher.
- The style in which the poem is written could be complex and you might need to do some detective work to unravel its meaning.

Some of these problems may be particularly apparent when studying poetry that was written in a different age. Perhaps the most extreme example of this that you might encounter in A-level study would be in the study of the works of Chaucer, which we will look at later (see page 71). However, the works of writers such as Shakespeare (see Unit 5) and Milton can also lead to feelings of apprehension.

So let us look at some examples of Milton's poetry and think about the kind of things you can do to help yourself when tackling such writers as this.

Milton lived and wrote in the Seventeenth Century, eventually siding with the Puritans during the English Civil War. He became their 'Secretary for the Foreign Tongues', translating political documents. He was also a leading author of the Puritan pamphlets which were issued to try to justify Cromwell's reign and the execution of Charles I.

Although he wrote poetry throughout his life, producing various works including *L'Allegro* (1632), *Il Penseroso* (1632), *Comus* (1634), and *Lycidas* (1637), it was in the latter part of his life that his great long, or 'epic', poems *Paradise Lost* (1667) and *Samson Agonistes* (1671), were written. These are the ones you are most likely to find set for study at AS- or A-level.

Paradise Lost concerns itself with the Fall of Adam and Eve and was originally published in ten books although later it was issued in twelve books – the traditional number for an 'epic'. When set for A-level two books are usually specified for study. Here is an extract from *Book IX* where Satan, in the form of the serpent, seeks his prey, Eve, and finds her gardening. Read it through carefully.

Paradise Lost

Book IX
Nearer he drew, and many a walk traversed
Of stateliest covert, cedar, pine, or palm;
Then voluble and bold, now hid, now seen,
Among thick-woven arborets, and flowers
Imbordered on each bank, the hand of Eve:
Spot more delicious than those gardens feigned

Or of revived Adonis, or renowned
Alcinous, host of old Laertes' son,
Or that, not mystic, where the sapient king
Held dalliance with his fair Egyptian spouse.
Much he the place admired, the person more.
As one who, long in populous city pent,
Where houses thick and sewers annoy the air,
Forth issuing on a summer's morn to breathe
Among the pleasant villages and farms
Adjoined, from each thing met conceives delight -
The smell of grain, or tedded grass, or kine,
Or dairy, each rural sight, each rural sound;

Milton

Activity

> **1** Write a brief summary of what Milton is saying here. (Limit this to a
> maximum of 45 words.)
> **2** What immediate problems, if any, did you encounter in terms of
> understanding the detail of this passage?

Summary

You may find that the following cause you some problems.
- Some of Milton's vocabulary consists of words that are unfamiliar to you
  – words like 'arborets', 'sapient', 'dalliance' or 'tedded'.
- Milton mentions characters that you have not heard of before –
  'Alcinous' or 'old Laertes', for example.
- The word order is sometimes different from that which you are used to.
- The passage consists mainly of description with very little action.

Obviously, one of the problems in reading and understanding poetry that was
written possibly hundreds of years ago is that the language we use today is not
quite the same as the language that was used then. Words may have changed
in meaning, hold different connotations, or may simply have been outmoded.

The second problem here is that the references or allusions used would have
been understood and have held some significance to a reader in the poet's
own age but often mean little to us today. These are not difficulties confined
to poetry written a long time ago (a reading of T. S. Eliot's *The Wasteland* will
convince you of that) but the chances of encountering them are probably
greater the older the poetry is. However, good editions usually contain notes
and glossaries to help the reader understand these more obscure references
and so appreciate the text more fully.

Milton uses many references and allusions to Classical literature and to the
Bible in his work and a knowledge of Greek and Roman mythology helps a
good deal in studying his poetry. His readers in the Eighteenth Century would
have possessed this kind of background and would understand immediately
the Biblical references and Classical allusions. For them they would serve, as

they were intended to do, to illuminate and illustrate the work. Today, most of us do not have this kind of background and so often such references can initially act as barriers to meaning rather than assisting our understanding.

The question is – what can you do to help yourself overcome these initial difficulties? Well, three things would help to begin with:

- Buy a good dictionary if you do not possess one already and use it. Make sure that you look up every word that you come across that you do not understand. It can be a good idea to make a list of these.
- Look up and make a note of references that you do not understand. You might need to consult Classical dictionaries or encyclopedias for some of these.
- Ask yourself questions. Never be satisfied with ignoring difficult words or references. Always ask yourself questions like 'Why is that reference used?', 'What does it mean?', 'What does it add to the sense or effect of the poem?'

Now, let's assume that you have had the chance to do a bit of research on the passage from *Paradise Lost* on page 68. How does it help you gain a deeper understanding of the extract?

Here are some definitions of 'difficult' words:

voluble – smoothly (flowing) or rolling
arborets – shrubberies
sapient – wise
dalliance – playing or exchanging caresses and embraces
tedded – new mown grass spread for drying

And here are some notes on the references Milton uses:

... *gardens of Adonis* – who was 'revived' by Prosperpina after being killed by a wild boar – to emphasize that Eden was even more 'delicious' than the garden in which Adonis was brought back to life.

... *garden of Alcinous* – he was the king of Phaecia who royally entertained Odysseus ('Old Laertes' son') – again comparing Eden with this garden.

... *sapient king* – King Solomon was the 'sapient king' and this is a reference to the garden in which he entertained his wife, the Pharaoh's daughter.

As you will see all three of these references are used to compare the beauty of the Garden of Eden with other splendid gardens from the Bible or mythology. You will have noticed that all these references form part of an elaborate simile which is used to create a vivid impression of the splendid nature of Eden, but this is not the only simile he uses in the extract.

Activity   Look back at the extract on page 68 again and with a partner or in a small group discuss Milton's use of imagery here.

The simile form is an important part of the imagery of Paradise Lost. Some of Milton's images are drawn on a grand scale and can be elaborate and quite complicated to unravel. The key thing is that very often poetry needs working at in order to arrive at some kind of understanding of it.

Summary

Here are some suggestions to help you with that process.
- Read the piece several times and adopt a systematic approach.
- Use the parts of the poetry that you understand as clues to help you understand more difficult sections.
- Highlight particularly difficult words, phrases, lines, images, etc.
- Look up words that you do not understand in a good dictionary.
- Refer to the notes or glossary that the text contains.
- Do some background reading about the writer and his or her period.

Geoffrey Chaucer

The language of Geoffrey Chaucer is even further removed from that of our own modern English than Milton's, although once that language barrier has been breached students generally find his work more accessible.

Chaucer is generally considered to be the most important writer of the Middle Ages and his work, especially *The Canterbury Tales*, certainly had a great influence on our literature and language, laying the foundations for many writers who were to come after him. It is no surprise, therefore, to find Chaucer featured on a variety of AS- and A-level English Literature specifications.

This section will examine ways of approaching the reading of Middle English and the context within which *The Canterbury Tales* are set. The final section suggests various things that you can do in order to help develop your understanding of the particular Chaucer text that you are studying.

Reading Middle English

In the initial stages of your study of Chaucer you may encounter problems of understanding that are not present in other types of poetry. When you first open your copy of whichever Chaucer text you are studying, probably the first thing to strike you will be that it appears to be written in another language. Initially, this can be quite unsettling. Do not be put off, though, because once you have become used to the language things will seem much simpler. The language itself is nowhere near as daunting as it can look at first sight.

The first thing to bear in mind is that it is not written in another language – it is very definitely written in English. Admittedly, it is a rather different form of English from our present-day language because it is the English that was used in the Fourteenth Century. It is called Middle English and evolved as a mixture of different language elements. French was influential in its development. From the time of the Norman Conquest in 1066 until the mid-Thirteenth Century, French was the language of the Court and the upper middle-classes. Latin also made an important contribution to Middle English, being the language of legal and ecclesiastical documents and the preferred language of scholarly communication in the Middle Ages. These elements, combined with the predominant east Midland dialect (the dialect of Chaucer), gradually evolved into Middle English. This is the form of language from which modern English developed. In some respects modern English is similar to Middle English but there are differences too.

In studying Chaucer for the first time your first task is to become familiar with these similarities and differences. There are a number of things that you can do to help you to quickly become quite fluent in reading Chaucer in the original. So let us start by having a closer look at some of the features of Chaucer's language.

Reading Chaucer

Let us begin by looking at the opening lines of Chaucer's *General Prologue*:

Whan that Aprill with his shoures soote
The droghte of March hath perced to the roote,
And bathed every veyne in swich licour
Of which vertu engendred is the flour;
Whan Zephirus eek with his sweete breeth
Inspired hath in every holt and heeth
The tendre croppes,

(Lines 1–7)

Activity

> **1** Read these few lines aloud pronouncing each word just as it looks and write down a 'translation' of what you think it means. Make a note of any words that puzzle you or cause you a problem in the translation.
> **2** Now do exactly the same thing with these lines from the opening of *The Franklin's Tale*.

In Armorik, that called is Britayne,
Ther was a knyght that had loved and dide his payne
To serve a lady in his beste wise;
And many a labour, many a greet emprise
He for his lady wroghte, er she were wonne.

(Lines 1–5)

Let's see how you got on. Translated literally the lines from the *General Prologue* could read:

When that April with his showers sweet
The drought of March hath pierced to the root,
And bathed every vein in such liquor
Of which energy engendered is the flower;
When Zephirus also with his sweet breath
Breathes upon every wood and heath
Upon all the tender crops;

Activity

> This still has some way to go before the meaning is clear in modern English.
> 1 Think carefully about the lines and then write your own version of what it means. You can write this in prose if you wish. Do not worry about an exact line-for-line translation.
> 2 First, compare your version with the one below and then compare both with your initial translation.

Here is one possible translation:

When the sweet showers of April have pierced the drought of March to its roots and bathed every vein in the powerful moisture that gives birth to the flowers; when Zephirus too, with his sweet breath, has breathed upon the delicate shoots in every wood and heath;

How did you get on? Your version will no doubt differ slightly. There are a number of ways that this could be written down and yet the sense would remain the same. One of the reasons for this is that sometimes the sense of a particular Middle English word can be expressed through a number of modern English alternatives. For example, 'vertu' can mean *virtue* in modern English, although here it conveys the sense of the rain having the power to give life to the plants. Similarly, 'engendred' can mean *engendering* or *procreation* although here we could translate it as *gives birth*, as we have done, or even *produces* would be in keeping with the sense of the line.

Here's a translation of the opening of *The Franklin's Tale*. Compare it with your version.

In Armorica, which is also known as Brittany, there lived a knight who loved and took trouble to serve his lady to the best of his ability. He undertook many labours and great enterprises for her before he won her.

Where did your problems with these lines occur? The place names of Armorik and Britaine perhaps caused you a little difficulty. 'Armorica' is simply another name, an ancient name for Brittany. 'Britaine' looks very similar to Britain so this might have misled you. Perhaps certain expressions, such as '... and dide his paine', also caused you some difficulty.

Activity

> From your work on these two short extracts, make a list of the ways in which you have found Chaucer's English to differ from modern English.

Summary

You may have noticed some, or all, of the following points.
- Some words are identical to their modern English counterparts (e.g. 'bathed', 'every', 'called', 'loved').
- Some words look and sound very similar to their modern English counterparts (e.g. 'whan', 'greet', 'wonne').
- Some words look completely unfamiliar (e.g. 'soote', 'swich', 'eek').

- Some words might remind you of modern English words but actually mean something different (e.g. 'inspired', 'holt').
- Some of the words seem to be in rather a strange order.
- There are references to people, places, etc. that you might not have come across before (e.g. 'Zephirus').

The context of the tales

If you study Chaucer for AS- or A-level it is likely that you will read one of the stories which make up *The Canterbury Tales*. Whichever particular tale you are studying, though, it is important that you are able to set the tale into the wider context of *The Canterbury Tales* as a whole rather than just look at it in isolation. Each of the tales is set within the fictional framework established by Chaucer in the *General Prologue to the Canterbury Tales* which is a kind of introduction in which Chaucer sets the scene, introduces the pilgrims, describes them, and so forth.

The basic background to the tales is straightforward. A group of pilgrims are travelling from London to Canterbury to worship at the shrine of Thomas à Becket. They meet at the Tabard Inn at Southwark in London ready to begin their journey and the landlord, or Host, as he is known, suggests that they all take part in a story-telling competition to help to pass the time on their journey. The Host will judge the stories and the winner will receive a free meal at the inn on their return from Canterbury.

You will probably find in your edition of the particular tale that you are studying other material which is not actually part of the tale itself but which will help you to establish some background to the character telling the tale. This material usually includes at least two extracts taken from elsewhere in *The Canterbury Tales*:

- most editions contain the section taken from the *General Prologue* which describes the particular pilgrim who is telling the tale
- most editions also contain the relevant lines that link the tale in question to the one that immediately precedes it. This often involves an exchange between the pilgrims and the Host and which can help to throw light on characters and how they relate to one another

The narrator's voice

The Canterbury Tales, then, is a story about a group of people telling stories. The characters are, of course, the invention of Chaucer but he also writes himself into the script by taking the role of one of the pilgrims. In fact, in his role as Sir Topas, he gives himself the worst tale of all to tell and is interrupted by the Host who can listen to no more and so he never actually finishes it.

Throughout the tales there is always the sense of the presence of two narrators; first of all the character telling the story but secondly, hidden somewhere behind the first narrator there is Chaucer himself, masterminding the whole scheme.

Activity

> What do you think Chaucer gains by having his tales narrated by fictitious characters within a fictitious framework rather than simply telling the tales directly himself?

There are several factors that you might consider here.

- The idea of the group of pilgrims gives a sense of unity and structure to what might otherwise have been a loosely linked collection of stories.
- Links can be made between the character telling the tale and the actual tale itself and this can add another dimension to both tale and teller.
- The whole narrative scheme is given a depth and complexity in terms of its overall effect on the audience that would have been lacking in a simple single narration scheme.
- It allows him to get away with telling stories and making comments that may be ribald or contentious by distancing himself from them and attributing them to his characters. This can add to the ironic effect he often creates.

In most parts of most of the tales Chaucer keeps to the background but watch out for his voice coming through. Sometimes he will comment or make an aside or observation or sometimes even endow his character with a language or mode of expression which is very much Chaucer's own. In other words he has it both ways. Using *The Miller's Tale* as an example again, here Chaucer is able to convince his audience of the Miller as an independent character that he has no control over and urges them to choose another tale if they are likely to be offended by the Miller's bawdy offering.

The key thing throughout is to be aware of the subtlety with which Chaucer uses a variety of narrative voices to achieve just the effect that he wants. To summarize, following these steps should help you to tackle your Chaucer text confidently.

Summary

- Read the tale you are studying through fairly quickly to get a general sense of what it is about. Do not worry too much at this first stage if there are words, phrases, or sections of it that you do not understand.
- Avoid using your glossary too much during this 'first read' stage. This can interrupt your reading and make it more difficult to get the overall 'feel' of the story.
- Then look back over the tale and focus on the individual words, phrases, or sections that gave you problems and use the glossary to help form a picture of their meaning.
- Most editions of a particular tale will contain quite detailed line-referenced notes. Make full use of these – they will help you establish the meaning of more difficult sections and also fill in some useful background information that will add to your understanding of the tale.

- Try listening to a recording of the tale read by a professional. This will help you to gain an impression of the sound of the language and you will hear rhymes and rhythms that are invisible when looking at the printed page.
- Avoid using a modern English translation. If you go straight to a translation this will really inhibit you from coming to terms with the language for yourself. It is far better to be able to read the original for yourself than have to rely on a ready-made translation.

Putting it into practice

Now have a look at a quite different kind of poem and see how you handle an appreciation of it. The poem is by Samuel Taylor Coleridge, probably most famous for his narrative poem, *The Ancient Mariner*. He also wrote some poems that became known as *Conversation Poems* because of the way that they seem to address the reader in the style of an intimate and private talk. Read the poem through carefully.

Frost At Midnight

The Frost performs its secret ministry,
Unhelped by any wind. The owlet's cry
Came loud – and hark, again! loud as before.
The inmates of my cottage, all at rest,
Have left me to that solitude, which suits
Abstruser musings: save that at my side
My cradled infant slumbers peacefully.
'Tis calm indeed! so calm, that it disturbs
And vexes meditation with its strange
And extreme silentness. Sea, hill, and wood,
With all the numberless goings-on of life,
Inaudible as dreams! the thin blue flame
Lies on my low-burnt fire, and quivers not;
Only that film,[1] which fluttered on the grate,
Still flutters there, the sole unquiet thing.
Methinks, its motion in this hush of nature
Gives it dim sympathies with me who live,
Making it a companionable form,
Whose puny flaps and freaks the idling Spirit
By its own moods interprets, everywhere
Echo or mirror seeking of itself,
And makes a toy of Thought.

      But O! how oft,
How oft, at school, with most believing mind,
Presageful, have I gazed upon the bars,
To watch that fluttering *stranger*! and as oft

With unclosed lids, already had I dreamt
Of my sweet birth-place, and the old church-tower,
Whose bells, the poor man's only music, rang
From morn to evening, all hot Fair-day,
So sweetly, that they stirred and haunted me
With a wild pleasure, falling on mine ear
Most like articulate sounds of things to come!
So gazed I, till the soothing things, I dreamt,
Lulled me to sleep, and sleep prolonged my dreams!
And so I brooded all the following morn,
Awed by the stern preceptor's face, mine eye
Fixed with mock study on my swimming book:
Save if the door half opened, and I snatched
A hasty glance, and still my heart leaped up,
For still I hoped to see the *stranger*'s face,
Townsman, or aunt, or sister more beloved,
My play-mate when we both were clothed alike!

    Dear Babe, that sleepest cradled by my side,
Whose gentle breathings, heard in this deep calm,
Fill up the interspersed vacancies
And momentary pauses of the thought!
My babe so beautiful! it thrills my heart
With tender gladness, thus to look at thee,
And think that thou shalt learn far other lore,
And in far other scenes! For I was reared
In the great city, pent 'mid cloisters dim,
And saw nought lovely but the sky and stars.
But thou, my babe! shalt wander like a breeze
By lakes and sandy shores, beneath the crags
Of ancient mountain, and beneath the clouds
Which image in their bulk both lakes and shores
And mountain crags: so shalt thou see and hear
The lovely shapes and sounds intelligible
Of that eternal language, which thy God
Utters, who from eternity doth teach
Himself in all, and all things in himself.
Great universal Teacher! he shall mould
Thy spirit, and by giving make it ask.

    Therefore all seasons shall be sweet to thee,
Whether the summer clothe the general earth
With greenness, or the redbreast sit and sing
Betwixt the tufts of snow on the bare branch
Of mossy apple-tree, while the nigh thatch
Smokes in the sun-thaw; whether the eave-drops fall
Heard only in the trances of the blast,
Or if the secret ministry of frost

Shall hang them up in silent icicles,
Quietly shining to the quiet Moon.

Samuel Taylor Coleridge
(Published 1798)

1 In all parts of the kingdom these films are called strangers and supposed to portend the arrival of some absent friend [Coleridge's note]

Activity

> **1** Discuss the poem with a partner or in a small group. Then, on your own, make a list of the key points arising from your discussion.
>
> **2** Now have a closer look at the poem. Consider the following questions about the early part of the poem. Discuss them with a partner making notes on the following as you go.
> - Why do you think Coleridge describes the Frost's ministry as secret?
> - What kind of atmosphere does he create in lines 1–7?
> - What kind of scene is set within the cottage?
> - How would you describe the poet's mood here?
> - Look at lines 15–23. What is the significance of '...that film, which fluttered on the grate'?
>
> **3** Now, on your own, look at the second section of the poem. Describe what is happening here. How has the mood changed?
>
> **4** The focus shifts again in the third section. How? Comment on Coleridge's use of imagery here.
>
> **5** How effective do you find the concluding section? Refer to the text to support your comments.
>
> **6** What use do you think Coleridge has made of rhythm here and what relationship does this have with the overall form of the poem?
> (A consideration of the kind of poem this is may help you here.)
>
> **7** Now write your own critical appreciation of this poem covering all the aspects of it that you feel are of significance. (Your essay should be 3 to 4 pages in length.)

Special Feature:
Carol Ann Duffy

Carol Ann Duffy was born in Glasgow in 1955. She grew up in Stafford and later moved to Liverpool. She graduated from Liverpool University with a degree in Philosophy and now lives in London where she works as a freelance writer. In 1977, she embarked on a career as a playwright and two of her plays were performed at Liverpool Playhouse. This led her into television where she worked as a freelance scriptwriter. However, it is for her poetry that Carol Ann Duffy is best known and she has gained acclaim in recent years, winning the Dylan Thomas Award in 1989 and the Whitbread Poetry Award in 1993. She is regarded now as one of Britain's leading contemporary poets, her work dealing with themes that have universal significance touching on the concerns of all people. Although it is easy to see some of her poetry reflecting her own life, in reading her work, it is a mistake to see it as autobiographical and to look for clues to its significance in Duffy's own life. The poems should be viewed in a much wider context than this and the voice of the poems should be seen as expressing concerns, experiences and emotions that lie deep within us all.

She has written several anthologies of poetry, perhaps the best known being her fourth, 'Mean Time'. In this Special Feature we will focus on poems from this collection to illustrate the nature of her poetry and the ideas, themes and issues that she explores through it. Remember, when you are thinking and writing about her poetry, that examiners are not interested in students 'spotting' features of language such as the use of similes or metaphors or alliteration. Just identifying such features really tells us nothing about how a poem works or the effect that it might create in the mind of the reader. What examiners really want you to look at is *how* poets use language and *why* they make the language choices that they do. In other words you need to be aware of the language choices the poet has made, be sensitive to why the poet has chosen a particular form of words and explain the effect that is created by the words that have been chosen.

Themes and issues in Duffy's poetry

Carol Ann Duffy has said that the title of her collection, 'Mean Time', can have a variety of interpretations.

Activity Think about this title and write down the different ideas that can be associated with the phrase, 'Mean Time'.

Here are some ideas that you may have thought about:

- The passage of time – 'in the mean time'
- Time is 'mean' – hard and ungiving
- Time is 'mean' – we don't get enough of it
- Time means something – the 'meaning' of time.
- Greenwich Meantime – this sets standard time for the world

Here is the title poem of the collection, 'Mean Time':

Mean Time

The clocks slid back an hour
and stole light from my life
as I walked through the wrong part of town,
mourning our love.

And, of course, unmendable rain
fell to the bleak streets
where I felt my heart gnaw
at all our mistakes.

If the darkening sky could lift
more than one hour from this day
there are words I would never have said
nor have heard you say.

But we will be dead, as we know,
beyond all light.
These are the shortened days
and the endless nights.

Activity

> Read the poem through carefully several times. What is it about, and why do you think Duffy chose this particular poem to provide the title for the whole anthology?

Here are some ideas you might have thought of:

- The poem opens with the clocks being 'put back' one hour, referring to the adjustment we make to our clocks in the autumn which changes them from BST (British Summer Time) to GMT (Greenwich Mean Time.) One obvious result when we do this is that it gets dark an hour earlier in the evenings. Note how she uses this image of 'stealing light' to reveal the poet's emotional state at the breakdown of a relationship. This darkness/loss idea is further reinforced by connotations of death introduced through her use of 'mourning'. The sense of disorientation the poet feels at this loss is emphasized in '*I walked through the wrong part of town.*'
- The second stanza continues this sense of despair and darkness with images such as '*unmendable rain*', and '*bleak streets, where I felt my*

heart gnaw / at all our mistakes.' The word 'gnaw' here is particularly powerful, implying a constant insidious eating away at the mistakes that cannot be changed. This heightens the sense of destructive pain the poet endures.

- In the third stanza we return to the idea of 'time' and again the mood is darkened, this time through the image of the '*darkening sky*' which reinforces the sense of hopelessness and resignation. Even the possibility of metaphorically 'turning back the clocks' could provide no solution.
- The finality of the situation is evoked in the last stanza through the bleak image of death. The poet uses this in both a literal sense (one day they will be dead) and a metaphorical sense (they are dead in the sense that they have lost the light in their lives). The poem ends with a return to the image of the taking away of light and the ensuing darkness.
- This poem encapsulates all the central themes that Duffy explores in the poems in this selection and, as such, can be seen as a poem that sounds the 'key note' of the anthology as a whole.

Activity | Write a list of the central themes that you think the poem explores.

Here is our list:

- The breakdown of a relationship
- Loss
- Time
- Change
- Emotional darkness
- Pain
- Love and the loss of it

Now read *Havisham.*

This will, perhaps, mean more to you if you have read Charles Dickens's *Great Expectations.* In that novel, Miss Havisham is an old woman who, many years previously, had been deserted by her fiancé on her wedding day. This experience leaves her a bitter and lonely woman who spends the rest of her life in solitude, shut off from the world.

Havisham

Beloved sweetheart bastard. Not a day since then
I haven't wished him dead. Prayed for it
so hard I've dark green pebbles for eyes,
ropes on the back of my hands I could strangle with.

Spinster. I stink and remember. Whole days
in bed cawing Nooooo at the wall; the dress
yellowing, trembling if I open the wardrobe;
the slewed mirror, full-length, her, myself, who did this

to me? Puce curses that are sounds not words.
Some nights better, the lost body over me,
my fluent tongue in its mouth in its ear
then down till I suddenly bite awake. Love's

hate behind a white veil; a red balloon bursting
in my face. Bang. I stabbed at a wedding-cake.
Give me a male corpse for a long slow honeymoon.
Don't think it's only the heart that b-b-b-breaks.

Activity | **What does this poem have in common with *Mean Time*? What message do you think Duffy wants to convey to her readers?**

The language of 'Mean Time'

When we examine Duffy's use of language in her poetry, every poem needs to be looked at individually. However, in talking about what she hopes to achieve through her writing she has drawn attention to several specific features that you might like to keep in mind when looking in detail at her work. These features include:

- her use of rhyme
- her use of 'echoes' and assonance
- the form of her poetry – the ways in which stanzas are organized to give an ordered shape to the poems
- the use of imagery
- the use of a language and vocabulary of her time

Now read the following poem carefully.

Confession

Come away into this dark cell and tell
your sins to a hidden man your guardian angel
works your conscience like a glove-puppet It
smells in here doesn't it does it smell
like a coffin how would you know C'mon
out with them sins those little maggoty things
that wriggle in the soul ... *Bless me Father* ...

Just how bad have you been there's no water
in hell merely to think of a wrong's as evil
as doing it ... *For I have sinned* ... Penance
will cleanse you like a bar of good soap so
say the words into the musty gloom aye
on your knees let's hear that wee voice
recite transgression in the manner approved ... *Forgive me* ...

You do well to stammer A proper respect
for eternal damnation see the flicker

of your white hands clasping each other like
Hansel and Gretel in the big black wood
cross yourself Remember the vinegar and sponge
there's light on the other side of the door ... *Mother
of God* ... if you can only reach it Jesus loves you.

Activity

> Look carefully at the form and structure and the poet's use of imagery
> here. What effect do the poet's choice of imagery and the overall form
> and structure create? (Note particularly the effect on the reader of the
> lack of punctuation.)

Here are some points that you might have noticed:

- The poem opens with a rather threatening image as the poet is invited to
  '*come away into this dark cell and tell your sins to a hidden man*'.
  Normally the religious idea of the confessional is associated with a
  comforting spiritual cleansing, but here the image is sinister and
  threatening. This feeling is increased through the image of the priest
  working '*your conscience like a glove-puppet*' which implies that the
  priest has total control, and the poet is helpless in his grip. The lack of
  punctuation here merge the voice of the priest and the voice of the poet
  into one, almost as if they have no separate identity. The image of sins as
  '*maggoty things that wriggle in the soul*' creates an unpleasant image of
  them eating away at the individual.
- Stanza two opens with what seems to be the voice of the priest again
  drawing the poet into the act of confession by evoking an image of hell
  and damnation. Penance, which is usually seen as an act of spiritual
  cleansing, is compared to being cleansed by a bar of soap. Through this
  imagery, Duffy is criticising the narrow, limited and perhaps shallow
  nature of the ritual of the confessional.
- The final stanza begins with the priest's reference to the poet's
  '*stammering*' through the confessional. Again punctuation marks are
  omitted, although capital letters are used to denote when the priest
  begins a new point. Again the poet's fear is played on, this time through
  the image of Hansel and Gretel alone '*... in the big black wood*'. This
  creates a sense of insecurity and alienation which is used to reinforce the
  need to 'cross yourself'. The image of the vinegar and the sponge brings
  to mind the crucifixion of Christ and complements the image of there
  being light on the other side of the door. However, the final line – '*... if
  you can only reach it Jesus loves you*' leaves the question hanging of
  whether the 'light' is attainable and, if it is, is the confession box the way
  to attain it?

Now read the following two poems.

First Love

Waking, with a dream of first love forming real words,
as close to my lips as lipstick, I speak your name,
after a silence of years, into the pillow, and the power
of your name brings me here to the window, naked,
to say it again to a garden shaking with light.

This was a child's love, and yet I clench my eyes
till the pictures return, unfocused at first, then
almost clear, an old film played at a slow speed.
All day I will glimpse it, in windows of changing sky,
in mirrors, my lover's eyes, wherever you are.

And later a star, long dead, here, seems precisely
the size of a tear. Tonight, a love-letter out of a dream
stammers itself in my heart. Such faithfulness.
You smile in my head on the last evening. Unseen
flowers suddenly pierce and sweeten the air.

Stuffed

I put two yellow peepers in an owl.
Wow. I fix the grin of Crocodile.
Spiv. I sew the slither of an eel.

I jerk, kick-start, the back hooves of a mule.
Wild. I hold a red rag to a bull.
Mad. I spread the feathers of a gull.

I screw a tight snarl to a weasel.
Fierce. I stitch the flippers on a seal.
Splayed. I pierce the heartbeat of a quail.

I like her to be naked and to kneel.
Tame. My motionless, my living doll.
Mute. And afterwards I like her not to tell.

Activity

Compare and contrast these two poems examining the following:

• the ways in which Duffy uses imagery
• the form and structure of the poems
• the themes and issues she examines through these poems

4 Drama

Objectives
- To prepare yourself for writing about drama
- To consider some of the features to look for in evaluating drama texts
- To prepare for studying set drama texts
- To prepare for a context-based question on a drama text

What is drama?

A dictionary definition will state that:

❝drama is something intended specifically for performance on stage in front of an audience. ❞

This definition points to the fact that drama is written to be seen rather than read and its meaning can only be fully appreciated when actually seen in performance. This makes it a much more 'public' form than prose or poetry in that the experience of the play in performance is a shared experience. This essential aspect of drama is easy to lose sight of when sitting in a classroom, or on your own, grappling with the language of a drama text.

Visualizing the script

It is essential, then, that you are aware in approaching a play that you are dealing with a work that is very different from, say, a novel and that you will need to employ quite different strategies to handle it. You must be able to visualize the play in your head – be able to bring the play alive in your mind and see and hear the action as if you were at the theatre. Developing the ability to do this can be difficult simply by reading from the printed page. However, there are things you can do, from the outset, to help.

- Recognize that reading a play is essentially a group activity and so work with others as much as possible.
- Go and see plays performed as often as possible. (Do not restrict yourself to the ones you are studying, or just to professional productions.)
- Keep a notebook or log of plays that you see noting your responses – thoughts and feelings about performances and ideas on production.
- Take part in 'acting out' parts of a play – this will help you to appreciate the staging implications of a text in a way that straight reading never can.
- Listen to audio tapes or watch video recordings of plays. (These do not replace seeing the play 'live' but they are better than only reading the scripts.)

With this key point in mind, let us consider some aspects of plays that you will need to examine in the texts that you study.

Opening scenes

The way that a play opens is obviously crucial to engaging the audience's attention and writers can take many options here depending on the effects that they wish to achieve. In looking at an opening scene, whether of a text you are studying for the examination, or a passage you are confronted with for the 'unseen', there are some key questions that are worth asking. The central questions are: 'What effect does the writer want this scene to have on the audience?' and 'What purpose does the scene serve to the play as a whole?'. Here are some possible answers to these questions.

- The scene provides an explanation of the plot so far, background information and details the audience need to understand what is going on. (This is sometimes called **exposition** [see page 95].)
- The scene creates a setting or background against which the play is set.
- The scene creates a mood or creates tension which captures the audience's attention immediately (the opening scene of *Hamlet* is a good example of this).
- The scene introduces characters, situations, and relationships.
- The scene provokes a sense of intrigue which captures the audience's attention and makes them want to know more.

Activity | **1** Read carefully the opening to Brian Friel's *Making History* on page 87. Think about what Friel hopes to achieve here and what effect it would have on the audience.

> **2** Discuss this opening with a partner focusing on these aspects:
> * your impression of the two characters and their concerns
> * the information conveyed to the audience here and the techniques that Friel uses to put it across
> * the kind of atmosphere created and how Friel creates it

Making History

Act I Scene 1
(A large living room in **O'Neill's** *home in Dungannon, County Tyrone, Ireland. Late August in 1591. The room is spacious and scantily furnished: a large, refectory-type table; some chairs and stools; a sideboard. No attempt at decoration.*
O'Neill *moves around this comfortless room quickly and energetically, inexpertly cutting the stems off flowers, thrusting the flowers into various vases and then adding water. He is not listening to* **Harry Hoveden** *who consults and reads from various papers on the table.*
O'Neill *is forty-one. A private, sharp-minded man at this moment uncharacteristically outgoing and talkative. He always speaks in an upper-class English accent except on those occasions specifically scripted.* **Harry Hoveden**, *his personal secretary, is about the same age as* **O'Neill**. **O'Neill** *describes him as a man 'who has a comforting and a soothing effect'.)*

Harry:	That takes care of Friday. Saturday you're free all day – so far. Then on Sunday – that'll be the fourteenth –
	O'Hagan's place at Tullyogue. A big christening party. The invitation came the day you left. I've said you'll be there. All right?
	(Pause)
	It's young Brian's first child – you were at his wedding last year. It'll be a good day.
	(Pause)
	Hugh?
O'Neill:	Yes?
Harry:	O'Hagan's – where you were fostered.
O'Neill:	Tell me the name of these again.
Harry:	Broom.
O'Neill:	Broom. That's it.
Harry:	The Latin name is *genista*. Virgil mentions it somewhere.
O'Neill:	Does he really?
Harry:	Actually that *genista* comes from Spain.
	*(**O'Neill** looks at the flowers in amazement.)*
O'Neill:	Good Lord – does it? Spanish broom – magnificent name, isn't it?
Harry:	Give them plenty of water.
O'Neill:	Magnificent colour, isn't it?
Harry:	A letter from the Lord Deputy –
O'Neill:	They really transform the room. Splendid idea of yours, Harry. Thank you.
	*(**O'Neill** silently mouths the word Genista again and then continues distributing the flowers.)*

Harry: A letter from the Lord Deputy 'vigorously urging you to have your eldest son attend the newly established College of the Holy and Undivided Trinity in Dublin founded by the Most Serene Queen Elizabeth'. That 'vigorously urging' sounds ominous, doesn't it?

O'Neill: Sorry?

Harry: Sir William Fitzwilliam wants you to send young Hugh to the new Trinity College. I'm told he's trying to get all the big Gaelic families to send their children there. He would like an early response.

O'Neill: This jacket – what do you think, Harry? It's not a bit ...excessive, is it?

Harry: Excessive?

O'Neill: You know ... a little too – too strident?

Harry: Strident?

O'Neill: All right, damn it, too bloody young?

Harry: (*Looking at his papers*) It's very becoming, Hugh.

O'Neill: Do you think so? Maybe I should have got it in maroon.
    (*He goes off to get more flowers.*)

Harry: A reminder that the Annual Festival of Harpers takes place next month in Roscommon. They've changed the venue to Roosky. You're Patron of the Festival and they would be very honoured if you would open the event with a short –
    (*He now sees that he is alone. He looks through his papers. Pause.* **O'Neill** *enters again with an armful of flowers.*)

Brian Friel

This opening scene starts the play off in quite a private and intimate setting. The stage directions at the beginning describe the setting and what is going on and this will help you to visualize the scene in your mind. Although the audience will not be so fully aware of what is happening here the activity taking place will capture their attention. The two characters, O'Neill and Harry, seem to have very different concerns at the opening of the play. O'Neill is immersed in the domestic – arranging the flowers in the room and seeking Harry's opinion about his attire. Harry, on the other hand, is concerned with imparting business and political news to O'Neill. Within this apparently low-key opening Friel makes it clear that O'Neill is a prominent public figure from the details that are mentioned – his presence being requested at important domestic and public occasions and the letter from the Lord Deputy trying to persuade him to send his son to Trinity College confirm this.

Notice how Friel's economical technique allows him to give the audience a good deal of information and establishes the central character of O'Neill right at the outset. If you were to study the whole of this play you would find that Friel also establishes one of the central themes of the play here – that of the conflict between O'Neill the private man and O'Neill the public figure. He is also able to give a clear indication of O'Neill's stature and importance both as a political figure and as a man with pastoral responsibilities towards his people.

Activity	1 Read the following extract which is the opening scene from Sheridan's comedy, *The Rivals*.
	2 Discuss the scene with a partner and consider these points:
	  • the effect of the opening on the audience
	  • the intention of the playwright
	  • the techniques used
	  • the purpose of any stage directions

The Rivals

Act I, Scene 1
(*Scene, a street in Bath.*
Coachman *crosses the stage. Enter* **Fag** *looking after him.*)

Fag:	What! – Thomas! – Sure 'tis he? – What! – Thomas! – Thomas!
Coachman:	Hey! – Odds life! – Mr Fag! – give us your hand, my old fellow-servant.
Fag:	Excuse my glove, Thomas: I'm devilish glad to see you, my lad: why, my prince of charioteers, you look as hearty! – but who the deuce thought of seeing you in Bath!
Coachman:	Sure, Master, Madam Julia, Harry, Mrs Kate, and the postillion be all come!
Fag:	Indeed!
Coachman:	Aye! Master thought another fit of the gout was coming to make him a visit: so he'd a mind to gi't the slip, and whip we were all off at an hour's warning.
Fag:	Aye, aye! hasty in everything, or it would not be Sir Anthony Absolute
Coachman:	But tell us, Mr Fag, how does young Master? Odd! Sir Anthony will stare to see the Captain here!
Fag:	I do not serve Captain Absolute now–
Coachman:	Why sure!
Fag:	At present I am employed by Ensign Beverley.
Coachman:	I doubt, Mr Fag, you ha'n't changed for the better.
Fag:	I have not changed, Thomas.
Coachman:	No! why didn't you say you had left young Master?
Fag:	No – Well, honest Thomas, I must puzzle you no farther: briefly then – Captain Absolute and Ensign Beverley are one and the same person.
Coachman:	The devil they are!
Fag:	So it is indeed, Thomas; and the *Ensign* half of my master being on guard at present – the *Captain* has nothing to do with me.
Coachman:	So, so! – what, this is some freak, I warrant! Do, tell us, Mr Fag, the meaning o't – you know I ha' trusted you.
Fag:	You'll be secret, Thomas.
Coachman:	As a coach-horse.
Fag:	Why then the cause of all this is – L, O, V, E, – love, Thomas, who (as you may get read to you) has been a masquerader ever since the days of Jupiter.
Coachman:	Aye, aye; I guessed there was a lady in the case: but pray, why does your master pass only for Ensign? – now if he had shammed General indeed –
Fag:	Ah! Thomas, there lies the mystery o'the matter. Harkee, Thomas, my master is in love with a lady of a very singular taste: a lady who likes him better as a half-pay

Ensign than if she knew he was son and heir to Sir Anthony Absolute, a baronet with three thousand a year.

Coachman: That is an odd taste indeed! – but has she got the stuff, Mr Fag; is she rich, hey?

Fag: Rich! – why, I believe she owns half the stocks! Zounds! Thomas, she could pay the national debt as easy as I could my washerwoman! She has a lap-dog that eats out of gold – she feeds her parrot with small pearls – and all her thread-papers are made of bank-notes!

Coachman: Bravo! – faith! – odd! I warrant she has a set of thousands at least: but does she draw kindly with the Captain?

Fag: As fond as pigeons.

Coachman: May one hear her name?

Fag: Miss Lydia Languish – but there is an old tough aunt in the way; though by the by – she has never seen my master – for he got acquainted with Miss while on a visit in Gloucestershire.

Coachman: Well – I wish they were once harnessed together in matrimony. But pray, Mr Fag, what kind of a place is this Bath? I ha' heard a deal of it – here's a mort o' merry-making – hey?

Fag: Pretty well, Thomas, pretty well – 'tis a good lounge. In the morning we go to the pump-room (though neither my master nor I drink the waters); after breakfast we saunter on the parades or play a game at billiards; at night we dance: but damn the place, I'm tired of it: their regular hours stupefy me – not a fiddle nor a card after eleven! – however Mr Faulkland's gentleman and I keep it up a little in private parties; I'll introduce you there, Thomas – you'll like him much.

Coachman: Sure I know Mr Du-Peigne – you know his master is to marry Madam Julia.

Fag: I had forgot. But Thomas you must polish a little – indeed you must: here now – this wig! – what the devil do you do with a wig, Thomas? None of the London whips of any degree of ton wear wigs now.

Coachman: More's the pity! more's the pity, I say. Odds life! when I heard how the lawyers and doctors had took to their own hair, I thought how 'twould go next – odd rabbit it! when the fashion had got foot on the Bar, I guessed 'twould mount to the Box! – but 'tis all out of character, believe me, Mr Fag and lookee, I'll never gi' up mine – the lawyers and doctors may do as they will.

Fag: Well, Thomas, we'll not quarrel about that.

Coachman: Why, bless you, the gentlemen of they professions ben't all of a mind – for in our village now tho'ff Jack Gauge the exciseman has ta'en to his carrots, there's little Dick the farrier swears he'll never forsake his bob, though all the college should appear with their own heads!

Fag: Indeed! well said Dick! but hold – mark! mark! Thomas.

Coachman: Zooks! 'tis the Captain – is that the lady with him?

Fag: No! no! that is Madam Lucy – my master's mistress's maid. They lodge at that house – but I must after him to tell him the news.

Coachman: Odd! he's giving her money! – well, Mr Fag -

Fag: Goodbye, Thomas – I have an appointment in Gyde's Porch this evening at eight; meet me there, and we'll make a little party.

(*Exeunt severally*)

Sheridan

Presenting character

A key element in the impact of a dramatic production is the extent to which the playwright achieves a convincing sense of character. However, the nature of drama is such that the playwright employs very different methods of characterization from those employed by a novelist. Novelists can provide the reader with as much background information as they wish. They can enter the minds of the characters, let their readers know what characters think, feel, are planning to do. A playwright does not have all these options.

Activity

> Focusing on a play that you are studying, think carefully about the ways the characters are presented to the audience to give a full and rounded impression of them. Make a list of these methods and devices.

Perhaps the most straightforward way in which a playwright can define exactly how he or she intends a character to appear to the audience is through detailed and explicit stage directions. So it is important that when you begin to study a play you pay close attention to this information. When watching the play on the stage, of course, you will not be reading stage directions but you will actually be seeing them in performance.

Some playwrights give a great deal of information through their descriptions of how characters are meant to appear. Look carefully at this description from the opening of John Galsworthy's *Strife*, for example:

Strife

Act I

(It is noon. In the Underwoods' dining-room a bright fire is burning. On one side of the fireplace are double doors leading to the drawing-room, on the other side a door leading to the hall. In the centre of the room a long dining-table without cloth is set out as a board table. At the head of it in the Chairman's seat, sits **John Anthony**, *an old man, big, clean shaven, and high-coloured, with thick white hair, and thick dark eyebrows. His movements are rather slow and feeble, but his eyes are very much alive. There is a glass of water by his side. On his right sits his son,* **Edgar**, *an earnest-looking man of thirty, reading a newspaper. Next to him* **Wanklin**, *a man with jutting eyebrows, and silver-streaked light hair, is bending over transfer papers.* **Tench**, *the secretary, a short and rather humble, nervous man, with side whiskers, stands helping him. On* **Wanklin's** *right sits* **Underwood**, *the Manager, a quiet man, with a long, stiff jaw, and steady eyes. Back to the fire is* **Scantlebury**, *a very large, pale, sleepy man, with grey hair, rather bald. Between him and the Chairman are two empty chairs.)*

Wilder: *(Who is lean, cadaverous, and complaining, with drooping grey moustaches, stands before the fire)* I say, this fire's the devil! Can I have a screen, Tench?

John Galsworthy

Activity | In a small group, read these stage directions carefully. Imagine you are a producer and a team of actors discussing preliminary views of these characters. Think about their appearances and personalities.

Galsworthy here presents anyone reading the text with a good deal of guidance on how to visualize the characters. Some playwrights provide little or no such direct guidance on how to interpret their characters but rely on other methods to convey a sense of character. These include:

- how characters speak (also embedded in stage directions)
- how characters are described by other characters
- what the characters say and do

Most playwrights (including Galsworthy) use a combination of all these methods in order to give a sense of fully-developed characters, although in some cases playwrights deliberately create stereotypical characters in order to achieve their particular effect. Some of the 'stock' characters to be found in Restoration Comedy, or a comedy of manners such as *The Rivals*, are examples of this.

Asides and soliloquies

To succeed in creating a convincing character, the dramatist needs to give the audience some sense of deeper, inner thoughts and feelings. Unlike the novelist, however, who can describe these as fully as desired to the reader, the dramatist has much more limited means at his or her disposal.

Two methods that are often used to provide some insight into characters' minds are the aside and the soliloquy. The aside is a kind of 'stage whisper', a behind-the-hand comment. Sometimes it is directed to another character but often it is aimed at the audience or characters 'speak to themselves'. Asides tend to be short, often a single sentence, sometimes a single word. They are used by the playwright to convey small pieces of information concerning the plot or character to the audience. For example, in Congreve's *The Way of the World* one of the central characters, Mirabell, has insincerely courted Lady Wishfort as a cover for his real love of her niece, Millamant. Lady Wishfort has discovered the truth and, although she gives nothing away in conversation, her aside shows that despite all she is still susceptible to his charms.

Lady Wishfort: (*Aside*) Oh, he has witchcraft in his eyes and tongue! When I did not see him, I could have bribed a villain to his assassination; but his appearance rakes the embers which have so long lain smothered in my breast.

Although asides are usually short comments, sometimes they can be more extended. In *The Rivals* the characters almost give the audience a running commentary on what is going on and how they are feeling. In the following extract Absolute has angered his father by refusing to marry the girl his father has selected for him. He then has found out that she is actually the same girl as the one he loves and so he decides to appear penitent to his father (without letting him in on what is really happening!). It is worth noting that lines which can be taken as asides in performance are not always marked (*Aside*) in the script. One television adaptation of this play actually had the characters addressing the camera directly as though speaking confidentially and directly to the viewers, making them privy to the intrigue.

The Rivals

Act III, Scene 1
(*Scene, the North Parade.*
Enter **Absolute**.)

Absolute: 'Tis just as Fag told me, indeed. Whimsical enough, faith! My father wants to force me to marry the very girl I am plotting to run away with! He must not know of my connection with her yet awhile. – He has too summary a method of proceeding in these matters – and Lydia shall not yet lose her hopes of an elopement. – However, I'll read my recantation instantly. My conversion is something sudden, indeed, but I can assure him it is very *sincere*. – So, so – here he comes. He looks plaguy gruff.
(*Steps aside*)
(*Enter Sir Anthony.*)

Sir Anthony: No – I'll die sooner than forgive him. Die, did I say? I'll live these fifty years to plague him. – At our last meeting, his impudence had almost put me out of temper. An obstinate, passionate, self-willed boy! Who can he take after? This is my return for getting him before all his brothers and sisters! – for putting him, at twelve years old, into a marching regiment, and allowing him fifty pounds a year, besides his pay ever since! But I have done with him – he's anybody's son for me. – I never will see him more – never – never – never – never.

Absolute: Now for a penitential face.
(*Advances*)

Sheridan

The aside is an extremely useful device by which the playwright can give hints concerning plot or character to the audience. Through the soliloquy, the playwright has much more scope for developing a character's thoughts and feelings aloud, allowing the audience to see into the mind of the character. The soliloquy is an expanded and more fully developed speech and is usually delivered when the character is alone on the stage. Often soliloquies allow characters to reveal their true feelings, plans, or motives as they do not need to maintain any public image that they may project in front of the other characters. We will consider the role of the soliloquy in Shakespearean drama on page 119 but many playwrights in many different kinds of play make use of asides and soliloquies to create the effect they want.

Returning to *The Rivals*, the maid, Lucy, who pretends to be a 'simpleton', is, in fact, a cunning operator. When she is left alone at the end of a scene, this soliloquy reveals her true nature to the audience and so adds to their amusement as they see how she is playing all the characters off against one another.

The Rivals

Act I, Scene 2

Lucy: Ha! ha! ha! So, my dear simplicity, let me give you a little respite – (*Altering her manner*) let girls in my station be as fond as they please of appearing expert, and knowing in their trusts; commend me to a mask of silliness, and a pair of sharp eyes for my own interest under it! Let me see to what account I have turned my simplicity lately – (*Looks at a paper*) *For abetting Miss Lydia Languish in a design of running away with an ensign – in money – sundry times – twelve pound twelve – gowns, five – hats, ruffles, caps, etc., etc. – numberless! From the said Ensign, within this last month, six guineas and a half* – about a quarter's pay! Item, *from Mrs Malaprop, for betraying the young people to her* – when I found matters were likely to be discovered – *two guineas, and a black paduasoy*. Item, *from Mr Acres, for carrying divers letters* – which I never delivered – *two guineas, and a pair of buckles*. Item, *from Sir Lucius O'Trigger – three crowns – two gold pocket-pieces – and a silver snuff-box!* – Well done, *simplicity!* – yet I was forced to make my Hibernian believe, that he was corresponding, not with the aunt, but with the niece: for, though not over rich, I found he had too much pride and delicacy to sacrifice the feelings of a gentleman to the necessities of his fortune. (*Exit*)

Sheridan

Soliloquies are frequently used at some special moment in the play or when a character is undergoing some kind of emotionally or psychologically heightened experience – for example, when a character is distressed or suffering some kind of confusion of mind or alternatively when a character is feeling exultant or wants to work through his or her own thoughts and feelings.

Although technically speaking we think of characters being alone on the stage, or at least out of earshot of other characters, when they deliver their soliloquy, a soliloquy-like effect can be created in other ways. Sometimes characters may be in the presence of others but they are so wrapped up in their own world that it is as though they are talking to themselves. Although technically speaking not a soliloquy, this can serve much the same function.

It has often been noted that both the aside and the soliloquy are artificial devices and that in 'real life' people do not go around delivering speeches to themselves. In fact, they are just two of many conventions that we accept when watching a play which can be termed 'dramatic licence'. In the context of the theatre we forget their artificiality and accept them quite naturally.

Activity

> **1** Working in pairs, select a character from a play that you are studying. One assumes the role of that character, the other the mirror image. The 'character' asks questions of the image about thoughts, feelings, motivations, etc. and the image answers. This role play should teach you as much about what your chosen character is not as what he or she is.
> **2** You can then select another character and swap roles.

Issues and themes

Complex though the formation and development of characters may be, they are themselves part of a more complex web that makes up the play as a whole. Within this web the playwright will have interwoven certain themes and issues. In studying a play, you will need to be able to identify these and to look at how the playwright explores them through the drama. Such ideas can be presented to the audience in two key ways. First, we can detect ideas, issues, thoughts, etc. expressed by the actual characters in a play. Secondly, we can detect themes, issues, or ideas that the playwright wants the play as a whole to project.

Sometimes a playwright will have major characters hold views or follow a philosophy that ultimately is shown to be counter to the message that the play as a whole conveys. This is often done to show the problems caused by or shortcomings of certain courses of action or philosophies. The issues that a play might raise can be many and varied but they are almost always presented via action centering on human relationships and conflicts.

Activity

> List the major characters in a play that you are studying. Draw up a chart which shows briefly the ideas, philosophies, values etc. held by each character, as shown through the action of the play. Then think about these ideas and against each jot down the dramatist's view.

Plot and structure

Obviously plot is central to most plays although there are certain kinds of play (some of Samuel Beckett's for example) where the very lack of a plot, or at least something that we would ordinarily recognize as a plot, is essential for the effect. At its simplest the **plot** is the story of the play – what actually happens. Having said that, there is much more to plot than simple 'story-line'. The whole notion of plot and its development is bound up with the way that the play is put together, with its structure. The creation of an order or pattern needs careful planning and the playwright needs to consider a number of factors. Generally speaking an effective plot should:

- maintain the interest of the audience from beginning to end
- move the action on from one episode to the next
- arouse interest of the audience in character and situation
- create high points or moments of crisis at intervals
- create expectation and surprise

Usually, the structure of a play follows a basic pattern which consists of a number of identifiable elements.

1 **Exposition:** this opens the play and often introduces the main characters and provides background information.
2 **Dramatic incitement:** the incident which provides the starting point for the main action of the play.

3 **Complication:** this usually forms the main action of the play in which the characters respond to the dramatic incitement and other developments that stem from it.

4 **Crisis:** the climax of the play.

5 **Resolution:** this is the final section of the play where things are worked out and some kind of conclusion is arrived at.

Let us look at this structure as applied to *The Rivals* to see how it works out. Sheridan's play, because of the complexities and confusions of the plot, may seem to have no structure at all on first reading (or viewing). However, a closer study of it reveals that it is very carefully structured indeed.

1 **Exposition:** the opening scene is a classic example of an exposition (see script on pages 89–90). Two servants, Fag and Thomas, through their conversation provide the audience with all the information that they need to follow the action. We are introduced to the stories of the two pairs of lovers (Jack and Lydia and Faulkland and Julia) whose fortunes run parallel to each other throughout the play and reach their resolution in the final scene.

2 **Dramatic incitement:** we are made aware of this through the exposition where we are told that Jack Absolute is wooing the beautiful Lydia Languish by pretending to be a character called Ensign Beverley.

3 **Complication:** there are many complications and twists to the plot – Jack's father, Sir Anthony, arranges for his son to marry a young woman (who happens to be Lydia), Lydia's aunt forbids her to see Ensign Beverley (although she would be happy if she knew he was, in fact, Sir Anthony's son) and many more complications develop.

4 **Crisis:** the main crisis comes when Lydia finds out who her beloved Ensign Beverley really is, thus shattering her notions of a romantic elopement and she refuses to have any more to do with him.

5 **Resolution:** the final scene brings the reconciliation of Jack and Lydia and other strands of the plot which have created problems and complications for most of the other characters are also resolved.

In addition to the main plot involving Lydia and Jack, Sheridan makes use of various sub-plots (the most obvious being the action involving Julia and Faulkland). **Sub-plots** are secondary plots, sometimes separate from the main action but often linked to it in some way. Sub-plots tend to echo themes explored by the main plot or shed more light on them. They contribute to the interest of the play but do not detract from the main plot.

The pace of the action is also integral to the idea of plot and structure. Varying the pace at which the plot unfolds is another factor in maintaining the interest of the audience. Variations in the lengths of scenes and in mood, setting, and action can all influence a play's dramatic effectiveness.

Activity   Examine carefully the structure of a play that you are studying. Draw a diagram to represent the way that the play develops, making brief notes of key moments.

Approaching your script

There are a number of things you can do to deepen your understanding of your drama text for the examination. Here are some suggestions.

Summary

Plays in performance
- See a live performance of the play.
- Failing that see a video recording or a film of it.
- Make notes on performances in a play log book to help you to remember those important initial impressions.
- Read your drama text thoroughly prior to seeing it performed.
- Listen to the play on audio tape.
- See as many other plays as you can to broaden your experience of drama and the theatre.

Directing the text
- Work with others dramatizing for yourselves scenes from the text.
- Talk to others about staging implications.
- Imagine you are a director – plan carefully how you would stage a production of the play, the kind of actors you would cast, how you would bring your own interpretation out live on the stage, etc.
- Use diagrams, drawings and models to work out sets, stage layout, and props for selected scenes.

Studying the text
- Think about the characters – look at key speeches, look for shifts in focus, different ways of interpreting what they do and say.
- Look for various possible 'meanings' and 'patterns' in the play.
- Consider how/if the theatrical effects are signalled.
- Think about the pace and variety of the action.
- Think about the overall shape and structure of the play and the impact that this could have on an audience.
- Consider the particular characteristics and qualities of the play you are studying.
- Think about relationships between these various elements of the play and how together they present a whole.
- Apply the broader knowledge you have about the nature of plays and drama.

All these activities will help you to formulate and develop your own informed critical response to the play and therefore fulfil the objectives which lie at the heart of your study of drama.

Special Feature: Christopher Marlowe

● ●

Christopher Marlowe was born in 1564 in Canterbury, Kent. The son of a shoemaker, he was awarded a scholarship at Corpus Christi College, Cambridge. To a large extent his life is still surrounded by mystery and speculation but it does seem that early in his life, possibly while still at university, Marlowe may have become an agent of Sir Francis Walsingham, who was in charge of Queen Elizabeth's 'secret service'.

What is known is that he took his BA in 1584 and his MA in 1587, when he left Cambridge for London and took up the profession of playwright. He met with immediate success, presenting the first part of *Tambourlaine the Great* at the London Theatre. The second part, too, was a great success and this work established his reputation as a playwright. His colourful private life, with accusations of atheism, blasphemy, subversion and homosexuality, added spice and notoriety to his reputation. His association with a group of radical thinkers led by Sir Walter Raleigh and the suspicion that he might have had leanings towards Catholicism added to the unfavourable view of him held by some.

Whether this reputation or his possible activities as a spy led in some way to his death will never be known. However, we do know that on 30 May 1593 Marlowe was involved in a brawl in a tavern at Deptford with a man called Ingram Frizar. Both men drew their daggers and in the ensuing fray Marlowe was stabbed in the right eye. He died very quickly from the wound.

Frizar was a servant of Thomas Walsingham, Francis's brother, and although he was arrested for the murder of Marlowe he was pardoned by Queen Elizabeth less than a month later. Marlowe was potentially Shakespeare's greatest rival, but we will never know what he might have gone on to achieve. At the age of twenty nine, Christopher Marlowe was dead.

Marlowe's works

After *Tambourlaine* Marlowe continued to write plays dramatizing the lives of heroes whose ambitions and aspirations cause them to overreach themselves. This bold defiance of social, political and religious morality invites the admiration of the audience while at the same time warranting condemnation. *The Jew of Malta* (c. 1589) is usually described as a tragedy but it can, through the murderous excess and the inflated rhetorical posturings of Christian authority, be looked on as parody. As in *Tambourlaine*, at the centre of the play is a hero/villain figure, in this case Barabas. *Edward the Second* (c. 1592) is sometimes regarded as Marlowe's most accomplished play, dealing with the defeat and eventual murder of a homosexual king by the powerful barons. This play is notable for the new, much plainer style that Marlowe adopted here. *Doctor Faustus* brings to a close the examination of the 'overreacher', and it is felt by many scholars to be the last of Marlowe's plays, although it could have been written at any time between 1588 and 1592. We will examine this play in a little more detail now.

Doctor Faustus

The story is set in Germany, where the brilliant scholar Dr John Faustus, wishing even greater challenges and power, agrees to sell his soul to the Devil. He strikes the agreement with Mephistophilis, the Devil's emissary. Faustus is given twenty-four years of luxurious life, magical power, and unlimited knowledge of the secrets of the universe in return for his denial of God. Faustus enjoys his twenty-four years but in the end the Devil comes to claim his soul and Faustus, being unable to turn to God, is dragged off to hell.

This story had been popularly recorded in ballads and folklore for many years, but Marlowe saw very different possibilities in it. He saw the story as a kind of parable epitomising the central spiritual dilemma posed by the temptation to taste forbidden fruits. The play explores two key areas: the temptation of power, and the dread of damnation as taught by the Christian doctrine. In Faustus we have the portrait of a man caught up in that dilemma.

Now look at the opening to the play:

Scene 1

Faustus:　Settle thy studies, Faustus, and begin
To sound the depth of that thou wilt profess;
Having commenc'd, be a divine in show,
Yet level at the end of every art,
And live and die in Aristotle's works.
Sweet Analytics, 'tis thou hast ravish'd me!
Bene disserere est finis logices.
Is to dispute well logic's chiefest end?
Affords this art no greater miracle?
Then read no more, thou hast attain'd that end;
A greater subject fitteth Faustus' wit.
Bid *on kai me on* farewell; Galen come,
Seeing *ubi desinit philosophus, ibi incipit medicus.*
Be a physician, Faustus, heap up gold,
And be eterniz'd for some wondrous cure.
Summum bonum medicinae sanitas,
The end of physic is our body's health.
Why, Faustus, has thou not attain'd that end?
Is not thy common talk sound aphorisms?
Are not thy bills hung up as monuments,
Whereby whole cities have escap'd the plague
And thousand desperate maladies been cur'd?

Yet art thou still but Faustus, and a man.
Couldst thou make men to live eternally
Or being dead raise them to life again,
Then this profession were to be esteem'd.
Physic, farewell! Where is Justinian?
Si una eademque res legatur duobus, alter rem, alter valorem
Rei, etc.
A petty case of paltry legacies!
Exhereditare filium non potest pater, nisi-
Such is the subject of the Institute
And universal body of the law.
This study fits a mercenary drudge
Who aims at nothing but external trash,
Too servile and illiberal for me.
When all is done, divinity is best.
Jerome's Bible, Faustus, view it well.
Stipendium peccati mors est. Ha! *Stipendium, etc.*
The reward of sin is death: that's hard.
Si peccasse negamus, fallimur, et nulla est in nobis veritas.
If we say that we have no sin, we deceive ourselves, and there's no truth in us.
Why, then, belike we must sin, and so consequently die.
Ay, we must die an everlasting death.
What doctrine call you this? *Che sera, sera*:
What will be, shall be! Divinity, adieu!
These metaphysics of magicians
And necromantic books are heavenly;
Lines, circles, letters, and characters:
Ay, these are those that Faustus most desires.
O, what a world of profit and delight,
Of power, of honour, of omnipotence,
Is promis'd to the studious artisan!
All things that move between the quiet poles
Shall be at my command: emperors and kings
Are but obey'd in their several provinces,
Nor can they raise the wind or rend the clouds;
But his dominion that exceeds in this
Stretcheth as far as doth the mind of man:
A sound magician is a demi-god;
Here tire, my brains, to get a deity!

Activity

Faustus is thinking aloud here and his soliloquy is designed to give the audience various information.

1 What is Faustus saying here, and what information does the audience gain?
2 Faustus approaches his decision systematically, by considering the purpose of each of the intellectual disciplines. Identify these disciplines and make notes on what Faustus has to say about each of them.
3 What is the dramatic effect of Faustus's opening speech?

Here are some points that you might have noted.

- Faustus lists the great authors he has read, but all now seem useless.
- He hopes that magic will make him godlike.
- The speech contains an analytical discussion of the things he no longer believes in.
- The audience is made aware of the strength of Faustus's desire for more.
- This opening scene creates the sense of man's unbounded potential by dismissing as insignificant all human achievement to date.
- Man's intellectual, spiritual and practical achievements are summed up in a few lines.
- Religion is dismissed in favour of magic.
- We gain an initial understanding of Faustus's character and motivation.

The disciplines he considers are:
- philosophy, through the achievements of the Greek philosopher Aristotle
- medicine, considered through the work of Galen
- law and the legal profession, in the form of Justinian's Laws
- religion, through Jerome's Bible

The effects created by the following:
- use of blank verse
- references to classical scholars
- Latin references
- use of imagery

Of course, you may well find the end result of this speech a foregone conclusion, because through his reasoning it seems clear that Faustus has already made up his mind and has decided on his course of action. He simply wants to justify it.

Having reached his decision, Faustus sends his servant to fetch Valdes and Cornelius, who will teach him the art of magic. Briefly, two Angels appear, one good and one evil, who try to persuade Faustus in opposite directions. Faustus seems to hear only what the evil Angel says, as he is promised power over the elements and becomes carried away by the idea of the possibilities that this power would open up to him.

Now look at this next extract, in which Faustus ponders what such power could mean to him.

Scene 1

Faustus: How I am glutted with conceit of this!
Shall I make spirits fetch me what I please,
Resolve me of all ambiguities,
Perform what desperate enterprise I will?
I'll have them fly to India for gold,
Ransack the ocean for orient pearl,
And search all corners of the new-found world
For pleasant fruits and princely delicates;

I'll have them read me strange philosophy
And tell the secrets of all foreign kings;
I'll have them wall all Germany with brass
And make swift Rhine circle fair Wittenberg;
I'll have them fill the public schools with silk
Wherewith the students shall be bravely clad;
I'll levy soldiers with the coin they bring
And chase the Prince of Parma from our land
And reign sole king of all our provinces;
Yea, stranger engines for the brunt of war
Than was the fiery keel at Antwerp's bridge
I'll make my servile spirits to invent.

Activity

> This is one of a number of richly poetic speeches in the play. Examine it carefully and make notes on the poetic techniques that Marlowe uses to create his effects.
> Here are some particular points to consider:
> • the repetition of the 'I' sound
> • the effect of words such as 'resolve', 'gold', 'pleasant'.
> • the imagery used
> • the vocabulary

In Scene 5, after repeated hesitations, Faustus is persuaded by Mephistophilis, the Devil's agent, to sign away his soul. Throughout this scene, Faustus repeatedly experiences doubts which are then overcome. This doubting and overcoming of doubt forms a pattern for the whole scene – it is repeated four times in all. This is the pattern that it follows:

- Faustus begins to doubt his actions.
- He is persuaded that his doubts are groundless.
- He regains his determination to go on with his bargain.
- He appears to gain by his decision.

The following extracts represent the second repetition of this cycle in the scene. Read them through carefully.

Scene 5

1

Faustus: Lo, Mephostophilis, for love of thee
Faustus hath cut his arm, and with his proper blood
Assures his soul to be great Lucifer's
Chief lord and regent of perpetual night.
View here this blood that trickles from mine arm,
And let it be propitious for my wish.

Meph.: But, Faustus,
Write it in a manner of a deed of gift.

Faustus:	Ay, so I do. But Mephostophilis,
	My blood congeals, and I can write no more.
Meph.:	I'll fetch thee fire to dissolve it straight. *Exit*
Faustus:	What might the staying of my blood portend?
	Is it unwilling I should write this bill?
	Why streams it not, that I may write afresh?
	'Faustus gives to thee his soul' : O, there it stay'd
	Why shouldst thou not? Is not thy soul thine own?
	Then write again : 'Faustus gives to thee his soul'.

2

Meph.:	[*Aside*] What will not I do to obtain his soul!
Faustus:	*Consummatum est* : this bill is ended,
	And Faustus hath bequeath'd his soul to Lucifer.
	But what is this inscription on mine arm?
	Homo fuge ! Whither should I fly?
	If unto God, he'll throw me down to hell. –
	My senses are deceiv'd, here's nothing writ.–
	O yes, I see it plain; even here is writ,
	Homo fuge ! Yet shall not Faustus fly.
Meph.:	[*Aside*] I'll fetch him somewhat to delight his mind. *Exit*

Enter **Devils**, *giving crowns and rich apparel*
to **Faustus**. *They dance and then depart.*
          Enter **Mephostophilis**.

3

Faustus:	What means this show? Speak, Mephostophilis.
Meph.:	Nothing, Faustus, but to delight thy mind
	And let thee see what magic can perform.
Faustus:	But may I raise such spirits when I please?
Meph.:	Ay, Faustus, and do greater things than these.
Faustus:	Then, Mephostophilis, receive this scroll,
	A deed of gift of body and of soul:
	But yet conditionally that thou perform
	All covenants and articles between us both.
Meph.:	Faustus, I swear by hell and Lucifer
	To effect all promises between us made.
Faustus:	Then hear me read it, Mephostophilis.

4

Faustus:	Nay, and this be hell, I'll willingly be damn'd:
	What, sleeping, eating, walking, and disputing!
	But, leaving this, let me have a wife, the fairest maid in
	Germany, for I am wanton and lascivious and cannot live
	Without a wife.
Meph.:	How, a wife! I prithee, Faustus, talk not of a wife.

Faustus: Nay, sweet Mephostophilis, fetch me one, for I will have One.
Meph.: Well, thou wilt have one. Sit there till I come; I'll fetch
Thee a wife in the devil's name.   [*Exit*]

Enter with a **Devil** *dressed like a woman,*
    With fireworks.

Tell me, Faustus, how dost thou like thy wife?
Faustus: Here's a hot whore indeed! No, I'll no wife.
Meph.: Marriage is but a ceremonial toy;
And if thou lov'st me, think no more of it.
I'll cull thee out the fairest courtesans
And bring them every morning to thy bed;
She whom thine eye shall like, thy heart shall have,
Were she as chaste as was Penelope,
As wise as Saba, or as beautiful
As was bright Lucifer before his fall.
Hold; take this book, peruse it thoroughly:
The iterating of these lines brings gold;
The framing of this circle on the ground
Brings thunder, whirlwinds, storm, and lightning;
Pronounce this thrice devoutly to thyself
And men in harness shall appear to thee,
Ready to execute what thou command'st

Activity

> Look carefully at each extract and write down what is happening in
> each one.
> **1** Why does Faustus begin to doubt?
> **2** How is he persuaded to overcome his doubts?
> **3** How is his determination to go on revealed?
> **4** What does he appear to gain by his decision?
> **5** What do you think would be the dramatic effect of the repetition of
>   this cycle throughout the whole scene?
>
> If you are studying this play for the exam try to identify the other three
> occasions when this pattern is repeated in Scene 5. Identify each stage
> and make notes on them.

The play develops many dramatic tensions and provides a broad vision of
Faustus's temptation and downfall, but it also contains moments of high
comedy. Some critics have found this a flaw in what is otherwise a master-
piece, and have commented that the ways in which Faustus exercises his
new-found powers trivialize the issues. Particular examples are the slapstick
of his humiliation of the Pope, the duping of the horse dealer and the
supplying of ripe grapes in winter. However, these lighter elements do form a
counter-balance to the learned questioning of Mephostophilis on the nature of
hell, and the poetic beauty of the apparition of Helen of Troy at the end.

The doubts that Faustus experienced at the beginning of the play return to
haunt him further at the end. In Scene 18 we see a return to the doubt/

persuasion structure that we looked at in Scene 5. This time, the Old Man acts as an advisor to Faustus and tries to persuade him to repent. Read the following extract carefully.

Scene 18

Enter an **Old Man**

Old Man:	O gentle Faustus, leave this damned art,
	This magic, that will charm thy soul to hell
	And quite bereave thee of salvation.
	Though thou hast now offended like a man,
	Do not persever in it like a devil.
	Yet, yet, thou hast an amiable soul,
	If sin by custom grow not into nature:
	Then, Faustus, will repentance come too late,
	Then thou art banish'd from the sight of heaven;
	No mortal can express the pains of hell.
	It may be this my exhortation
	Seems harsh and all unpleasant; let it not,
	For, gentle son, I speak it not in wrath
	Or envy of thee, but in tender love
	And pity of thy future misery;
	And so have hope that this my kind rebuke,
	Checking thy body, may amend thy soul.
Faustus:	Where art thou, Faustus? wretch, what hast thou done?
	Damn'd art thou, Faustus, damn'd; despair and die!
	Mephostophilis *gives him a dagger.*
	Hell claims his right and with a roaring voice
	Says, 'Faustus, come; thine hour is almost come';
	And Faustus now will come to do thee right.
	[**Faustus** *goes to use the dagger*]
Old Man:	O, stay good Faustus, stay thy desperate steps!
	I see an angel hovers o'er thy head
	And with a vial full of precious grace
	Offers to pour the same into thy soul:
	Then call for mercy, and avoid despair.
Faustus:	O friend, I feel
	Thy words to comfort my distressed soul.
	Leave me awhile to ponder on my sins.
Old Man:	Faustus, I leave thee, but with a grief of heart,
	Fearing the enemy of thy hapless soul. *Exit*
Faustus:	Accursed Faustus, where is mercy now?
	I do repent, and yet I do despair;
	Hell strives with grace for conquest in my breast.
	What shall I do to shun the snares of death?
Meph.:	Thou traitor, Faustus, I arrest thy soul
	For disobedience to my sovereign lord:
	Revolt, or I'll in piecemeal tear thy flesh.

Faustus:	I do repent I e'er offended him.
	Sweet Mephostophilis, entreat thy lord
	To pardon my unjust presumption,
	And with my blood again I will confirm
	The former vow I made to Lucifer.
Meph.:	Do it, then, Faustus, with unfeigned heart,
	Lest greater dangers do attend thy drift.
Faustus:	Torment, sweet friend, that base and aged man
	That durst dissuade me from thy Lucifer,
	With greatest torment that our hell affords.
Meph.:	His faith is great; I cannot touch his soul;
	But what I may afflict his body with
	I will attempt, which is but little worth.
Faustus:	One thing, good servant, let me crave of thee
	To glut the longing of my heart's desire:
	That I may have unto my paramour
	That heavenly Helen which I saw of late,
	Whose sweet embraces may extinguish clear
	Those thoughts that do dissuade me from my vow,
	And keep mine oath I made to Lucifer.
Meph.:	This or what else my Faustus shall desire
	Shall be perform'd in twinkling of an eye.

Enter **Helen** *again, passing over between two* **Cupids**

Faustus:	Was this the face that launch'd a thousand ships
	And burnt the topless towers of Ilium?
	Sweet Helen, make me immortal with a kiss.
	Her lips suck forth my soul: see where it flies!
	Come, Helen, come, give me my soul again.
	Here will I dwell, for heaven is in these lips,
	And all is dross that is not Helena.

Enter **Old Man**

I will be Paris, and for love of thee
Instead of Troy shall Wittenberg be sack'd,
And I will combat with weak Menelaus
And wear thy colours on my plumed crest,
Yea, I will wound Achilles in the heel
And then return to Helen for a kiss.
O, thou art fairer than the evening's air
Clad in the beauty of a thousand stars,
Brighter art thou than flaming Jupiter
When he appear'd to hapless Semele,
More lovely than the monarch of the sky
In wanton Arethusa's azur'd arms,
And none but thou shalt be my paramour.

Exeunt [**Faustus**, **Helen**, *and the* **Cupids**].

Old Man: Accursed Faustus, miserable man,
That from thy soul exclud'st the grace of heaven
And fliest the throne of his tribunal seat!

Enter the **Devils**.

Satan begins to sift me with his pride:
As in this furnace God shall try my faith,
My faith, vile hell, shall triumph over thee.
Ambitious fiends, see how the heavens smiles
At your repulse and laughs your state to scorn!
Hence, Hell! for hence I fly unto my God.   *Exeunt*

Activity: Examine this extract carefully and comment on the dramatic structure of it. (Remember the structure that we looked at in Scene 5.)

What is the dramatic effect of the Old Man's death at the end of the scene?

The stage is now set for the death of Faustus himself. Here is his final speech.

Scene 19

Faustus: Ah, Faustus,
Now hast thou but one bare hour to live,
And then thou must be damn'd perpetually.
Stand still, you ever-moving spheres of heaven,
That time may cease, and midnight never come;
Fair nature's eye, rise, rise again, and make
Perpetual day; or let this hour be but
A year, a month, a week, a natural day,
That Faustus may repent and save his soul.
O, lente lente currite noctis equi!
The stars move still, time runs, the clock will strike,
The devil will come, and Faustus must be damn'd.
O, I'll leap up to my God! Who pulls me down ?
See, see where Christ's blood streams in the firmament!
One drop would save my soul, half a drop. Ah, my Christ! –
Rend not my heart for naming of my Christ;
Yet will I call on him. O, spare me, Lucifer! –
Where is it now ? 'Tis gone: and see where God
Stretcheth out his arm and bends his ireful brows.
Mountains and hills, come, come, and fall on me,
And hide me from the heavy wrath of God!
No, no:
Then will I headlong run into the earth.
Earth, gape! O, no, it will not harbour me.
You stars that reign'd at my nativity,
Whose influence hath allotted death and hell,

Now draw up Faustus like a foggy mist
Into the entrails of yon labouring cloud,
That, when you vomit forth into the air,
My limbs may issue from your smoky mouths,
So that my soul may but ascend to heaven.   *The watch strikes.*
Ah, half the hour is pass'd: 'twill all be pass'd anon.
O God,
If thou wilt not have mercy on my soul,
Yet for Christ's sake, whose blood hath ransom'd me,
Impose some end to my incessant pain;
Let Faustus live in hell a thousand years,
A hundred thousand, and at last be sav'd.
O, no end is limited to damned souls.
Why wert thou not a creature wanting soul ?
Or why is this immortal that thou hast ?
Ah, Pythagoras' *metempsychosis*, were that true,
This soul should fly from me and I be chang'd
Unto some brutish beast: all beasts are happy,
For when they die
Their souls are soon dissolved in elements;
But mine must live still to be plagu'd in hell.
Curs'd be the parents that engendered me!
No, Faustus, curse thyself, curse Lucifer
That hath depriv'd thee of the joys of heaven.
                    The clock strikes
O, it strikes, it strikes! Now, body, turn to air,
Or Lucifer will bear thee quick to hell!
                    Thunder and lightning
O soul, be changed into little water drops,
And fall into the ocean, ne'er be found.
          Enter **Devils**.

My God, my God! Look not so fierce on me!
Adders and serpents, let me breathe awhile!
Ugly hell, gape not! Come not, Lucifer;
I'll burn my books!-Ah, Mephostophilis!
              Exeunt with him. [*Exeunt* **Lucifer** *and* **Beelzebub**.]

Activity: Write an essay comparing the Faustus we see in this final speech with the Faustus portrayed in his opening speech of the play. You should consider in your answer:
• the content of what Faustus has to say
• the language of each speech
• the dramatic impact of each speech

5 Shakespeare

Objectives
- To identify ways in which you can approach the study of Shakespeare
- To prepare yourself for writing about Shakespeare
- To consider some of the features to look for in Shakespearean drama
- To prepare for studying set Shakespearean texts

Shakespeare has always held a dominant position in the drama element of English Literature at AS- and A-level. By the time you reach this stage in your studies you will probably have encountered several Shakespeare plays already. It is likely that you will have studied Shakespeare for Key Stage 3 and Key Stage 4, so you will already be aware of some of the features that characterize his plays.

Exactly which play (or plays) you study will depend on which particular texts are offered in your Exam Board's specification, which are selected by your teacher or lecturer, or which texts are covered by your learning modules.

Shakespeare and drama

Obviously Shakespeare is a dramatist, and it follows that his plays have a great deal in common with those of other dramatists. In this respect, much of what you learned from the unit on drama is applicable to Shakespeare's plays too.

They follow the clear structural pattern that we discussed in some detail earlier:

EXPOSITION → DRAMATIC INCITEMENT→COMPLICATION→CRISIS→RESOLUTION

Similarly, Shakespeare's plays also make use of sub-plots or secondary plots which, although separate from the main action, link with it in some way.

Approaching your text

In approaching the Shakespeare text you are studying, make use of the knowledge you already possess as to the nature of drama generally. This can help you understand the plot of your Shakespeare text when reading it for the first time. For example, it will help if you know that Shakespeare's plays follow this pattern:

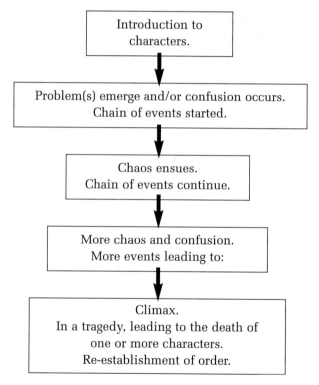

Introduction to characters.

Problem(s) emerge and/or confusion occurs.
Chain of events started.

Chaos ensues.
Chain of events continue.

More chaos and confusion.
More events leading to:

Climax.
In a tragedy, leading to the death of
one or more characters.
Re-establishment of order.

Knowledge of this general structure can help you to follow the storyline of any play, but more than this, it can provide you with a framework for your analysis of the play as a whole. One of the problems that students frequently encounter when studying a Shakespeare text is that they focus so closely on detailed summaries of scene, character and theme that they sometimes lose sight of the fact that the play is an integrated whole. Being able to see the play in terms of its overall framework can help you to appreciate the broad pattern of the text, thus helping you to make sense of the detail when it emerges through more detailed study.

Shakespeare's plays

There are various ways in which the plays of Shakespeare can be categorized but a useful and simple method is to divide them into Histories, Tragedies and Comedies.

The main texts set for study at AS- and A-level are as follows:

Histories	**Tragedies**	**Comedies**
Richard II	*Hamlet*	*The Taming of the Shrew*
Henry IV (Part 1)	*Macbeth*	*Love's Labour's Lost*
Henry IV (Part 2)	*Othello*	*A Midsummer Night's Dream*
Henry V	*King Lear*	*Much Ado About Nothing*
Richard III	*Romeo and Juliet*	*The Merchant of Venice*
Antony and Cleopatra		*As You Like It*
Coriolanus		
Julius Caesar		

In addition, there are two further categories for a handful of plays that do not fit easily in the three broad areas.

Problem comedies	**Romances**
Troilus and Cressida	*Cymbeline*
All's Well That Ends Well	*The Winter's Tale*
Measure for Measure	*The Tempest*

Let's have a closer look at some of the features of plays in each of these categories.

The histories

The main history plays that you are likely to encounter in studying English at AS or A-level are *Richard II*, *Henry IV Part 1*, *Henry IV Part 2*, *Henry V*, and *Richard III*, all of which focus on a specific period of English history. Added to these five are the Roman history plays, *Coriolanus*, *Julius Caesar*, and *Antony and Cleopatra*. It appears that Shakespeare was the first playwright to write a real history play and to treat his material as a drama rather than a mere chronicle of events. His development of character, ideas and themes in these plays makes them far more than simple chronicles, because he adapts historical facts to suit his dramatic purpose.

Although each of Shakespeare's histories is very different from the others in many respects, they do have certain features in common. For example, history plays usually:

- present famous historical figures at moments of crisis in their lives
- concern themselves with the order and stability of the state
- portray rebels who create problems
- have heroes who are fallible
- examine the gap between an ideal notion of kingship and the less tidy reality

- accept the inevitability of disorder
- show that the failings and ambitions of individuals can disrupt the social order

Activity
> Take the history play that you are studying for your course, or one you have studied in the past, and decide how many of the above features you can identify in it. Make a note of how each feature can be seen in the particular play you have chosen.

The tragedies

The idea of disorder also lies at the heart of the tragedies. The Roman history plays are often included in the list of tragedies. The four plays that are regarded as 'the great' tragedies are *Hamlet*, *King Lear*, *Othello*, and *Macbeth*. These plays are very frequently set for study at A-level. At the heart of each of these plays is the central character after whom the play is named – **the eponymous hero**, to give the technical term – and the action focuses very much on this character. However, other characters are important too, and often several innocent victims are claimed before the play reaches its end.

Overall, Shakespeare's tragedies have many of the key features we associate with the concept of dramatic tragedy in general.

- At the beginning of the play something occurs that disrupts the normal order of things.
- Chaos or disorder in society results.
- Extreme emotions are involved.
- Social restraint disintegrates.
- A climax is reached, usually with the death of the main character (and several others), before order is restored. The purging of emotions that affects the audience at the end of a tragedy is sometimes referred to as **catharsis**.

Activity
> If you are studying one of Shakespeare's tragedies think about how the play fits this general pattern. Note down one thing that happens in the play which corresponds to each of the above features.

The comedies

The term 'comedy' in modern usage tends to be associated with something fairly lightweight that makes us laugh. However, in its original sense, and certainly as applied to the plays of Shakespeare, the term simply means a play that has a happy ending; the action that leads to this ending may be funny and light in tone, but equally it could deal with serious, even dangerous and life-threatening situations. Shakespearean comedy can deal with issues that are just as serious as those raised by other kinds of plays.

Shakespeare's comedies vary considerably both in style and the mood the play creates. Early comedies such as *The Taming of the Shrew, Love's Labour's Lost, A Midsummer Night's Dream*, and *Much Ado About Nothing*, or the later comedies, *As You Like It*, and *Twelfth Night*, might reasonably be called romantic comedies as love plays a central role in them. The general pattern for these comedies is as follows.

- Life is going on as normal.
- Characters fall in love.
- Various mishaps and misunderstandings threaten the happy outcome.
- The problems are resolved.
- The play ends happily with the various lovers united.

However, in some – notably *Much Ado About Nothing* – a good deal in the play verges on the tragic and in some ways is reminiscent of *Romeo and Juliet*. This serious edge is clearly there in *The Merchant of Venice* too, so much so that although the play ends happily for all except Shylock – almost a tragic figure at the end – the term tragicomedy has been applied to it. The basic pattern, then, is very similar to that of the tragedies.

- An event occurs.
- This leads to disorder and disruption.
- Confusion results.
- The problems are resolved.

The difference comes in the way that the action is resolved and the focus that is maintained. In a comedy, serious issues may be raised and addressed but the focus is very much on the foolishness of human behaviour, and the audience usually feels confident that all will turn out well. However, within this structure evil influences may be at work and the play may deal with the powerful negative forces that motivate characters – sexual appetite, lust for power, greed, and envy. These forces are nowhere more evident than in what are referred to as the problem comedies.

The problem comedies

Generally the problem comedies are taken to be *Measure for Measure, Troilus and Cressida*, and *All's Well That Ends Well*. In many ways these plays fall somewhere between tragedy and comedy – they avoid becoming tragic because they end 'happily', at least in so far as no one dies at the end of the play. They are also known as the **problem plays** or **dark comedies**.

A dark tone and flawed characters are typical of these plays. They are more likely to disturb the audience than amuse them, as they raise unsettling issues about the darker side of human nature. Like the other types of plays we have looked at, they centre on disorder within society, but whereas the comedies operate in a world of fantasy and make-believe, these plays take place in a very much bleaker and often coldly realistic environment.

It has been said that in writing these plays Shakespeare was experimenting with a dramatic form which brought together comedy and tragedy. If this is so, his experimentation culminated in the romance plays, written towards the end of his career.

The romance plays

The romances (or 'last plays'), *Pericles*, *Cymbeline*, *The Winter's Tale*, and *The Tempest*, are once again concerned with the idea of disorder. Unlike the problem comedies, which have a harshly realistic setting, these plays make much use of fantasy elements and magic to explore their central ideas. They operate in make-believe worlds and the plots often take improbable or incredible turns and twists. However, these features of the plays are essential to the effects that they create and the purpose they hope to achieve.

Certain key ideas can be seen emerging through all four of these plays.

- The play centres on a noble family and a king.
- An evil or misguided deed is done.
- This causes great suffering to characters and they endure years of separation.
- Through the suffering, something new and positive begins to emerge.
- In the end this new element transforms the old evil.
- An act of forgiveness resolves the problems, and reconciliation takes place.

In simple terms the general pattern can be seen as:

In many ways the unusual (sometimes bizarre) events that occur in the romances can present added difficulties when you are trying to establish the plot and characters in your mind. However, at their heart are the same features that are present in the other kinds of plays we have discussed. There is order versus disorder; love and harmony versus conflict and discord; and life falls short of the ideal because of human imperfection.

Activity | What type of Shakespeare play are you studying? Draw up a table of the key events and describe the plot structure, thinking about the overall pattern that is created.

Shakespeare's plots

As we have seen the plots of Shakespeare's plays adhere to a general pattern common to many plays. However, when studying your text one of the first things you will need to do is to get to grips with the details of the plot. Very often your first encounter with the play will be through a reading, perhaps in class, with students taking the various parts. When reading the play either to yourself or as part of a group, though, it is easy to lose sight of the fact that you are studying a drama. The text you are reading was written to be performed and therefore brought to life on the stage. Although we now read Shakespeare's plays as 'literary texts', we must not forget this central fact, and you should view the 'text' as a 'script'. A 'script' suggests something that in itself is incomplete because it needs a dramatic enactment to achieve its purpose. This opens up the whole question of how the play is to be enacted, and touches on the fact that the play has many rather than a single meaning.

In coming to terms with the plot of a Shakespeare play, therefore, you first need to understand generally what is happening, and then think about ways in which this could be enacted on the stage. To help you appreciate the variety of ways that a play can be interpreted, you should try to see as many performances of it (live in the theatre, on film, or video, etc.) as you can.

Activity

> In **ten** sentences summarize the plot of the Shakespeare play you are studying. Then take the opening scene of that play and describe two possible, but contrasting, ways in which that scene could be enacted on the stage.

Structure

The structure of each play is integral to the way in which Shakespeare develops its central issues. The structure of his plays (or any play) can be viewed in two ways. What is sometimes called the **dynamic structure** of the play consists of the sequence of events which builds up in a 'cause and effect' fashion to create the plot of the play, and so drives the play forward.

Underlying this obvious structure, however, it is often possible to detect another that is less prominent but just as important. This second structure consists of various parallels and cross-references, or repeated images, symbols, and language that create a network of threads running through the play. This kind of structure is sometimes called the **symmetric structure**, and it can exert a powerful influence on the overall effect of a play.

In *Hamlet*, for example, the repeated parallels between Hamlet and Laertes as avenging sons, and Hamlet's repeated contemplation of death with its associated imagery, are just two elements that help to form a web of patterning developed throughout the play. Similarly, in *King Lear*, the theme of 'blindness' to the truth as well as physical blindness, presented through Gloucester and Lear, create parallels that give another kind of structure on the play.

Activity

> Draw two diagrams, one to represent the dynamic structure of the Shakespeare play you are studying, the other to represent the symmetric structure.

Character in Shakespeare's plays

An essential part of the study of any play will be to study the characters and Shakepeare's methods of creating and presenting them.

To put it simply, Shakespeare uses three main techniques to create characters. They reveal themselves:

- through their actions
- by what others say about them
- through their own language

Let's have a look at this in practice.

Activity | Examine the following extracts from *Othello*. Iago is the focus of them all.

Othello
Act II Scene 1

Iago: That Cassio loves her, I do well believe't:
That she loves him, 'tis apt and of great credit.
The Moor – howbeit that I endure him not –
Is of a constant, loving, noble nature,
And, I dare think, he'll prove to Desdemona
A most dear husband. Now, I do love her too;
Not out of absolute lust – though peradventure
I stand accountant for as great a sin –
But partly led to diet my revenge
For that I do suspect the lusty Moor
Hath leaped into my seat, the thought whereof
Doth, like a poisonous mineral, gnaw my inwards,
And nothing can, or shall, content my soul
Till I am evened with him, wife for wife;
Or failing so, yet that I put the Moor
At least into a jealousy so strong
That judgement cannot cure. Which thing to do
If this poor trash of Venice, whom I leash
For his quick hunting, stand the putting on,
I'll have our Michael Cassio on the hip,
Abuse him to the Moor in the rank garb –
For I fear Cassio with my night-cap too –
Make the Moor thank me, love me, and reward me
For making him egregiously an ass,
And practising upon his peace and quiet,
Even to madness. 'Tis here, but yet confused:
Knavery's plain face is never seen till used.   *Exit*

Act III Scene 3

Enter **Othello** *and* **Iago**

Emilia:	Madam, here comes my lord.
Casio:	Madam, I'll take my leave.
Desdemona:	Why, stay and hear me speak.
Cassio:	Madam, not now: I am very ill at ease,
	Unfit for mine own purposes.
Desdemona:	Well, do your discretion. *Exit* **Cassio**
Iago:	Ha! I like not that.
Othello:	What dost thou say?
Iago:	Nothing, my lord; or if – I know not what.
Othello:	Was not that Cassio parted from my wife?
Iago:	Cassio, my lord? No, sure, I cannot think it
	That he would sneak away so guilty-like,
	Seeing you coming.
Othello:	I do believe 'twas he.
Desdemona:	How now, my lord?
	I have been talking with a suitor here,
	A man that languishes in your displeasure.

Act V Scene 1

He wounds **Roderigo**

Roderigo:	O, I am slain!
	Iago *wounds* **Cassio** *in the leg, and exit*
Cassio:	I am maimed for ever. Help, ho! Murder, murder!

Enter **Othello**, *above*

Othello:	The voice of Cassio: Iago keeps his word.
Roderigo:	O, villain that I am!
Othello:	It is even so.
Cassio:	O, help, ho! A surgeon!
Othello:	'Tis he! O brave Iago, honest and just,
	That hast such noble sense of thy friend's wrong,
	Though teachest me! Minion, your dear lies dead,
	And your unblest fate lies. Strumpet, I come!
	Forth of my heart those charms, thine eyes, are blotted;
	Thy bed, lust-stained, shall with lust's blood be spotted.
	Exit **Othello**

Enter **Lodovico** *and* **Gratiano**

Cassio:	What, ho! No watch? No passage? Murder, murder!
Gratiano:	'Tis some mischance: the cry is very direful.
Cassio:	O, help!
Lodovico:	Hark!
Roderigo:	O wretched villain!
Lodovico:	Two or three groan. It is a heavy night.

	These may be counterfeits. Let's think't unsafe
	To come in to the cry without more help.
Roderigo:	Nobody come? Then shall I bleed to death.
Lodovico:	Hark!

Enter **Iago,** *with a light*

Gratiano:	Here's one comes in his shirt, with light and weapons.
Iago:	Who's there? Whose noise is this that cries on murder?
Lodovico:	We do not know.
Iago:	Did you not hear a cry?
Cassio:	Here, here: for heaven's sake help me!
Iago:	What's the matter?
Gratiano:	This is Othello's Ancient, as I take it.
Lodovico:	The same indeed, a very valiant fellow.
Iago:	What are you here, that cry so grievously?
Cassio:	Iago? O, I am spoiled, undone by villains!
	Give me some help.

Act V Scene 2

Lodovico:	Where is this rash and most unfortunate man?
Othello:	That's he that was Othello: here I am.
Lodovico:	Where is that viper? Bring the villain forth.
Othello:	I look down towards his feet; but that's a fable.
	If that thou be'st a devil, I cannot kill thee.

He wounds **Iago**

Lodovico:	Wrench his sword from him.
Iago:	I bleed, sir, but not killed.
Othello:	I am not sorry neither; I'd have thee live,
	For in my sense 'tis happiness to die.
Lodovico:	O, thou Othello, that wast once so good,
	Fallen in the practice of a damned slave,
	What shall be said to thee?
Othello:	Why, anything:
	An honourable murderer, if you will:
	For naught did I in hate, but all in honour.
Lodovico:	This wretch hath part confessed his villainy.
	Did you and he consent in Cassio's death?
Othello:	Ay.
Cassio:	Dear General, I never gave you cause.
Othello:	I do believe it, and I ask your pardon.
	Will you, I pray, demand that demi-devil
	Why he hath thus ensnared my soul and body?
Iago:	Demand me nothing; what you know, you know:
	From this time forth I never will speak word.

Activity

> What does each of the extracts tell you about the nature of Iago's character and the nature of Othello's character? Make a note how each feature is revealed.

Activity

> Choose one of the central characters from the Shakespeare play that you are studying. Imagine that you are an actor who has been offered that part in a forthcoming production. Collect evidence from the play to support your view of the character and the way that you intend to play him or her on stage. Your evidence should consist of the following:
>
> - what the character says about himself or herself
> - what others say about the character
> - what the character does when speaking
> - what the character does when silent
> - how the character's words match his or her actual deeds or underlying motives
> - how the character is viewed by those around him or her

This activity should help you form your own view of a character. Remember, though, there is more than one way of looking at a character. Characters in plays, like living people, can rarely be seen in clear-cut, black-and-white terms. As part of your preparation for the examination, it would be useful for you to make notes on each of the characters in the play(s) you are studying, making sure that you cover the points in the following summary.

Summary

- Consider all possible interpretations of the character.
- Assess the role or function that the character performs in the play.
- Examine in detail the key speeches the character makes and the scenes in which he or she appears.
- Gather a range of evidence from the play to support your view of the character.

Soliloquies and asides

In most of his plays Shakespeare makes full use of the dramatic devices of asides and soliloquies as a means of developing aspects of character.

In Shakespeare's *Othello* there is substantial use of both long and short asides. Often they reveal to the audience the wicked plan developing in Iago's mind, and give a glimpse into his thoughts and the delight he takes in his evil. In this unusually long aside we are shown his thoughts taking shape as he watches Desdemona and Cassio.

Othello

Act II Scene 1

Iago: (*Aside*) He takes her by the palm. Ay, well said, whisper. With as little web as this will I ensnare as great a fly as Cassio. Ay, smile upon her, do. I will gyve thee in thine own courtship. You say true, 'tis so indeed. If such tricks as these strip you out of your lieutenantry, it had been better you had not kissed your three fingers so oft, which now again you are most apt to play the sir in. Very good: well kissed, an excellent courtesy! 'Tis so indeed. Yet again your fingers to your lips? Would they were clyster-pipes for your sake!

The repeated use of asides also give us an insight into Othello's growing torment. For example, in this extract Iago urges Othello to secretly observe his own conversation with Cassio, to convince Othello (quite wrongly) that Cassio and Desdemona are lovers. In fact, Iago and Cassio are talking about Bianca.

Act IV Scene 1

Othello: (*Aside*) Look, how he laughs already!
Iago: I never knew a woman love man so.
Cassio: Alas, poor rogue! I think i'faith she loves me.
Othello: (*Aside*) Now he denies it faintly, and laughs it out.
Iago: Do you hear, Cassio?
Othello: (*Aside*) Now he importunes him to tell it o'er.
Go to, well said, well said!
Iago: She gives it out that you shall marry her.
Do you intend it?
Cassio: Ha, ha, ha!
Othello: (*Aside*) Do you triumph, Roman? Do you triumph?
Cassio: I marry her! What! A customer! Prithee bear some charity to my wit: do not think it so unwholesome. Ha, ha, ha!
Othello: (*Aside*) So, so, so, so: they laugh that win.

And so Othello's jealousy builds and is communicated to the audience through the cumulative tension created by the asides.

Soliloquies, too, are used extensively to convey both information and inward emotion to the audience. In *Hamlet*, for example, it is possible to trace the development of Hamlet's shifting emotions during the course of the play through the sequence of soliloquies he delivers at various points in the action.

In *Henry IV Part 1* the following soliloquy allows us, the audience, to see the true nature of Prince Hal early on in the play. We see him in a light that none of the other characters can see. He has been a complete disappointment to his father, King Henry, and all the 'responsible' authority figures in the play, because of the wild and dissolute life he has been leading in the company of an old reprobate, Falstaff, and his dubious tavern and whorehouse companions. However, at the end of Act I Scene 2, after bantering with these companions in the tavern and becoming involved in the planning of a robbery, the Prince is left alone on the stage and delivers this soliloquy.

Henry IV Part 1

Act I Scene 2

Prince: I know you all, and will awhile uphold
The unyok'd humour of your idleness.
Yet herein will I imitate the sun,
Who doth permit the base contagious clouds
To smother up his beauty from the world,
That, when he please again to be himself,
Being wanted he may be more wonder'd at
By breaking through the foul and ugly mists
Of vapours that did seem to strangle him.
If all the year were playing holidays,
To sport would be as tedious as to work;
But when they seldom come, they wish'd-for come,
And nothing pleaseth but rare accidents:
So, when this loose behaviour I throw off,
And pay the debt I never promised,
By how much better than my word I am,
By so much shall I falsify men's hopes;
And, like bright metal on a sullen ground,
My reformation, glittering o'er my fault,
Shall show more goodly, and attract more eyes
Than that which hath no foil to set it off.
I'll so offend to make offence a skill,
Redeeming time when men think least I will.

In the second soliloquy taken from *Henry IV Part 2* we see the Prince at the bedside of his father as he sleeps. His father is ill and the Prince is likely to succede to the throne.

Henry IV Part 2

Act IV Scene 5

Prince: Why doth the crown lie there upon his pillow,
Being so troublesome a bedfellow?
O polish'd perturbation! golden care!
That keep'st the ports of slumber open wide
To many a watchful night! Sleep with it now!
Yet not so sound and half so deeply sweet
As he whose brow and homely biggen bound
Snores out the watch of night. O majesty!
When thou dost pinch thy bearer, thou dost sit
Like a rich armour worn in the heat of day
That scald'st with safety. By his gates of breath
There lies a downy feather which stirs not.
Did he suspire, that light and weightless down
Perforce must move. My gracious lord! my father!

This sleep is sound indeed; this is a sleep
That from this golden rigol hath divorc'd
So many English kings. Thy due from me
Is tears and heavy sorrows of blood
Which nature, love, and filial tenderness,
Shall, O dear father, pay thee plenteously.
My due from thee is this imperial crown,
Which, as immediate from thy place and blood,
Derives itself to me. [*Putting on crown.*] Lo where it sits –
Which God shall guard; and put the world's whole strength
Into one giant arm, it shall not force
This lineal honour from me. This from thee
Will I to mine leave as 'tis left to me.

Activity

> Look at Prince Hal's first soliloquy.
>
> **1** What is the Prince saying here?
> **2** What does he reveal to the audience?
> **3** Why do you think Shakespeare has placed this soliloquy at such an early point in the play?
>
> Now look at the second soliloquy.
>
> **1** What is the Prince saying here?
> **2** What differences in content, mood and tone can you detect between the two soliloquies?

The soliloquy, then, is one key way in which Shakespeare lets us, the audience, know what a character is really like. Through a soliloquy characters tell us directly about themselves and can inform us about a whole range of issues, such as what is in their minds, why they are acting as they are, what they intend to do in the future.

Activity

> This soliloquy is taken from *Othello*, and in it Iago reveals a good deal about his own attitudes. Read it carefully and make a list of the key points that Iago reveals about himself here.

Othello

Act I Scene 3

Iago: Thus do I ever make my fool my purse:
       For I mine own gained knowledge should profane
       If I would time expend with such a snipe
       But for my sport and profit. I hate the Moor,
       And it is thought a broad that 'twixt my sheets
       He's done my office. I know not if't be true
       But I, for mere suspicion in that kind,

Will do as if for surety. He holds me well:
The better shall my purpose work on him.
Cassio's a proper man: let me see now;
To get his place and to plume up my will
In double knavery. How? How? Let's see.
After some time, to abuse Othello's ear
That he is too familiar with his wife;
He hath a person and a smooth dispose
To be suspected, framed to make women false.
The Moor is of a free and open nature,
That thinks men honest that but seem to be so,
And will as tenderly be led by th'nose
As asses are.
I have't. It is engendered. Hell and night
Must bring this monstrous birth to the world's light.

Exit

Activity | Now look at the play you are studying. Make a list of the soliloquies in it and what those soliloquies tell you about the characters who speak them.

Shakespeare's themes and ideas

Each of Shakespeare's plays is concerned with certain ideas or issues that recur and develop as the play progresses. These topics with which the play is preoccupied are the play's 'themes'. They are the subject that Shakespeare explores through the events, characters and language of the play. It is the themes that give a shape and pattern to the play and give it a significance beyond the events it describes.

The themes are developed through the language of the play, and often Shakespeare creates powerful images. For example, in *Othello* one of the themes of the play is 'honesty' and Iago's 'dishonesty'. The language itself draws attention to this theme in a variety of ways, one of which is the repetition of the word 'honest' to emphasize Othello's complete belief in Iago's 'honesty' and Desdemona's 'dishonesty'.

It has often been said that one of the reasons that Shakespeare's plays have remained so popular for so long, lies in the fact that they deal with great and universal themes that were of concern to people in Shakespeare's time, and are of no less significance to us today. His plays often deal with themes such as love, hate, envy, jealousy, death, revenge, guilt, corruption, destiny.

Certain themes seem to have particularly interested Shakespeare and can be seen in one form or another in all of his plays. These themes are:

- conflict
- appearance and reality

- order and disorder
- change
- love

Conflict

Conflict, of one type or another, is the starting point for many dramas, and it can take many forms. In *Othello*, for example, we have the conflict between Iago and Othello (a conflict that Othello is unaware of until it is too late), and the inner conflict that Othello experiences as he battles to control his growing jealousy. In *Henry IV Part 2*, conflict exists externally as Henry faces rebellion.

Appearance and reality

In all of Shakespeare's plays there is a mis-match between how things seem to be and how they actually are. In *Othello*, for example, everyone thinks Iago is 'honest' but in fact he is completely the opposite. In *Twelfth Night*, Viola disguises herself as a boy, while in *Hamlet* the apparently popular and effective King, Claudius, is, in reality guilty of the murder of his brother and seduction of his brother's wife. *Measure for Measure* is very concerned with 'seeming' as the Duke leaves his apparently incorruptible deputy, Angelo, in charge of the state, to see 'If power change purpose, what our seemers be.' He certainly finds out, when it is revealed that Angelo attempted to seduce the innocent Isabella.

Order and disorder

In all of Shakespeare's plays there is some kind of breakdown in order, and some form of confusion temporarily gains the upper hand. Sometimes the breakdown is in the order of the state, as in *Macbeth*, where the murder of Duncan plunges the state into turmoil and war. In *Henry IV* (Parts 1 and 2), King Henry faces rebellion and civil war, while *Twelfth Night* begins with Olivia's rejection of Orsino's suit and Viola shipwrecked on the coast of Illyria. The causes of the disruption vary from play to play, but they tend to include key causes such as jealousy, love, hate, and ambition. Very often the protagonist undergoes some kind of learning process during the course of the play before order is re-established.

Change

In all Shakespeare plays the characters undergo some kind of change. Sometimes the ultimate result of this change is death, as in *Othello*, where Othello changes from a respected military leader to a man eaten away by jealousy who murders his wife and then, realising the terrible mistake he has made, takes his own life. In *Twelfth Night*, Malvolio changes from a puritan figure into a foolish lover.

Love

For Shakespeare, one of the instruments of change is love, which has a transforming power and is often at the heart of his plays. *Twelfth Night* begins with the words 'If music be the food of love, play on.' It goes on to present a world of romantic love. In *A Midsummer Night's Dream* we see young men and women who love each other but who also have to endure crosses and frustrations in love. In Othello we see a quite different portrayal of love, as Othello's love for Desdemona is corrupted into jealousy and hate by the scheming Iago.

Development of themes

Of course, there are many specific themes that can be traced in individual plays, but in one way or another they will relate to the four key areas discussed above.

The themes in Shakespeare's plays often develop in one of three ways:

- An individual character or characters experience some personal difficulties or inner turmoil, perhaps moral or spiritual, that causes some mental conflict. For example, Hamlet struggles to come to terms with events and revenge his father.
- The family, society, or the country is affected by turmoil. For example, the feuding Capulets and Montagues disrupt Verona in *Romeo and Juliet*, and Rome is at war with Egypt in *Antony and Cleopatra*.
- Nature or the universe may be disordered, or supernatural events may be involved. Examples are the appearance of the witches and Banquo's ghost in *Macbeth*, or the storm imagery in *King Lear*.

At the heart of the development of the themes of a play is Shakespeare's rich and complex use of language.

Shakespeare's language

Often students encounter difficulties when first studying a Shakespeare play because they find the language of Shakespeare different in a number of ways from the kind of English they are used to. This difficulty is particularly evident when reading the text rather than watching the play being performed, when actions are brought to life and give the words much more meaning.

At first, concentrate on arriving at a broad understanding of what is happening, in terms of the plot of the play. Once this basic knowledge has been established, you will very soon progress to a more detailed study of the language of the play and the effects that it creates to bring the drama to life.

Here are some of the uses to which Shakespeare puts language:

- creating atmosphere
- opening scenes

- in songs
- in dialogue
- in puns and wordplay

Creating atmosphere

You should remember that in Shakespeare's time theatres did not have the elaborate scenery, backdrops and the sophisticated technology that is used to create effects in modern theatres. If you have ever visited Shakespeare's Globe in London or seen drawings of the Elizabethan theatre, you will know that they had little more than a bare stage, and in that sense theatregoers went to 'hear' a play rather than to 'see' a play as we would say today. The plays would also usually take place in daylight, without the elaborate lighting effects we are used to today.

Apart from all its other important functions, language was therefore essential to the creation of setting and atmosphere. In a Shakespeare play the atmosphere and setting are created through words.

Look at the following extract from the opening scene of *Hamlet*.

Hamlet

Act I Scene 1

Scene I. *Enter* **Barnardo** *and* **Francisco***, two sentinels*

Barnardo:	Who's there?
Francisco:	Nay, answer me. Stand and unfold yourself.
Barnardo:	Long live the King.
Francisco:	Barnardo?
Barnardo:	He.
Francisco:	You come most carefully upon your hour.
Barnardo:	'Tis now struck twelve. Get thee to bed, Francisco.
Francisco:	For this relief much thanks. 'Tis bitter cold, And I am sick at heart.
Barnardo:	Have you had quiet guard?
Francisco:	Not a mouse stirring.
Barnardo:	Well, good night. If you do meet Horatio and Marcellus, The rivals of my watch, bid them make haste.

Enter **Horatio** *and* **Marcellus**

Francisco:	I think I hear them. Stand, ho! Who is there?
Horatio:	Friends to this ground.
Marcellus:	And liegemen to the Dane.

Francisco:	Give you good night.
Marcellus:	O, farewell honest soldier,
	Who hath relieved you?
Francisco:	Barnardo hath my place.
	Give you good night.

[*Exit*

Marcellus:	Holla, Barnardo!
Barnardo:	Say,
	What, is Horatio there?
Horatio:	A piece of him.
Barnardo:	Welcome, Horatio. Welcome, good
	Marcellus.
Marcellus:	What, has this thing appeared again
	tonight?
Barnardo:	I have seen nothing.
Marcellus:	Horatio says 'tis but our fantasy,
	And will not let belief take hold of him
	Touching this dreaded sight, twice seen of us.
	Therefore I have intreated him along
	With us to watch the minutes of this night,
	That, if again this apparition come,
	He may approve our eyes and speak to it.
Horatio:	Tush, tush, 'twill not appear.
Barnardo:	Sit down awhile,
	And let us once again assail your ears,
	That are so fortified against our story,
	What we have two nights seen.
Horatio:	Well, sit we down,
	And let us hear Barnardo speak of this.
Barnardo:	Last night of all,
	When yon same star that's westward from
	the pole,
	Had made his course t'illume that part of
	heaven
	Where now it burns, Marcellus and myself,
	The bell then beating one –

Activity

> Read the extract carefully and try to 'feel' the atmosphere that is being created.
>
> Identify the ways in which Shakespeare creates a sense of the atmosphere through the language.

Here are some points you may have noted:

- The opening challenge "Who's there?" creates a sense of tension.

- The darkness (remember, Shakespeare's plays were performed in daylight) is created through the language.

- There is a sense of fear about what is to happen next.

- The fact that it is midnight is clearly signalled.

Activity

Now think about the play you are studying. Find **four** parts of the play where Shakespeare creates an atmosphere through the language. Examine these sections carefully showing how the language creates a sense of the atmosphere.

Opening scenes

Shakespeare was very aware of the necessity to capture the audience's attention at the beginning of the play, and the opening of *Hamlet*, which you have just looked at, is a prime example of this. Obviously the creation of atmosphere is an integral part of the impact of the opening of the play in terms of capturing the audience's interest right from the outset.

Look now at the opening of *Antony and Cleopatra*.

Antony and Cleopatra

Act I Scene 1

[*Alexandria,* **Cleopatra's** *palace.*]

Enter **Demetrius** *and* **Philo.**

Philo: Nay, but this dotage of our General's
          O'erflows the measure. Those his goodly eyes
          That o'er the files and musters of the war
          Have glowed like plated Mars, now bend, now
              turn
          The office and devotion of their view
          Upon a tawny front. His captain's heart,
          Which in the scuffles of great fights hath burst
          The buckles on his breast, reneges all temper
          And is become the bellows and the fan
          To cool a gypsy's lust.

          Flourish. Enter **Antony**, **Cleopatra**, *her* **Ladies**,
              The Train, with Eunuchs fanning her.

                    Look where they come:
          Take but good note, and you shall see in him
          The triple pillar of the world transformed
          Into a strumpet's fool. Behold and see.

Cleopatra: If it be love indeed, tell me how much.
Antony: There's beggary in the love that can be
                  reckoned.

Cleopatra:	I'll set a bourn how far to be beloved.
Antony:	Then must thou needs find out new heaven, new earth.

Enter a **Messenger**

Messenger:	News, my good lord, from Rome.
Antony:	Grates me! The sum.
Cleopatra:	Nay, hear them, Antony. Fulvia perchance is angry; or who knows If the scarce-bearded Caesar have not sent His pow'rful mandate to you, "Do this, or this; Take in that kingdom, and enfranchise that. Perform't, or else we damn thee."
Antony:	How, my love?
Cleopatra:	Perchance? Nay, and most like: You must not stay here longer, your dismission Is come from Caesar; therefore hear it, Antony. Where's Fulvia's process? Caesar's I would say? Both? Call in the messengers. As I am Egypt's Queen, Though blushest, Antony, and that blood of thine Is Caesar's homager: else so thy cheek pays shame When shrill-tongued Fulvia scolds. The messengers!
Antony:	Let Rome in Tiber melt, and the wide arch Of the ranged empire fall! Here is my space, Kingdoms are clay: our dungy earth alike Feeds beast as man. The nobleness of life Is to do thus; when such a mutual pair And such a twain can do't, in which I bind, On pain of punishment, the world to weet We stand up peerless.
Cleopatra:	Excellent falsehood! Why did he marry Fulvia, and not love her? I'll seem the fool I am not. Antony Will be – himself.
Antony:	But stirred by Cleopatra. Now for the love of Love and her soft hours, Let's not confound the time with conference harsh. There's not a minute of our lives should stretch Without some pleasure now. What sport tonight?
Cleopatra:	Hear the ambassadors.
Antony:	Fie, wrangling queen! Whom everything becomes – to chide, to laugh, To weep; whose every passion fully strives To make itself, in thee, fair and admired. No messenger but thine; and all alone Tonight we'll wander through the streets and note The qualities of people. Come, my queen;

> Last night you did desire it. [*To Attendants*] Speak
>   not to us.
>   *Exeunt* [**Antony** *and* **Cleopatra**] *with the Train.*

Demetrius: Is Caesar with Antonius prized so slight?

Philo: Sir, sometimes, when he is not Antony,
He comes too short of that great property
Which still should go with Antony.

Demetrius: I am full sorry
That he approves the common liar, who
Thus speaks of him at Rome; but I will hope
Of better deeds tomorrow. Rest you happy! *Exeunt.*

Activity

> How does Shakespeare capture the audience's attention at the outset of the play?

This scene is particularly interesting as an opening to the play because, it presents, in terms of language, theme and technique, a kind of summary of the play itself. Here are some points you might have noticed about Shakespeare's use of language in the opening speech here:

- Philo's 'Look where they come:/Take but good note' invites us to view the scene as if through his eyes.
- His introductory speech creates a picture of Antony as a man with mythic rather than human qualities.
- There is vivid imagery in the description, for example he 'glowed like plated Mars' in his armour.
- At the same time, Philo disparages him in vulgar terms, describing him as being no more than the 'bellows and the fan/To cool a gypsy's lust.'
- The use of the word 'gypsy' derived from 'Egyptian', presents us with the Rome/Egypt contrast.
- Contemptuous terms are used to describe Cleopatra.

Activity

> Now look at the opening scene of the play you are studying and write about the kind of impact it would have on an audience and how Shakespeare achieves this through his use of language.

Songs

At first sight, songs may not seem particularly important in the plays of Shakespeare, but it is interesting to note that twenty-six of his thirty-seven plays contain songs or parts of songs. Each of these is used quite deliberately to create a particular effect such as influencing the mood, giving us an insight into character, or echoing a theme.

In *The Tempest*, for example, the spirit Ariel sings the following song to Ferdinand:

Full fathom five thy father lies,
Of his bones are coral made;
Those are pearls that were his eyes;
Nothing of him that doth fade,
But doth suffer a sea-change
Into something rich and strange.
Sea-nymphs hourly ring his knell.
Hark, now I hear them, 'ding dong bell.'
        [*Spirits echo burden 'ding dong bell'*]

Activity

> Look carefully at the words of this song.
> Write down the themes that it seems to deal with.

You may have noted the following:

- The song addresses the theme of death.
- It deals with something being magically transformed into something else.

This gives a forecast of what will happen in the play where Alfonso, through suffering, will be transformed into something better and will come to regret his past wrongdoings.

Activity

> Look at the play you are studying as part of your course. Does it have any songs in it? If it does, look at them carefully and make notes on why Shakespeare uses a song or songs, and what they contribute to the play.

Dialogue

Dialogue is the means by which the characters communicate with each other, and it can take many different forms. For example, in *Othello*, Shakespeare uses the technique of rapidly alternating single lines in the scene where Othello accuses Desdemona of being unfaithful, and she responds.

Othello

Act V Scene 2

Othello: That handkerchief which I so loved and gave thee,
Thou gav'st to Cassio.
Desdemona: No, by my life and soul!
Send for the man and ask him.
Othello: Sweet soul, take heed,
Take heed of perjury; thou art on thy death-bed.
Desdemona: Ay, but not yet to die.

Othello:	Yes, presently.
	Therefore confess thee freely of thy sin;
	For to deny each article with oath
	Cannot remove nor choke the strong conception
	That I do groan withal. Thou art to die.
Desdemona:	Then Lord have mercy on me!
Othello:	I say, amen.
Desdemona:	And have you mercy too! I never did
	Offend you in my life; never loved Cassio
	But with such general warranty of heaven
	As I might love. I never gave him token.
Othello:	By heaven, I saw my handkerchief in's hand!
	O perjured woman! Thou dost stone my heart,
	And mak'st me call what I intended to do
	A murder, which I thought a sacrifice.
	I saw the handkerchief.
Desdemona:	He found it then.
	I never gave it to him. Send for him hither.
	Let him confess a truth.
Othello:	He hath confessed.
Desdemona:	What, my lord?
Othello:	That he hath used thee.
Desdemona:	How? Unlawfully?
Othello:	Ay.
Desdemona:	He will not say so.
Othello:	No, his mouth is stopped:
	Honest Iago hath ta'en order for't.
Desdemona:	O, my fear interprets! What, is he dead?
Othello:	Had all his hairs been lives, my great revenge
	Had stomach for them all.
Desdemona:	Alas, he is betrayed, and I undone.
Othello:	Out, strumpet! Weep'st thou for him to my face?
Desdemona:	O banish me, my lord, but kill me not!
Othello:	Down, strumpet!
Desdemona:	Kill me tomorrow: let me live tonight!
Othello:	Nay, if you strive –
Desdemona:	But half an hour!
Othello:	Being done, there is no pause.
Desdemona:	But while I say one prayer.
Othelllo:	It is too late

The sharpness of Othello's words here, and the increasing desperation of Desdemona's pleading, clearly work to increase the tension as it builds towards the climax.

By contrast, the following extract of dialogue from *Romeo and Juliet* shows the tender expression of the love between them.

Romeo and Juliet

Act II Scene 1

Juliet:	My ears have not yet drunk a hundred words
	Of thy tongue's uttering, yet I know the sound
	Art thou not Romeo, and a Montague?
Romeo:	Neither, fair maid, if either thee dislike.
Juliet:	How cam'st thou hither, tell me, and wherefore?
	The orchard walls are high, and hard to climb,
	And the place death, considering who thou art,
	If any of my kinsmen find thee here.
Romeo:	With love's light wings did I o'erperch these
	walls,
	For stony limits cannot hold love out,
	And what love can do, that dares love attempt.
	Therefore thy kinsmen are no stop to me.
Juliet:	If they do see thee, they will murder thee.
Romeo:	Alack there lies more peril in thine eye
	Than twenty of their swords; look thou but sweet,
	And I am proof against their enmity
Juliet:	I would not for the world they saw thee here.
Romeo:	I have night's cloak to hide me from their eyes,
	And but thou love me, let them find me here.
	My life were better ended by their hate,
	Than death prorogued, wanting of thy love.
Juliet:	By whose direction found'st thou out this place?
Romeo:	By love that first did prompt me to inquire;
	He lent me counsel, and I lent him eyes.
	I am no pilot, yet wert thou as far
	As that vast shore washed with the farthest sea,
	I should adventure for such merchandise.

Every exchange is different, with rhythm patterns, tone and vocabulary suited to the context and the mood that Shakespeare wants to express.

Activity
> Look at the play you are studying and find three or four examples of contrasting uses of dialogue.

Puns and wordplay

Wordplay was much admired in Elizabethan England, and so it is no surprise that it is frequently used in the plays of Shakespeare. Puns were a particularly popular kind of wordplay. A pun is created when a word has two or more different meanings and the ambiguity is used to witty effect.

An example in *The Taming of the Shrew* is where Petruchio tells his servant, Grumio, to knock on the door of Hortensio. Grumio deliberately misunderstands his master's order.

The Taming of the Shrew

Act I Scene 2

Petruchio:	Verona, for awhile I take my leave,
	To see my friends in Padua; but, of all,
	My best beloved and approved friend,
	Hortensio; and I trow this is his house, –
	Here, sirrah Grumio, knock, I say.
Grumio:	Knock sir! Whom should I knock? Is there any man has re-
	bused your worship?
Petruchio:	Villain, I say, Knock me here soundly.
Grumio:	Knock you here, sir! Why, sir, what am I, sir, that I should
	Knock you here, sir?
Petruchio:	Villain, I say, knock me at this gate.
	And rap me well, or I'll knock your knave's pate
Grumio:	My master is grown quarrelsome. – I should knock you first,
	And then I know after who comes by the worst.
Petruchio:	Will it not be?
	Faith, sirrah, an you'll not knock, I'll wring it;
	I'll try how you can sol, fa, and sing it.
	(He wrings him by the ears)

In *Hamlet*, the gravedigger insists on a precise interpretation of words.

Hamlet

Act V Scene 1

Hamlet:	Whose grave's this, sirrah?
I Clown:	Mine, sir –
[*sings*]	O, a pit of clay for to be made
	For such a guest is meet.
Hamlet:	I think it be thine, indeed, for thou liest in't.
I Clown:	You lie out on't sir, and therefore 'tis not yours; for my part I do
	not lie in't, and yet it is mine.
Hamlet:	Thou dost lie in't, to be in't and say it is thine.
	'Tis for the dead, not for the quick – therefore thou liest.
I Clown:	'Tis a quick lie, sir, 'twill away again from
	me to you.
Hamlet:	What man dost thou dig it for?
I Clown:	For no man, sir.
Hamlet:	What woman then?
I Clown:	For none neither.
Hamlet:	Who is it to be buried in't?
I Clown:	One that was a woman, sir, but rest her
	soul she's dead.
Hamlet:	How absolute the knave is! We must speak
	by the card or equivocation will undo us.

Activity

> Now look at the play you are studying and find some examples of wordplay. Explain what the wordplay consists of. What function does the wordplay serve in the context of the play?

Shakespeare's imagery

The use of imagery, designed to conjure up vivid images in the mind, is a very important aspect of the way in which Shakespeare works with language. Such imagery plays a key part in every Shakespeare play and very often it is closely linked to central themes of the play. For example, as Othello becomes convinced of Desdemona's infidelity, his jealousy is expressed in increasingly unpleasant animal imagery.

In *King Lear*, certain images recur time and again. Here, too, there is an abundance of animal imagery, often used to stress the inhuman behaviour of Lear's daughters. Here, Lear complains to Regan about the treatment he has received from Goneril.

King Lear

Act II Scene 4

Regan:	Good sir, no more; these are unsightly tricks.
	Return you to my sister.
Lear:	[*Rising*] Never, Regan.
	She hath abated me of half my train;
	Looked black upon me; struck me with her tongue,
	Most serpent-like, upon the very heart.
	All the stored vengeances of Heaven fall
	On her ungrateful top! Strike her young bones,
	You taking airs, with lameness!
Cornwall:	Fie, sir, fie!
Lear:	You nimble lightnings, dart your blinding flames
	Into her scornful eyes! Infect her beauty,
	You fen-sucked fogs, drawn by the pow'rful sun,
	To fall and blister her!
Regan:	O the blest Gods! so will you wish on me,
	When the rash moods is on.
Lear:	No, Regan, thou shalt never have my curse:
	Thy tender-hefted nature shall not give
	Thee o'er to harshness: her eyes are fierce, but thine
	Do comfort and not burn. 'Tis not in thee
	To grudge my pleasures, to cut off my train,
	To bandy hasty words, to scant my sizes,
	And, in conclusion to oppose the bolt
	Against my coming in:

Storm imagery also plays an important part in the language of the play, reflecting the chaos and breakdown caused to society and the mental chaos created within Lear's mind.

King Lear

Act III Scene 2

Another part of the heath. Storm still
*Enter **Lear** and **Fool**.*

Lear: Blow, winds, and crack your cheeks! rage! blow!
You cataracts and hurricanoes, spout
Till you have drenched our steeples, drowned the
    cocks!
You sulph'rous and thought-executing fires,
Vaunt-couriers of oak-cleaving thunderbolts,
Singe my white head! And thou, all-shaking
    thunder,
Strike flat the thick rotundity o'th'world!
Crack Nature's moulds, all germens spill at once
That makes ungrateful man!

Fool: O Nuncle, court holy-water in a dry house is
better than this rain-water out o'door. Good
Nuncle, in, ask thy daughters blessing; here's a
night pities neither wise men nor Fools.

Lear: Rumble thy bellyful! Spit, fire! spout, rain!
Nor rain, wind, thunder, fire, are my daughters:
I tax you not, you elements, with unkindness;
I never gave you kingdom, called you children,
You owe me no subscription: then let fall
Your horrible pleasure; here I stand, your slave,
A poor, infirm, weak, and despised old man.
But yet I call you servile ministers,
That will with two pernicious daughters join
Your high-engendered battles 'gainst a head
So old and white as this. O, ho! 'tis foul.

Activity

> 1 Find examples of vivid imagery in the play you are studying.
> 2 Are there any links between the kind of imagery the play contains and
>   the themes of the play?
> 3 Pick **two** examples of imagery and analyse the ways in which
>   Shakespeare uses language to achieve his effects.
> 4 Now write an essay in which you analyse the imagery patterns in the
>   play you are studying.

Verse and prose

It has often been said that Shakespeare's greatness is rooted in his ability to
use language to suit all moods, occasions, and characters. Much of his work
is written in blank verse (see Unit 3, page 62) – a flexible form which he
adapts to suit many purposes, from moments of intense passion to bawdy

bantering. However, we must not lose sight of the fact that Shakespeare makes substantial use of prose, too, which prompts the question 'Why does he switch between verse and prose in his plays?'

A common answer to this question is that the 'high' characters use poetry, in keeping with their elevated natures and the substance of their dialogue, while the 'low' or comic characters use the more plebeian prose. An alternative answer is that Shakespeare uses prose for sub-plots, or to indicate madness or a highly-wrought emotional state in a character. It is easy to find examples to support these ideas, but it is also easy to find examples to disprove them. The truth is that all these explanations are too general and simplistic to help us much, and the real explanation is rather more complex.

For example, *Hamlet* begins with the guards, Francisco and Barnardo, who are 'ordinary' and minor characters, speaking in verse (see page 126). This helps to create a solemn and dignified tone with which to open the play, in keeping with the serious events that are about to unfold with the appearance of the Ghost. When Ophelia becomes mad she speaks prose but she also speaks prose in the 'play-within-the-play' scene where she is perfectly sane. Hamlet himself speaks both prose and verse depending on the situation and who he is speaking to. The Players speak prose when they are not performing and verse when they are in role.

In looking at Shakespeare's use of verse and prose, therefore, you need to look at the context of the specific episode to determine why Shakespeare has chosen to use language in the form he has. In every instance there will be a good dramatic reason on which his decision is based. Remember also that Shakespeare's prose is not an unplanned, casual form of writing. It is as much an art-form as his verse, and is just as carefully structured and organized.

Activity

> Make a note of where switches between verse and prose occur in the text you are studying. Choose four of these points. Give reasons why you think the switch is made in each case.

Types of questions

The following are given as examples of question types but obviously wording and focus can vary.

1 *Comment on the effectiveness of this extract.*
Although superficially this may appear a fairly open-ended question, it is really looking for some quite specific comments about any or all of the following features:

- language – the effectiveness of vocabulary, imagery, etc.
- action – the way the plot develops and links to other parts of the play
- character – significant or revealing points with regard to character
- themes – the relevance of the passage to the themes expressed through the play

- form – the way the passage is written, e.g. verse or prose, and the effect created by the particular form used

2 *What does the passage reveal about the speaker's character and state of mind at this point in the play?*
This kind of question suggests that there is something in the extract which is of particular significance in terms of character. Avoid just writing all you know about that character and focus on what is specifically shown through the passage.

3 *What is the dramatic significance of this passage?*
The idea of dramatic significance can be a little puzzling at first, but it is quite straightforward. It really is a signal to let you know that you should comment on some or all of the following:

- how the content of the passage relates to and contributes to the whole plot
- what and how it contributes to your understanding of character(s)
- its relevance to the underlying themes of the play
- its contribution to the creation of atmosphere and mood
- its contribution to the overall impact on the audience both at this point in the play and in the play as a whole

4 *Comment on the language used in the passage.*
This question is sometimes phrased as *Comment on the way in which the passage is expressed*, and is asking you to focus in detail on the language used in the passage in terms of the effect it creates. The key here is to avoid general comments and to deal with specific words, phrases, and images, writing about the particular effects that they create. Here are some points to consider for this kind of question:

- the tone of the language
- the mood created
- the images used and their effect
- the way the language is structured and the impact this has
- the effect of the particular form chosen, e.g. blank verse, prose, etc.
- the rhythm created and its effect

Critical notes and commentaries

There have probably been more critical works written on Shakespeare than any other writer. This can give the impression that in order to understand his plays it is necessary to be familiar with the massive body of scholarship that attaches itself to his works. This is not true.

When studying a Shakespeare play for AS- or A-level the first thing to do is to try to make sense of it in your own terms. Reading the writings of literary critics can help to show the range of views that it is possible to take on almost any aspect of a Shakespeare play, but you must not let these views become substitutes for your own. Be aware that other views exist, and often can be well supported. Use them to help form your own ideas and sometimes to revise them, but do not be overawed by them. Words in print are not automatically 'true'. If you support your view with direct reference to the text, then you have a valid view.

Many students seek the security of prepared commentaries, particularly in the early stages of their studies. There are various commentaries on the market but most of them have the same basic format of a scene-by-scene summary of the play and then sections on basic features such as 'themes', 'character', and 'style'. Most include some kind of 'specimen questions'. This type of commentary is sometimes frowned upon by teachers, but nevertheless many students do use them and providing you are aware of their limitations they can help you come to terms with a text early on in your studies. Be aware, however, that in order to be successful at A-level you need to go far beyond the level of discussion that they provide.

Which edition?

If you are working on AS- or A-level Literature in a class, the edition of the Shakespeare text may well be chosen for you by your teacher. If you are working in isolation or if you are providing your own text for your class, then you might find yourself puzzling over which edition to choose. The Arden edition is usually regarded as the most 'academic' and is packed with detailed notes covering a whole variety of issues. Many of these notes can be useful, but a great many of them are more relevant to undergraduate study and beyond.

There are several editions (New Penguin, New Swan, Cambridge, Oxford, etc.) which contain some notes, usually at the back of the book, in a more accessible form. Some are specifically aimed at school or college students and contain activities, suggested essay questions, etc. Finally, there are editions that simply contain the text alone. There are no notes or other 'trimmings' in these editions, and they are very inexpensive.

The key thing to remember is that although notes might help, they are by no means essential. Indeed, sometimes they can even interfere with you coming to grips with the text itself. It would be easy to get the impression that Shakespeare study is so arcane that you can only understand it and engage with it if you have notes to unlock the meaning for you. That would be a wrong impression. The two essential requirements are your mind and the text itself.

Special Feature: Shakespearean Comedy

• •

As mentioned earlier in this Unit, there are three kinds of Shakespearean comedy:

- the romantic comedies, which include *The Taming of the Shrew, Love's Labour's Lost, A Midsummer Night's Dream, Much Ado About Nothing, The Merchant of Venice, As You Like It* and *Twelfth Night*
- the romances – *Cymbeline, The Winter's Tale, The Tempest*
- the problem comedies – *Troilus and Cressida, All's Well that Ends Well, Measure for Measure*

In this Special Feature we will focus on the study of romantic comedy illustrated through extracts from *Twelfth Night*.

Very often the romantic comedies are looked on as the 'lightweights' of Shakespearean drama, and it is true that they do not deal with serious issues in the way that the tragedies focus on them. However, it is important to realize that despite their apparently light nature and their comic characters and situations, they are 'serious' plays with real substance.

Thinking about the nature of Shakespeare's comedies will help you to understand what he is doing with this kind of drama. In many ways the structure follows the general structure of drama, which we discussed earlier:

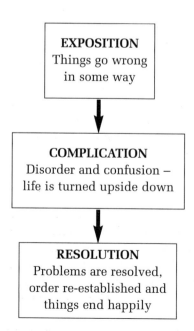

EXPOSITION
Things go wrong
in some way

↓

COMPLICATION
Disorder and confusion –
life is turned upside down

↓

RESOLUTION
Problems are resolved,
order re-established and
things end happily

The pattern of the comedies, then, follows the pattern of other Shakespearean drama, but there are key differences to do with how things work out within the general pattern.

- The actions of the characters create chaos and confusion, but whereas in a tragedy this chaos disturbs the audience, in romantic comedy the audience laughs at it.
- The perspective on events is one that focuses on comic rather than tragic views. A tragedy could very easily be changed into a comedy, and vice versa, by changing this perspective.

Activity | Think about the last statement carefully. Choose one tragedy and one comedy that you know. Now write a brief synopsis showing how you would convert the tragedy into a comedy and the comedy into a tragedy.

The following brief plot summary will show you how the plot structure works out in *Twelfth Night*.

The play opens with Orsino, the Duke of Illyria, in love with Olivia but she does not return his love. Twins Viola and Sebastian are shipwrecked off the Coast of Illyria. Viola believes Sebastian drowned.	The exposition
Viola disguises herself as a boy (Cesario) and is welcomed at Orsino's court. Orsino sends Cesario to woo Olivia on his behalf. Olivia is not moved by Orsino's declaration of love sent via Cesario, but she does feel attracted to Cesario.	Complications
Sebastian has been saved from the shipwreck by Antonio and is on his way to Orsino's court. Antonio, though, is an enemy of Orsino's. Orsino is very unhappy at Olivia's rejection and it is clear that she is in love with Cesario. However, her love is rejected by Cesario.	Complications
There then follows a variety of incidents involving the mistaking of Viola (Cesario) for Sebastian and vice versa. Olivia mistakes Sebastian for Cesario – Sebastian in turn is amazed to be invited home by a beautiful woman. She gives him a jewel and proposes marriage to him and he agrees.	Complications

Orsino confronts Antonio, who tells him he has only come to Illyria to be with his friend. Olivia enters and thinks she has just married Cesario. Viola is amazed as she knows nothing of this. The comic confusion reaches its height when Sebastian enters. Slowly the confusion begins to unravel.	Complications

All is resolved at last as Orsino realizes he is in love with Viola and he declares a double celebration when he will marry Viola, and celebrate Olivia's marriage to Sebastian.	Resolution

Activity   If you are studying a Shakespeare comedy, work out a brief synopsis of the plot to see in what ways it follows this pattern.

Shakespeare and the Fantasy World

One of the features often found in Shakespeare's comedies is that the action takes place in an imaginary world. This is certainly true in *Twelfth Night*, which is set in the fictional land of Illyria. The fantasy setting allows the audience more readily to suspend their disbelief and enter a world where characters act in curious ways, and where events are not governed by the normal rules that regulate our society. There are, of course, points in the play where the characters experience sadness and pain, and they have to deal with realistic emotions. But the play is very much a fantasy in a number of ways:

- adults behave like unruly children
- the behaviour of the lovers as they fall in and out of love is not rational
- the storyline of the play is basically absurd – there are many unlikely events and coincidences that do not bear close scrutiny
- Malvolio, the one apparently serious person, is made a complete fool of

It is worth noting that Feste's song at the end of the play recognizes that while the audience has temporarily escaped from reality into a fantasy world, they will have to emerge from the theatre into a less happy world.

Act V Scene 1

Feste: [*Sings*] When that I was and a little tiny boy
            With hey, ho, the wind and the rain,
        A foolish thing was but a toy,
            For the rain it raineth every day.

But when I came to man's estate,
   With hey, ho, the wind and the rain,
'Gainst knaves and thieves men shut their gate,
   For the rain it raineth every day.

But when I came, alas, to wive,
   With hey, ho, the wind and the rain,
By swaggering could I never thrive,
   For the rain it raineth every day.

But when I came unto my beds,
   With hey, ho, the wind and the rain,
With toss-pots still had drunken heads,
   For the rain it raineth every day.

A great while ago the world begun,
   With hey, ho, the wind and the rain,
But that's all one, our play is done,
   And we'll strive to please you every day.　　　　　　*[Exit*

Openings

In the tragedies the opening scenes prepare us for what to expect. For example, in *Romeo and Juliet* the servants of the Capulet and Montague families come into conflict, which foreshadows the deeper conflict that is to come. Similarly, the openings of *Macbeth* and *Hamlet* prepare us for the troubling events that are to be portrayed.

The openings of comedies work in much the same way, in that they prepare the audience for what is to come. The opening of *Twelfth Night* prepares us, but in this case the things that are about to happen come about through coincidence, mistaken identity, disguise and strange adventures.

Now look at the opening of the play.

Act I Scene 1

The Duke's Palace
Music. Enter **Orsino**, *Duke of Illyria,* **Curio**, *and other Lords*

Duke: If music be the food of love, play on,
Give me excess of it; that, surfeiting,
The appetite may sicken, and so die.
That strain again – it had a dying fall.
O, it came o'er my ear like the sweet sound
That breathes upon a bank of violets,
Stealing and giving odour. Enough, no more,
'Tis not so sweet now as it was before.
O spirit of love, how quick and fresh art thou,
That, notwithstanding thy capacity

Receiveth as the sea, nought enters there,
Of what validity and pitch soe'er,
But falls into abatement and low price,
Even in a minute! So full of shapes is fancy,
That it alone is high fantastical.

Curio: Will you go hunt, my lord?
Duke: What, Curio?
Curio: The hart.
Duke: Why so I do, the noblest that I have.
O when mine eyes did see Olivia first,
Methought she purged the air of pestilence.
That instant was I turned into a hart,
And my desires, like fell and cruel hounds,
E'er since pursue me.

    Enter **Valentine**

        How now, what news from her?
Valentine: So please my lord, I might not be admitted,
But from her handmaid do return this answer:
The element itself, till seven years' heat,
Shall not behold her face at ample view;
But like a cloistress she will veiled walk,
And water once a day her chamber round
With eye-offending brine; all this to season
A brother's dead love, which she would keep
    fresh
And lasting, in her sad remembrance.
Duke: O she that hath a heart of that fine frame
To pay this debt of love but to a brother,
How will she love, when the rich golden shaft
Hath killed the flock of all affections else
That live in her; when liver, brain, and heart,
These sovereign thrones, are all supplied and
    filled,
Her sweet perfections, with one self king.
Away before me to sweet beds of flowers:
Love-thoughts lie rich when canopied with
    bowers.

Activity

Look at this opening to *Twelfth Night*.

1 What do you make of Orsino's profession of love here?
2 What sort of mood does the play open with?
3 What power does music have?
4 Olivia, the woman Orsino is love-sick for, has said that she will not stop mourning for her brother for seven years. What effect does this have on the opening of the play?
5 What comfort does Orsino draw from this?

Now look at the opening of the second scene.

Act I Scene 2

A Sea Coast
Enter **Viola**, *a* **Captain**, *and Sailors*

Viola:	What country, friends, is this?
Captain:	This is Illyria, lady.
Viola:	And what should I do in Illyria?
	My brother he is in Elysium.
	Perchance he is not drowned – what think you,
	sailors?
Captain:	It is perchance that you yourself were saved.
Viola:	O my poor brother, and so perchance may he be.
Captain:	True, madam, and to comfort you with chance,
	Assure yourself, after our ship did split,
	When you and those poor number saved with
	you
	Hung on our driving boat, I saw your brother,
	Most provident in peril, bind himself –
	Courage and hope both teaching him the practice –
	To a strong mast that lived upon the sea;
	Where, like Arion on the dolphin's back,
	I saw him hold acquaintance with the waves
	So long as I could see.
Viola:	For saying so, there's gold.
	Mine own escape unfoldeth to my hope,
	Whereto thy speech serves for authority,
	The like of him. Know'st thou this country?
Captain:	Ay, madam, well, for I was bred and born
	Not three hours' travel from this very place.
Viola:	Who governs here?
Captain:	A noble duke, in nature as in name.
Viola:	What is his name?
Captain:	Orsino.
Viola:	Orsino – I have heard my father name him.
	He was a bachelor then.
Captain:	And so is now, or was so very late;
	For but a month ago I went from hence,
	And then 'twas fresh in murmur – as, you know,
	What great ones do the less will prattle of –
	That he did seek the love of fair Olivia.
Viola:	What's she?
Captain:	A virtuous maid, the daughter of a count
	That died some twelvemonth since, then leaving
	her
	In the protection of his son, her brother,
	Who shortly also died; for whose dear love,

> They say, she hath abjured the company
> And sight of men.

Viola: O that I served that lady
> And might not be delivered to the world,
> Till I had made mine own occasion mellow
> What my estate is.

Captain: That were hard to compass,
> Because she will admit no kind of suit,
> No, not the Duke's.

Viola: There is a fair behaviour in thee, captain,
> And though that nature with a beauteous wall
> Doth oft close in pollution, yet of thee
> I will believe thou hast a mind that suits
> With this thy fair and outward character.
> I prithee – and I'll pay thee bounteously –
> Conceal me what I am, and be my aid
> For such disguise as haply shall become
> The form of my intent. I'll serve this duke;
> Thou shalt present me as an eunuch to him
> It may be worth thy pains, for I can sing
> And speak to him in many sorts of music
> That will allow me very worth his service.
> What else may hap to time I will commit,
> Only shape thou thy silence to my wit.

Captain: Be you his eunuch, and your mute I'll be.
> When my tongue blabs, then let mine eyes not
>   See.

Viola: I thank thee. Lead me on.

[Exeunt

Activity

> What information do you draw from this scene? What clues do you get from these opening two scenes as to what might happen later? Use the information you gain about the characters, as well as the clues from the dialogue.

Thematic development

As the plot of *Twelfth Night* develops, various themes begin to emerge. These echo some of Shakespeare's central concerns in many of his plays:

- love
- appearance and reality
- order and disorder

In *Twelfth Night* Viola is disguised as a boy in the service of Orsino. He sends her to try to woo Olivia for him. Viola has by this time fallen in love with

Orsino. However, Viola now begins to realize that Olivia has fallen in love with her, believing her to be a man. Look carefully at this extract.

Act II Scene 2

Viola: Poor lady, she were better love a dream.
Disguise, I see thou art a wickedness
Wherein the pregnant enemy does much.
How easy is it for the proper false
In women's waxen hearts to set their forms.
Alas, our frailty is the cause, not we.
For such as we are made of, such we be.
How will this fadge? My master loves her dearly.
And I, poor monster, fond as much of him;
And she, mistaken, seems to dote on me.
What will become of this? As I am man,
My state is desperate for my master's love;
As I am woman, – now alas the day –
What thriftless sighs shall poor Olivia breathe.
O time, thou must untangle this, not I;
It is too hard a knot for me t'untie.

[*Exit*

Activity

> **1** What does Viola have to say in this soliloquy?
> **2** How does what she says relate to the theme of appearance and reality?

Another thematic strand that is commonly found in the plays of Shakespeare is that of order and disorder. In *King Lear* or *Macbeth* this disruption of order has far-reaching and ultimately tragic consequences. In a comedy such as *Twelfth Night* the disruption of order ultimately adds to the comedy.

Sir Toby Belch is a key character associated with disorder. However, the sense of disorder within the play is much more deeply embedded in the play than merely in the superficial disruption of Sir Toby. The whole essence of *Twelfth Night* implies a relaxation of order and a liberal, 'festive' attitude. This is reinforced by the play's subtitle – 'What You Will'. In more subtle ways Feste, the clown, subverts order and even Viola and Sebastian play roles that contribute to disorder, in that through them conventional distinctions are broken down.

Activity

> Think about the play that you are studying and write about the ways in which the theme of order/disorder is relevant to it.

Endings

At the end of a Shakespearean comedy there is always some kind of resolution, a sorting out of the confusions and misunderstandings that have developed through the action. In *Twelfth Night* the long, single closing scene of Act V resolves all the problems of the play. In this lengthy concluding scene all the various plot entanglements are disentangled and the confusions of identity are sorted out.

Even in a comedy there may be some bitter moments to be endured during this period of resolution. For example, read this extract from the closing of *Twelfth Night*.

Act V Scene 1

Duke:	Is this the madman?
Olivia:	Ay, my lord, this same.
	How now, Malvolio?
Malvolio:	Madam, you have done me wrong,
	Notorious wrong.
Olivia:	Have I, Malvolio? No.
Malvolio:	Lady, you have. Pray you peruse that letter.
	You must not now deny it is your hand;
	Write from it if you can, in hand or phrase;
	Or say 'tis not your seal, not your invention;
	You can say none of this. Well, grant it then,
	And tell me, in the modesty of honour,
	Why you have given me such clear lights of favour,
	Bade me come smiling and cross-gartered to you,
	To put on yellow stockings and to frown
	Upon Sir Toby and the lighter people;
	And, acting this in an obedient hope,
	Why have you suffered me to be imprisoned,
	Kept in a dark house, visited by the priest,
	And made the most notorious geck and gull
	That e'er invention played on? Tell me why.
Olivia:	Alas, Malvolio, this is not my writing,
	Though, I confess, much like the character;
	But out of question 'tis Maria's hand.
	And now I do bethink me, it was she
	First told me thou wast mad; then cam'st in smiling,
	And in such forms which here were presupposed
	Upon thee in the letter. Prithee be content,
	This practice hath most shrewdly passed upon thee.
	But when we know the grounds and authors of it,
	Thou shalt be both the plaintiff and the judge
	of thine own cause.
Fabian:	Good madam, hear me speak,
	And let no quarrel nor no brawl to come
	Taint the condition of this present hour,
	Which I have wondered at. In hope it shall not,

	Most freely I confess myself and Toby
	Set this device against Malvolio here,
	Upon some stubborn and uncourteous parts
	We had conceived against him. Maria writ
	The letter at Sir Toby's great importance,
	In recompense whereof he hath married her.
	How with a sportful malice it was followed
	May rather pluck on laughter than revenge,
	If that the injuries be justly weighed
	That have on both sides passed.
Olivia:	Alas, poor fool, how have they baffled thee!
Feste:	Why, 'Some are born great, some achieve greatness,
	and some have greatness thrown upon them.' I was
	one, sir, in this interlude, one Sir Topas, sir; but
	that's all one. 'By the Lord, fool, I am not mad.'
	But do you remember? – 'Madam, why laugh you
	at such a barren rascal? An you smile not he's
	gagged.' And thus the whirligig of time brings in
	his revenges.
Malvolio:	I'll be revenged on the whole pack of you. [*Exit*
Olivia:	He hath been most notoriously abused.
Duke:	Pursue him, and entreat him to a peace;
	He hath not told us of the captain yet.

[*Exit* **Fabian** *or some other*]

Activity	Think about the comedy that you are studying or one that you have studied in the past. How does it end? Make notes on the ways in which which it fits in with the patterns we have seen with *Twelfth Night*. Now write an essay on the nature of Shakespearean comedy, based on two plays that you have read or seen.

6 The Short Story

Objectives

- To prepare yourself for writing about short stories
- To consider some of the particular features of short stories
- To examine examples of the work of short story writers who often feature on examination syllabuses
- To prepare for studying set short story texts

What is a short story?

In one sense the answer to this question is so obvious it hardly seems worth a thought. A 'short story' is clearly a story that is short! Perhaps we need to rephrase the question and pose the question that the critic, Norman Friedman, once asked – 'What makes a short story?'

Activity

> Think carefully about the short stories that you have read. Make a list of the differences between these stories and novels that you have studied (apart from the obvious point to do with length!).

Friedman answers this question by identifying two key features.

- A short story may be short because the material itself is narrow in its range or area of interest.

- A short story may be short because although the material has a potentially broad range the writer cuts it down to focus on one aspect and maximize the story's impact or artistic effect.

Many short stories do focus on a single incident, moment in time, or experience, but that is not always the case. Not all short stories are deliberately crafted by the writer as a vehicle for a single effect. In fact some stories gain their impact because they do not operate on a 'single effect' structure. Indeed, in some instances the 'single effect' type of story can appear contrived.

For many years the short story has suffered a good deal of critical neglect and has been regarded as an academically lightweight genre when measured against the much 'weightier' and prestigious novel form. However, recently there has been a recognition that the short story is something more than the novel's poor relation and it is not now uncommon to find a range of short stories on A-level syllabuses. If you are studying a short story text there are a number of areas that you will need to have some ideas about. Examination questions can be phrased in different ways but it is likely that they will focus on one or more of the following.

- **Plot and structure** You will need a clear understanding of what happens in the story, the basic ideas that it deals with, how it is structured, and how the various elements of it relate to one another. How the story is structured can be of particular interest to the examiner if it varies from a straightforward chronological pattern.
- **Narrative viewpoint** The question of who is telling the story is a very important one and raises questions about why the writer has chosen to present the story from this particular viewpoint and what effect this has on the reader's response.
- **Characters** This is a favourite area for A-level questions. They often focus on one or more of the characters in the story or stories and may ask you to examine how the writer presents or develops the characters or to explore how they relate to each other.
- **Language and style** You will also need a clear idea about the distinctive qualities of the writer's style. This will involve focusing closely on the specific detail and the writer's choice of language (the way this is used, and the effects that it creates).

Plot and structure

Activity

> Think carefully about a short story that you have read and make a list of the features that you think are important in terms of making this story 'work'.

One thing you may have noted about short stories is that very often the story focuses on a single character in a single situation rather than tracing a range of characters through a variety of situations and phases of development as novels often do. However, often the focus for the story is a moment at which the central character(s) undergoes some important experience which presents a significant moment in their personal development. It can be seen as a 'moment of truth' in which something or some perception, large or small, changes within the character. In some stories, though, this 'moment of truth' is evident only to the reader and not the character(s).

Not all stories reach a climax, though. Some stories may offer a kind of 'snapshot' of a period of time or an experience – a 'day in the life of...' kind of story might be like this. Other stories end inconclusively leaving the reader with feelings of uncertainty, while other kinds of story do not seem to have a discernible plot at all. This may lead the reader to feel completely baffled by what he or she has read and subsequently to tentatively explore a range of possible interpretations in his or her head. This might, of course, have been exactly the response that the writer intended.

This diagram presents one way of thinking about how alternative plots and structures of short stories work:

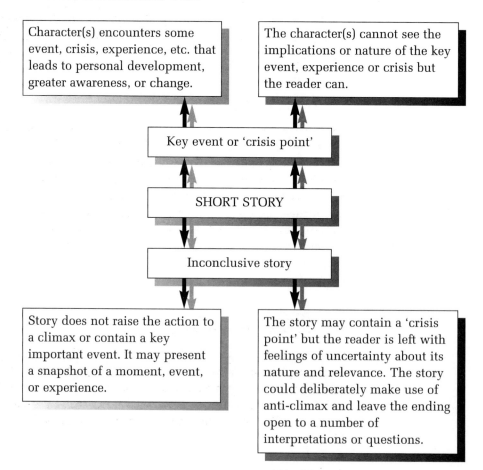

Character(s) encounters some event, crisis, experience, etc. that leads to personal development, greater awareness, or change.

The character(s) cannot see the implications or nature of the key event, experience or crisis but the reader can.

Key event or 'crisis point'

SHORT STORY

Inconclusive story

Story does not raise the action to a climax or contain a key important event. It may present a snapshot of a moment, event, or experience.

The story may contain a 'crisis point' but the reader is left with feelings of uncertainty about its nature and relevance. The story could deliberately make use of anti-climax and leave the ending open to a number of interpretations or questions.

Beginnings

Our very earliest experiences of stories (the fairy tales we listen to, and then the vast range of stories that we hear, read, and see presented in film and television as adults) teach us one thing – stories have a 'beginning', a 'middle', and an 'end'. Strictly speaking, though, it is not entirely true. There are stories that do not seem to have a beginning or an ending in the conventional sense. We will look at stories like these which seem to be 'all middle', so to speak, a little later. The vast majority of stories, however, do have some kind of beginning or opening section; a middle, where the characters, situation, and ideas are developed; and an ending that draws the story to a conclusion.

Here are some possible ways in which stories can open:
- the writer launches straight into the narrative
- the writer sets the scene by giving explicit background information
- the writer informs the reader using suggestion or implication rather than direct description
- the opening is direct and holds the reader's attention, perhaps capturing attention with a word or short phrase

Activity Read the following openings to four short stories. Then, in a small group, discuss your responses to them. Think carefully about how each writer approaches the opening to their story and try to identify the techniques that they use.

1 The Boarding House

Mrs Mooney was a butcher's daughter. She was a woman who was quite able to keep things to herself: a determined woman. She had married her father's foreman and opened a butcher's shop near Spring Gardens. But as soon as his father-in-law was dead Mr Mooney began to go to the devil. He drank, plundered the till, ran headlong into debt. It was no use making him take the pledge: he was sure to break out again a few days after. By fighting his wife in the presence of customers and by buying bad meat he ruined his business. One night he went for his wife with the cleaver and she had to sleep in a neighbour's house.

James Joyce

2 In Memoriam Brian Rosenfeld

'1939. It wasn't just the outbreak of war to us, but the fact that my mother decided to leave my father that week. Just like that. A personal holocaust. Fear was in the air, muted excitement; the measured tones of Neville Chamberlain oozed out of the dark brown canvas-webbed wireless set, gently, softly. He was an appeaser, like my ma, but he'd lost patience, as she had. The future would be different now.'

Elizabeth Troop

3 The Snow Pavilion

The motor stalled in the middle of a snowy landscape, lodged in a rut, wouldn't budge an inch. How I swore! I'd planned to be snug in front of a roaring fire by now, a single malt on the mahogany wine-table (a connoisseur's piece) beside me, the five courses of Melissa's dinner savourously aromatizing the kitchen; to complete the décor, a labrador retriever's head laid on my knee as trustingly as if I were indeed a country gentleman and lolled by rights among the chintz. After dinner, before I read our customary pre-coital poetry aloud to her, my elegant and accomplished mistress, also a connoisseur's piece, might play the piano for her part-time pasha while I sipped black, acrid coffee from her precious little cups.

Angela Carter

4 Dual Control

'You ought to have stopped.'
'For God's sake, shut up, Freda.'
'Well, you should have. You ought to have made sure she was alright.'
'Of course she's alright.'
'How do you know? You didn't stop to find out, did you?'
'Do you want me to go back? We're late enough as it is, thanks to your fooling about getting ready, but I don't suppose the Bradys'll notice if we're late. I don't suppose they'll notice if we never turn up, though after the way you angled for the invitation...'
'That's right, blame it all on me. We could have left half an hour ago if you hadn't been late home from the office.'
'How often do I have to tell you that business isn't a matter of nine to five?'
'No it's a matter of the Bradys, isn't it? You were keen enough we should get asked. Where were you anyway? Drinking with the boys? Or smooching with some floozie?'

Elizabeth Walter

Obviously the opening of a story is vital. If readers' attention is not captured immediately the story contains no initial impact to encourage them to continue, to draw them into the story. However, bearing in mind the constraints of length under which the short story operates, it is also important that the opening compresses information that might have taken some time to explain so that the reader quickly and effectively gains a picture of what is going on. Short story writers are often faced with this question of how much they can omit while at the same time creating the impression of completeness and continuity in their stories.

Going back to the extracts that you have just discussed, you may have noticed that Extract 3 launches straight into the narrative. The car getting stuck in the snow captures the reader's attention straight away. This opening paragraph goes on to give quite a bit of information to set the scene very economically as the narrator reflects on the plans he had made for his evening.

In Extract 1, Joyce begins by setting the scene and providing the reader with some background information necessary to understand the context of the story. This opening paragraph concentrates on providing the reader with details of Mrs Mooney's background and her situation through succinct and straightforward description.

In Extract 4, on the other hand, we are told very little directly and we have to work out for ourselves what is happening or what has happened using clues suggested through the narrative. This approach can provide us with just as much information as straightforward description. In this instance we learn about the characters – what they are doing and what has happened – through the dialogue but it leaves a good deal to the reader's imagination too. (In fact, this story is told entirely through dialogue with no direct description.)

In contrast, Extract 2 begins with the arresting '1939' which immediately captures our attention. The short and direct paragraph clearly sets the context for the story and indicates to us the personal and domestic scene reflected against the magnitude of world events.

Narrative line

Short stories, like other fictional works, order the events that they describe in a particular way. Through the story-line the writer can create a wide range of effects, such as creating suspense, raising the action to a climax point, resolving problems, leading (or misleading) the reader in particular ways, and leaving endings open to a variety of interpretations.

Very often the narrative structure is a straightforward progression with one event following another and moving towards a conclusion where all is resolved. However, sometimes a writer might play around with this structure to create particular effects. Here are some points to consider when you focus on the narrative structure of a story.

- Make a list of the key events in the story.
- Look at the order in which these events are related by the writer.
- Look at the time structure of the story – is it told in simple chronological order or is there use of flashbacks or cutting back and forth?
- Are there any details or pieces of information that the writer omits or particular points that are emphasized?

Short stories often have a moment in the plot upon which the whole structure of the story turns and which affects the outcome of the tale. Sometimes this trigger can be a quite trivial incident or experience but it signifies a moment of revelation to the central character. *Hassan's Tower* by Margaret Drabble contains just such a moment for newly-married Kenneth on honeymoon with his wife, Chloë, in Morocco. They are a wealthy couple who appear to have everything that they could want in life but Kenneth is disappointed in his new wife and disillusioned with life in general. He is ill-at-ease in Morocco and goes about in constant fear of being robbed. Against his will his wife takes him to Hassan's Tower and wants to climb to the top to see the view. Reluctantly, he accompanies her and during the course of this seemingly unremarkable excursion he experiences a revelation that changes his whole outlook on his wife, his life, and those around him.

Hassan's Tower

The more he looked, the more he realized that the people on top of the tower were in their own way as astonishing a view as the more evidently panoramic vistas. The whole of the top of the tower was thick and covered with people: small children were crawling about, mothers were feeding their babies, young men were holding the hands of girls and indeed the hands of other young men, boys were sitting on the very edge and dangling their feet into space, and old women who would need a day to recover from the climb were lying back in the sun, for all the world as though they were grandmothers on a beach in England ... and as he gazed he felt growing within him a sense of extraordinary familiarity that was in its own way a kind of illumination ... He saw these people, quite suddenly, for what they were, for people, for nothing other than people; their clothes filled out with bodies, their faces took on expression, their relations became dazzlingly clear, as though the details of their strangeness had dropped away, as though the terms of common humanity (always before credited in principle, but never before perceived) had become facts before his eyes.

Margaret Drabble

Endings

There are as many ways of ending a story as there are of beginning it and the ending is clearly a very important element in the overall structure of a piece. In a short story it is often the ending which reveals meaning, points up a significant theme, or provides a resolution. This kind of ending should leave the reader contented and satisfied with a sense of a tale completed.

Equally though, a writer might create an 'open' ending, one that does not provide answers, an ending that might leave the reader pondering on what it all means or unsettle them. This could be, of course, just the kind of response that the writer is aiming for.

The ending with 'a sting in the tail' has become very popular in recent years, being popularized through the short stories of Roald Dahl. It is worth noting, though, that with this kind of ending we need to distinguish between a device which is merely used as a kind of 'trick' and a twist at the end which causes us to see something fundamental in the story as a whole.

Activity

> Choose three short stories that you know and reread them. Discuss the
> ending of each with a partner, thinking about the following questions.
> • Does the story have what you would recognize as a definite ending?
> • How does the ending relate to the rest of the story?
> • Does the writer draw attention to any specific points in the ending?
> • How would you have ended the story?

Narrative viewpoint

You will already be familiar with the term viewpoint in the sense of 'from
whose point of view we see the events of the story'. However, it is perhaps
worth bearing in mind that this term can encompass two related but distinct
ideas. In addressing viewpoint we need to consider the question of who is
actually seeing the events described and who is narrating them. They may be
one and the same or quite separate and the question is rather more complex
than it might first appear.

It may be possible to approach the question of viewpoint by distinguishing
between narrators who seem to address the reader directly from within the
story (**internal narrators**) or those who have a more 'external' narrative
viewpoint. As readers you need to be aware of how writers use viewpoint
within their stories, be sensitive to subtle shifts and aware of the effects this
can have on the narrative and your perception of it.

For more discussion of narrative viewpoint see Unit 2.

Activity

> Look at these two extracts and think about the narrative viewpoints
> used in each.

1 Missy

'There you are, Mrs Ebbs, hold the cup steady. Can you manage, dear? Whoops!
That's it. Now sit up properly, you'll slip down in the bed again, sit up against
your pillows. That's it. Don't nod off again, will you? Now careful, Mrs Ebbs, I
haven't got all day, dear. That's it, good girl.'
The voice came roaring towards her. The face was bland as suet. The face was a
cow's face. An ox.
'Ox-face,' she said, but she had not said it.
She tipped the spoon and sucked in her soup, little bits of carrot and soft lentil
sieving through the spaces between her teeth.
'All right now, Mrs Ebbs?'
Ox-face.
'I'm not deaf.'
Was she?

Susan Hill

2 A Tradition of Eighteen Hundred and Four, Christmas 1882

The widely discussed possibility of an invasion of England through a Channel Tunnel has more than once recalled old Solomon Selby's story to my mind.
The occasion on which I numbered myself among his audience was one evening when he was sitting in the yawning chimney-corner of the inn-kitchen, with some others who had gathered there, and I entered for shelter from the rain.
Withdrawing the stem of his pipe from the dental notch in which it habitually rested, he leaned back in the recess behind him and smiled into the fire. The smile was neither mirthful nor sad, not precisely humorous nor altogether thoughtful.
We who knew him recognized it in a moment: it was his narrative smile. Breaking off our few desultory remarks we drew up closer, and he thus began ...

Thomas Hardy

In Extract 2 you will notice immediately that Hardy is writing in the first person here. He is recounting a particular evening when he heard a story told by Solomon Selby. You obviously cannot tell from this brief opening but the bulk of the story is told as if by Solomon Selby as reported by Hardy. Think about what effect this has on the narrative. Notice too how Hardy economically sets the context of the story through implication – the title providing the date, 1804, coupled with the idea of an invasion through a 'Channel Tunnel' clearly sets the story against the background of the Napoleonic Wars. Hardy also economically sets the story in its more immediate context – the cosy inn of 1882, sheltering from the rain with others gathered round the fire, and the anticipation of a good story well told – all these details help to set the mood and draw the reader into the narrative.

Compare this with the approach adopted by Hill in Extract 1. She chooses a quite different way of telling her story. It is written in the third person and we are launched, without any preamble, into a 'situation'. It is not immediately clear what that situation is but it seems that someone, perhaps a nurse, is feeding soup to Mrs Ebbs. Although Hill partially adopts the stance of external narrator, some of the narrative views the scene through the eyes of Mrs Ebbs as she sees the face of the nurse peering towards her.

Activity   Look at three or four short stories that you have studied. With a partner, discuss the narrative viewpoint that the writer adopts in each. Now write a short essay, illustrated by examples, on the way in which narrative viewpoint contributes to the overall effect of these stories.

Character

Although some critics argue that it is absurd to consider fictitious characters as if they were 'real' people, on the other hand, when we read stories we do create our own mental image of them based on our experiences of real life.

However, we must not lose sight of the fact that they are creations of the writer and do not have an existence outside the text. In many cases writers create their characters to serve particular functions within the narrative and present them in ways that give particular impressions. Therefore, we should look carefully at the kinds of characters the writer portrays, how they are presented, which of their features are stressed, and what role they perform. We must also think about how the characters interlock with all the other elements of the story to create a unified whole and how we respond to them as readers.

In Unit 2 you considered ways in which characters can be revealed to us in novels and these points also apply to the short story. It would be useful to look back at these points to refresh your memory (see page 17). Read the following extract and think about how the two characters are presented.

Halloran's Child

He was eating the rabbit he had shot himself on the previous day, separating the small bones carefully from the flesh before soaking lumps of bread in the dark salt gravy. When they were boys, he and his brother, Nelson Twomey, used to trap rabbits and other animals too, weasels and stoats – it was sport, they thought nothing of it, it was only what Farley the gamekeeper did.
Then, Nate had gone by himself into the wood and found a young fallow deer caught by the leg, and when he had eventually got it free the animal had stumbled away, its foot mangled and dropping a trail of fresh blood through the undergrowth. Nate had gone for his brother, brought him back and shown him. 'Well, it'll die, that's what,' Nelson had said, and shrugged his thin shoulders. It was the first glimpse Nate had of his brother's true nature, his meanness.
'Die of gangrene. That's poison.'
He had wept that night, one of the few occasions in his life, and he got up at dawn and gone out to search for the wounded animal, remembering the trembling hind quarters and the sweat which had matted its pale coat, the eyes, where the sticky rheum had begun to gather in the corners. He found only the blood, dried dark on the bracken. It led him towards where the bank of the stream fell away at his feet, and he could not follow further.

Susan Hill

Activity   What impressions do you get of Nelson and Nate Twomey in this extract? Use specific references from the passage to support your ideas.

One of the first striking things about this passage is the way that Hill emphasizes Nate's sensitivity and concern for the suffering of an innocent and helpless creature. He does, however, continue to shoot and eat rabbits and to kill chickens for food but these things are all part of the natural order of things and do not involve unnecessary or drawn-out suffering. What seems significant here is that it is not the killing but the pointless suffering of the innocent animal in the trap that appals him. In this respect he is quite different to his older brother, Nelson, who not only appears indifferent to the suffering of the animals but actually relishes the cruelty inherent in his work as a rat-catcher. There is a violence within Nelson that seems to simmer below the surface and that makes Nate in some way afraid of him. One of the effects of the description of the two brothers in this passage is to focus attention more closely on the characteristics of Nate. If you were to read the rest of the story you would find that Nate is the central character.

Activity

> **1** Now look back at the two extracts on pages 157–158 that you considered in terms of narrative viewpoint. Read them again but this time focus on any clues or hints that they might give concerning the characters. Discuss your ideas with a partner and jot down the main points of your discussion.
>
> **2** Choose two stories that you have read and studied and write brief notes on how the writer(s) reveal and present the central character(s).

Language and imagery

The style in which a story is written – the choices that writers make in the language they use and the ways in which they use it – is a key element in the overall effect that is created by a story in the mind of the reader. It might be written quite plainly using little figurative language or the writer might use imagery to help create the desired effect.

In *Halloran's Child*, Hill very often uses groups of images to build up a particular effect. Look at this passage, for example, which describes the Hallorans' daughter, Jenny.

Halloran's Child

They had only one child, the daughter, Jenny. She had never been truly well since the day she was born, and when she was a year old and began to walk her limbs seemed incapable of holding her up, she was unsteady and sickly. At the age of four she had rheumatic fever and almost died, and Halloran had said in public hearing that he wished for it, wished to have it over with, for who wanted an invalid for a child and how could he bear the anxiety? She had been forbidden to run or even walk far, though she went to school when she was five and there was treated like a fragile doll by the others, who had been put in awe of her. She played with no one, though sometimes, as she sat in a corner of the playground, one of them would take pity on her and bring pick-sticks or a jigsaw and do it with her for a little while. But she seemed to be separated from them, almost to be less than human, because of the transparency of her skin and her thin, delicate bones, because of the fine blueness tinging her lips and the flesh below her nervous eyes.

Susan Hill

Activity

> Read this extract carefully and pick out any images that are particularly effective. Describe what impressions are created by each of these and then compare your ideas with a partner.

Notice how Hill emphasizes the frailty of Jenny through a variety of images that build up to create a vivid impression of the sick child. She tells us that Jenny '... was treated like a fragile doll' that she seemed '... almost to be less than human, because of the transparency of her skin and her thin, delicate bones, because of the fine blueness tinging her lips and the flesh below her nervous eyes'. This creates an image of a fragile, young, featherless baby bird and gives an impression of vulnerability, of someone with a tenuous grip on life.

Later on in the story Jenny goes into hospital and when she comes out the fragility of her body is re-emphasized by Hill who describes her '... small legs poking out like sticks', her '... neck bent like a stalk', and introduces the idea that she is dying as Nate sees '... the deadness within the child's eyes'.

Nate goes to visit Jenny, and again Hill uses description relating to skin and eyes and bones to show the child's deteriorating condition:

'... she seemed to have shrunk, her flesh was thinner, scarcely covering her bones, and the skin was tight and shiny. Her eyes were very bright and yet dead, too.'

Again Hill uses imagery suggestive of a helpless creature:

'He looked down at her hand, resting on the sheet. It was like a small claw.'

and again images that hint of death:

'Her lips moved and there was no blood in them, they were thin and dry and oddly transparent, like the skin of a chrysalis.'

This technique of using recurring images to build up a picture or atmosphere is a feature typical of Hill's style.

Activity

> Choose two or three stories that you have studied and think carefully about how they are written. Note down what seem to you to be particular features of the style of each. Include examples to illustrate your points.

The whole story

Annotation can be a very useful aid to exploring a text. It allows you to record those tentative first responses or ideas that are suggested to you as you read a text. Indeed, the process of noting points on the text itself can help you to focus on the meaning and implications of individual words and phrases.

Often these 'first impressions' tend to be lost or forgotten later but they do play a very important part in the development of your ideas about a particular text. Here is an example of a second year student's notes around the short story *I Spy* by Graham Greene. In this instance the student read the story and then began annotating it prior to a small group discussion in which students compared their ideas. Read *I Spy* for yourself and think about the annotations made around the text.

I Spy

Sense of secrecy

Charlie Stowe waited until he heard his mother snore before he got out of bed. Even then he moved with caution and tiptoed to the window. The front of the house was irregular, so that it was possible to see a light burning in his mother's room. But now all the windows were dark. A searchlight passed across the sky, lighting the banks of cloud and probing the dark deep spaces between, seeking enemy airships. The wind blew from the sea, and Charlie Stowe could hear behind his mother's snores the beating of the waves. A draught through the cracks in the window-frame stirred his nightshirt. Charlie Stowe was frightened.

But the thought of the tobacconist's shop which his father kept down a dozen wooden stairs drew him on. He was twelve years old, and already boys at the County School mocked him because he had never smoked a cigarette. The packets were piled twelve deep below, Gold Flake and Players, De Reszke, Abdulla, Woodbines, and the little shop lay under a thin haze of stale smoke which would completely disguise his crime. That it was a crime to steal some of his father's stock Charlie Stowe had no doubt, but he did not love his father; his father was unreal to him, a wraith, pale, thin, indefinite, who noticed him only spasmodically and left even punishment to his mother. For his mother he felt a passionate demonstrative love; her large boisterous presence and her noisy charity filled the world for him; from her speech he judged her the friend of everyone, from the rector's wife to the 'dear Queen', except the 'Huns', the monsters who lurked in Zeppelins in the clouds. But his father's affection and dislike were as indefinite as his movements. Tonight he had said he would be in Norwich, and yet you never knew. Charlie Stowe had no sense of safety as he crept down the wooden stairs. When they creaked he clenched his fingers on the collar of his nightshirt.

At the bottom of the stairs he came out quite suddenly into the little shop. It was too dark to see his way, and he did not dare touch the switch. For half a minute he sat in despair on the bottom step with

Annotations (left margin):
- Sense of secrecy
- Searchlight – airships – wartime
- 1st World War
- Cold – out of bed! – darkness emphasized
- Not modern
- 'Manly' to smoke – grown up
- Brands of cigarettes
- Why?
- Father does not seem to bother with him – different to mum
- Zeppelins – bombing raids

Annotations (right margin):
- Sense of mystery, menace, potential danger, etc
- Sleeping mother – repetition of snore
- What is Charlie up to?
- Mention of father
- More info about Charlie
- Pressure from peers
- A 'crime' stealing, guilty conscience
- What does all this mean?
- Contrast with father
- Something mysterious about father
- A sign of fear!
- A sense almost of surprise
- What to do next!

his chin cupped in his hands. Then the regular movement of the searchlight was reflected through an upper window and the boy had time to fix in memory the pile of cigarettes, the counter, and the small hole under it. The footsteps of a policeman on the pavement made him grab the first packet to his hand and dive for the hole. A light shone along the floor and a hand tried the door, then the footsteps passed on, and Charlie cowered in the darkness. At last he got his courage back by telling himself in his curiously adult way that if he were caught now there was nothing to be done about it, and he might as well have his smoke. He put a cigarette in his mouth and then remembered that he had no matches. For a while he dared not move. Three times the searchlight lit the shop, while he muttered taunts and encouragements. 'May as well be hung for a sheep,' 'Cowardy, cowardy custard,' grown-up and childish exhortations oddly mixed.

But as he moved he heard footfalls in the street, the sound of several men walking rapidly. Charlie Stowe was old enough to feel surprise that anybody was about. The footsteps came nearer, stopped; a key was turned in the shop door, a voice said: 'Let him in,' and then he heard his father, 'If you wouldn't mind being quiet, gentlemen, I don't want to wake up the family.' There was a note unfamiliar to Charlie in the undecided voice. A torch flashed and the electric globe burst into blue light. The boy held his breath; he wondered whether his father would hear his heart beating, and he clutched his nightshirt tightly and prayed, 'O God, don't let me be caught.' Through a crack in the counter he could see his father where he stood, one hand held to his high stiff collar, between two men in bowler hats and belted mackintoshes. They were strangers. 'Have a cigarette,' his father said in a voice dry as a biscuit. One of the men shook his head. 'It wouldn't do, not when we are on duty. Thank you all the same.' He spoke gently, but without kindness. Charlie Stowe thought his father must be ill. 'Mind if I put a few in my pocket?' Mr Stowe asked, and when the man nodded he lifted a pile of Gold Flake and Players from a shelf and caressed the packets with the tips of his fingers. 'Well,' he said, 'there's nothing to be done about it, and I may as well have my smokes.' For a moment Charlie Stowe feared discovery, his father stared round the shop so thoroughly; he might have been seeing it for the first time. 'It's a good little business,' he said, 'for those that like it. The wife will sell out, I suppose. Else the neighbours'll be wrecking it. Well, you want to be off. A stitch in time. I'll get my coat.'

Marginal annotations (left):

Fear of discovery builds up atmosphere of tension

Panic

Relief

Recovers

Gone so far, might as well go through with it

Still afraid

Why this word?

Tension again

'Gentlemen' – very polite and formal

Something out of the ordinary happening

Police?

Police again!

Stocking up – may not be back for some time

Why 'caressed'?

A bit like Charlie, 'if he were caught now there would be nothing to be done about it'

Marginal annotations (right):

Fear of his 'crime' being found out

Tension

Why 'curiously' adult? – he is realistic about what is happening

Mixture of adult and child

Supposed to be in Norwich

Why not?

Fear of being caught

Like Charlie clenching his nightshirt

Is he under arrest?

Fear, uncertainty

Why 'gently'/without kindness'? – an unusual combination

Has to ask permission – under arrest?

Or the last!

The end of his family life

Why would the neighbours do that?

Daren't let him out of their sight –
serious charges maybe

'One of us'll come with you, if you don't mind,' said the stranger

'Gently' again — gently.

'You needn't trouble. It's on the peg here. There, I'm all ready.'

Doesn't want to say goodbye – afraid, ashamed?

The other man said in an embarrassed way, 'Don't you want to   Feels awkward
speak to your wife?' The thin voice was decided, 'Not me. Never
do today what you can put off till tomorrow. She'll have her chance
later, won't she?'—— When?

Sounds serious

'Yes, yes,' one of the strangers said and he became very cheerful   Trying to jolly him along
and encouraging. 'Don't you worry too much. While there's life...'
and suddenly his father tried to laugh.   ...There's hope – could suggest long sentence or worse

When the door had closed Charlie Stowe tiptoed upstairs and got

We see everything through Charlie's eyes

into bed. He wondered why his father had left the house again so
late at night and who the strangers were. Surprise and awe kept him   What had he done?
for a little while awake. It was as if a familiar photograph had
stepped from the frame to reproach him with neglect. He
remembered how his father had held tight to his collar and fortified   Just like Charlie
himself with proverbs, and he thought for the first time that, while
his mother was boisterous and kindly, his father was very like —— Something has
himself doing things in the dark which frightened him. It would   happened to change Charlie's view
have pleased him to go down to his father and tell him that he
loved him, but he could hear through the window the quick steps
going away. He was alone in the house with his mother, and he fell
asleep.   Returns to the beginning

Graham Greene

Special Feature: Jane Gardam

• •

Jane Gardam was born in Yorkshire in 1928 and after studying literature at London University she became a journalist and writer. She is well known for her novels for children and adults as well as for short stories in which she experiments with different forms and ideas. She won the Winifred Holtby Memorial Prize in 1976, was runner-up for the Booker Prize in 1978, won the Whitbread Literary Award in 1981 and her collection of short stories, *Pangs of Love and Other Stories*, from which *Stone Trees* is taken, received the Katherine Mansfield Award in 1984.

Stone Trees reflects both her urge to experiment with the short story form and her exploration of the inner emotions of her central character. Read the story through carefully.

Stone Trees

So now that he is dead so now that he is dead I am to spend the day with them. The Robertsons.
On the Isle of Wight. Train journey train journey from London. There and back in a day.
So now that he is dead –
They were at the funeral. Not their children. Too little. So good so good they were to me. She – Anna – she cried a lot. Tom held my arm tight. Strong. I liked it. In the place even the place where your coffin was, I liked it, his strong arm. Never having liked Tom that much, I liked his strong arm.
And they stayed over. Slept at the house a night or two. Did the telephone. Some gran or someone was with their children. Thank God we had no children. Think of Tom/Anna dying and those two children left –
So now that you are dead –
It's nice of them isn't it now that you are dead? Well, you'd have expected it. You aren't surprised by it. I'm not surprised by it. After all there has to be somewhere to go. All clean all clean at home. Back work soon someday. Very soon now for it's a week. They broke their two week holiday for the funeral. Holiday Isle of Wight where you/I went once. There was a dip, a big-dipper dip, a wavy line of cliffs along the shore, and in this dip of the cliffs a hotel – a long beach and the waves moving in shallow.
Over stone trees.
But it was long ago and what can stone trees have been? Fantasy.
So now that you are dead so now –

Sweetie love so now that you are dead I am to spend the day with the Robertsons alone and we shall talk you/I later. So now –

The boat crosses. Has crossed. Already. Criss-cross deck. Criss-cross water. Splashy sea and look – ! Lovely clouds flying (now that you are dead) and here's the pier. A long, long pier into the sea and gulls shouting and children yelling here and there and here's my ticket and there they stand. All in a row – Tom, Anna, the two children solemn. And smiles now – Tom and Anna. Tom and Anna look too large to be quite true. Too good. Anna who never did anything wrong. Arms stretch too far forward for a simple day.

They stretch because they want. They would not stretch to me if you were obvious and not just dead. Then it would have been, hullo, easy crossing? Good. Wonderful day. Let's get back and down on the beach. Great to see you both. So now that you are dead –

We paced last week. Three

Tom. Anna. I.

And other black figures wood-faced outside the crematorium in blazing sun, examining shiny black-edged tickets on blazing bouquets. 'How good of Marjorie – fancy old Marjorie. I didn't even know she –' There was that woman who ran out of the so-called service with handkerchief at her eyes. But who was there except you my darling and I and the Robertsons and the shiny cards and did they do it then? Were they doing it then as we read the flowers? Do they do it at once or stack it up with other coffins and was it still inside waiting as I paced with portly Tom? Christian Tom – Tom we laughed at so often and oh my darling now that you are dead –

Cambridge. You can't say that Tom has precisely changed since Cambridge. Thickened. More solid. Unshaken still, quite unshaken and – well, wonderful of course. Anna hasn't changed. Small, specs, curly hair, straight-laced. Dear Anna how we sat and worked out all. Analysed. Girton. We talked about how many men it was decent to do it with without being wild and when you should decide to start and Anna said none and never. Not before marriage you said. Anna always in that church where Tom preached and Tom never looking Anna's way, and how she ached. So now that –

Sweet I miss you so. Now that you are –. My darling oh my God!

In the train two young women. (Yes thanks Anna, I'm fine. Nice journey. First time out. It's doing me good. Isn't it a lovely day?) There were these two women talking about their rights. They were reading about all that was due to them. In a magazine.

'Well, it's only right isn't it?'

'What?'

'Having your own life. Doing your thing.'

'Well–'

'Not – you know. Men and that. Not letting them have all the freedom and that. You have to stand up for yourself and get free of men.'

We come to the hotel and of course it is the one. The one in the dip of the cliffs almost on the beach, and how were they to know? It's typical though, somehow. We didn't like them my darling did we, after Cambridge very much? We didn't see them – dropped them in some way. We didn't see them for nearly two years. And we wondered, sometimes, whatever it was we had thought we had had in common – do-good, earnest Tom, healthy face and shorts, striding out over mountains singing snatches of Berlioz and stopping now and then to pray. And you were you and always unexpected – alert, alive, mocking, and forever young and now that you are –

But they were there again. In California. You at the university and I at the university, teaching a term; and there – behold the Robertsons, holding out their arms to save America. Little house full of the shiny-faced, the chinless – marriage counsellors, marriage-enrichment classes oh my God! And one child in Anna and one just learning to walk. We were taken to them by somebody just for a lark not knowing who they'd turn out to be and we said – 'Hey! Tom and Anna.'

And in Sacramento in a house with lacy balconies and little red Italian brick walls and all their old Cambridge books about and photographs we half-remembered, we opened wine and were very happy; and over the old white-washed fireplace there was Tom's old crucifix and his Cambridge oar. And I sat in the rocking chair she'd had at Girton and it felt familiar and we loved the Robertsons that day in sweaty, wheezing Sacramento because they were there again. This is no reason. But it is true.

We talked about how we'd all met each other first. Terrible party. Jesus College. Anna met Tom and I met you my darling and it was something or other – Feminism, Neo-Platonism, Third World – and there you were with bright, ridiculous, marvellous, mocking eyes and long hard hands and I loved you as everyone else clearly loved you. And the Robertsons talked sagely to one another. They were not the Robertsons then but Tom and Anna. We never became the anythings, thank God. There was no need because we were whatever the appearance might be one person and had no need of a plural term and now that –

Sweetie, do you remember the *smell* of that house? In Cambridge? And again in Sacramento? She liked it you know. She left dishes for a week and food bits and old knickers and tights in rolls on the mantelpiece and said, 'There are things more important.' Under the burning ethic there was you know something very desperate about Anna. Tom didn't notice her. Day after day and I'd guess night after night.' He sat in the rocking chair and glared at God. And meeting them again just the same, in Sacramento, you looked at the crucifix and the oar and at me, your eyes like the first time we met because there we both remembered the first time, long ago. Remembering that was a short return to each other because by then, by America, I knew that you were one I'd never have to myself because wherever you were or went folk turned and smiled at you and loved you. Well, I'd known always. I didn't face it at first, that one woman would never be enough for you and that if I moved in with you you would soon move on.

Everyone wanted you. When we got married there was a general sense of comedy and the sense of my extraordinary and very temporary luck.

It is not right or dignified to love so much. To let a man rule so much. It is obsession and not love, a mental illness not a life. And of course, with marriage came the quarrelling and pain because I knew there were so many others, and you not coming home, and teasing when you did and saying that there was only me but of course I knew it was not so because of – cheap and trite things like – the smell of scent. It was worst just before the Robertsons went away.

But then – after California – we came here to this beach once and it was September like now, and a still, gold peace. And the hotel in the dip, and the sand white and wide and rock pools. And only I with you. You were quieter. You brought no work. You lay on the beach with a novel flapping pages and the sand gathering in them. We held hands and it was not as so often. It was not as when I looked at you and saw your eyes looking at someone else invisible. God, love – the killing sickness. Maybe never let it start – just mock and talk of Rights. Don't let it near. Sex without sentiment. Manage one's life with dignity. But now that you are dead –

And one day on that year's peaceful holiday we walked out to the stone trees which now I remember. They told us, at the hotel, that in the sea, lying on their stone sides, on their stone bark and broken stone branches, were great prehistoric trees, petrified and huge and broken into sections by the millennia and chopped here and there as by an infernal knife, like rhubarb chunks or blocks of Edinburgh candy, sand coloured, ancient among the young stones.

Trees so old that no one ever saw them living. Trees become stone. I said, 'I love stone' and you said, 'I love trees,' and kicked them. You said, 'Who wants stone trees?' And we walked about on them, a stone stick forest, quite out to sea, and sat and put our feet in pools where green grasses swayed and starfish shone. And you said – despising the stone trees – there is only ever you – you know – and I knew that the last one was gone and the pain of her and you and I were one again. It was quite right that you loved so much being so much loved and I am glad, for now that you are dead –

I shall never see you any more.

I shall never feel your hand over my hand.

I shall never lean my head against you any more.

I shall never see your eyes which now that you are –

'The sandwiches are egg, love, and cheese, and there's chocolate. We didn't bring a feast. It's too hot.'

'It's lovely.'

'Drink?'

'I don't like Ribena, thanks.'

'It's not. It's wine. In tumblers. Today we're having a lot of wine in very big tumblers.'

(Anna Robertson of evangelical persuasion, who never acts extremely, is offering me wine in tumblers. Now that you are dead.)

'It's nice wine. I'll be drunk.'

The children say, 'You can have some of our cake. D'you want a biscuit?' They've been told to be nice. The little girl pats sand, absorbed, solemn, straight-haired, grave like Tom. The older one, the boy, eats cake and lies on his stomach aware of me and that my husband has died and gone to God.

And you have gone to God?

You were with God and you were my god and now that you –

The boy has long legs. Seven-year-old long legs. The boy is a little like you and not at all like Tom. He rolls over and gives me a biscuit. I'm so glad we had no children. I could not have shared you with children. We needed nobody else except you needed other girls to love a bit and leave – nothing important. You moved on and never mind. I didn't. I did not mind. The pain passed and I don't mind and I shall not mind now that you are dead.

The boy is really – or am I going mad altogether – very like you.

The boy is Peter.

Says, 'Are you coming out on the rocks?'

'I'm fine thanks, Peter. I'm drinking my wine.'

'Drink it later and come out on the rocks. Come on over the rocks.'

See Anna, Tom, proud of Peter being kind to me and only seven. They pretend not to see, fiddling with coffee flask, suntan oil. 'Wonderful summer,' says Anna. 'Wonderful.'

'Come on the rocks.'

'Peter – don't boss,' says Anna.

'Leave your wine and come,' says Peter, 'I'll show you the rocks.'

Do I go with this boy over the rocks my darling now that you are dead and I have no child and I will never see you any more.

Not any more.

Ever again.

Now that you are –

It is ridiculous how this boy walks.

How Anna wept.

'Look, hold my hand,' says Peter, 'and take care. We're on old trees. What d'you think of that? They were so old they turned to stone. It's something in the atmosphere. They're awful, aren't they? I like trees all leafy and sparkly.'

'Sparkly trees?'

'Well, there'd be no pollution. No people. Now just rotten stone.'

'I like stone.'

He kicks them, 'I like trees.'

And I sit down my love because I will not see you any more or hold your hand or put my face on yours and this will pass of course. They've told me that this sort of grief will pass.

But I don't want the grief to change. I want not to forget the feel and look of you and the look of your live eyes and the physical life of you and I do not want to cease to grieve.

'Look, hey, look,' says Peter and stops balancing. 'The tide is coming in.' The water slaps. The dead stone which was once covered with breathing holes for life takes life again, and where it looked like burned out ashy stone there are colours, and little movements, and frondy things responding to water, which laps and laps.

'Look,' says Peter, 'there's a starfish. Pink as pink. Hey – take my hand. Mind out. You mustn't slip.' (This boy has long hard hands.) 'The tide is coming in.'

How Anna cried.

The tide is coming in and it will cover the stone trees and then it will ebb back again and the stone trees will remain, and already the water is showing more growing things that are there all the time, though only now and then seen. And Peter takes my hand in yours and I will never see you any more – How Anna cried. And things are growing in the cracks in the stones. The boy laughs and looks at me with your known eyes. Now that you are.

Jane Gardam

Activity

1 Discuss the plot of *Stone Trees*, making a note of the key points and any features that particularly strike you. Consider the story's structure. How do flashbacks and time shifts contribute to this? Draw a chart or a diagram to illustrate the structure of the story.

2 Now focus on the characters in the story and the ways in which Gardam creates and presents them. Using specific references from the text, show how she portrays them.

3 What ideas does Gardam explore through the story? Do you think she has a message for the reader? If so, what do you think it is?

4 Now write an essay discussing your interpretation of and responses to this short story. Use your ideas from questions 1–3 and ensure that you comment on the effect of the following:
   • characterization
   • plot and structure
   • use of language
   • theme

Section II
Developing Your Language of Criticism

7 Preparing for Writing

●●

Objectives
- To introduce strategies for planning writing
- To practise using different strategies
- To settle on the best planning methods for own writing

Applying the rules

In Willy Russell's play *Educating Rita*, Rita – a young woman from a working-class background – begins to study English Literature through the Open University. She decides that an 'education' will give her more choices in life. After her first unsuccessful attempts at essays, her tutor Frank explains:

Frank: There is a way of answering examination questions that is expected. It's a sort of accepted ritual, it's a game, with rules. And you must observe those rules.

Later, the play suggests that in order to write according to the rules, Rita will have to give up some aspects of herself and her own natural, emotional responses to what she reads. Frank does not believe this will be altogether a good thing. Similarly, the challenge of writing about literature at A-level is to learn the 'rules of the game' so as to write in the appropriate way for examination questions without losing the ability to respond in a personal way.

Through the units in Section II, we will consider those 'rules' and identify strategies for developing your language of criticism. As we work through these, we will look at some examples of planning and writing activities based on a scene from the play *A Streetcar Named Desire* by Tennessee Williams, which is often set for AS- or A-level study.

Planning strategies

Whether you are writing an essay for classwork, in an examination, or beginning a major piece of coursework, it can often be difficult to get started. However, there are several measures you can take to make this easier. There are also ways of thinking and planning beforehand that can help you feel more confident and secure about essay writing.

Many students find it best to develop their own preparing and planning methods which feel familiar and which can be used in examinations as well as for less formal pieces of writing. However, it is a good idea to try out several different methods and then choose those that work best for you. Your choice will depend on your 'learning style'. For example, some people naturally find it easier to grasp information when it is presented using pictures and diagrams, while others are more comfortable with words, and prefer information written in list or note form. The remainder of this unit presents some strategies for planning your work. Experiment to find which ones are most helpful to you.

Analysing the question

After reading the text or passage at least twice, consider the question you plan to answer very carefully. Check that you understand it fully. (If you do not, ask for help or if possible choose a question that you feel more confident about.) What are its key words and ideas? Underline them, like this:

Chaucer: *The Miller's Tale*
Someone once described *The Miller's Tale* as a <u>rude story</u> told with <u>speed</u> and <u>wit</u>. To what extent do you agree?
or this:
Toni Morrison: *Beloved*
What <u>features</u> of this novel did you find <u>disturbing</u>?

The underlined words represent the ideas that you will need to keep in mind while you plan and write your answer. In addition to identifying these specific points, do not forget that the 'hidden message' in almost all questions is that you need to write about *how* the writer has used language to create effects. For more on analysing question types see Unit 14, pages 297–308.

Activity

> Look at the following question on Scene 3 of *A Streetcar Named Desire* and decide which key words you would underline:
> Write as fully as you can about Scene 3, 'The Poker Night', focusing on the way the male and female characters are presented.

Annotating the text

When you are preparing to write an essay, annotating your text can be very useful. It can help you to remember certain details and enable you to find them again, especially in a long text. This is true whether the text is a poem or a passage set for unseen practical criticism, or a complete novel or play. However, there are some factors you need to bear in mind before you fill the margins of your text with notes.

- If you are studying the text for an 'Open Book' examination (where you are allowed to take your text into the examination with you), you will probably need to have a 'clean copy' of the text, with no marginal notes at all. Since annotation is still a very useful aid to revision and essay preparation, you might consider buying a second copy in which you can write as many notes as you like. This will work best if the two copies of the text are the same edition, so that the general layout of the clean copy is familiar to you. Alternatively, you could perhaps make photocopies of a few key pages to annotate in detail, but check copyright regulations first. You are usually allowed to copy a small proportion of a text, provided you are using it for educational purposes. Otherwise, you will have to rely on notes written separately from the text.

- If you are studying the text for an examination where you cannot have access to the text, there should be no problem about annotating your copy for practice essays or revision, unless you have borrowed the book from your college or school and they wish to keep the texts 'clean'. If that is the case, you may find it worthwhile to buy a copy of your own to annotate.

If you already have an essay question or a topic to focus on when you read and annotate, it will be easier to recognize the information, lines, and phrases from the text which are relevant for you to underline or highlight.

The following annotations on the opening stage directions for Scene 3 of *A Streetcar Named Desire*, and a brief excerpt from later in the scene, have been made in preparation for the question from the activity above.

To set the scene, Blanche Dubois, a complex woman with much to hide, is staying with her sister Stella and Stella's husband Stanley in New Orleans. Their life is very different from the unrealistic expectations she carries from her girlhood as a 'Southern Belle'. Here, she and Stella return from an evening out to find Stanley playing poker with his friends.

A Streetcar Named Desire

Scene 3
The Poker Night

(There is a picture of Van Gogh's of a billiard-parlour at night. The kitchen now suggests that sort of lurid nocturnal brilliance, the raw colours of childhood's spectrum. Over the yellow linoleum of the kitchen table hangs an electric bulb with a vivid green glass shade. The poker players – **Stanley, Steve, Mitch,** *and* **Pablo** *– wear coloured shirts, solid blues, a purple, a red-and-white check, a light green, and they are men at the peak of their physical manhood, as coarse and direct and powerful as the primary colours. There are vivid slices of watermelon on the table, whisky bottles, and glasses. The bedroom is relatively dim with only the light that spills between the portières and through the wide window on the street. The sisters appear around the corner of the building.)* ...

Colours bold, bright, simple, modern

'Raw' suggests uncultivated

(Brilliant light where the men are)

Colour of watermelon could suggest raw flesh

(Where the women will be is 'dim': only light from outside)

Stella: The game is still going on.

Blanche: How do I look?

Stella: Lovely, Blanche.

Blanche concerned with her appearance. Stella gives the answers she needs to hear

Blanche: I feel so hot and frazzled. Wait till I powder before you open the door. Do I look done in?

Stella: Why no. You are as fresh as a daisy.

(**Stella** *opens the door and they enter.*)

Stella: Well, well, well. I see you boys are still at it!

Stanley: Where you been?

Stella: Blanche and I took in a show. Blanche, this is Mr Gonzales and Mr Hubbel.

Blanche: Please don't get up. *Old-fashioned – she expects courtesy*

Stanley: Nobody's going to get up, so don't be worried. *She doesn't get it!*

Stella: How much longer is this game going to continue? *Stan takes no account of Stella's wishes. His responses to both women are abrupt, rude.*

Stanley: Till we get ready to quit.

Blanche: Poker is so fascinating. Could I kibitz? = *Look over someone's shoulder and sit in on their hand of cards*

Trying to get 'in' with the men

Stanley: You could not. Why don't you women go up and sit with Eunice?

Stella: Because it is nearly two-thirty. *Derogatory tone*

Stan will have none of it

He wants them out of the way – poker is a man's world. Women excluded

(**Blanche** *crosses into the bedroom and partially closes the portières.*)

Stella: Couldn't you call it quits after one more hand?

Stella trying to be reasonable

'loud whack' – Stanley is solid, boisterousness

(*A chair scrapes.* **Stanley** *gives a loud whack of his hand on* **Stella's** *thigh.*)

Chauvinistic reaction – treats Stella roughly, disrespectfully, as his possession

Stella: (*Sharply*) That's not fun, Stanley.

(*The men laugh.* **Stella** *goes into the bedroom.*)

She dislikes this; at least she expresses her anger – but she gets no support – the men think her annoyance is funny. All she can do is walk out

Tennessee Williams

Colour coding

One additional useful way of annotating, which keeps your text fairly uncluttered but helps you to find the parts that you want quickly, especially in a longer text, is to use a system of colour-coding. Using this system you can underline or sideline references relating to different themes, topics, characters, and so on in different colours. As long as you know what the colour signifies and you do not overdo it, it can really help you to find your way around the text quickly. This is useful whether you are preparing for an essay or revising for an examination.

Listing key points

Quickly make a list of 4 to 6 points which you would need to cover in order to answer the different aspects of the question posed on page 173. Try to arrange them in a logical order, so that you can move easily from one to another as you write. Often, it is best to begin with the most general point, and then move on to more specific ones. If you are answering an examination question, 4 to 6 points should be sufficient. (If you are writing a larger-scale essay for coursework, you will probably need a longer list.)

Taking our question on *A Streetcar Named Desire*, here is a possible list of topics, jotted down quickly.

> **MEN:** dominant, forceful, violent
>
> **POKER:** a man's world – women excluded
>
> **WOMEN:** feminine – much less powerful
>
> **BLANCHE:** nervous, flirtatious
>
> **SETTING:** men – 'lurid' kitchen; women – 'dim' bedroom
>
> **COLOURS:** men – bold; women – white, delicate

An answer which included a paragraph on each of these would cover the main points appropriate to the essay question.

Using diagrams

Try writing your key words or topic headings in the middle of a blank sheet of paper. Write phrases for related ideas around them, working outwards towards more detailed points, as shown in the spider diagram below. Link the words in as many ways as possible and circle or highlight ideas of most importance. Some people who use these say that you can begin your essay with any point on your diagram and find a way to work through all your ideas. Others prefer to start from one of the topic headings, for example, 'Men' or 'Women' in this case.

A Streetcar Named Desire: Scene 3

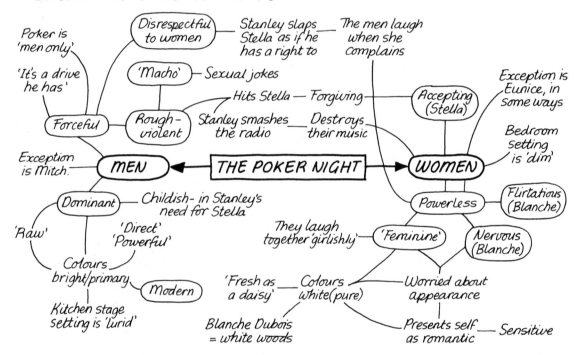

Charting information

Devise your own ways of arranging information in diagram form. For example, family trees can help sort out complex relationships, or you could use a graph to plot the ups and downs of a character's life.

If the essay question asks you to consider two 'sides' argumentatively, or involves a comparison, listing the opposing ideas like this in a table can help.

Male characters	Female characters
Dominant; powerful.	Powerless; can't change the men.
Rough, violent, macho.	'Feminine'; Blanche presents an image of herself as sensitive and well-bred.
Disrespectful to women; see them as objects, don't take them seriously and are amused when they are annoyed.	Blanche flirtatious with men; Stella accepts violence as 'normal' and continues to love Stanley; strong sexual bond holds them together.

Arranging ideas on cards

Write important points and related quotations, or notes for the individual paragraphs you want to include on cards. You can then arrange these, like jigsaw pieces, in different ways until you work out the best order in which to write about them. An example, taking characters from *A Streetcar Named Desire* is shown below.

Blanche – wants to appear respectable, thoughtful, sensitive to Mitch.

'I can't stand a naked light bulb, any more than a rude remark or a vulgar action.'

'I am not accustomed to having more than one drink.'

Uses sentimental, clichéd expressions – 'Sorrow makes for sincerity, I think.'

to tease Mitch about other – embarrass him.

...ck and we'll fix you
...tit.'

...is spineless, mean, not mother's boy.

...get ants when they win.'
...when he goes home he'll deposit them one by one in a piggy bank his mother give him.'

This technique is not suitable for examination situations! It is most useful when you are working on a long text and need to collect notes and examples on a theme or character as you read. An alternative is to use a reading log for each text you study, as suggested in Unit 2, page 9.

Finding your own strategies

Activity

> Having seen the various planning strategies in action in this unit, try out at least three using an extract from one of your set texts.
>
> As you work on each technique decide how successful it is for you and which methods you find most fruitful in your interpretation of the text.

We do need to remember, however, that sometimes the process of writing is in itself an exploration. At times we need to throw away all our plans and plunge into the writing before we can find out exactly what our ideas are; some arguments and ideas only take shape when we have worked through them in writing. Some writers always work this way and are not comfortable with planning in advance.

The most important thing is that you discover planning strategies that work for you, and use them so that they become a natural part of your writing process. Then you will have a familiar starting point when faced with the pressure of exam conditions. (For more on planning exam essays see Unit 15, pages 313–315.)

8 Formulating Views in Writing

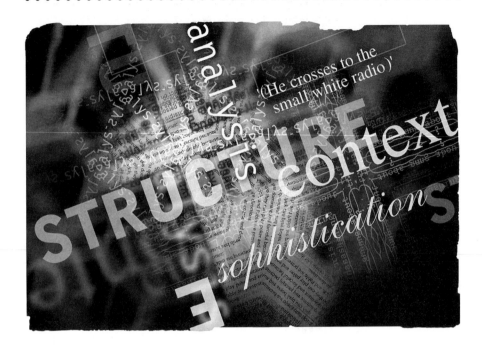

Objectives

- To consider the features of clear structure in literary essays
- To use a student's written response as a model for learning
- To study the effective use of quotation in essays

Writing a considered essay

Another moment from Willy Russell's *Educating Rita*, will get us thinking about what is meant by a considered essay.

Frank: In response to the question, 'Suggest how you would resolve the staging difficulties inherent in a production of Ibsen's *Peer Gynt*, you have written, quote, 'Do it on the radio', unquote.

Rita: Precisely.

Frank: Well?

Rita: Well what?

Frank: Well I know it's probably quite naïve of me but I did think you might let me have a considered essay.

Rita's answer is not wrong, but as Frank tells her, she has not yet learned the rules she needs to follow in order to write a 'considered essay'.

Activity | Your understanding of essay writing will be far more sophisticated than Rita's is at this stage! Working in a small group, create an advice sheet for her about the dos and don'ts of writing literary criticism.

Using evidence from the text effectively

Once you have done some thinking and planning for the question you will be writing about, you will have established the main points that you want to convey in your essay, and perhaps even feel you have an 'answer', as Rita does. However, as you write, it is essential that you provide some good reasons and evidence to support what you say. Evidence in this sense means examples and quotations from the text. It is not very useful, for example, to write that a poet 'uses a great deal of alliteration' in a poem. That would be to make an assertion without giving any grounds for it. All it would demonstrate is that you can recognize alliteration and that you know the technical term for it. You need to follow this statement with some quotations from the poem which contain alliteration. From there you will need to go on and analyse the quotation and comment on the effect created by the alliteration.

So, broadly speaking, the process of literary comment has three stages.
1 State the point you wish to make.
2 Follow this with your quotation, making sure the context of the quotation is clear, by briefly explaining the situation, or who is speaking and to whom. Quotations should be presented in speech marks or clearly differentiated from the rest of your writing.
3 Analyse the quotation in detail, commenting on individual words or phrases and explaining how and why they are used and with what effect.

For example, *The Laboratory* by Robert Browning is a poem, in the form of a monologue, spoken by a jealous woman who plans to murder the woman who is her rival. At the time she speaks she is in the laboratory of an alchemist who is mixing some arsenic for her to use, and her words are addressed to him. (Apparently this situation was not that uncommon in Renaissance France and Italy!)

1 In stanza three, as the alchemist works on preparing the poison, she comments on his actions, and seems to be enjoying the process. Her words include some alliteration which heightens this effect:
2 'Grind away, moisten and mash up thy paste,
    Pound at thy powder – I am not in haste.'
3 The repeated 'm' sounds of 'moisten' and 'mash' suggest her almost chewing these words with relish, while the 'p' sounds not only suggest the actual sound of the pestle and mortar, but, because of their explosive quality, express her spiteful pleasure at the thought of her rival's death.

Of course, you will not want to keep rigidly to this three-stage process of Statement, Quotation, Analysis; that would produce rather mechanical essays. However, it is useful to bear it in mind until it becomes integrated into your writing.

These are two of the most common difficulties that students have with essay-writing.

- **Context:** not providing enough information to make sense of quotations, i.e. sprinkling quotations in essays without providing crucial details about the situation. However do not fall into the trap of spending all your time paraphrasing the text. It is a fine balance to achieve.
- **Analysis:** students usually find this third stage of the process the most challenging. However, its importance is shown in the A-level marking criteria where it is the ability to be analytical to a high degree that gains candidates higher grades.

In any case, you will no doubt find your study of literature more rewarding when you know how to recognize and comment on the important details of how writers use language. It will also help you to become more aware of the language choices you make when you are writing.

Structuring an essay

There is no one structure that will work for every essay. Each question will demand a slightly different approach as the following guidelines, using a basic framework, illustrate.

1 Introduction
Briefly outline the subject of the essay; it can be useful to refer to the question and its key words and ideas.

Sometimes in coursework it can be useful to give a very concise introduction to the text(s) you are writing about. This might include one or two sentences to establish the context of the question, for example, in terms of plot or character. It is vital that you do not tell the story at length. All your time and effort should be devoted to answering the question.

2 Main section
This could take several different forms, depending on the type of question that you are answering.
- If the question has several key words or ideas, or asks you to explore more than one aspect of the text, you may be able to see a ready-made structure for the main part of your essay.
- If you have already thought about the question and made a plan, in one of the ways suggested in Unit 7 (pages 172–178), you can then set about working through the topics in your list or diagram, presenting them in an order which allows you to move easily from one to another.
- If the question requires you to consider two sides of an argument before concluding with your own views, you can organize your writing in one of two ways:

Present all the arguments on one side first, making sure you always support your ideas with evidence. Then repeat the process for the other side of the argument.

or

Make a table showing the arguments on each side of the question, then work through them 'zig-zag' fashion, presenting an argument from one side followed by one from the other side, and so on until you have covered all the points you wish to make. This may seem harder to do, but can often have more impact.

3 Conclusion

Once you have explored all the ideas or arguments you want to mention, finish by explaining the conclusion you have reached and/or briefly summing up the most important points you have made. Sometimes it is useful to restate the key words and ideas from the question in your conclusion. Try to express your conclusion clearly. An otherwise good essay can be marred by a weak ending, and you want to leave your reader with a good impression!

Adding more sophistication

The above essay structure is quite straightforward. You will often find, however, that in following a line of argument, it is necessary to explore a side issue or a related topic before returning to your central theme. It is vital that you can do this without becoming sidetracked and never returning to the main path, or jumping jarringly from one idea to another.

Let us look again at the question on *A Streetcar Named Desire* which featured in Unit 7:

Write as fully as you can about Scene 3 *The Poker Night*, focusing on the way the male and female characters are presented.

We know from the planning activities that the central theme for discussion is the contrast between the male characters – presented as dominant, hard, and forceful – and the female characters – portrayed as gentler and less powerful. Yet, in the course of the essay, we are likely to explore several side issues, some of which will contribute to the main argument while others offer exceptions to it or alternative views. It is important to find ways of incorporating these while maintaining a strong sense of direction and flow in the writing. Using connecting devices like the ones shown in the following examples can help achieve this successfully.

A

One aspect of Williams' presentation in the scene, which contributes to our sense that the men are more powerful than the women, is the way in which he uses colours ...
[... discussion of the use of colour and its effect ...]
Having examined the use of colours in the scene, we can see that it reinforces the impression that the men are dominant here.

B

The relative powerlessness of the female characters is demonstrated by the fact that neither Blanche nor Stella commands any respect from the poker players.

However, the two women are different in the ways in which they respond to the men ...

[... comparison of the behaviour of Blanche and Stella ...]

Although the female characters differ in the ways they react to the situation, they are presented in general as less forceful than the male characters.

C

Although we have seen that for the most part the men are harder and more forceful than the women, there are some exceptions ...

[... First ... discussion of Mitch's character ...

Second ... examine how Stanley becomes like a pathetic small boy in his need for Stella once she has left ...

Third ... example of Eunice shouting roughly and angrily ...]

There are, therefore, some occasions when male characters seem weaker. On the whole, however, they are presented as powerful.

In each of these examples the writer moves temporarily away from the central line of argument to discuss a side issue, but each time returns to the central question, pointing out how the side issue relates to it. This leaves the writer back on track, ready either to continue the main argument or to explore another 'by way'.

If you are tackling an unseen text for practical criticism, these structures may still be useful. We will look in more detail at ways of organizing your ideas for close reading in Unit 10, pages 193–195.

Activity

> With a partner, look at how one student answers the question on Scene 3 *The Poker Night*. As you read, take note of the annotations given and discuss how this student has structured his work.

Write as fully as you can about *Scene 3 The Poker Night*, focusing on the way the male and female characters are presented.

A fair introductory paragraph which refers to the question and leads into his discussion of the characters

It has been said that Scene 3, which is the poker scene, actually represents the whole play and acts as a miniature version of the play. *The Poker Night* is an important scene because it shows how the male and female characters are presented by Tennessee Williams.

An interesting point in this opening sentence which could do with more explanation

The male characters as a group are presented as dominant and forceful because they have ordered the women out for the night so they can play poker and enjoy themselves. The group of men, Stanley, Steve, Mitch, and Pablo are presented as strong, powerful, and coarse. This is said in the stage directions:

'They are men at the peak of their physical manhood, as coarse and direct as the primary colours.'

'The primary colours' are the colours of the shirts the men are wearing. The colours are 'solid blues, a purple, a red-and-white check, a light green'. Also from these colours and the shirts being worn these are modern men unlike the type Stella and Blanche would have been used to in their past.

The group of men are seen as brutes of men as they sit around the poker table. Here the men start to 'argue hotly':

'I didn't hear you name it.'

'Didn't I name it, Mitch?'

Several good points about the men as a group, including some discussion of the significance of the colours they wear. Next Ian focuses on individual male characters, which makes good sense

The group of men argue over a simple game of cards. This is almost like a children's squabble.

Stanley is the prime example of a forceful modern man in a world where Stella and Blanche must do as he says. He is the most dominating male character in the group of four. Here, Stella comes in and complains to Stanley about the time they are still playing poker at. Stanley shows he isn't respectful of Stella's wishes.

'A chair scrapes. Stanley gives a loud whack of his hand on her thigh.'

Structure works quite well here. Ian conveys a sense of how the men behave as a group and also draws a contrast between them

Stanley shows his masculinity and authority over Stella by slapping her thigh in a manly way. Stanley is showing off around his friends, proving how much of a man he is. Stanley again shows his dominance over the females when he demands Blanche turns the radio off and when she doesn't do so on his word he becomes fierce.

'Stanley stalks fiercely through the portières into the bedroom. He crosses to the small white radio and snatches it off the table. With a shouted oath, he tosses the instrument out of the window.'

Even the way Stanley approaches the radio before he acts presents him in a fierce and forceful light. The words 'stalks', as if he was a primitive caveman stalking his prey, and 'fiercely', which is his anger, show how Stanley is going to act before he acts. Stanley acts more

He uses appropriate quotations and attempts more detailed analysis in places (for example, where he comments on the significance of individual words such as 'stalks')

like a modern barbarian around women than a modern gentleman.

Mitch is the only exception to the group. Mitch is sympathetic and much more considerate to what Blanche and Stella want than Stanley. Mitch shows he is more gentle in these stage directions:

'..coughing a little shyly. He realizes he still has the towel in his hands and with an embarrassed laugh hands it to Stella.'

This is the first time we see Mitch around females and he shows he is different to the other men around him by the way he embarrassedly laughs at his little mistake. This shows a kinder and gentler side to the male populace and is a contrast to Stanley's hard, rough and ready nature. Mitch is presented as a fine character who is more suitable to Blanche and Stella and is more like the men they once knew. Here Blanche waltzes to the music with romantic gestures to Mitch.

'Mitch is delighted and moves in awkward imitation like a dancing bear.'

The point here is although Mitch didn't know how to waltz he gladly made a fool of himself dancing strangely just to please Blanche. Stanley, from what we know of him, would have laughed and walked away.

The female characters are quite similar in the way they are presented. Stella is presented as strong by the way she stands up to Stanley over the card game:

'Drunk – drunk – animal thing you! All of you – please go home! If any of you have one spark of decency in you ...'

Stella confronts the group of males playing poker and challenges them. Also, Stella is shown as wanting to be treated with respect. Stanley slaps Stella's thigh and she reacts sharply and then tells Blanche:

'It makes me so mad when he does that in front of people.'

Stella is showing how she wants to look as if she is respected in front of people.

Quotations usually introduced quite neatly, providing enough information to place them in context but Ian fails to do this when he quotes Mitch's moment of embarrassment. To make the situation fully clear to the reader, he needs to say: '...in these stage directions when he comes out of the bathroom and has to pass the women, who are in the bedroom...'

Ian also slightly misreads Mitch's character here, not picking up that, although he is relatively gentle, he is also rather naïve and undignified in the way he responds to Blanche's flirtation

This section is less successful: the first sentence is ambiguous. Does he mean that the women are similar to each other, or to the men? He needs to round off his discussion of the men and then lead into his discussion of the women, like this: 'Although Mitch seems different from Stanley and the others, on the whole the men are strong and rough and form a powerful group. On the other hand, the women, although different from each other, seem much less forceful...'

Stella may be presented as strong and brave and trying to gain respect, but she is also weak when it comes down to what Stanley wants. After Stanley hits her and she and Blanche go up to Eunice's, when Stanley stands downstairs crying, she gives in and goes to Stanley, showing she needs him no matter what he's done.

Ian's essay continues with a discussion of Blanche's character and actions and concludes like this...

Blanche shows or presents another image of the female which is provocative, flirty and deceitful ...

This is rather disappointing. The essay just stops, without a conclusion to draw the ideas together. The mention of the previous scene is a red herring – not relevant to the question here

...Blanche is easily older than Stella and has blatantly lied about her age so that Mitch will become more interested in her. Blanche always tries to present herself in a better light:

'I can't stand a naked light bulb, any more than I can a rude remark or a vulgar action.'

Blanche is trying to sound much more refined than she actually is. She is being provocative and flirtatious, exactly as she was in the previous scene when she was alone with Stanley.

Ian

Ian has not really made use of opportunities to analyse details in his later paragraphs. For example, Blanche's statement that she 'can't stand a naked light bulb' deserves much more attention. As Ian has pointed out, she is deceitful. The naked light bulb would reveal too much literally – she lies about her age – and metaphorically – it also represents the fact that she has a lot more to hide

Activity

> 1 Swap answers to a recent essay with a partner. Assess the structure of your partner's essay. Annotate it to show where the structure is clear and informative and where it could be improved. (Use the notes around Ian's essay as models for your own.)
> 2 Hand back the annotated essay and discuss your comments on it with your partner.

9 Getting Tone and Style Right

Objectives
- To develop personal writing style
- To implement formal and objective elements of style
- To look at style in literary criticism

Being 'objective'

Until you are familiar with the conventions for writing literary criticism, it may be difficult to grasp exactly what kind of tone or style is appropriate. One way to approach this is to read some good critical writing to get the 'feel' of it. Collections of critical writing which contain essays and reviews relating to a particular author or to specific texts can be useful in this respect. These often illustrate widely differing points of view and so serve as good reminders that there is rarely only one way to interpret a text. As well as introducing you to some different ways of thinking about the texts you are studying, they will help you to develop your awareness of the accepted language of criticism.

Some of these points are brought out in this extract from *Educating Rita*.

Educating Rita

Frank: Now the piece you wrote for me on – what was it called ...?
Rita: *Rubyfruit Jungle.*
Frank: Yes, it was – erm ...

Rita: Crap?

Frank: No. Erm – the thing is, it was an appreciation, a descriptive piece. What you have to learn is criticism.

Rita: What's the difference?

Frank: Well. You must try to remember that criticism is purely objective. It should be approached almost as a science. It must be supported by reference to established literary critique. Criticism is never subjective and should not be confused with partisan interpretation. In criticism sentiment has no place. (*He picks up the copy of* Howards End) Tell me, what did you think of *Howards End?*

Rita: It was crap.

Frank: What?

Rita: I thought it was crap!

Frank: Crap? And who are you citing in support of your thesis, F. R. Leavis?

Rita: No. Me!

Frank: What have I just said? 'Me' is subjective.

Rita: Well it's what I think.

Willy Russell

Perhaps Frank's assertion that literary criticism is 'purely objective' and like a science, is going too far. In studying A-level Literature there should be opportunities for you to express your own responses to texts as well as writing objectively about them. However, the more objective approach always needs to form the backbone of your critical writing, and when you do express your opinions or feelings about the effectiveness of a piece of writing, you still need to support them with reasoned evidence. Usually this evidence will take the form of quotations from the text, as was shown in Unit 8. Beware of writing statements like 'The imagery in stanza 2 is extremely evocative and effective.' or 'I found this chapter very moving.' – and leaving it at that. You need to provide specific examples or quotations and explain how the lines are effective and why.

In the extract, Frank also suggests that Rita should make 'reference to established literary critique'. In other words, she should refer to the views held by well-known academics who have already written about the text. A word of warning here. Reading the work of experienced literary critics can be useful in developing your awareness of style and also in introducing you to some different ways of approaching your text. However, it is very important that you do not write about other critics' ideas at the expense of expressing your own ideas about the text.

Examiners will always look for well-supported ideas and interpretations that you have worked out for yourself. They may also look for your understanding of other people's readings of the text, particularly if you are writing about a text in terms of its historical or critical context (see Unit 12). However, when you include the views of other critics, these need to be presented as quotations and acknowledged. Otherwise you run the risk of plagiarizing: 'borrowing', or even stealing, someone else's ideas and presenting them as your own. For more on other critical views see Unit 12, page 245.

Here is a sample of critical writing to give a sense of an appropriate tone and style and to demonstrate the use and analysis of quotations. It is an extract from an essay on Tennessee Williams' *A Streetcar Named Desire* by an American scholar, Felicia Hardison Londre in which she comments on the scene used as an example in Units 7 and 8.

On 'The Poker Night'

Scene 3 stands out from the others in several ways. It has its own title, 'The Poker Night.' Its pictorial atmosphere of 'lurid nocturnal brilliance, the raw colors of childhood's spectrum' is inspired by a picture of Van Gogh's of a billiard parlour at night, which Henry I. Schvey has identified as *All Night Cafe* (1888). It is one of few ensemble scenes in a play composed largely of two- or three-character sequences. And most importantly, it is the scene in which Blanche and Stanley truly begin to see each other as a threat. The opening line, spoken by one of the men at the card table, serves as a pointer: 'Anything wild in this deal?'
Stanley has been losing at cards and displays a volatile irritability even before Stella and Blanche come in. Mitch sets himself apart from the other card-players by his anxiety over his sick mother. The association with sickness and the dread of loneliness in his comment that 'I'll be alone when she goes' convey a subtle thematic linkage with Blanche, to whom he is introduced by Stella. Blanche quickly senses that Mitch is a prospective conquest. When she changes out of her dress, she deliberately stands in the light so the men can see her through the portieres. When Stella exits into the bathroom, Blanche turns on the radio and sits in a chair ... as if confident of her power to attract Mitch to her. First, however, it is Stanley who crosses to the bedroom and turns off the radio, but 'stops short at the sight of Blanche in the chair. She returns his look without flinching', and he returns to the poker table. Thus with great economy of means, by a simple dramatic gesture, Williams demonstrates the staking out of territory.
Mitch soon leaves the card game to chat with Blanche. He shows her the inscription on his silver cigarette case, given to him by a girl who knew she was dying. Blanche homes in on his vulnerabilities: 'Sick people have such deep, sincere attachments.' She asks him to cover the light bulb with a paper lantern she bought on Bourbon Street: 'I can't stand a naked light bulb, any more than I can a rude remark or a vulgar action.' Her equation of the naked bulb with vulgarity implies its opposite: the soft glow of filtered light as the refined sensibility by which she identifies herself. It recalls her comment to Stanley in Scene 2: 'I know I fib a good deal. After all, a woman's charm is fifty per cent illusion ...' Blanche's desire for illusion in opposition to the harsh realities that surround her is probably the play's most obvious thematic value. It is significant that Mitch is the one who both installs the paper lantern and, in Scene 9, removes it, for these actions define the period during which he sees Blanche as she wants him to see her, under the spell of an illusion she creates ... Blanche ... is an artist who dramatizes herself as if she were a stage character, playing roles detached from the reality of her situation, costuming herself from the trunk containing fake furs and costume jewelry, designing the lighting effects that will show her to advantage. With Mitch as her enthralled audience, she adds musical underscoring: she turns on the radio and 'waltzes to the music with romantic gestures'.

The radio galvanizes Stanley into aggressive action, though the actual source of his action undoubtedly lies deeper. Here in his own home, where he is cock of the roost and host of the poker party, the intruder Blanche has lured both his wife and his best friend into her orbit. She has appropriated his radio for her kind of music. In a drunken rage, he throws the radio out of the window.

Felicia Hardison Londre

Formality of style

As well as saying that she should be more objective, Frank hints that Rita needs to develop a more formal style of writing before her essays will be acceptable (see page 188). This can be difficult to define, but there are some things to avoid.

Summary

• **The first person**   Generally, avoid *over-using* the first person in your responses. For example, rather than saying 'I think Louisa is imaginative because', try to use expressions like 'It appears that Louisa has a vivid imagination, because ...' or 'Louisa seems to be imaginative because ...' Having said that, the occasional use of 'I' or 'me' in a piece of critical commentary to reinforce an important point can be most effective.

• **Slang**   Avoid using slang expressions (unless, of course, they appear in quotations from your text!). Colloquial language is the language of informal speech. Try to develop your awareness of the differences between spoken English and written English.

• **Dialect and local usage**   Some words or expressions may be used only in some parts of the country; these are appropriate in some forms of writing, but in a formal essay Standard English is preferable. Try to develop your awareness of your local dialect and, if you can, substitute Standard English equivalents in your essays. This will also avoid confusions in meaning. For example, 'to get wrong' (North-east England) = 'to get into trouble' (Standard English).

• **Abbreviations**   It is better not to use abbreviated forms in formal writing. For example, write 'did not' rather than 'didn't'; and avoid using 'etc.'.

• **Numbers**   These should be written in word form, for example, 'thirty-seven' rather than '37', unless the figure is very large.

However, do use:

• **The present tense**   Most literary criticism is written in the present tense. This is because the text itself, whether a novel or a poem, always exists in the same way, even though the narrative may be in the past tense. Aim to keep your writing in the present tense. For example, 'The opening scenes of the play take place in ...' not '... took place in ...'. It is even more important to be consistent: whether you use present or past tense, make sure you use the same one throughout. There are many examples of critical responses written in the present tense throughout this book.

Activity

> Here is part of a draft student essay on 'The Poker Night' where the style needs quite a lot of attention. Redraft it, improving the style in as many ways as possible. Compare your version to that of another student in your group.

In the scene of the poker night the men and women were presented very differently. Stanley seems to me to be presented in a very macho style character. This is shown in the way that Stanley gets very drunk and this is seen to be the manly thing to do. Also the way he mocks Mitch about having to go home and see his Mam. Stanley says 'Hurry back and we'll fix you a sugar-tit'. He's also shown as a hard and nasty character when he hits Stella because she wants them to stop playing poker. This shows Stanley to be a harsh and hard character because he hits his wife because she asks them to stop playing poker.

Whereas in contrast with the other 3 men, Mitch is shown to be a very sensitive and understanding person. This is shown in the fact that he goes home early to see his Mam because she's ill. Mitch says, 'I gotta sick mother. She don't sleep until I come in at night. She says go out, so I do, but I don't enjoy it. I just keep wondering how she is.' I think this shows Mitch is sensitive and caring and thinks about his mother a lot.

Mitch also shows his sensitivity when after Stanley had hit Stella he said, 'This is terrible. Poker should not be played in a house with women.' This showed Mitch felt very sorry and awful about what had happened to Stella.

The craft in your writing

As your study of literature progresses, you will develop an awareness of the variety of ways in which writers use language. You may begin to think of writing as a 'craft', something which most writers think about and work at with great care and attention to detail, rather than something which simply happens rather haphazardly.

Try to think about your own writing in the same way.

- Make deliberate choices about the vocabulary you use, choosing the best word for the job, rather than the first one that comes to mind.
- Try out different lengths and types of sentences.
- Think about the different ideas you wish to include in your paragraphs.
- Try to weigh ideas against each other when you are writing argumentatively.

Some fortunate people – usually those who have read very widely – seem to have an innate sense of how to write appropriately for different purposes. Others only develop a sense of style with practice. The aim is to reach the point where you know you can communicate ideas clearly and that you are in complete control of your writing.

Activity

1 Reread some of your own recent essays. What are the strengths and weaknesses of your written style? Think about this carefully yourself and/or ask a teacher for feedback. Choose one weakness (for example, not putting quotations properly in context; changing tense; poor punctuation) and focus on correcting it in your next essay.

2 In a group of four, swap essays or other written work. Work in pairs to read and discuss a partner's work. Consider these points.
- Is it easy to read and understand?
- Has the question been answered?
- Are quotations used effectively?

Make a note of positive comments and advice about improvements before giving each other feedback.

10 Encountering Texts

Objectives

- To establish a strategy for approaching unprepared texts
- To practise close reading of poetry and prose texts
- To look closely at what makes a distinctive style

Close reading

Skills in close reading are essential for AS- and A-level Literature study. Whenever you encounter a literary text for the first time – whether it is a text you are reading for coursework, a set text, or a poem or extract you have been asked to analyse in an examination – all the habits and skills of close reading that you have learned will enable you to discover more for yourself about the text. 'Close reading' means exactly what it says. It is the art of reading closely, paying great attention to details of language, in order to come to the best possible understanding of texts and of how writers create meaning.

Developing your skills

The best way to develop your ability to read closely is to practise, by reading and analysing as wide a variety of texts as you possibly can. The more familiar you can become with a broad range of literary texts, the more you will be able to recognize the features of different types of writing and to see the similarities and differences between them.

In the course of your A-level studies you will probably be given opportunities to practise your close reading skills by working on a variety of short texts on a particular theme (see also Unit 13, Reading for Meaning) or by doing what used to be called 'practical criticism,' 'unseen criticism'. or 'critical commentary'. This means that you are presented with poems or short prose extracts you have not seen before, and asked to discuss them or to write about them, with only a short time to prepare your response. Altneratively, you may be presented with a selection of material in a 'pre-release anthology' and given some time to become familiar with it before tackling questions on it in an examination (again, see Unit 13 for more on this). These are good ways of developing abilities like the following, which you can apply to all aspects of your studies:

- to read and make sense of a text and recognize its most important features quickly – a kind of instant 'research' where you have to 'think on your feet'.
- to apply your own literary understanding rather than ideas you have read or been taught
- to know about 'how writers write', in terms of style and structure
- to organize your ideas in writing quickly

Approaching unprepared texts

There are some methods of planning your approach which can help you feel more confident about the close reading of unprepared texts. First, it is important not to be daunted by a poem or prose extract you are given to analyse. There will be good reasons why a particular piece has been set, and with close reading you will be able to discover them. Texts about which there is nothing to say are not usually chosen!

Once you have the text in front of you, it is helpful to have a strategy that will allow you to examine it in detail. Here is a suggested checklist of the things you need to consider as you read it. As this list suggests, it is a good idea to begin with an overview or general point, such as the theme of the text, and go on to look at the details. If a written response is required, it can be structured in this way too.

Summary

1 **Subject or theme**   What is the text about? (This may seem too obvious, but it is a good broad starting point.) What other information do you have, for example the writer's name or a date?

2 **Speaker and/or situation**   Whose 'voice' do you hear in the text? Is it in the third- person or the first-person? If it is first-person writing, is it the voice of the author, or are they taking on a role? In poems, in particular, writers sometimes write with the voice of an object (for example a mountain/the wind), an animal, or even a god, as well as with the voices of people or characters.

Next ascertain to whom the text is addressed, and the situation in which it is set. (For example, Thomas Hardy's poem *God-forgotten* is written from the point of view of a messenger sent from Earth to ask God to help the human race, only to discover He has forgotten He ever created the planet. The poem consists of the messenger's dialogue with God.)

3 Form   What is the overall structure of the piece? Is it in a recognizable poetic form? Are there any obvious ways in which it could be divided into sections, either by its layout, its meaning, or by changes in the way language is presented at different points?

4 Ideas and messages   Look for ideas which are embedded 'below the surface' of the text. Think about the author's aims and purposes. Are there any signs of irony or satire?

5 Tone and atmosphere   How would you describe the writer's 'tone of voice'? Is there an atmosphere or feeling which pervades the poem, such as sadness, gloom, or joy? If so, what is it about the writing that creates this effect? (For example, long sentences, with soft consonant sounds and repeated use of 'oo' and 'o' vowels, tend to create a sombre effect.)

6 Imagery   What kinds of visual images or 'word-pictures' does the text present? How does the writer use simile or metaphor? Comment both on individual examples and on patterns of images which you notice. Be careful to explain and analyse these examples in terms of their contribution to the overall meaning of the text.

7 Vocabulary   What do you notice about the individual words and phrases which the writer has chosen? Are there types of words which recur? (For example, there may be several words relating to death, or fire, or childhood.) Are there words which seem unexpected or out of place? What effect do they create?

8 Rhyme, rhythm, and sound effects   If the text is a poem, has it got a rhyme-scheme and what is its effect? (Beware of simply describing a rhyme-scheme without going on to say why you think the poet has chosen it and how far this aim is achieved.) Rhythm can be important in prose as well as in poetry. Are the lines/sentences flowing or short and jerky? Does the rhythm change at key points in the text? Other sound effects or aural images are created through the use of devices like alliteration. Remember to comment on the *effect* of these. If you cannot see any particular effect, it is better not to mention these features at all.

9 Conclusion   Finally, return to an overview of the text. Sum up how the effects and details of style you have analysed come together to create a 'whole' piece of writing. What has your reading of it contributed to your understanding of the subject that it deals with? Does it offer a way of looking at things which you had not considered before? If the question invites you to give a personal response to the text, this is the place for it.

Please note that this is *not* intended as a formula to be applied rigidly in every situation. Not every unseen text requires detailed analysis of every one of these points, but this checklist can act as a starting point and you can easily omit any aspects that are not relevant.

Poetry

Let us consider a poem using this close reading strategy.

Activity

> **1** Working alone or with a partner, read the question and *Swifts* carefully, making notes under each of the headings 1–9 given above. The poet Ted Hughes said that his aim in some of his poems was 'capturing animals' in words. How does he set about doing so in the following poem?
>
> **2** Then compare your notes with those that follow on from the poem. What are the main similarities and differences in interpretation? You will no doubt have noticed different effects and meanings.

Swifts

Fifteenth of May. Cherry blossom. The swifts
Materialize at the tip of a long scream
Of needle. 'Look! They're back! Look!' And they're gone
On a steep

Controlled scream of skid
Round the house-end and away under the cherries. Gone.
Suddenly flickering in sky summit, three or four together,
Gnat-whisp frail, and hover-searching, and listening

For air-chills – are they too early? With a bowing
Power-thrust to left, then to right, then a flicker they
Tilt into a slide, a tremble for balance,
Then a lashing down disappearance

Behind elms.
They've made it again,
Which means the globe's still working, the Creation's
Still waking refreshed, our summer's
Still all to come –
And here they are, here they are again
Erupting across yard stones
Schrapnel-scatter terror. Frog-gapers,
Speedway goggles, international mobsters –

A bolas of three or four wire screams
Jockeying across each other
On their switchback wheel of death.
They swat past, hard fletched,

Veer on the hard air, toss up over the roof,
And are gone again. Their mole-dark labouring,
Their lunatic limber scramming frenzy
And their whirling blades
Sparkle out into blue –

Not ours any more.
Rats ransacked their nests so now they shun us.
Round luckier houses now
They crowd their evening dirt-track meetings,

Racing their discords, screaming as if speed-burned,
Head-height, clipping the doorway
With their leaden velocity and their butterfly lightness,
Their too much power, their arrow-thwack into the eaves.

Every year a first-fling, nearly-flying
Misfit flopped in our yard,
Groggily somersaulting to get airborne.
He bat-crawled on his tiny useless feet, tangling his flails

Like a broken toy, and shrieking thinly
Till I tossed him up – then suddenly he flowed away under
His bowed shoulders of enormous swimming power,
Slid away along levels wobbling

On the fine wire they have reduced life to,
And crashed among the raspberries.
Then followed fiery hospital hours
In a kitchen. The moustached goblin savage

Nested in a scarf. The bright blank
Blind, like an angel, to my meat-crumbs and flies.
Then eyelids resting. Wasted clingers curled.
The inevitable balsa death.
Finally burial
For the husk
Of my little Apollo –

The charred scream
Folded in its huge power.

Ted Hughes

One interpretation

1 **Subject or theme**   As the title tells us, the poem is almost entirely devoted
   to describing and 'capturing' in writing the appearance, movements, and
   behaviour of the swifts. (Fast-moving, forked-tailed birds related to swallows
   and martens, they are summer visitors to Britain.)
2 **Speaker and/or situation**   The poem is written in the first person. There is
   no reason to question that the poet is writing in his own voice and that he
   is addressing the reader directly. Although his chief purpose is to convey
   the characteristics of the birds in words, there are also elements of a 'story'
   in the poem. Watching and describing the punctual arrival of the swifts in
   May, Hughes reacts with excitement:

'Look! They're back! Look!'

For him, they signal the beginning of summer. As he puts it:

'... our summer's
Still all to come –'

Placing 'Still all to come' on a separate line seems to convey his pleasure in anticipating the summer that lies ahead.

Later in the poem, Hughes reminisces about previous seasons and tells the story of how each year a young bird would fail to manage its first flight, be rescued and cared for, wrapped in a scarf and offered 'meat-crumbs and flies', only to die later and be buried.

3 **Form**   For the most part, four-line stanzas are used, but rather freely. Line lengths vary. Lines are quite frequently broken or interrupted, or run on to the next line, suggesting the fast, erratic flight of the birds.

4 **Ideas and messages**   This poem does not seem to carry a hidden message but it does hold some thought-provoking ideas. For Ted Hughes, the annual arrival of the swifts is a reminder that life goes in cycles; they are a signal that the seasons continue to change and spring and summer will follow winter.

'They've made it again,
Which means the globe's still working, the Creation's
Still waking refreshed ...'

The phrase 'Which means the globe's still working' contains a touch of humour, suggesting, perhaps, that he had begun to doubt whether summer would come again.

In his description of his vain attempts to keep the helpless small birds alive each year and his tone of resignation as they reach 'The inevitable balsa death', he may be reminding us that there is little point in trying to interfere with the inexorable course of nature. The rule of the survival of the fittest would ensure that the weak bird did not live long.

5 **Tone and atmosphere**   Most of the poem has a tone of excitement and haste. The swifts move with such speed that

'... they're gone
On a steep
Controlled scream of skid
Round the house-end and away under the cherries. Gone.'

almost before you have seen them. The way in which they dart in and out of sight is reflected in these short, broken lines. They give the poem an almost breathless quality, enforced by repetitions of '... gone' and '... here they are again ...'

The second half of the poem is slightly more subdued, but the feeling of great speed continues whenever Hughes focuses on the movements of the birds. Many lines run into each other without punctuation, adding to the effect of fast, perpetual motion.

6 **Imagery**   As you might expect in a poem whose main aim is descriptive, the use of imagery is particularly powerful here. Most noticeable is the repeated use of metaphors likening the birds to machines (a device typical

of Hughes). Many words and phrases suggest the flight of planes – fast fighter-planes in particular – or speedway driving. For example:

'On a steep
Controlled scream of skid'

and

'... With a bowing
Power-thrust to left, then to right, then a flicker they
Tilt into a slide ...'

would not be out of place in an account of an air display. Words like 'Power-thrust', 'Erupting', and 'Schrapnel-scatter terror' suggest something violent and frightening.

However, there is a contradictory quality to the swifts. As well as making them sound powerful and dangerous, Hughes also draws attention to their delicacy: they 'flicker' and 'tremble' and are 'Gnat-whisp frail'. He repeatedly uses paradox to contrast their speed, which seems blundering and uncontrolled, a 'lunatic, limber scramming frenzy', with their tiny size and grace which is very much under control. They have 'leaden velocity' and 'butterfly lightness'.

Another aspect which Hughes captures is the swifts' cry – a high-pitched screaming sound. Somehow he manages to combine their sound with their movement. It is as if the birds are faster than their sounds, which they leave trailing behind them like wires:

'A bolas of three or four wire screams'

When they come into view they:

'Materialize at the tip of a long scream
Of needle ...'

So conversely sometimes they are heard first and then seen. The word 'needle' conveys the sharp, piercing quality of their cry and their movement.

7 **Vocabulary**   In addition to these metaphors, there are other interesting choices of words. When Hughes describes the injured young bird, he emphasizes its mysterious, wild, and rather awe-inspiring qualities by referring to it as a 'moustached goblin savage' and as 'my little Apollo'. This suggests that he worships it like a little god. Apollo, the sun god, was one of the more powerful gods of Greek mythology; 'goblin' also suggests something supernatural, but rather mischievous too. Hughes refers to the bird's 'balsa death'. Balsa wood is very light and brittle, so this word encapsulates the feel of the bird's corpse, little more than feathers and bones.

8 **Rhyme, rhythm, and sound effects**   Formal rhyme does not feature in this poem. As we have noted, some lines and sentences run on fluently, while others are abrupt and broken. The rhythmic pattern emulates the darting movements of the swifts.

Hughes does also use some sound effects to contribute to his imagery. In particular, when he describes the young bird which fails to fly, it is a 'first-fling, nearly flying misfit' which 'flopped' in the yard. The alliterative repetition of the soft 'f', 'l' and 's' sounds creates an aural image which helps to suggest the bird's floundering as well as representing the fluttering sound of its wings.

9 Conclusion   To sum up, Hughes's main concern here is to 'capture' and convey as clearly as possible his impressions of the swifts. Through his use of metaphor and choice of words he gives an impression both of their incredible speed, power, and vivacity and of their tiny lightness of touch.

If you were to omit the headings from these notes and adapt them slightly, you would have a reasonable analysis of the poem in essay form. Of course, not every detail of the poem has been examined here; probably you noted other ideas or other examples of imagery that you would include in an answer. However, with a poem of this length, it is advisable to be selective in the details you choose to analyse.

Activity

> Working alone or with a partner, now look at the following student response to *Swifts* and compare it with your own notes and the ideas given above.
> • Which aspects of the poem has James covered thoroughly and which need more attention?
> • Has he supported his ideas by quoting details from the text?
> • Has he analysed details of the text closely? Can you find places where he needs to do more of this?
> • Is his written style clear and appropriate?

The poet Ted Hughes said that his aim in some of his poems was 'capturing animals' in words. How does he set about doing this in the following poem?

Ted Hughes begins the poem by describing the time and one aspect of the natural surroundings associated with that time when the birds return.
'Fifteenth of May. Cherry blossom.'
The poet also shows how excited he is to see the returning swifts. This is shown by the use of exclamation marks and the repetition of the word 'Look!' Almost immediately the poet goes on to discuss the speed of the swifts. He does this by saying that by the time a step has been taken the swifts are out of sight. This is a sign of the tone of the poem, the most striking feature is that of the way the poet describes the speed with which the swifts fly. The speed of the swifts is also shown by the poet by the way the different stanzas are written. The sentences are fragmented as they use exclamation marks, dashes, commas, and question marks. This gives the poem a sense of pace which is reflected by the way the swifts fly. The language the poet uses in the first stanza shows how the swifts use power and agility to fly. This is best described in the line
'Power-thrust to left, then to right, then a flicker they
Tilt into a slide'.
The swifts manage to use both power and agility to fly, which is something that man-made machines fail to achieve. A rocket has power but agility is reserved for machines such as gliders.
The poet also uses metaphors of nature to explain how the swifts arrived.
'They've made it again.
Which means the globe's still working'.

This gives the connotation that the arrival of the swifts signifies that nature will continue to develop as long as they arrive after their winter break.

In the next few stanzas sporting metaphors are used and this helps again to highlight the speed at which the swifts fly. Examples of these are 'Speedway goggles', 'Jockeying', and 'Veer on the hard air.' These are used because of the speed associated with them, speedway for fast motorbikes, jockeying as for jockeying for a position in a race, and veering hard as in some other form of motor sport. These all help to give a sense of realism to the reader who may be unfamiliar with the sight of a swift flying.

The poet feels saddened when they have gone. He tries to find something to blame. In this case it is the rats who have destroyed their nests. The poet seems jealous that the swifts have gone, this is shown in the line that says they are 'Round luckier houses now'.

This also shows the fondness which the poet has for the birds.

The next stanza best highlights the speed of the swifts. Again dashes are used in the sentence structure which adds to the sense of speed. The way the poet describes how the swifts are

'clipping the doorway'

shows that the birds are flying so quickly that there is hardly any margin for error. They try to take short-cuts to reach their destination quicker and this could prove fatal.

The final few stanzas show the youth of the swift and how frail and vulnerable they can be. This is in great contrast to the agility and power with which they are described early in the poem.

The poet describes how in the early days, swifts, like any other birds, find it hard to fly. He uses language which again is in contrast to the language used earlier. Words such as 'crawled', 'useless feet', and 'tangling' are in vast contrast with the sure and certain movements such as 'erupting' and veering. These also show the power the young swift has to come.

The poet also describes how he once found a swift that had 'crashed among the raspberries', he attempted to care for it in his kitchen but the bird died. The poet describes the death of the swift as

'The inevitable balsa death'.

This shows both the benefits and drawbacks of being, as balsa wood is when used for model planes, swift and light through the air but also frail.

The life the swifts lead is best described by

'the fine wire'.

This shows that they live on the edge risking their life by flying so quickly through the air.

James

Activity   Now try applying the same procedure to Hughes' poem, *Second Glance at a Jaguar* on page 202. Again, his main purpose is to 'capture' the characteristics of an animal in words. Make notes under each of the nine headings before writing a short critical essay to answer the same question that was asked on *Swifts*:

> The poet Ted Hughes said that his aim in some of his poems was 'capturing animals' in words. How does he set about doing so in the following poem?

Second Glance at a Jaguar

Skinful of bowls he bowls them
The hip going in and out of joint, dropping the spine
With the urgency of his hurry
Like a cat going along under thrown stones, under cover,
Glancing sideways, running
Under his spine. A terrible, stump-legged waddle
Like a thick Aztec disembusheller,
Club-swinging, trying to grind some square
Socket between his hind legs round,
Carrying his head like a brazier of spilling embers
And the black bit of his mouth, he takes it
Between his back teeth, he has to wear his skin out,
He swipes a lap at the water-trough as he turns,
Swivelling the ball of his heel on the polished spot,
Showing his belly like a butterfly.
At every stride he has to turn a corner
In himself and correct it. His head
Is like the worn down stump of another whole jaguar,
His body is just the engine shoving it forward,
Lifting the air up and shoving on under,
The weight of his fangs hanging the mouth open,
Bottom jaw combing the ground. A gorged look,
Gangster, club-tail lumped along behind gracelessly,
He's wearing himself to heavy ovals,
Muttering some mantrah, some drum-song of murder
To keep his rage brightening, making his skin
Intolerable, spurred by the rosettes, the Cain-brands,
Wearing the spots off from the inside,
Bounding some revenge. Going like a prayer-wheel,
The head dragging forward, the body keeping up,
The hind legs lagging. He coils, he flourishes
The blackjack tail as if looking for a target,
Hurrying through the underworld, soundless.

Ted Hughes

Prose extracts

The close reading strategy can also be applied to prose passages, although you may find you need to focus on different aspects of the texts. You will be examining many of the same literary techniques, such as imagery, choice of vocabulary, and rhythm, but these will probably be more 'dilute' in prose writings than in poetry. This may mean you need to concentrate even harder, when studying prose passages, noticing how the writer uses language as well as commenting on the ideas that are expressed.

For the most part, prose passages will be extracts from longer works rather than complete texts, although occasionally very short essays or short stories are set. The next piece we will look at is the opening of a novel, *The Crow Road*, by Iain Banks.

Activity

> First, read the following extract carefully. Working with a partner, make notes in preparation for answering this question.
> Write an assessment of the beginning of *The Crow Road* by Iain Banks, commenting on its effectiveness as the opening of a novel.

The Crow Road

It was the day my grandmother exploded. I sat in the crematorium, listening to my Uncle Hamish quietly snoring in harmony to Bach's Mass in B Minor, and I reflected that it always seemed to be death that drew me back to Gallanach. I looked at my father, sitting two rows away in the front line of seats in the cold, echoing chapel. His broad, greying-brown head was massive above his tweed jacket (a black arm-band was his concession to the solemnity of the occasion). His ears were moving in a slow oscillatory manner, rather in the way John Wayne's shoulders moved when he walked; my father was grinding his teeth. Probably he was annoyed that my grandmother had chosen religious music for her funeral ceremony. I didn't think she had done it to upset him; doubtless she had simply liked the tune, and had not anticipated the effect its non-secular nature might have on her eldest son.

My younger brother, James, sat to my father's left. It was the first time in years I'd seen him without his Walkman, and he looked distinctly uncomfortable, fiddling with his single earring. To my father's right my mother sat, upright and trim, neatly filling a black coat and sporting a dramatic black hat shaped like a flying saucer. The UFO dipped briefly to one side as she whispered something to my father. In that movement and that moment, I felt a pang of loss that did not entirely belong to my recently departed grandmother, yet was connected with her memory. How her moles would be itching today if she was somehow suddenly reborn!

'Prentice!' My Aunt Antonia, sitting next to me, with Uncle Hamish snoring mellifluously on her other side, tapped my sleeve and pointed at my feet as she murmured my name. I looked down.

I had dressed in black that morning, in the cold high room of my aunt and uncle's house. The floorboards had creaked and my breath had smoked. There had been ice inside the small dormer window, obscuring the view over Gallanach in a crystalline mist. I'd pulled on a pair of black underpants I'd brought especially from Glasgow, a white shirt (fresh from Marks and Sparks, the pack-lines still ridging the cold, crisp cotton) and my black 501s. I'd shivered, and sat on the bed, looking at two pairs of socks; one black, one white. I'd intended to wear the black pair under my nine-eye Docs with the twin ankle buckles, but suddenly I had felt that the boots were wrong. Maybe it was because they were matt finish ...

The last funeral I'd been to here – also the first funeral I'd ever been to – this gear had all seemed pretty appropriate, but now I was pondering the propriety of the Docs, the 501s, and the black biker's jacket. I'd hauled my white trainers out of the bag, tried one Nike on and one boot (unlaced); I'd stood in front of the tilted full-length mirror, shivering, my breath going out in clouds, while the floorboards creaked and a smell of cooking bacon and burned toast insinuated its way up from the kitchen.

The trainers, I'd decided.

So I peered down at them in the crematorium; they looked crumpled and tea-stained on the severe black granite of the chapel floor. Oh-oh; one black sock, one white. I wriggled in my seat, pulled my jeans down to cover my oddly-packaged ankles. 'Hell's teeth,' I whispered. 'Sorry, Aunt Tone.'

My Aunt Antonia – a ball of pink-rinse hair above the bulk of her black coat, like candy floss stuck upon a hearse – patted my leather jacket. 'Never mind, dear,' she sighed. 'I doubt old Margot would have minded.'

'No,' I nodded. My gaze fell back to the trainers. It struck me that on the toe of the right one there was still discernible the tyre mark from Grandma Margot's wheelchair. I lifted the left trainer onto the right, and rubbed without enthusiasm at the black herring-bone pattern the oily wheel had left. I remembered the day, six months earlier, when I had pushed old Margot out of the house and through the courtyard, past the outhouses and down the drive under the trees towards the loch and the sea.

Iain Banks

Activity | Read this student's response to the question and then study the comments on its strengths and weaknesses which follow.

Write an assessment of the beginning of *The Crow Road*, by Iain Banks, commenting on its effectiveness as the opening of a novel.

The extract from the novel, 'The Crow Road' by Iain Banks is rather unusual. The passage describes his family at his grandmother's cremation in his home town of Gallanach. The piece is unusual as it is written in a jovial style which is not often connected with death except in Black comedy. However, this is not a comedy so is unusual. The opening sentence, 'It was the day my grandmother exploded.' is so surprising when put in context with the rest of the passage.

The narrator does not dwell on the grief of losing a member of his family, but more so on his isolation from his parents. In a movement his mother makes to his father he feels 'a pang of loss that did not entirely belong to my recently departed grandmother'.

The fact he has had to stay at his aunt and uncle's house and is sitting with them shows his isolation from his parents. The narrator does not seem to 'fit in' with the rest of his family. His clothes are different and his whole attitude towards the funeral is distracted.

This distraction of the narrator is shown in his digressions from the funeral. How he notices his father's ears move, as he grinds his teeth, like 'John Wayne's shoulders when he walks'. He notices his brother James is not wearing his Walkman for the first time in years and that his mother's dramatic hat is shaped like a UFO. There do not seem to be many emotions shown by the narrator, nor any of the other characters. He remarks how his father is probably angry his grandmother had chosen religious music for her funeral ceremony instead of secular, as he would have wanted. His Uncle Hamish has fallen asleep and is snoring 'In harmony to Bach's Mass in B Minor'; he is obviously oblivious or uncaring of the situation around him.

The narrator tries to create a cold atmosphere, one traditionally associated with death. They are sitting in the cold 'echoing chapel' which emulates a feeling of emptiness and loss. The cold temperature of his bedroom, however, which the author embellishes upon, seems to be more related to his isolation from his family. The fact he is not in his parents' home shows how they have excluded him from their lives. Also that they do not sit with him at the chapel. The atmosphere is not maintained as the author makes comical asides which are more light-hearted, for example the references to John Wayne and the UFO and the fact his boots didn't look right because they had a matt finish. Also, how he has odd socks on and his description of his Aunt Antonia being like 'candy floss stuck upon a hearse'.

From this passage, the narrator shows himself to be a young man who has moved away from his home town, possibly without his parents' blessing as they have become disassociated. The narrator shows that he did love his grandmother Margot as he describes a fond memory of her at the end of the passage, yet shows no real signs of grief.

This passage is quite effective as the opening of a novel as it makes me want to read on. It provides details of what are, presumably, the main characters (his family) and it would be interesting to find out what happens next. His jovial style is easy to read and understand, it being quite light-hearted.

Julia

Comments on the strengths and weaknesses of Julia's response

Julia provides a clear introductory paragraph, giving enough information to put the passage in context without wasting time on paraphrasing. She could say more to make it clear that the narrator is a fictional character.

She describes the style as 'jovial'. This may be a good way to describe it, but she will need to clarify what she means by explaining fully later in the essay. The reference to black comedy is very useful. Again she needs to pick out examples of this later, even though she has stated that the passage as a whole is not comedy.

She comments on the surprising first sentence in relation to the rest of the passage. A fuller analysis would improve this. For example, she could point out the strangely matter-of-fact tone of the sentence and the shocking effect of the word 'exploded' when applied to a 'grandmother'!

Julia's point in paragraph 3 about the narrator seeming isolated from his parents is a good one. We have to be careful, though, not to speculate too far. From this extract, we do not know that the whole family were not staying with the aunt and uncle! It's best to keep to points for which you can find evidence in the passage. However, within the extract, there is a sense of his distance from his parents.

Julia has pointed out that his clothes are different, but could expand on this. What do the details of his clothes tell us about him? They could suggest an image or stereotype: 'Nine-eye Docs, 501s and the black biker's jacket'?

She makes a good point about the narrator's 'digressions' in paragraph 4, giving examples of how his attention wanders to dwell on the people around him. Again, she could comment more analytically about these, on what they tell us about the members of his family and also, through his choice of words, about himself. For example, the similes he uses, referring to John Wayne and UFOs, suggest the popular culture of film stars and science fiction, which contrasts with the sombre music his grandmother has chosen. It seems that his brother, too, with his earring, but without his Walkman, has made concessions for the occasion.

In paragraph 5, Julia's remarks on atmosphere are apt, the quotation is helpful, and she has added some further comment. She could also go on to say something about the use of colour in the passage. Repeated 'black' and 'white' are appropriate for cold and death. Having mentioned the aunt's pink hair, she could go on to explain why this is humorous: its inappropriateness among all the black, which is captured by the candy-floss/hearse image.

The penultimate paragraph is disappointing. Julia is rather too concerned with inventing theories about the young man's background at the expense of paying close attention to the details that are provided.

This highlights a broader point. If you are familiar with the whole text from which the extract has been set, this will have advantages and disadvantages. You will be able to relate key points from the extract to your wider knowledge of the text, but will need to make it clear that you have read the full text. However, you will need to beware of your wider knowledge distracting you from focusing on and making deductions from the details of the passage itself. Julia does begin to explore the narrator's reference to his grandmother at the end; however, we are not given any evidence in the extract that the memory is a 'fond' one.

The passage has obviously captured Julia's interest, and her final paragraph provides a fair summing up of her response.

However, there is more to notice about the young man in relation to his family and the scene at the crematorium:

- his outward 'style' and image, which suggest rebellious youth, could lead to his being labelled uncaring. It contrasts with the conventional dress of his older relatives. As Julia points out, he does not overtly declare his emotions or much sense of loss, although we do not detect much emotion in the other characters either.
- in opposition to this, his painful preoccupation with 'getting it right'. He is very concerned that his dress should be appropriate, so he does care. In a strange sense, what seemed inappropriate is in fact fitting: the white trainers his aunt objects to carry the mark of his grandmother's wheelchair, and serve as a record of their last meeting, and of his having shown his care of her. The 'adults', on the other hand, may be dressed more conventionally, but seem, if anything, less involved in the proceedings.

Activity

Now look at Richard's answer, which has different qualities. Read this carefully, noting its strengths and suggesting some ways in which his work could be improved. In particular, look at:
- major points he has noticed about the passage
- how well his ideas are supported with evidence
- appropriateness of quotations from the text
- his analysis of the writer's style
- clarity of expression: is it easy to follow? Is the writing well organized or chaotic?
- technical accuracy: punctuation, paragraphing, and spelling

Write an assessment of the beginning of *The Crow Road*, by Iain Banks, commenting on its effectiveness as the opening of a novel.

This passage is an effective opening to the novel, as the first sentence 'It was the day my grandmother exploded' grabs the reader's attention instantly. This opening line also establishes the mood of the piece, a quite darkly humorous style – the various family members present at the crematorium are described in a lot of detail – the images created of them are expanded upon (the narrator's mother is said to be wearing a hat that looks like a flying saucer – this is furthered when we are given the image of it 'dipping' to the side when she talks). There is a very sarcastic tone to the passage in places, such as when the narrator tells us his father is probably 'annoyed that my grandmother had chosen religious music for her funeral ceremony', and the constant references to Uncle Hamish snoring in the background – this style of humor fits in quite well with the proceedings as it isn't (for want of a better term) 'Har-de-har-har' humor – it is subtle, and certain points about it are written in such a way, that they could just be taken as extra description of the events (the flashback to the narrator getting dressed is a good example – with him rattling off precise descriptions of his clothes, and where they are from). The atmosphere, despite the humor, is retained: the formal mood is (kind of) still there, and there are references to the cold atmosphere to add to this (although this refers to the morning, it still has an effect on the scene at hand) also, a lot of the comments from the narrator (who seems to be taking the event as a sort of 'family reunion' – or a freak show, depending) are linked with death, even if in an obscure way such as referring to somebody as looking like candy floss stuck on a hearse – which in itself, is mixing something associated with fun & something associated with death – much like the whole passage.

PS – is the 'smell of cooking bacon & burned toast' line a really sick reference to the cremation taking place?

Richard

Examining writers' styles

Throughout this book you are being asked to think not only about what writers are saying – the content of their work – but also about *how* they write. This means examining the particular combination of literary devices, structures, and vocabulary which a writer uses and which go together to form that writer's individual 'style'. From your own reading you will know that some writers' work is easy to recognize immediately because they have a distinctive 'style'. However, it can be more difficult to explain exactly which characteristics make a writer's style recognizable.

As a student of A-level Literature, you will need to develop the ability to analyse and write about style. One shortcoming noted by examiners is that students fail to take account of this and do not engage in enough detailed analysis of how texts are written. It is easier to concentrate on the writer's use of language when studying poetry, but it can be tempting, when writing about novels or other longer prose works, to focus on the plot or the ideas and neglect to examine the features that make up the author's style.

Try thinking of 'style' as the product of many choices the writer makes about these elements.

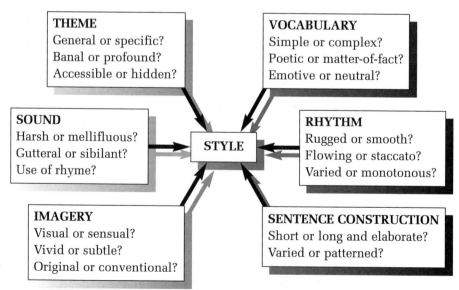

THEME
General or specific?
Banal or profound?
Accessible or hidden?

VOCABULARY
Simple or complex?
Poetic or matter-of-fact?
Emotive or neutral?

SOUND
Harsh or mellifluous?
Gutteral or sibilant?
Use of rhyme?

STYLE

RHYTHM
Rugged or smooth?
Flowing or staccato?
Varied or monotonous?

IMAGERY
Visual or sensual?
Vivid or subtle?
Original or conventional?

SENTENCE CONSTRUCTION
Short or long and elaborate?
Varied or patterned?

These are only some examples of the choices writers make, but they are a helpful reminder of the questions we need to ask when considering style.

Thinking or feeling

'Style' can also be viewed as the expression of a writer's personality and preoccupations. The way in which a writer experiences the world and the things which are most important to them are bound to affect how and what they write.

The psychologist Carl Jung puts forward the theory that people tend towards being **introverted** (more concerned with the 'inner' world of thought or imagination) or **extraverted** (more grounded in the external world of physical reality and other people). Stemming from this, he maintains that some people are thinking types, most at home with thoughts and ideas and perhaps less comfortable with the experience and expression of emotions; others use their intuition. A third group are feeling types, relying on their feelings more than their thoughts to guide them through life and a final group are sensation types, experiencing the world via their physical senses.

This is a partial and simplistic explanation of Jung's ideas, and many other people have created models to try and understand the human personality. However, factors like these are bound to influence the choices authors make when they write, in terms of content and style. They may also account for the fact that most of us respond or 'relate' better to some writers than others. We naturally feel more at home with the work of a writer who experiences the world as we do, while reading the work of a writer who experiences it very differently may feel like struggling to understand a foreign culture.

Of course, most writing – the act of putting ideas and experiences into words – involves a rather cerebral or 'thinking' activity. Most writers 'craft' their work carefully even if their aim is to use words to convey emotional or sensual experiences, but there are some who use more intuitive or free-writing techniques, allowing their words to flow without judging or altering them.

Now let us consider how these ideas might help us in gaining a sense of an author's personal 'style'.

First, read the following passage from *The Rainbow*. This novel by D. H. Lawrence traces the patterns of love and relationships through three generations of the Brangwens, a family of farmers in the East Midlands. Here, in the early part of the book, Tom Brangwen struggles with his sense of being both close to and distant from the woman he will marry.

The Rainbow

Chapter 1
Then, as he sat there, all mused and wondering, she came near to him, looking at him with wide, grey eyes that almost smiled with a low light. But her ugly-beautiful mouth was unmoved and sad. He was afraid.

His eyes, strained and roused with unusedness, quailed a little before her, he felt himself quailing and yet he rose, as if obedient to her, he bent and kissed her heavy, sad, wide mouth, that was kissed, and did not alter. Fear was too strong in him. Again he had not got her.

She turned away. The vicarage kitchen was untidy, and yet to him beautiful with the untidiness of her and her child. Such a wonderful remoteness there was about her, and then something in touch with him, that made his heart knock in his chest. He stood there and waited, suspended.

Again she came to him, as he stood in his black clothes, with blue eyes very bright and puzzled for her, his face tensely alive, his hair dishevelled. She came close up to him, to his intent, black-clothed body, and laid her hand on his arm. He remained unmoved. Her eyes, with a blackness of memory struggling with passion, primitive and electric away at the back of them, rejected him and absorbed him at once. But he remained himself. He breathed with difficulty, and sweat came out at the roots of his hair, on his forehead.

'Do you want to marry me?' she asked slowly, always uncertain.

He was afraid lest he could not speak. He drew breath hard, saying:

'I do.'

Then again, what was agony to him, with one hand lightly resting on his arm, she leaned forward a little, and with a strange, primeval suggestion of embrace, held him her mouth. It was ugly-beautiful, and he could not bear it. He put his mouth on hers, and slowly, slowly the response came, gathering force and passion, till it seemed to him she was thundering at him till he could bear no more. He drew away, white, unbreathing. Only, in his blue eyes was something of himself concentrated. And in her eyes was a little smile upon a black void.

She was drifting away from him again. And he wanted to go away. It was intolerable. He could bear no more. He must go. Yet he was irresolute. But she turned away from him.

With a little pang of anguish, of denial, it was decided.

'I'll come an' speak to the vicar to-morrow,' he said, taking his hat.

She looked at him, her eyes expressionless and full of darkness. He could see no answer.

'That'll do, won't it?' he said.

'Yes,' she answered, mere echo without body or meaning.

'Good night,' he said.

'Good night.'

He left her standing there, expressionless and void as she was. Then she went on laying the tray for the vicar. Needing the table, she put the daffodils aside on the dresser without noticing them. Only their coolness, touching her hand, remained echoing there a long while.

They were such strangers, they must for ever be such strangers, that his passion was a clanging torment to him. Such intimacy of embrace, and such utter foreignness of contact! It was unbearable. He could not bear to be near her, and know the utter foreignness between them, know how entirely they were strangers to each other. He went out into the wind. Big holes were blown into the sky, the moonlight blew about. Sometimes a high moon, liquid-brilliant, scudded across a hollow space and took cover under electric, brown-irridescent cloud-edges. Then there was a blot of cloud and shadow. Then somewhere in the night a radiance again, like a vapour. And all the sky was teeming and tearing along, a vast disorder of flying shapes and darkness and ragged fumes of light and a great brown circling halo, then the terror of a moon running liquid-brilliant into the open for a moment, hurting the eyes before she plunged under cover of cloud again.

D. H. Lawrence

Activity

Having read the passage carefully, make notes on the following questions.

1 To what extent is Lawrence concerned with:
- his character's thoughts and ideas
- his character's feelings and emotions
- his character's experience of the physical world around him
- relationships?

2 What choices does Lawrence make relating to:
- theme
- vocabulary
- sentence structures
- rhythm
- sound?

Lawrence is a writer deeply concerned with human relationships, particularly those between men and women. He tries to articulate the effect people have on each other and presents an ambivalent view of close relationships, which can bring great happiness, but may also be very threatening or destructive.

You will probably have noticed in this extract that he seems to be chiefly aiming to convey Brangwen's feelings, both in a physical and in an emotional sense. Brangwen feels sexual desire for the woman, but is also fearful of losing himself in love, of being 'absorbed' by it. Lawrence sometimes describes this in terms of the actual physical sensations in his body:

'He breathed with difficulty, and sweat came out at the roots of his hair, on his forehead.'

However, when he describes their kiss, he can no longer be quite so concrete. To convey the emotional and physical sensations Brangwen feels here, Lawrence uses the image of her seeming to be 'thundering' at him, which suggests something both powerful and threatening, but is much less direct. It is the nearest he can get to an impression of his character's feelings.

Some of Lawrence's work was originally banned for being too sexually explicit, but often, as he tries to convey his characters' experiences of love and sex, his descriptions have this rather impressionistic quality. Powerful images and metaphors from nature are used to portray emotional and sexual needs as something almost mystical. Something of this is present in the final paragraph of the extract above, where his description of the stormy night sky mirrors Brangwen's experience with the woman. The moon, which scuds behind the clouds, appears intermittently, 'hurting the eyes' and causing 'terror', reminds us of the moments when he fully feels the presence of the woman and their mutual desire, or looks into her eyes and sees 'a little smile upon a black void'. Both are elusive, beautiful, and frightening.

Having recognized that Lawrence's 'style' has its basis in the emotional, physical, and sensual exploration of life, we can go on to examine in detail some of the choices he makes in using language. You may have noticed some of these.

- Predictably, perhaps, he uses 'feeling' words in almost every sentence: 'unmoved and sad', 'afraid', 'fear', 'agony', and 'anguish' are just a few.
- Although this is a third-person narrative, everything is filtered through Brangwen's emotional responses.
- Colours, and other adjectives, are sometimes used repeatedly, reinforcing their effect, creating patterns, or even giving a ritualistic effect. His eyes are blue and very bright, while hers are grey, black, or 'full of darkness' and her 'sad, wide' mouth is 'ugly-beautiful'.
- Sentence lengths are varied. This too contributes to the portrayal of Brangwen's feelings. Moments of tension and uncertainty are made up of short or incomplete sentences, which give a sense of pain, urgency, and indecision:
  'She was drifting away from him again. And he wanted to go away. It was intolerable. He could bear no more. He must go. Yet he was irresolute.'
- The description of the ragged sky is similarly broken up, but there are other moments when the sentences flow more freely, usually when the two characters seem more connected. The use of sentence patterns to enhance a sense of drama is typical of Lawrence.
- The sound qualities of the words are fairly varied, with a few alliterative patterns. Hard consonants are used and, in the case of the image of the disordered sky 'teeming and tearing along', add to the sense of confusion.

Exaggerating style

One interesting – and amusing – way of becoming more aware of a writer's style is to look at a pastiche or parody. The parodist usually takes the most obvious features of a writer's style and exaggerates them, as a cartoonist exaggerates physical features in visual images. A successful parody can make it obvious what a writer's stylistic 'habits' are and help you to recognize them when you return to the original. Writing parody yourself encourages you to concentrate hard on the features which make a writer's style distinctive.

Activity | What features of Lawrence's writing do you recognize in this short parody?

Sons and Aztecs

She lay, motionless, in the burning heat. She gave herself to the sun in an act of supreme worship. Her body was the sacrament.

He watched and was thrilled to the soul. A dark primeval shout resounded through his whole being. To him, she was the true female spirituality. Not the whimpering, cloying, tendrilled feminine grasp of demand and duty, not the empty ache of sentiment, but the pure lambent flame of passion. He warmed to her flame. She basked in his primitive mooncold light. She was the sun, and he the moon.

He lay down beside her. Then he climbed on top of her and did it to her.

Richard Curtis

A 'thinking' style

Now we will look at how a very different writer, Henry James, presents a scene of courtship. In his novel *Washington Square*, Catherine Sloper, a like-able, but rather plain and naïve young woman who is heiress to a great fortune, receives a visit from her 'lover' Morris Townsend, of whom her father disapproves. Mrs Penniman is her sentimental, meddling aunt.

Washington Square

Chapter 10
Catherine received the young man the next day on the ground she had chosen – amidst the chaste upholstery of a New York drawing-room furnished in the fashion of fifty years ago. Morris had swallowed his pride, and made the effort necessary to cross the threshold of her too derisive parent – an act of magnanimity which could not fail to render him doubly interesting.
'We must settle something – we must take a line,' he declared, passing his hand through his hair and giving a glance at the long narrow mirror which adorned the space between the two windows ... If Morris had been pleased to describe the master of the house as a heartless scoffer, it is because he thought him too much on his guard, and this was the easiest way to express his own dissatisfaction – a dissatisfaction which he had made a point of concealing from the Doctor. It will probably seem to the reader, however, that the Doctor's vigilance was by no means excessive, and that these two young people had an open field. Their intimacy was now considerable, and it may appear that, for a shrinking and retiring person, our heroine had been liberal of her favours. The young man, within a few days, had made her listen to things for which she had not supposed that she was prepared; having a lively foreboding of difficulties, he proceeded to gain as much ground as possible in the present. He remembered that fortune favours the brave, and even if he had forgotten it, Mrs Penniman would have remembered it for him. Mrs Penniman delighted of all things in a drama, and she flattered herself that a drama would now be enacted. Combining as she did the zeal of the prompter with the impatience of the spectator, she had long since done her utmost to pull up the curtain. She, too, expected to figure in the performance – to be the confidante, the Chorus, to speak the epilogue. It may even be said that there were times when she lost sight altogether of the modest heroine of the play in the contemplation of certain great scenes which would naturally occur between the hero and herself.

What Morris had told Catherine at last was simply that he loved her, or rather adored her. Virtually, he had made known as much already – his visits had been a series of eloquent intimations of it. But now he had affirmed it in lover's vows, and, as a memorable sign of it, he had passed his arm round the girl's waist and taken a kiss. This happy certitude had come sooner than Catherine expected, and she had regarded it, very naturally, as a priceless treasure. It may even be doubted whether she had ever definitely expected to possess it; she had not been waiting for it, and she had never said to herself that at a given moment it must come. As I have tried to explain, she was not eager and exacting; she took what was given her from day to day; and if the delightful custom of her lover's visits, which yielded her a happiness in which confidence and timidity were strangely blended, had suddenly come to an end, she would not only not have spoken of herself as one of the forsaken, but she would not have thought of herself as one of the disappointed. After Morris had kissed her the last time he was with her, as a ripe assurance of his devotion, she begged him to go away, to leave her alone, to let her think. Morris went away, taking another kiss first. But Catherine's meditations had lacked a certain coherence. She felt his kisses on her lips and on her cheeks for a long time afterward; the sensation was rather an obstacle than an aid to reflection. She would have liked to see her situation all clearly before her, to make up her mind what she should do if, as she feared, her father should tell her that he disapproved of Morris Townsend.

Henry James

Activity

> Now ask yourself these questions about the style of this extract.
> **1** To what extent, would you say, is James concerned with:
> • his characters' thoughts and ideas
> • his characters' feelings and emotions?
> **2** Where do you think he stands in relation to his characters? What is his attitude towards them?

Probably you will have noticed the enormous difference between this extract and the one from *The Rainbow* on pages 209–211. Both depict an encounter between a man and a woman where marriage is in question, yet the writers are poles apart in the ways they approach this subject. Where Lawrence is so intent on conveying a sense of his characters' emotions and sensations, James is much more concerned with what they are thinking, or with analysing what is going on.

The effect is that reading Lawrence can be a powerful emotional experience: we are presented with such a close view of the characters that it can almost feel as if we are 'inside' their skins. Reading James, however, is often more of an intellectual challenge. It is not that his characters do not have feelings, but that they stop and think about them – or James does – for several pages sometimes. Situations are weighed up and the rights and wrongs of their responses pondered. James maintains a good distance between himself and his characters, leaving himself space to comment and judge, to use irony, or to gently mock. (It is almost impossible, incidentally, to imagine Lawrence being ironic or mocking his characters.) As a result, we as readers also feel more remote from James' characters.

There are other factors in James' writing which contribute to this very different 'style'. Asking some further questions about the details of how he uses language should reveal these.

Activity

Look again at the passage from *Washington Square*.
1 What are James' choices with respect to:
 • vocabulary
 • imagery
 • sentence structures
 • sound?
 What do these choices contribute to his 'style'?
2 What words would you use to describe his 'style'?

These are some of the points you may have noted.

• James' vocabulary tends to be demanding or 'inflated': he often deliberately chooses words which are complex or latinate (derived from Latin), when simpler words would convey his meaning equally well. Morris is not 'worried', for example, but has 'a lively foreboding of difficulties' (and this extract is a relatively straightforward example!) This gives a sense of formality, and adds to the feeling of distance mentioned earlier: only someone who steps back and weighs his words would make these choices. Also, James' tone becomes ironic or mocking as he uses long words when his characters and subjects do not really merit them. They may be foolish, like Mrs Penniman, or dishonest or ordinary, but think themselves grander than they really are.
• There is little imagery in the extract, but what there is is deliberately clever. For example, the extended metaphor which describes Mrs Penniman's propensity for acting as if life is a stage drama ('Combining as she did the zeal of the prompter ... between the hero and herself.') goes on a bit, as we may imagine Mrs Penniman herself does.
• On the whole, James' sentence structures also tend to be complex. (More extreme examples can be found elsewhere in his work.) He is renowned for producing sentences with multiple clauses which temporarily digress from their subject. These require us to hold several ideas in mind simultaneously which demands concentration. You will find this aspect of his style particularly noticeable if you try to read the passage aloud.
• There is no evidence that James chooses words in order to create deliberate sound effects. However, the complex and latinate vocabulary does perhaps give a rather dry, crisp effect to his style, but precision in meaning is his chief aim.
• There can be little doubt that James' main purpose is to present us with something to think about. It is the meanings and ideas contained in his long, precisely constructed sentences, carefully chosen vocabulary, and clever metaphors which are important, never sensual effects like

alliteration or visual imagery. It is as difficult to imagine James writing to appeal to the senses as it is to imagine Lawrence being ironic.

To conclude, here is another example of parody, this time of Henry James. It tells of two children awakening on Christmas morning.

The Mote in the Middle Distance

It was with the sense of a, for him, very memorable something that he peered now into the immediate future, and tried, not without compunction, to take that period up where he had, prospectively, left it. But just where the deuce had he left it? The consciousness of dubiety was, for our friend, not this morning, quite yet clean-cut enough to outline the figures on what she had called his 'horizon', between which and himself the twilight was indeed of a quality somewhat intimidating. He had run up, in the course of time, against a good number of 'teasers'; and the function of teasing them back – of, as it were, giving them, every now and then, 'what for' – was in him so much a habit that he would have been at a loss had there been, on the face of it, nothing to lose. Oh, he always had offered rewards, of course – had ever so liberally pasted the windows of his soul with staring appeals, minute descriptions, promises that knew no bounds. But the actual recovery of the article – the business of drawing and crossing the cheque, blotched though this were with tears of joy – had blankly appeared to him rather in the light of sacrilege, casting, he sometimes felt, a palpable chill on the quest. It was just this fervour that was threatened as, raising himself on his elbow, he stared at the foot of his bed. That his eyes refused to rest there for more than the fraction of an instant, may be taken – was, even then, taken by Keith Tantalus – as a hint of his recollection that after all the phenomenon wasn't to be singular. Thus the exact repetition, at the foot of Eva's bed, of the shape pendulous at the foot of his was hardly enough to account for the fixity with which he envisaged it, and for which he was to find, some years later, a motive in the (as it turned out) hardly generous fear that Eva had already made the great investigation 'on her own'. Her very regular breathing presently reassured him that, if she had peeped into 'her' stocking, she must have done so in sleep. Whether he should wake her now, or wait for their nurse to wake them both in due course, was a problem presently solved by a new development. It was plain that his sister was now watching him between her eyelashes. He had half expected that. She really was – he had often told her that she really was – magnificent; and her magnificence was never more obvious than in the pause that elapsed before she all of a sudden remarked, 'They so very indubitably are, you know!'

Max Beerbohm

Activity

1 What features of James' style are being exaggerated here? (If you have read *The Turn of the Screw*, this parody may have a familiar ring.)

2 Look at other texts you are reading where the author has a distinctive style. Analyse the details which create this style and use your findings to write your own parody.

11 Literary Connections: Comparing Texts

Objectives
- To develop the ability to explore relationships and comparisons between literary texts
- To practise the skills of comparative writing

Making connections

Becoming skilful at making connections between things which may on the surface seem unrelated can be a useful way of making sense of some of the situations you encounter in real life, as well as in literature. In another conversation from Willy Russell's play *Educating Rita*, Rita reveals that, like many people, she has a natural ability to do this:

Rita: ... everyone behaves as though it's normal, y'know inevitable that there's vandalism an' violence an' houses burnt out an' wrecked by the people they were built for. There's somethin' wrong. An' like the worst thing is that y'know the people who are supposed to like represent the people on our estate, y'know the *Daily Mirror* an' the *Sun,* an' ITV an' the Unions, what are they tellin' people to do? They just tell them to go out an' get more money; it's like me, isn't it? y' know, buyin' new dresses all the time, isn't it? The Unions tell them to go out an' get more money an' ITV an' the papers tell them what to spend it on so the disease is always covered up.

Frank *swivels round in his chair to face* **Rita**.

Frank: (*after a pause*) Why didn't you take a course in politics?

Rita: Politics? Go way, I hate politics. I'm just tellin' y' about round our way. I wanna be on this course findin' out. You know what I learn from you, about art an' literature, it feeds me, inside. I can get through the rest of the week if I know I've got coming here to look forward to. Denny tried to stop me comin' tonight. He tried to get me to go out to the pub with him an' his mates. He hates me comin' here. It's like drug addicts, isn't it? They hate it when one of them tries to break away. It makes me stronger comin' here. That's what Denny's frightened of.

Frank: 'Only connect.'

Rita: Oh, not friggin' Forster again.

Frank: 'Only connect.' You see what you've been doing?

Rita: Just tellin' y' about home.

Frank: Yes, and connecting, your dresses/ITV and the *Daily Mirror*. Addicts/you and your husband.

Rita is hardly aware of what she is doing, but the study of literature provides you with the opportunity to practise making connections more consciously. Learning to relate literary texts to each other by linking their themes, or spotting how the human situations they present can appear different and yet be parallel, or by analysing how authors can deal with the same topic in radically different ways, can be fascinating and satisfying.

For Advanced Level courses, particularly at A2 level, you will be expected to demonstrate that you can recognize and understand literary connections like these and explore them effectively in writing. There are several situations in which your ability to compare texts may be assessed.

- Some examination papers or questions focus specifically on the comparison of two (or more) full-length set texts. These are most likely to be two novels that share a common theme, although it is possible that collections of short stories or poetry or non-fiction texts could also be set.

- If your syllabus includes an optional coursework module, the written assignments will probably include a comparative study of two full-length texts.

- Examination papers that test your close reading of shorter texts or extracts usually have a comparative element. You may prepare for these by reading a variety of texts around a particular theme (see Unit 13, Reading for Meaning) or by studying an anthology of pre-release material. Alternatively, the texts may be completely 'unseen' and new to you. In all these cases you will be asked to compare and contrast at least two short texts or extracts, which can be of any genre.

Prepare to compare

Writing comparatively about two texts is inevitably a more complex process than writing about a single one. Sometimes, particularly when under pressure in an examination, it may seem easier to resort to writing first about one text and then about the other, perhaps making an attempt to link them with a short summary in the final paragraph. However, this is not true comparative writing and rarely produces a satisfactory result. It is much better to develop the skill of weaving together your ideas and arguments about both texts throughout your writing even if this seems more difficult initially. There are some strategies you can use when preparing to write comparatively, which may help to make this easier.

If you are working on two full-length texts for an examination paper or a coursework assignment, you need to know them both well enough to find material as you need it and to be comfortable moving backwards and forwards from one to the other. If they are unseen texts or extracts, your reading and annotations should be geared towards highlighting the similarities and differences between them. Once you have studied each text, you need to find ways of organizing your thoughts and ideas effectively, not just about one text at a time but about both together.

Clarify your ideas

It is usually helpful to focus first on the **connections**.

1 Establish the major links between the texts first, making sure that you are clear about any similarities in themes, characters or their situations.
2 You can then go on to note more specific or detailed similarities. These may be to do with
   • the settings or 'worlds' the novels present
   • the writers' attitudes to the same subject or theme
   • the narrative viewpoints they use
   • how the texts are structured
   • the tone of the writing, e.g. serious, humorous, satirical, ironic, tragic etc.
   • the use of imagery or its absence
   • vocabulary
   • other stylistic features

Then turn your attention to the **contrasts**. Concentrate on noting what makes the texts different in any of the above ways.

For example, look at a few of the ways we can connect and contrast two novels about the experiences of British visitors to India: E.M. Forster's *A Passage to India* and *Heat and Dust*, by Ruth Prawer Jhabvala.

Connections
   • Both are set (at least partly) in India around 1923, when it was still part of the British Empire, but when the fight for Independence was

beginning. They show India in transition. The resulting racial tension contributes to the plot and atmosphere of both novels.

- Both novels portray the world of the 'British Raj' – the expatriate community of officials who governed India at that time.

- Both have main characters who are English women new to the country and eager to experience 'the real India'. They find Anglo-India disturbing, cross the boundaries of expected behaviour and become 'too involved' with Indians.

- The women's concerns are disregarded by experienced Anglo-Indians – especially men – and put down to the climate or old age.

- 'India always changes people,' says the narrator of *Heat and Dust*. This is illustrated in both novels.

- The 'heat and dust' of India are significant in both novels. They are part of the 'personality' of India and are often used symbolically; rising temperatures and suffocating dust parallel and heighten the tension between individuals and races; the British struggle to keep the heat and dust (India) at bay, with barred windows and shutters.

Contrasts
- *A Passage to India* was written mainly in 1923–4, at the same time as the events it depicts. *Heat and Dust* was written in the 1970s, and with the benefit of hindsight it can present the transition in India in terms of the contrast between 'modern' India and India in the days of the Empire.

- Forster writes as an omniscient third-person narrator who sees into the minds of all his important characters, whether English or Indian, and moves freely from one perspective to another. *Heat and Dust* is a dual narrative. The story of Olivia, from 1923, is told in the third person, but placed within a first person 'frame' or context. It is presented as if it has been researched and reconstructed from her letters by the main first-person narrator, her step-grand-daughter, who intersperses it with entries from her diary of her own experience of travelling in India in the 1970s.

- Because of these narrative viewpoints, in *A Passage to India* Forster can describe English characters as they are seen by Indian characters as well as the other way round, while in *Heat and Dust* Indians and Anglo-Indians are presented only as they are observed by English characters and not vice versa.

Organize

In order to keep track of your ideas about two (or more) texts, you may find it helpful to use a diagram or table to organize them before you start to write. (Some ways of doing this have already been suggested in Unit 7.)

Sometimes, you will find that the contrasts between texts become more apparent once you have made the connections. The differences grow out of the similarities. This is one possible way of organizing your ideas. Here is an example, using another pair of novels which share a theme: *The Color Purple* by Alice Walker and *Oranges Are Not the Only Fruit* by Jeanette Winterson.

A woman's struggle: *The Color Purple/Oranges Are Not the Only Fruit*

Connections		Contrasts
Both novels trace a girl's struggle to grow up and achieve independence in a hostile, prejudiced or limiting environment.	**But**	They are set in very different environments and contexts. Celie in *The Color Purple* grows up as a black woman in the Deep South of America in the 1930s facing the oppression not just of her sex but of her race. Jeanette, in Lancashire, England, in the 1960s has to contend with the overpowering domination of her mother and the narrow-minded beliefs of the religious sect in which she is brought up.
Both novels explore feminist themes and feature strong female characters (Jeanette's mother/Sofia). Jeanette and Celie both have female 'mentors' or role models who encourage them to find their own inner strength (e.g. Elsie/Shug Avery)	**But**	Sofia and Shug are sympathetic characters who are powerful and assert their own rights, while Jeanette's mother is oppressive as well as impressive.
Male characters are weak	**But**	They show it in different ways. Jeanette's father is hardly there at all – he simply opts out of asserting himself. Men like Mr___ and Harpo hide their feelings of impotence behind violence and vindictiveness – usually against women. The men in *Oranges Are Not the Only Fruit* do not develop, but in *The Color Purple*, men learn something too.
Celie and Jeanette are both empowered by lesbian relationships.	**But**	Celie's relationship with Shug is life-enhancing and leads through to greater acceptance of herself and a greater ability to relate comfortably on an equal basis with both men and women. Jeanette discovers her sexuality, an important part of her identity, through her relationship with Melanie, but has to cope with betrayal and denunciation before

going on alone to find her own way in the world as a lesbian.

Both challenge the traditional forms of the Christian religion which have restricted their freedom to grow.

But   In Celie's case this means ridding herself of the image of a white, male, judgemental God and replacing it with a more inclusive loving presence, while Jeanette concludes by questioning the existence of God altogether.

Both are narrated in the first person and both use some unconventional narrative techniques.

But   Most of *Oranges Are Not the Only Fruit* is fairly traditional, past-tense narrative; this is interrupted by reflective passages and fairy tales or fables, told in the third person, which run parallel or act as a commentary. *The Color Purple* is constructed as a series of letters, a device that makes possible the immediacy of the present tense.

Both writers challenge us with their use of language.

But   Winterson uses a great deal of religious and Biblical vocabulary and allusion. Without some knowledge of this, some of her ideas and humour will be lost on us. *The Color Purple* is not 'difficult' in this way, but is written in a form of Black English that may be unfamiliar to some readers.

Comparing poems

To see another method in action, we will work through an example of a comparison of two short poems, making use of the strategy for tackling the close reading of unseen texts which was suggested in Unit 10. We will think about features such as theme, situation, 'speaker', atmosphere or use of imagery as they appear in *both* texts.

Activity

1 Read these two poems on the theme of anger. Use the close reading strategy from Unit 10, pages 193–195, to make notes on each poem.
2 Combine your findings in a table.
3 Compare your ideas with the table that follows the poems.
4 Use your notes to write a short essay to answer this question:
   Examine the similarities and the differences in the ways Elizabeth Daryush and William Blake describe feelings of anger in the following poems.

'Anger lay by me all night long'

Anger lay by me all night long,
   His breath was hot upon my brow,
He told me of my burning wrong,
   All night he talked and would not go.

He stood by me all through the day,
   Struck from my hand the book, the pen;
He said: 'Hear first what I've to say,
   And sing, if you've the heart to, then.'

And can I cast him from my couch?
   And can I lock him from my room?
Ah no, his honest words are such
   That he's my true-lord, and my doom.

Elizabeth Daryush

A Poison Tree

I was angry with my friend:
I told my wrath, my wrath did end.
I was angry with my foe:
I told it not, my wrath did grow.

And I watered it in fears,
Night & morning with my tears;
And I sunned it with smiles,
And with soft deceitful wiles.

And it grew both day and night,
Till it bore an apple bright.
And my foe beheld it shine,
And he knew that it was mine.

And into my garden stole,
When the night had veiled the pole:
In the morning glad I see
My foe outstretched beneath the tree.

William Blake

	Daryush	**Blake**
Subject	The experience of anger and its effects	The effects of anger; the results of expressing or suppressing anger.
Speaker/ Situation	First person; poet describes being overpowered by anger, which is personified as a male character. She resists her anger at first, then seems to accept it as justified, though still threatening ('doom').	First person; poet tells of being angry, with a friend, and then an enemy. The symbol of a tree represents unexpressed anger, which, nurtured, grows and bears the fruit of revenge. The story is fable-like, and the speaker is more an archetype or representative human being than an individual.
Form	3 rhyming, 4-line stanzas which convey the point neatly in few words.	4 x 4-line stanzas with simple rhythm and rhyme, like a nursery rhyme; the simplicity is deceptive.
Ideas/Messages	Anger can take hold of a person and dominate life. The poet lives, works, and sleeps with anger which she cannot release: 'And can I lock him from my room? Ah no ...' Describing it as a separate person suggests her inability to control the anger. If we dwell on angry thoughts and words this only increases our rage. Her mind is full of a sense of being a victim of some wrongdoing: 'He told me of my burning wrong, All night he talked and would not go.'	Anger which is openly expressed quickly passes, while hidden anger grows. Nursing a grudge can make one vengeful and destructive. The poet's anger is nurtured, becomes poisonous and eventually destroys the enemy, leaving him jubilant: 'In the morning glad I see/My foe outstretched beneath the tree.'
Tone/ Atmosphere	Sense of urgency, being swept along by the anger; punctuation pushes each stanza on towards its last line, especially the last, making her 'doom' seem inevitable.	Simple language gives an unemotional quality; rather cold, distanced from the anger, with a sense that his revenge is deliberate, premeditated, and enjoyed ('soft deceitful wiles'; 'glad').

	Daryush	Blake
Imagery	Personification of anger extends throughout; image of powerful, violent man who is persistent and demands attention. 'Hear first what I've to say, And sing, if you've the heart to, then.'	Symbolic image of hidden anger as the destructive 'Poison Tree' throughout. He nurtures anger like a gardener with a favourite plant ('watered'; 'sunned'). Image of tree/apple is biblical, suggesting Adam and Eve; the Tree of Knowledge of good and evil, with overtones of loss of innocence, and betrayal.
Vocabulary	Words like 'hot' and 'burning' suggest, perhaps, a devilish quality; also a feverishness, adding to the sense of urgency. 'Honest' and 'true-lord' are a surprise: as if she now accepts her anger as genuine and justifiable.	Mainly simple; words reminiscent of the Bible (in older translations): 'foe' 'wrath'; 'bore'; these enhance the timeless, fable-like quality.
Rhyme, Rhythm, and Sound Effects	Strong rhythmic movement; 4 stressed 'beats' in each line, driving poem forward to its conclusion and emphasizing rhymes – they seem unavoidable, like the anger. Use of hard consonant sounds, sometimes alliteratively, suggests her struggle, (breath/brow/burning; cast/couch; struck/lock/book) while the repeated 'oo' sound in the final line (true/doom) slows the pace, suggesting resignation.	Simple 4-beat lines; rhyming couplets with final words stressed emphasizing contrasting ideas. (friend/foe/end/grow; smiles/wiles; night/bright) Some alliteration and sound patterns. Deceit is emphasized by repeated soft 's' sounds (sunned/smiles/soft/deceitful); many lines begin with 'I' while others echo its sound, also giving a 'sly' quality – or revealing the self-absorption of the speaker.

Now try tackling another comparison of poems. You could use the same approach, or experiment with devising your own ways of organizing your ideas.

Activity | Write as fully as you can about the similarities and differences between the following poems.

To My Mother

You were gutting herring in distant Yarmouth and the salt sun in the morning rising out of the sea, the blood on the edge of your knife, and that salt so coarse that it stopped you from speaking and made your lips bitter.

I was in Aberdeen sucking new courses, my Gaelic in a book and my Latin at the tiller, sitting there on a chair with my coffee beside me and leaves shaking the sails of scholarship and my intelligence.

Guilt is tormenting me because of what happened and how things are. I would not like to be getting up in the morning on the shore and that savage sea to be roaring down my gloves without cease.

Though I do that in my poetry it is my own blood that is on my hands, and every herring that the high tide gave me palpitating till I make a song, and instead of a cooper my language always hard and strict on me, and the coarse salt on my ring bringing animation to death.

Iain Crichton Smith

Digging

Between my finger and my thumb
The squat pen rests; snug as a gun.

Under my window, a clean rasping sound
When the spade sinks into gravelly ground:
My father, digging. I look down

Till his straining rump among the flower-beds
Bends low, comes up twenty years away
Stooping in rhythm through potato drills
Where he was digging.

The coarse boot nestled on the lug, the shaft
Against the inside knee was levered firmly.
He rooted out tall tops, buried the bright edge deep
To scatter new potatoes that we picked
Loving their cool hardness in our hands.

By God, the old man could handle a spade.
Just like his old man.

My grandfather cut more turf in a day
Than any other man on Toner's bog.
Once I carried him milk in a bottle
Corked sloppily with paper. He straightened up
To drink it, then fell to right away

Nicking and slicing neatly, heaving sods
Over his shoulder, going down and down
For the good turf. Digging.

The cold smell of potato mould, the squelch and slap
Of soggy peat, the curt cuts of an edge
Through living roots awaken in my head.
But I've no spade to follow men like them.

Between my finger and my thumb
The squat pen rests.
I'll dig with it.

Seamus Heaney

You can use a similar approach with short prose extracts, whether they are new to you or whether they are taken from longer texts you have already prepared.

Comparing novels or other full-length texts

Earlier, we looked at some examples of the ways connections can be made between novels that share a theme. However, you are unlikely to be asked to write about all those aspects of the texts at the same time. Although you will need to know about different ways the texts can be linked, questions for examinations or coursework will probably ask you to focus on only one or two of these. Once you have a clear idea of these broad connections, therefore, you may need to repeat the process of connecting and contrasting, this time looking for more detailed similarities and differences which are relevant to your question. You will also need to find passages and quotations from the texts to illustrate your ideas.

In examinations where you compare two set texts you will quite often be given the option of answering a question based on a comparison of two extracts. Although you will also be expected to write about these in relation to their contexts, this can be a useful way of focusing your mind on particular themes and on details of language that could be overlooked in answering a more general question. The extracts will have been selected because they are key passages illustrating one or more of the ways the texts can be connected and compared.

As you study the texts, it is a good idea to look out for and make a note of passages like these. Look for places where there are clear parallels, where a particular theme stands out or where characters in both texts are placed in similar situations. Study these episodes closely and make sure you can find them easily. If you have your own annotated copies of the texts, you can make marginal notes on links between them.

As an example, we will look more closely at one of the themes common to *The Color Purple* and *Oranges Are Not the Only Fruit*: religion. First we will begin the process of looking for connections in detail, and then compare the way the theme is treated in some extracts from the novels.

In her preface to the tenth anniversary edition of *The Color Purple*, Alice Walker has some things to say about religion in her novel, which could apply almost equally well to *Oranges Are Not the Only Fruit*. Quotations like these can provide useful starting points if you are devising your own topic for a coursework assignment, and are often used in examination questions too – so look out for them in introductions and book-jacket blurbs.

Sample questions

Quotation A is more general and would provide a good basis for a coursework assignment, while B is more tightly focused and could head an examination question.

A

... the book's intent ... [is to] ... explore the difficult path of someone who starts out in life already a spiritual captive, but who, through her own courage and the help of others, breaks free ...'

Discuss the ways in which Alice Walker's words about her purpose in her novel *The Color Purple* could also be applied to Jeanette Winterson's *Oranges Are Not the Only Fruit.*

B

To what extent is the following statement true of both *The Color Purple* and *Oranges Are Not the Only Fruit?*

'*The Color Purple* ... [is a] ... theological work examining the journey from the religious back to the spiritual ...'

Key words and phrases in quotations or questions can be used to guide you through the comparison and to keep your answer relevant.

Activity

> 1 Look at quotation A above and decide which are the key words or phrases (for example, 'difficult path').
> 2 Think about the meaning of each of the key words in relation to each of the texts, and about any questions that might arise from them (for example, In what ways does each character follow a difficult path? Who are the 'others' and how do they help?).
> 3 Look back at quotation B. Make a note of the key words and think carefully about their meanings. (Clue: It is particularly important that you have a clear understanding of the difference between 'religious' and 'spiritual'.)

> **4** Now read the extracts that follow. Even if you have not read the texts, you should be able to see that these episodes are central to the issue in quotation B.
> **5** Working with a partner, choose one text each and make detailed notes on how your chosen passage(s) relates to the quotation and its key words. Pay attention to language – *how* the text is written – as well as content. For example, look at the significance of colour.
> **6** Now present your ideas to each other, share your notes and discuss the similarities and differences between your findings.
> **7** Use your notes to write a short essay in response to sample question B.

These extracts are concerned with how, in the course of the novels, both Celie and Jeanette find that their religious faith and their conceptions of God are being altered irrevocably. As they reflect on these changes, they also question the meaning of love and its relationship to religion.

The Color Purple

This letter to her sister Nettie marks a turning point in Celie's life. She explains how Shug Avery, her friend, lover and mentor, introduces her to a new way of thinking about God, religion and spirituality. Mr____ (Albert) is the man to whom Celie's stepfather arranged her marriage, after using her sexually himself. Nettie ran away to escape a similar fate when they were still young girls, and is now in Africa working with a missionary family.

Dear Nettie,

I don't write to God no more, I write to you.
What happen to God? ast Shug.
Who that? I say.
She look at me serious.
Big a devil as you is, I say, you not worried bout no God, surely.
She say, Wait a minute. Hold on just a minute here. Just because I don't harass it like some peoples us know don't mean I ain't got religion.
What God do for me? I ast.
She say, Celie! Like she shock. He gave you life, good health, and a good woman that love you to death.
Yeah, I say, and he give me a lynched daddy, a crazy mama, a lowdown dog of a step pa and a sister I probably won't ever see again. Anyhow, I say, the God I been praying and writing to is a man. And act just like all the other mens I know. Trifling, forgitful and lowdown.
She say, Miss Celie. You better hush. God might hear you.
Let 'im hear me, I say. If he ever listened to poor colored women the world would be a different place, I can tell you.
She talk and she talk, trying to budge me way from blasphemy. But I blaspheme much as I want to.
All my life I never care what people thought bout nothing I did, I say. But deep in my heart I care about God. What he going to think. And come to find out, he

don't think. Just sit up there glorying in being deef, I reckon. But it ain't easy, trying to do without God. Even if he ain't there, trying to do without him is a strain. ...

She say, Celie, tell the truth, have you ever found God in church? I never did. I just found a bunch of folks hoping for him to show. Any God I ever felt in church I brought in with me. And I think all the other folks did too. They come to church to *share* God, not find God.

Some folks didn't have him to share, I said. They the ones didn't speak to me while I was there struggling with my big belly and Mr.____ children.

Right, she say.

Then she say: Tell me what your God look like, Celie.

Aw naw, I say. I'm too shame. Nobody ever ast me this before, so I'm sort of took by surprise. Besides, when I think about it, it don't seem quite right. But it all I got. I decide to stick up for him, just to see what Shug say.

Okay, I say. He big and old and tall and graybearded and white. He wear white robes and go barefooted.

Blue eyes? she ast.

Sort of bluish-gray. Cool. Big though. White lashes, I say.

She laugh.

Why you laugh? I ast. I don't think it so funny. What you expect him to look like, Mr.____?

That wouldn't be no improvement, she say. Then she tell me this old white man is the same God she used to see when she prayed. If you wait to find God in church, Celie, she say, that's who is bound to show up, cause thart's where he live.

How come? I ast.

Cause that's the one that's in the white folks' white bible.

Shug! I say. God wrote the bible, white folks had nothing to do with it.

How come he look just like them, then? she say. Only bigger? And a heap more hair. How come the bible just like everything else they make, all about them doing one thing and another, and all the colored folks doing is gitting cursed? ...

Ain't no way to read the bible and not think God white, she say. Then she sigh. When I found out I thought God was white and a man, I lost interest. You mad cause he don't seem to listen to your prayers. Humph! Do the mayor listen to anything colored say? Ask Sofia, she say.

But I don't have to ast Sofia. I know white people never listen to colored, period. If they do, they only listen long enough to be able to tell you what to do.

Here's the thing, say Shug. The thing I believe. God is inside you and inside everybody else. You come into the world with God. But only them that search for it inside find it. And sometimes it just manifest itself even if you not looking, or don't know what you looking for. Trouble do it for most folks, I think. Sorrow, lord, Feeling like shit.

It? I ast.

Yeah, It. God ain't a he or a she, but a It.

But what do it look like? I ast.

Don't look like nothing, she say. It ain't a picture show. It ain't something you can look at apart from anything else, including yourself. I believe God is everything, say Shug. Everything that is or ever was or ever will be. And when you can feel that, and be happy to feel that, you've found It.

Shug a beautiful something, let me tell you. She frown a little, look out cross the yard, lean back in her chair, look like big rose.

She say, My first step from the old white man was trees. Then air. Then birds. Then other people. But one day when I was sitting quiet and feeling like a motherless child, which I was, it come to me: that feeling of being part of everything, not separate at all. I knew that if I cut a tree, my arm would bleed. And I laughed and I cried and I run all round the house. I knew just what it was. In fact, when it happen, you can't miss it. It sort of like you know what, she say, grinning and rubbing high up on my thigh.

Shug! I say.

Oh, she say. God love all them feelings. That's some of the best stuff God did. And when you know God loves 'em you enjoys 'em a lot more. You can just relax, go with everything that's going, and praise God by liking what you like.

God don't think it dirty? I ast.

Naw, she say. God made it. Listen, God love everything you love – and a mess of stuff you don't. But more than anything else, God love admiration.

You saying God vain? I ast.

Naw, she say. Not vain, just wanting to share a good thing. I think it pisses God off if you walk by the color purple in a field somewhere and don't notice it.

What it do when it pissed off? I ast.

Oh, it make something else. People think pleasing God is all God care about. But any fool living in the world can see it always trying to please us back.

Yeah? I say.

Yeah, she say. It always making little surprises and springing them on us when us least expect.

You mean it want to be loved, just like the bible say.

Yes, Celie, she say. Everything want to be loved. Us sing and dance, make faces and give flower bouquets, trying to be loved. You ever notice that trees do everything to git attention we do, except walk?

Well, us talk and talk bout God, but I'm still adrift. Trying to chase that old white man out of my head. I been so busy thinking bout him I never truly notice nothing God make. Not a blade of corn (how it do that?) not the color purple (where it come from?). Not the little wildflowers. Nothing.

Now that my eyes are opening, I feels like a fool. Next to any little scrub of a bush in my yard, Mr.____ 's evil sort of shrink. But not altogether. Still, it is like Shug say, you have to git man off your eyeball, before you can see anything a'tall.

Alice Walker

Oranges Are Not the Only Fruit

1 Here, Jeanette has become involved with another young woman, Melanie. Although she finds the relationship 'a much happier thing' than the rest of her life, she is beginning to feel 'uncomfortable'. Her mother has just found out about their intimacy and has instructed her to 'come to church in the morning'.

Over breakfast the next morning [Melanie] told me she intended to go to university to read theology. I didn't think it was a good thing on account of modern heresies. She thought she should understand how other people saw the world.

'But you know they're wrong,' I insisted.

'Yes, but it might be interesting, come on, we'll be late for church. You're not preaching are you?'

'No,' I said. 'I was supposed to, but they changed it.'

We bustled through the kitchen and I stood on the stairs to kiss her.

'I love you almost as much as I love the lord,' I laughed.

She looked at me, and her eyes clouded for a moment. 'I don't know', she said.

By the time we got to church, the first hymn was under way. My mother glared at me, and I tried to look sorry. We had slid in next to Miss Jewsbury who told me to keep calm.

'What do you mean?' I whispered.

'Come and talk to me afterwards,' she hissed. 'But not till we're out of sight.'

I decided she had gone mad. The church was very full as usual, and every time I caught someone's eye they smiled or nodded. It made me happy. There was nowhere I'd rather be. When the hymn was over I squeezed a bit closer to Melanie and tried to concentrate on the Lord. 'Still,' I thought, 'Melanie is a gift from the Lord, and it would be ungrateful not to appreciate her.' I was still deep in these contemplations when I realised that something disturbing was happening. The church had gone very quiet and the pastor was standing on his lower platform, with my mother next to him. She was weeping. I felt a searing pain against my knuckles; it was Melanie's ring. Then Miss Jewsbury was urging me to my feet saying, 'Keep calm, keep calm,' and I was walking out to the front with Melanie. I shot a glance at her. She was pale.

'These children of God,' began the pastor, 'have fallen under Satan's spell.'

His hand was hot and heavy on my neck. Everyone in the congregation looked like a waxwork.

'These children of God have fallen foul of their lusts.'

'Just a minute ...,' I began, but he took no notice.

'These children are full of demons.'

A cry of horror ran through the church.

'I'm not,' I shouted, 'and neither is she.'

'Listen to Satan's voice,' said the pastor to the church, pointing at me. 'How are the best become the worst.'

'What are you talking about?' I asked, desperate.

'Do you deny you love this woman with a love reserved for man and wife?'

'No, yes, I mean of course I love her.'

'I will read you the words of St Paul,' announced the pastor, and he did, and many more words besides about unnatural passions and the mark of the demon.

'To the pure all things are pure,' I yelled at him. 'It's you not us.'

'Do you promise to give up this sin and beg the Lord to forgive you?'

'Yes.' She was trembling uncontrollably. I hardly heard what she said.

'Then go into the vestry with Mrs White and the elders will come and pray for you. It's not too late for those who truly repent.'

He turned to me.

'I love her.'

'Then you do not love the Lord.'

'Yes, I love both of them.'

'You cannot.'

'I do, I do, let me go.' But he caught my arm and held me fast.

'The church will not see you suffer, go home and wait for us to help you.'

I ran out on to the street, wild with distress.

2   In the final chapter, Jeanette returns to her home town for Christmas, her first visit since she left to establish her independence after her rift with the church.

I didn't go straight home, I went up on to the hill. No one else was there, with the weather like this. If I still lived there, I'd be indoors too. It's a visitor's privilege to be foolish. Right to the top I climbed, where I could watch the circling snow fill up the town till it blotted it out. All the black blotted out. I could have made a very impressive sermon ... 'My sins like a cloud hung over me, he blotted them out when he set me free ...' that sort of thing. But where was God now, with heaven full of astronoughts, and the Lord overthrown? I miss God, I miss the company of someone utterly loyal. I still don't think of God as my betrayer. The servants of God, yes, but servants by their very nature betray. I miss God who was my friend. I don't even know if God exists, but I do know that if God is your emotional role model, very few human relationships will match up to it. I have an idea that one day it might be possible, I thought once it had become possible, and that glimpse has set me wandering, trying to find the balance between earth and sky. If the servants hadn't rushed in and parted us, I might have been disappointed, might have snatched off the white samite to find a bowl of soup. As it is, I can't settle, I want someone who is fierce and will love me until death and know that love is as strong as death, and be on my side for ever and ever.

Jeanette Winterson

....

Summary   These are some of the points you may have noted:

- The key words here are 'theological', 'religious' and 'spiritual', which may seem all to be rather similar in meaning. 'Theology' is 'the study of God, religion and revelation'. All of these feature in both novels, so the term 'theological' is apt. **Religious** suggests organised religion: the systems of belief, the doctrines, rules and forms of worship of churches – which have been devised by human beings. **Spiritual** is something much broader and more open, but also suggests a more personal, inner conviction, which springs from experience rather than from the teachings of a church. One dictionary defines 'spiritual' as 'naturally looking to things of the spirit' and lists among its definitions of 'spirit', the phrase 'vital principle', which means, approximately, what life springs from and what keeps life going.

- The phrase 'the journey from the religious back to the spiritual' suggests that traditional, organised religion can take people away from their original, natural spirituality. The novels chart the 'journeys' Celie and Jeanette have to make in order to return. Both learn that their churches are exclusive, not inclusive: Celie realizes that she has worshipped an 'old white man' who doesn't listen to 'poor colored women', while Jeanette is rejected because of her sexual orientation.

- Rejection leads both of them to question the existence of God altogether, but they both struggle with the idea of doing without 'him'. Celie says,

  'It ain't easy, trying to do without God. Even if he ain't there, trying to do without him is a strain.'

  Jeanette says something almost identical. Having decided, in one of Winterson's humorous puns, that heaven is 'full of astronoughts' she finds

  'I miss God, I miss the presence of someone utterly loyal ... I miss God who was my friend.'

- In both novels, the idea of a judgemental God who would disapprove of sexual love is called into question. Celie asks if 'God don't think it dirty?', but Shug tells her:

  'God love all them feelings. That's some of the best stuff God did. And when you know God loves 'em you enjoys 'em a lot more. You can just relax, go with everything that's going, and praise God by liking what you like.'

  Jeanette echoes this when she says 'Melanie is a gift from the Lord, and it would be ungrateful not to appreciate her'. When the pastor accuses her of 'unnatural passions', she responds, 'To the pure all things are pure,' but where Celie has Shug to support her and lead her to a new understanding, Jeanette has only her own inner sense of what is right to guide her.

- Jeanette and Celie both reach a point when they can begin to separate God 'himself' from the church and the people who represent 'him'. Jeanette realizes that she doesn't think of God as her betrayer. 'The servants of God, yes, but servants by their very nature betray.' When Shug suggests that you don't find God in church, just people who have 'come to *share* God,' Celie realizes that she too has been betrayed not by God, but by his 'servants':

  'Some folks didn't have him to share, I said. They the ones didn't speak to me while I was there struggling with my big belly and Mr.____ children.'

- By the end of these extracts, both characters have travelled some distance on their 'journey' and are grappling with new perceptions of God. Celie is learning to 'chase that old white man out of [her] head' and that 'like Shug say, you have to git man off your eyeball, before you can see anything a'tall.' She is experimenting with Shug's vision of God which is beyond gender and race, an 'it' rather than a 'he'; a God which is 'everything that is or ever was or ever will be.' She realizes she has not seen the beauty and colour in the world around her and begins to open her eyes to 'the color purple'. Jeanette is less certain about the role of God in her future, wondering whether any human relationship will ever meet her needs or live up to the love of God which she had relied on in the past. We leave her 'wandering, trying to find the balance between earth and sky.'

The experience of India

Here are two passages to give you an opportunity to work in a similar way with the two novels about India which were mentioned earlier in the unit.

Activity

> Read the following extracts and use any of the ideas and strategies we have suggested to prepare a response to the following question:
>
> In each of these texts we find Indians discussing the English or the English giving their opinions of Indians. Compare and contrast the ways in which each author presents these situations.

A Passage to India

Early in the novel, Aziz, a young Indian doctor, arrives to share a meal with friends.

Abandoning his bicycle, which fell before a servant could catch it, the young man sprang up onto the veranda. He was all animation.
'Hamidullah, Hamidullah! Am I late?' he cried.
  'Do not apologize,' said his host. 'You are always late.'
  'Kindly answer my question. Am I late? Has Mahmoud Ali eaten all the food? If so I go elsewhere. Mr Mahmoud Ali, how are you?'
  'Thank you, Dr Aziz, I am dying.'
  'Dying before your dinner? Oh, poor Mahmoud Ali!'
  'Hamidullah here is actually dead. He passed away just as you rode up on your bike.'
  'Yes, that is so,' said the other. 'Imagine us both as addressing you from another and a happier world.'
  'Does there happen to be such a thing as a hookah[1] in that happier world of yours?'
  'Aziz, don't chatter. We are having a very sad talk.'

The hookah had been packed too tight, as was usual in his friend's house, and bubbled sulkily. He coaxed it. Yielding at last, the tobacco jetted up into his lungs and nostrils, driving out the smoke of burning cow-dung that had filled them as he rode through the bazaar. It was delicious. He lay in a trance, sensuous but healthy, through which the talk of the two others did not seem particularly sad – they were discussing as to whether or not it is possible to be friends with an Englishman. Mahmoud Ali argued that it was not, Hamidullah disagreed, but with so many reservations that there was no friction between them. Delicious indeed to lie on the broad veranda with the moon rising in front and the servants preparing dinner behind, and no trouble happening.
  'Well, look at my own experience this morning.'
  'I only contend that it is possible in England,' replied Hamidullah, who had been to that country long ago, before the big rush, and had received a cordial welcome at Cambridge.
  'It is impossible here. Aziz! The red-nosed boy has again insulted me in court. I do not blame him. He was told that he ought to insult me. Until lately he was quite a nice boy, but the others have got hold of him.'

'Yes, they have no chance here, that is my point. They come out intending to be gentlemen, and are told it will not do. Look at Lesley, look at Blakiston, now it is your red-nosed boy, and Fielding will go next. Why, I remember when Turton came out first. It was in another part of the Province. You fellows will not believe me, but I have driven with Turton in his carriage – Turton! Oh yes, we were once quite intimate. He has shown me his stamp collection.'

'He would expect you to steal it now. Turton! But red-nosed boy will be far worse than Turton!'

'I do not think so. They all become exactly the same – not worse, not better. I give any Englishman two years, be he Turton or Burton. It is only the difference of a letter. And I give any Englishwoman six months. All are exactly alike. Do you not agree with me?'

'I do not,' replied Mahmoud Ali, entering into the bitter fun, and feeling both pain and amusement at each word that was uttered. 'For my own part I find such profound differences among our rulers. Red-nose mumbles, Turton talks distinctly, Mrs Turton takes bribes, Mrs Red-nose does not and cannot, because so far there is no Mrs Red-nose.'

'Bribes?'

'Did you not know that when they were lent to Central India over a canal scheme some rajah or other gave her a sewing machine in solid gold so that the water should run through his state?'

'And does it?'

'No, that is where Mrs Turton is so skilful. When we poor blacks take bribes, we perform what we are bribed to perform, and the law discovers us in consequence. The English take and do nothing. I admire them.'

'We all admire them. Aziz, please pass me the hookah.'

'Oh, not yet – hookah is so jolly now.'

'You are a very selfish boy.' He raised his voice suddenly, and shouted for dinner. Servants shouted back that it was ready. They meant that they wished it was ready, and were so understood, for nobody moved. Then Hamidullah continued, but with changed manner and evident emotion.

'But take my case – the case of young Hugh Bannister. Here is the son of my dear, my dead friends, the Reverend and Mrs Bannister, whose goodness to me in England I shall never forget or describe. They were father and mother to me, I talked to them as I do now. In the vacations their rectory became my home. They entrusted all their children to me – I often carried little Hugh about – I took him up to the funeral of Queen Victoria, and held him in my arms above the crowd.'

'Queen Victoria was different,' murmured Mahmoud Ali.

'I learn now that this boy is in business as a leather merchant at Cawnpore. Imagine how I long to see him and to pay his fare that this house may be his home. But it is useless. The other Anglo-Indians will have got hold of him long ago. He will probably think that I want something, and I cannot face that from the son of my old friends. Oh, what in this country has gone wrong with everything, Vakil Sahib? I ask you.'

Aziz joined in. 'Why talk about the English? Brrrr ...! Why be either friends with the fellows or not friends? Let us shut them out and be jolly. Queen Victoria and Mrs Bannister were the only exceptions, and they're dead.'

'No, no, I do not admit that, I have met others.'

'So have I,' said Mahmoud Ali, unexpectedly veering. 'All ladies are far from alike.' Their mood was changed, and they recalled little kindnesses and courtesies. 'She said "Thank you so much" in the most natural way.' 'She offered me a lozenge when the dust irritated my throat.' Hamidullah could remember more important examples of angelic ministration, but the other, who only knew Anglo-India, had to ransack his memory for scraps, and it was not surprising that he should return to 'But of course all this is exceptional. The exception does not prove the rule. The average woman is like Mrs Turton, and Aziz, you know what she is.' Aziz did not know, but said he did. He too generalized from his disappointments – it is difficult for members of a subject race to do otherwise. Granted the exceptions, he agreed that all Englishwomen are haughty and venal. The gleam passed from the conversation, whose wintry surface unrolled and expanded interminably.

E. M. Forster

1 *hookah*: a tobacco pipe in which the smoke is inhaled through water

Heat and Dust

Olivia, the young wife of Douglas, a British official, is still new to India. She finds Anglo-India stifling and has become friendly with the Nawab, an Indian prince, and his retinue. Concerned about the health of Harry, an English friend of the Nawab, she wants to ask the British Dr Saunders to visit the palace.

The Nawab laughed at the idea of bringing in Dr Saunders. He said, if a European doctor was needed, he would of course send for the best specialist – if necessary, all the way to Germany or England. However, to humour Olivia and Harry, he consented to send a car for Dr Saunders.

Dr Saunders, pleased and flattered to be called in by royalty, laid his finger-tips together and used many technical terms. He puffed while he spoke and with each word blew out the hairs of his moustache so that they fluttered around his mouth as if stirred by a breeze. The Nawab treated him with that exaggerated courtesy that Olivia had learned to recognise as his way of expressing contempt: but it made Dr Saunders, who took it at face value, expand even further inside his tight shantung suit. The sight of the two of them seated opposite each other – the Nawab leaning forward deferentially while the doctor expounded and expanded – gave Harry the giggles and, seeing him, Olivia too could not stop. Dr Saunders did not notice but the Nawab did and, glad to provide such good entertainment for his friends, he insisted that the doctor stay for luncheon.

Dr Saunders reached new heights at the dining table. Flushed with enjoyment of his host's food and drink, he allowed himself to be prompted into expressing his considered opinion of India and Indians. He had many anecdotes to relate in illustration of his theme, mainly drawn from his hospital experience. Although Olivia had heard most of them before, she shared Harry's amusement at the Nawab's way of eliciting them.

'Then what did you do, Doctor?'

'Then, Nawab Sahib, I had the fellow called to my office and, no further argument, smartly boxed his ears for him, one-two, one-two.'

'You did quite right, Doctor. Quite right. You set a good example.'

'It's the only way to deal with them, Nawab Sahib. It's no use arguing with them, they're not amenable to reason. They haven't got it here, you see, up here, the way we have.'

'Exactly, Doctor. You have hit the – what is it, Harry?'

'Nail on the head.'

'Quite right. The nail on the head.' The Nawab nodded gravely.

After a while Olivia ceased to be amused. Dr Saunders was too blatantly stupid, the joke had gone on too long. Harry also became weary of it. With his usual sensitivity, the Nawab at once became aware of the change in atmosphere. He threw down his napkin and said 'Come, Olivia and Harry.' Leaving the doctor unceremoniously behind, he led the other two upstairs to Harry's suite. There he threw himself into a chair and, laying back his head, gave way to loud laughter. He was quite hurt when the other two did not join in: 'I have worked so hard and done so much only to amuse you two,' he complained.

'It's cruelty to animals.'

'But he calls us animals,' the Nawab pointed out.

Harry said 'He's just an old bore. Why ever did you bring him?'

'It was she,' the Nawab said, pointing at Olivia. But when she looked embarrassed, he tried to make it up to her: 'He is not a bore. He is very amusing. "We doctors at home in England",' he said, laying his fingertips together and blowing out an imaginary moustache. It was not a very good imitation, but to oblige him the other two laughed. At first he was gratified but then his mood changed and he said with disgust 'You are right. He is a bore. Tcha, why did we bring him, let's send him away.'

Olivia felt compelled to say: 'He really is exceptionally obnoxious. Don't judge by him.'

The Nawab looked at her rather coldly: 'Don't judge what by him?'

'All of us.'

'Who's us?' Harry asked her. He too sounded hostile. Olivia felt herself floundering – it was the same sensation she had had at the Crawford's dinner party, of not knowing where she stood.

'I don't know how you feel about it,' Harry pursued, 'but please don't lump me in with all that lot.'

'But, Harry, the Crawfords – for instance – they are not like Dr Saunders, you know they're not. Or the Minnies. Or for that matter Douglas and –'

'You?'

'All are the same,' the Nawab said suddenly and decisively.

Olivia had a shock – did he mean her too? Was she included? She looked at his face and was frightened by the feelings she saw so plainly expressed there: and it seemed to her that she could not bear to be included in these feelings, that she would do anything not to be.

Ruth Prawer Jhabvala

12 Texts in Context

Objectives
- To learn about various ways of placing texts in context
- To develop the ability to recognize and make use of relevant contextual information

What do we mean by context?

When we study a poem, a play, a novel or any other piece of writing we usually give most of our attention to exploring and analysing the text we see in front of us. However, no literary text can exist in a vacuum, or entirely on its own. All kinds of factors influence the way authors write and affect the way we read their work. Becoming aware of this background information can enhance our understanding and enjoyment of texts by enabling us to see them as part of a wider picture. In other words, we place them in context.

Relevant contexts

If you are studying literature at advanced level, you are expected to learn to recognize and comment on aspects of context that are relevant to the texts you have read. At AS level, you may be asked to demonstrate that you are aware of these, while at A2 level a deeper understanding of their significance is required. There are several ways of placing texts in context. We can consider

- how a text interrelates with the events of the **author's life** or **biography**
- the place of a particular text in the **author's** *oeuvre* or **writings as a whole**
- how the text reflects the **historical period** and/or the **place** in which it was written
- the text as an example of its **genre** or of a particular **literary style** or **period**
- the ways in which the **language** of a particular time or place is reflected in the text
- how our reading of the text might be influenced by the way other readers or critics have reacted to it recently or in the past, that is its **reception**
- the place and significance in the work as a whole of an **extract**, such as a passage from a novel or one poem from a collection.

The author's biography

It can certainly be interesting and increase our enjoyment of texts if we learn something about the lives of the people who wrote them. Indeed, it can be difficult to make any sense at all of some writing without any such knowledge. There can be two sides to this issue, however. Some critics believe that a text should stand alone and that as students of literature we should concern ourselves only with the words on the page, while others suggest that we should learn as much as possible about an author's life and times in order to understand the work fully. For AS- and A-level, we need to aim somewhere between these two extremes.

Some awareness of a writer's biography may be essential, but it cannot take the place of thorough knowledge of the texts themselves and it can create some pitfalls. For example, it may be tempting to begin an essay by telling the writer's life story, if you have spent time learning about it. However, unless you have specifically been asked to provide such information or to write about the text in relation to the author's life, this is unlikely to be relevant and will simply waste valuable time. It is more likely that you will want to demonstrate your understanding in more subtle ways, including facts or background details only when they are clearly relevant or they support points you want to make about the text.

Finding biographical information

As a starting point, editions intended for study, particularly of classics or older texts, often include an introduction with some biographical material. The best way to gain a deeper understanding of an author's life and times, however, is to read a good biography, or better still if one exists, an auto-biography. Biographies can vary enormously. Some can be thoroughly researched and packed with information but very dry and dull to read, while others may be enjoyable – even scandalous – but less accurate. It is worth dipping into a few, if they are available. You could also try the following:

- **Encyclopaedias**
- **Diaries** or **letters** from the author, published in book form. These can give fascinating insights into a writer's life, and how and why he or she writes. If you are studying Keats's poetry, for example, it is helpful to read some of his letters.
- **Television documentaries** or **films** about the lives of famous writers.
- The **Internet**. Contemporary writers, and associations of people interested in particular authors, often have websites, although you may have to search carefully for genuinely useful information.

If biography captures your imagination and you wish to explore this genre further, you could consider making a study of two contrasting biographies of the same writer for a coursework assignment. It is amazing how different the same person can appear through different pairs of eyes!

Activity

> **1** Choose a writer whose work you are currently studying. Arrange for each member of your group to research one possible source of information about this author, and bring notes to your next session.
>
> **2** Discuss what you have discovered, noting any differences in your findings. Combine your information and create a handout on the life of your chosen writer.

The author's *oeuvre*

It can be important to know not only about the lives of writers but about their other works, so that you can see whether the text you are studying is typical of its author or whether it stands out for some reason. You may be asked to show that you are aware that authors can have 'favourite' themes or features of style, which crop up regularly in their writings. For example, *The Handmaid's Tale* (see Unit 2) is typical of Margaret Atwood's work in that she frequently writes prose fiction about the roles and experiences of women in modern society. It is unusual, however, because it is the only novel in which she chooses to explore these ideas in a futuristic or 'science fiction' setting.

Activity

> Find out what you can about other works by the author of the text you are currently studying. Read synopses or summaries of them or skim read them if you have time.
>
> - Does this author have any favourite themes and concerns?
> - Do you think your set text is typical of its author?

Time and place

Some knowledge of the historical background to a text and the location in which it is written can help you to make sense of aspects of the writing that might otherwise be baffling. Different times and places or cultures have conventions, styles or variations of language which, with experience, we can begin to learn to recognize. The poet Shelley tries to explain how this comes about in the next extract:

There must be a resemblance, which does not depend upon their own will, between all the writers of any particular age. They cannot escape from subjection to a common influence which arises out of an infinite combination of circumstances belonging to the times in which they live; though each is in a degree the author of the very influence by which his being is thus pervaded.

Percy Bysshe Shelley (from his introduction to *Laon and Cythna*)

Shelley points out that not only are writers moulded – whether they like it or not – by the historical period in which they live and work, but they have the power to influence that age and contribute to creating the culture in which they live. It is a two-way process.

Activity

> At the back of this book (see pages 333–340) there is a Chronology listing important historical, political and social events in parallel with literary developments. Choose a text that you are studying or have read recently, and make sure that you know the dates when it was written and/or published. Refer to the Chronology to find out some of the key historical events that occurred around that time. If you can, use an encyclopaedia or other reference materials to expand your knowledge. Discuss whether you can find any evidence that your text reflects what was happening at the time when it was written.

For more on how texts can be related to their historical context, see the Special Feature on Romantic Poetry at the end of this unit.

'Place' can be as important as time. In recent years there has been a surge of interest in the work of British writers who can trace their roots to other cultures, and in the literature of other English-speaking countries. Some of this is what we call 'post-colonial' writing, by authors from nations which were previously colonies under the rule of European powers like the British Empire. Writers from the West Indies, India, and several African states, as well as from Canada and Australia, may fit this category. In a colony, the 'native' or indigenous culture may have been partly suppressed to make way for that which was imposed by the European invaders. With independence, there may be efforts to reassert the original culture. In any case, such societies are complex mixtures, often carrying the weight of the memory of oppression.

Some writers from this sort of background whose work is studied at A-level are:

Maya Angelou
Toni Morrison ⎫ – the American South and the legacy of slavery
Alice Walker ⎭

Margaret Atwood – Canada

Jean Rhys – the West Indies

If you are studying a text like this, find out what you can about the writer's cultural situation and/or the setting of the text. You will also need to be aware that some of these writers use different forms of the English language.

Genre, style and literary period

As well as relating texts to a historical period, we sometimes put them in the context of a **literary period** or style, which is not quite the same thing. Texts written around the same time are likely to have at least some similarities, as Shelley suggested in the passage above, but texts from a particular literary period are connected at a deeper level. Their authors are likely to share particular ideas about life, art and literature which are reflected in their work. They may be part of a 'movement' – a group of people who share a philosophy or belief system. Such groups tend to arise in response to political or social events, or out of a desire for change. For example, in the years after the First World War, the 'Modernists' experimented with artistic forms and styles. The old styles of art and writing no longer seemed appropriate in a world that had changed beyond recognition and had ceased to make sense in the way it had done in the past. The Special Feature at the end of this unit explores another literary period, that of the 'Romantics'.

When we talk about **literary genre**, we simply mean the particular kind or form of text we are reading: a play, a novel, a short story, a biography or a poem, for example. We might also focus on narrower categories, such as the Gothic novel, or Shakespearean tragedy.

Language

Language evolves continuously over time. We can see enormous differences between the language of our time and that of Chaucer or Shakespeare, but even in relatively recent texts, vocabulary and usage may be unfamiliar.

Language also alters with place. Within the United Kingdom, there are many varieties of English and quite a number of writers have experimented with these, from Emily Bronte's representation of Yorkshire dialect in *Wuthering Heights* to James Joyce's Irish English, or from Lewis Grassic Gibbon's Lowland Scots in *Sunset Song* to the broad Glaswegian of Irvine Welsh's *Trainspotting*. Also, as we have already mentioned, writers from other cultures may use forms of English other than Standard English. These are not 'wrong' or 'inferior', but are languages in their own right, with their own rules and structures.

Activity

> Read the following poem with a partner. Try reading it aloud, or at least try to imagine how it would sound. You may even be able to listen to a taped performance by the author. Discuss how the language differs from Standard English – but enjoy the poem too!

The poet, Grace Nichols, was born in Guyana in the West Indies in 1950, but came to live in the United Kingdom in her twenties. Often, she writes about the challenges of keeping a sense of identity while living in a culture very different from that of her past. Her work is written to be heard, not just to be read, and is best appreciated in live performance.

The Fat Black Woman Goes Shopping

Shopping in London winter
is a real drag for the fat black woman
going from store to store
in search of accommodating clothes
and de weather so cold

Look at the frozen thin mannequins
fixing her with grin
and de pretty face salesgals
exchanging slimming glances
thinking she don't notice

Lord is aggravating

Nothing soft and bright and billowing
to flow like breezy sunlight
when she walking

The fat black woman curses in Swahili/Yoruba
and nation language under her breathing
all this journeying and journeying

The fat black woman could only conclude
that when it come to fashion
the choice is lean

    Nothing much beyond size 14

Grace Nichols (from *The Fat Black Woman's Poems*)

Working on an extract

Sometimes, examination questions will ask you to write about an extract in detail, while also showing that you know how it fits into or is significant in the context of the text as a whole. This could be an important episode from a novel or play, or one poem or short story from a collection. As with the other aspects of context, you need a good understanding of the 'wider picture' in order to be able to assess this 'sample'. With an individual poem, you may be asked to consider whether it is typical of the collection in which it is published, or whether it differs from the 'norm'. With extracts from plays or novels, you will also have to think about how the drama or plot is carried forward by the scene or passage concerned. It may be a turning point for a particular character, or an incident that sets off a whole chain of events. In the first part of this book you will already have encountered many examples of extracts that have been related to their contexts in various ways.

Reception and critical context

As well as knowing something about the context in which a text is *written*, we also need to be aware that there is someone else in the equation: the *reader*. The background, culture or period in which we read a text may significantly influence how we react to it and what we 'receive' from it. If we think for a minute about texts written in our own time, such as modern novels, we will see that it is not really possible to categorize them or place them in context in quite the same way as we do with texts from the past, which have already been allocated to a 'period' that has been given a name, like 'Romantic' or 'Victorian'. With older texts, we can also read the comments of critics, both those who wrote their responses when the text was first published and those who write with many years of hindsight, and all these ideas contribute something to our overall impression of the text. For example, it is interesting to learn that some of the first readers of Emily Bronte's famous novel *Wuthering Heights* called it respectively:

'The weirdest story in the English Language ...'
'A nightmare.'
'A world of brilliant figures in an atmosphere of mist ...'
'One of the most repellent books we ever read'
[a book that] 'shows more genius ... than you will find in a thousand novels.'

Critics and readers ever since have continued to respond to the novel in different ways, depending on their own backgrounds and ideas.

When we turn to a modern text, however, we may have the remarks of a few reviewers or literary scholars to consider, but we cannot yet see how readers of the future might read and categorize it. There is less material to influence our opinions, but also less to get in the way of our own responses.

Reading the 'critics'

As part of your A-level course you may read some critical writing and come into contact with different interpretations of literary texts. Probably, you will form your own opinions of these different views. It is important, however, that you do not allow the ideas of the critics or other readers to confuse or take the place of your own thoughts and feelings about a text.

If you go on to study literature at a higher level, you will have more exposure to the writings of literary critics and various literary theories. The ideas and approaches that these offer can be useful in stimulating new ways of looking at texts and can often prompt ideas that might not have occurred to you had you not read them. It does not matter whether you agree or disagree with the ideas you read. Challenging the things that you read is just as important as agreeing with them when you are developing your ideas about the texts you are studying.

Literary theory

Many of the critics you will read, in studying Literature at a higher level, will approach their analysis of the text using a particular theory that they apply to all texts. There are many of these literary theories, most of which have been developed by academics over the past three or four decades, and sometimes they run counter to one another. The main thing to remember is that each one looks at a text from a particular point of view or focuses on a particular aspect of it. This is because the theory regards one particular aspect of the text as being more significant than anything else. It is important to bear this in mind when reading literary analysis based on individual literary theories. What follow are brief descriptions of the more important literary theories. You may well have already come across some of these. (Bear in mind, though, that these descriptions only give you a very simple definition of very complex theories.)

Structuralism

This is a complex theory but basically it involves the reader giving up his or her right to a personal response or interpretation and focusing on the text alone, describing how the text operates. The theory involves taking a much more 'scientific' approach by looking at texts with the view that all texts attempt to create a view of the world by ordering it through the structure of language. The effect of a structuralist approach can be to look closely at the language structures of a text and to place less emphasis on the ideas of what a text tells us about life, the world, and the characteristics of human nature; the latter are more common approaches at A-level.

Post-structuralism or deconstructive criticism

Post-structuralism covers a whole range of activities, so again the ideas are very much simplified here. Post-structuralism questions the structuralist idea that the reader must have knowledge of the 'literary code' of language in order to gain access to the 'meaning' of a text. It does not regard the meaning in language as being stable. It also argues that the reader's perceptions of a text are necessarily subjective so that the idea of any kind of literary objectivity is brought into question. Although post-structuralist criticism seeks to 'destabilize' the text by, amongst other means, demonstrating its contradictions and problems – and as such has sometimes been regarded as a quite destructive form of criticism – it can have more positive aspects. For example, it can encourage you to consider alternative meanings and treat the text as something that is dynamic and not as something that has finite or 'closed' meanings.

Psychoanalytical theory

Psychoanalytical theory has made a major contribution to post-structuralist theory, taking as its starting point the ideas of Freud who sought to provide universal models and explanations for the unconscious drives and desires that motivate human behaviour. Lacan developed Freud's theories further through his view that language is the major force in shaping human identity. These theories have been applied to literature study and can provide new angles on the ways in which texts are constructed and presented.

Marxist criticism

Unlike Structuralist and Post-structuralist literary theories, which have nothing to do with history, society, and class in relation to a text, the Marxist critic brings to a text Marx's view of history in which the idea of class struggle is central. It promotes analysis of a text by creating connections between the text itself and the social and economic structure of the society in which it was written. The theory regards these connections as being fundamental to the nature of the literature produced. Necessarily, Marxist criticism challenges many of the traditional views of texts which interpret them according to the values of a bourgeois or middle-class culture. It seeks to get away from the idea that texts present universal truths about human nature, looking instead to question and reinterpret a text in the light of the period in which it was written and the nature of the society within which it was produced and which influenced it.

Feminist criticism

Like Marxist criticism, Feminist criticism also concerns itself with social and political issues, in this case with the presentation of women in literature. The Feminist critic is particularly interested in seeking to affirm feminine qualities within what is regarded as a male-dominated society. Most Feminist criticism takes as its starting point the idea that society is and always has been patriarchal (i.e. where men assume the dominant role) and examines texts from this perspective.

An important element within feminist criticism is that of Black, Women-of-Colour, and Lesbian critical theory. Writers and critics involved in this area are very much concerned with the interrelationship between race, sexuality, and oppression of one kind or another.

An overview

This very brief look at some of the key critical theories that you might come across shows just a few examples of the varying ways in which texts can be considered through different critical theories. Your understanding of such theories can contribute to your overall understanding of literature but you should always be aware that they all approach the analysis of texts from a very particular, even partisan, point of view.

As you take your studies further, your awareness and sensitivity to the layers of meaning within literary texts will continue to grow but never forget that the fundamental element in this process is to develop your own view. Your view of a text is as valid as anyone else's, so long as it is based firmly on a study of the text itself – a view that presents your 'informed, independent opinions and judgements' is vital.

In A-level examinations, a question which focuses on the critical aspect of context is likely to present you with a statement of opinion from a critic, in the form of a quotation, and ask you to assess the validity of that opinion by referring closely to the text. You may also be expected to explain whether you agree or disagree with the critic, so you will need to have your own views and responses clear in your mind.

Special Feature: Romantic Poetry

. . . .

What do we mean by 'Romantic'?

Initially, perhaps, the word 'romantic' will bring to your mind images of romantic love, the stereotypical, idealized 'romance' of modern popular fiction or film. However, in the study of literature, we use the word to refer to something rather different.

When we talk about the **Romantic period** in literature, we are usually referring to writing produced in a specific period of time, usually the years between about 1780 and 1830. However, not all literature written at that time is 'Romantic': Jane Austen wrote her novels then, and they are not 'Romantic' in this sense at all, even though they are love stories. Date is not the only factor to consider.

'Romanticism' refers to a new set of ways of thinking and feeling about the world which swept through Europe in the later part of the Eighteenth Century and remained important for much of the Nineteenth, influencing music and painting as well as literature. These ways of thinking and feeling were apparent in most aspects of life, including politics, religion and science. If you look at the pages dealing with the years 1775 to 1850 in the Chronology (pages 336–337) you will see that the era in which the Romantics wrote was a very stormy one: an age of war, upheaval, and in particular, an age of revolution. Without some knowledge of this context, we cannot fully understand Romantic writing.

Traditionally in English Literature, the most important Romantic writers were six great male poets who were writing in the years between about 1780 and 1830:

'First Generation'	William Blake (1757–1827) Samuel Taylor Coleridge (1772–1834) William Wordsworth (1770–1850)
'Second Generation'	Lord Byron (1788–1824) John Keats (1795–1821) Percy Bysshe Shelley (1792–1822)

The novelist Sir Walter Scott is also sometimes included, as is Mary Shelley, the author of *Frankenstein*. Now, too, the work of some other women writers of the time, such as Joanna Baillie and Hannah More, is gaining recognition.

Revolution

There were political revolutions in several European countries in the late Eighteenth Century, as well as a War of Independence – from Britain – in America. The most influential was the French Revolution, which captured the imagination and support of many people in Britain when it began in 1789.

The revolutions aimed to bring an end to traditional systems of government, which involved remote monarchs and wealthy aristocrats ruling over populations who were largely poor and uneducated, and to create instead societies based on ideals like those of the French republic: 'Liberte, Egalite, Fraternite' – freedom, equality and the brotherhood of man. Power was seized by people who previously had not even been allowed to vote.

However, in France, revolutionary idealism soon tipped over into revenge and violence. In 1793, Louis XVI and his queen, Marie Antoinette (who is supposed to have been so out of touch with reality that she said 'Let them eat cake' when starving peasants complained that they had no bread) were guillotined along with many other aristocrats. France plunged not into a better future, but a reign of terror. Many of those in Britain who had supported the aims of the revolution were shocked and disillusioned, while others continued to sympathize in secret. Since Britain was at war with France by this time, supporting the revolution was regarded as treason.

The 'first generation' Romantic poets, Blake, Coleridge and Wordsworth, lived through the events of the French Revolution, and its effects can be seen in their work. For example, Wordsworth visited France during the Revolution and later recorded his impressions in his long autobiographical poem, *The Prelude*. Much of Blake's work is written and illustrated using complex and obscure symbolism, which is partly a way of expressing – in disguise – the visions and ideals of revolution. Even the much more approachable *Songs of Innocence and of Experience*, published in 1789 and 1794 respectively, parallel 'innocent' belief in revolution with the disillusionment of 'experience'. The disguise was not sufficient to protect Blake from being charged with offences against the State.

Political revolution was mirrored in social and cultural changes. In the previous decades, everything that was fancy and artificial had been admired. Elaborate clothing and enormous wigs were fashionable, and both men and women powdered their faces; architecture and furnishings were very ornate; literary style was rather dry, clever and witty, or satirical, and tended to be of the head rather than the heart. Revolutionary thought was about making people more equal. With it came a taste for what was simpler and more natural. Literature changed too.

William Wordsworth

In his preface to *Lyrical Ballads*, a collection of poems by himself and Coleridge, William Wordsworth wrote a kind of 'revolutionary manifesto' for literature, in which he outlines some of the ideas that lie behind what we now call Romantic poetry.

- **Nature**   The natural world should be the most important source of inspiration for poets. Being 'natural' or 'at one' with nature is seen as an ideal state, a paradise that human beings have lost and to which they yearn to return. This is a little like the political revolutionaries' wish to create ideal nation-states.
- **Feelings**   Being 'natural' involved being able to feel and respond spontaneously, from the heart. Logical thinking, or 'reason', is a limited or inadequate way of responding to the world.
- **Imagination**   Imagination is a quality that enables you to see something special in ordinary things. It casts a glow over everyday events or memories.
- **Power to the people**   People who are in some way powerless or on the fringes of society are given a voice: the poor, particularly those who live and work in the countryside, the uneducated, the 'mad', women, and especially children begin to feature in poetry. They are seen as more 'natural' and more in touch with their feelings; their imaginations are not hampered by too much 'reason' or education. Educated, city-dwelling adults could learn something from them.
- **Individual experience** and the private lives of ordinary people are suitable subject-matter for poetry, not just the public exploits of kings, politicians, or the famous.
- **Real language**   Wordsworth suggests that the 'real language of men' – by which he means the clear, simple, natural language of ordinary people, men, women and children – is the best way to express feelings and describe experiences in poetry. Complicated, 'flowery' or witty language only gets in the way. The language of poetry needs to get back to nature and down to earth.

Here are some of Wordsworth's own words on the subject, from the Preface to *Lyrical Ballads*:

The principal object, then, which I proposed to myself in these poems was to choose incidents and situations from common life and to relate or describe them, throughout, as far as was possible, in a selection of language really used by men; and at the same time, to throw over them a certain colouring of imagination, whereby ordinary things should be presented to the mind in an unusual way.

Activity   Read the following short poem by Wordsworth. Write a few paragraphs about the poem, saying how far you think it is an example of some of the 'revolutionary' ideas above. Discuss your work with the rest of your group.

My heart leaps up

My heart leaps up when I behold
  A rainbow in the sky:
So was it when my life began;
So is it now I am a man;
So be it when I shall grow old
  Or let me die!
The Child is father of the Man;
And I could wish my days to be
Bound each to each by natural piety.

William Wordsworth

The natural world was always important to Wordsworth, who grew up close to the English Lake District. He studied at Cambridge and travelled in France during the Revolution, before devoting himself to poetry. He was supported in this by his friendship with Samuel Taylor Coleridge and the devoted companionship of his sister Dorothy.

One of the ways in which Wordsworth revolutionized poetry was to direct his attention to his own 'self': rather than looking only to the world outside himself for topics, as poets had generally done in the past, he wrote about his own subjective experiences. Nowhere is this more apparent than in his long autobiographical poem *The Prelude*, which is subtitled 'The Growth of a Poet's Mind'.

Lyrical or narrative?

Most Romantic poetry can be described by one of these terms:

- **Lyrical** poems tend to be reflective. Often, the poet tries to capture a particular moment from his or her experience and then goes on to ponder about its deeper meaning or significance. *My Heart Leaps Up* is a lyric poem, and so is Wordsworth's famous *Daffodils*.
- **Narrative** poems, as you would expect, are those that tell a story. They have their roots in the old oral traditions of storytelling, and some of the oldest written poems such as the epic tales of ancient Greece and Rome. They range from the ballads of folksong to long, complex poems like Spenser's *Faerie Queene* in the Sixteenth Century or Milton's *Paradise Lost* in the Seventeenth. Coleridge's *The Rime of the Ancient Mariner* is a narrative poem, while the later Romantic poets often drew on characters and ideas from Greek and Roman myths and epics. Later in this feature we will look at a narrative poem by Keats.

Perhaps you can see by the title that in *Lyrical Ballads* Wordsworth and Coleridge were attempting to cross one with the other: they write poems that are both narrative *and* personal and reflective. This is also true of *The Prelude*, in which Wordsworth tells the story of his life and regularly pauses to reflect on significant moments in his experience.

In addition to the ideas we have already considered, Wordsworth believed that there can be certain moments in our lives in which we go beyond, or transcend, everyday 'reality' and experience ourselves and the world around us more vividly or in a different way. These 'spots of time', as he calls them, stand out in our memories and have the power to strengthen us in difficult times. For him, childhood was particularly rich in these moments, many of which are recorded in the first books of *The Prelude*. His description of skating on a frozen lake at nightfall, part of which was introduced briefly in Unit 3 to illustrate the use of blank verse (see page 63), is one of these.

William Blake

Blake, the son of a London tradesman, was a talented artist, and left school at the age of ten to concentrate on drawing, but could not afford to pursue his ambition of becoming a painter. Instead, through an apprenticeship, he learned the craft of engraving, at which he became highly skilled, and continued to educate himself, reading literature and philosophy to a high level and writing poetry.

He blended creativity with craftsmanship, devising a way of etching his poems on copper printing plates and combining them with illustrations which he later coloured by hand. If you are studying Blake's poetry, it is important to look at these designs and not just the plain printed text. They are the 'context' in which he intended his work to be read, and sometimes the illustrations convey almost as much meaning as the words.

Blake was very unconventional and something of a rebel. His work looks strange to our eyes, and very different from Wordsworth's, yet he too was one of the first Romantics. Why?

- He was very concerned with what was 'natural' and hated anything pompous or artificial. He had educated himself, but felt that conventional teaching, whether in schools or the church, restricted people and stopped them thinking for themselves. He felt children should be allowed to be spontaneous and express themselves freely.
- He thought human feelings and energies were crushed by too much 'reason'.
- To him, revolution signified the spontaneity and joy of youth rebelling against conventional, rational, materialistic 'civilization'.
- He prophesied a 'New Age' in which these values would flourish and wrote a kind of 'Bible of Hell' to put forward his ideas.
- He believed imagination was the most important quality for an artist and hated traditional art which merely aimed to represent or copy 'real' life.

Here is a short extract from one of his 'prophecies', to give a flavour of his language and symbolism. Enitharmon (the 'feminine') and Los (the spirit of prophecy) have given birth to the child Orc ('feeling') who is going to rebel against the ancient Urizen ('reason'). Notice how the voice of feeling, the child Orc, has the effect of awakening people from a kind of 'death'. Urizen, on the other hand, is oppressive and must measure and calculate everything. Not even 'the Abyss' can remain mysterious or sacred.

The Book of Urizen

1 They named the child Orc; he grew,
Fed with the milk of Enitharmon.

2 Los awoke her. O sorrow & pain!
A tight'ning girdle grew
Around his bosom. In sobbings
He burst the girdle in twain,
But still another girdle
Oppress'd his bosom. In sobbings
Again he burst it. Again
Another girdle succeeds.
The girdle was form'd by day,
By night was burst in twain.

3 These falling down on the rock
Into an iron Chain,
In each other link by link lock'd.

4 They took Orc to the top of a mountain.
O how Enitharmon wept!
They chain'd his young limbs to the rock
With the Chain of Jealousy
Beneath Urizen's deathful shadow.

5 The dead heard the voice of the child
And began to awake from sleep;
All things heard the voice of the child
And began to awake to life.

6 And Urizen, craving with hunger,
Stung with the odours of Nature,
Explor'd his dens around.

7 He form'd a line & a plummet
To divide the Abyss beneath;
He form'd a dividing rule.

8 He form'd scales to weigh,
He form'd massy weights,
He form'd a brazen quadrant,
He form'd golden compasses,
And began to explore the Abyss;
And he planted a garden of fruits.

9 But Los encircled Enitharmon
With fires of Prophecy
From the sight of Urizen & Orc,

10 And she bore an enormous race.

William Blake

Activity

> Look at the following two short poems from Blake's *Songs of Innocence and of Experience*. They will appear much simpler. In what ways do they reflect Blake's ideas? Make notes and/or discuss your thoughts with your group.

Infant Joy (From *Songs of Innocence, 1789*)

'I have no name:
I am but two days old.'
What shall I call thee?
'I happy am,
Joy is my name.'
Sweet joy befall thee!

Pretty joy!
Sweet joy but two days old,
Sweet joy I call thee:
Thou dost smile,
I sing the while
Sweet joy befall thee.

Infant Sorrow (From *Songs of Experience, 1794*)

My mother groan'd! my father wept,
Into the dangerous world I leapt,
Helpless, naked, piping loud,
Like a fiend hid in a cloud.

Struggling in my father's hands,
Striving against my swadling bands,
Bound and weary, I thought best
To sulk upon my mother's breast.

William Blake

The second generation

In the years after the French Revolution and the long period of war with France that followed it, political and social issues continued to stimulate Romantic thought.

Activity

> With a partner, read and discuss the following poem. What do you think the poem is about? What feelings does it convey? What do you make of the last two lines?

An old mad, blind, despised, and dying King;
Princes, the dregs of their dull race, who flow
Through public scorn – mud from a muddy spring;

Rulers who neither see, nor feel, nor know,
But leech-like to their fainting country cling
Till they drop, blind in blood, without a blow.
A people starved and stabbed in th'untilled field;
An army, whom liberticide and prey
Makes as a two-edged sword to all who wield;
Golden and sanguine laws which tempt and slay;
Religion Christless, Godless – a book sealed;
A senate, times worst statute, unrepealed –
Are graves, from which a glorious phantom may
Burst, to illumine our tempestuous day.

Percy Bysshe Shelley

Activity

> Here is some more information about the above poem. First, its title: *England in 1819*.
>
> Next, look at this extract from the Chronology on page 336, with some more detail filled in. Does knowing something about its context help you to make more sense of the poem?

1815 Napoleon defeated at Waterloo.
War with France ends.
Corn Laws are passed.

In the previous 25 years, the combined effects of war with France, bad harvests and legislation designed to protect landowners had led to crises of starvation and food riots. The Corn Laws of 1815, which set fixed prices for grain, made things even worse: landowners would leave land uncultivated if it was not profitable, increasing food shortages.

1819 'Peterloo' massacre in Manchester.

People were discontented with the unfair electoral system of the time. Only the wealthy could vote, and bribery and corruption were rife. A large crowd gathered to protest at St Peter's Fields, in Manchester. The demonstration was peaceful, but troops were sent in. They massacred the protestors in a 'battle' sarcastically nicknamed after the Battle of Waterloo.

1820 Death of George III.
Succeeded by the Prince Regent, George IV.

George III, who had reigned for almost 60 years, suffered from a disease which made him 'mad'. His son had already ruled as Regent since 1810. (You can gain a flavour of life in this period from Alan Bennett's play, which has also been filmed, *The Madness of George III*.)

Summary

- Probably you caught the mood of anger at the state of the country and disgust with its rulers at your first reading. Now you know that King George was 'mad, blind, despised and dying' and the poem tells you people didn't think much of his son, the Regent, either. He is 'mud from a muddy spring' and like a 'leech', he feeds on the blood of his country, oblivious to the needs of his subjects.
- The people were starving as a result of the Corn Laws and other problems, and were 'stabbed' at St Peter's Fields, where the army committed 'liberticide' – they murdered liberty. The laws are 'Golden' and 'sanguine' because money is at the root of the nation's corruption, and bloodshed is the result.
- The Church seemed corrupt and hypocritical too – 'Christless, Godless'; remote and closed off from the people, it is 'a book sealed'.
- In the last two lines the mood alters. From this picture of utter corruption and decay, Shelley suggests that something or someone, 'a glorious phantom', may emerge and change everything. Whatever this is, it is full of energy and light: it will 'burst' out and 'illumine' the 'tempestuous' world.

The final point shows that although the age of political revolutions had more or less passed, the idea that there could be some 'revolutionary' person or power, that might change the world and bring about a better future, continued to be important in later Romanticism.

Shelley, along with Lord Byron and John Keats, belonged to a younger generation of Romantic poets who had not been around at the time of the French Revolution and the horrors that followed. These young men accused the older poets like Wordsworth, who became rather staid later in life, of betraying revolutionary values. In contrast, they adopted what is seen as the stereotypical Romantic lifestyle, travelling abroad or living in exile, experimenting with open relationships, challenging social conventions, being revolutionary in their own way – and dying at a young age.

John Keats

Keats was born in London. His family was reasonably well off, but not wealthy enough to enable him to live without a profession as Byron and Shelley did. His parents died when he was young, and he was apprenticed to a surgeon before going on to study medicine at Guy's Hospital. However, his heart was in poetry, and he found time to read and write a considerable amount, and to go on mountain walking tours in Scotland and the Lake District. In his early twenties his health began to break down and he developed tuberculosis. He made a frantic voyage to Italy in the hope that the warmer climate would be beneficial, but he died aged only twenty-five. He had fallen deeply in love with a young woman, Fanny Brawne, and the letters he wrote to her and to others in his last months, when he knew he was doomed, are heart-breaking.

As we have seen, as well as imagining a better future, Romantics also tended to idealize aspects of the past. Though the Industrial Revolution was irrevocably changing the landscape and social systems of Britain, they mourned the passing of what Blake called 'England's green and pleasant land.' They were also drawn to the 'pastoral' world of shepherds, shepherdesses, nymphs and fauns from the myths of Ancient Greece and Rome. Keats had read these as a boy, along with the legends of Medieval and Renaissance Italy, and the works of earlier English poets like Spenser and Milton. He found in them a rich storehouse of ideas and starting points for his poetry. You will probably find that some knowledge of these is required to understand and enjoy his work, but most modern editions will include annotations and explanations to help you.

More than any other writer, Keats has been idealized as the typical Romantic poet and many people respond warmly to his work. His poems range from long, ambitious narratives such as *Endymion*, through intense odes and sonnets, to humorous, entertaining verses which he sometimes included in letters to his sister and brothers.

Keats's life was shadowed by life-threatening illness. His beloved youngest brother, Tom, who also had tuberculosis, died aged only 19 and he knew his own fate would be similar, so he was painfully aware of the transience and fragility of human life. This is the central theme of his poetry, together with the message that since life is short and things change, we should 'sieze the day', live life to the full and find what joy we can in the time we do have. As one critic, Jack Stillinger, expresses it,

Keats's significant poems center on a single problem, the mutability [or 'changeableness'] inherent in nature and human life.

We can see these themes clearly, even in an early work, written for his brother Tom's seventeenth birthday in 1816.

Activity   Read this poem carefully, with a partner. Discuss the picture Keats creates of this evening spent with his brothers. What 'birthday wish' does he express in the sestet (the final six lines) of this sonnet?

To my Brothers

Small, busy flames play through the fresh-laid coals,
   And their faint cracklings o'er our silence creep
   Like whispers of the household gods that keep
A gentle empire o'er fraternal souls.
And while, for rhymes, I search around the poles,
   Your eyes are fixed, as in poetic sleep,
   Upon the lore so voluble and deep,
That aye at fall of night our care condoles.
This is your birth-day Tom, and I rejoice
   That thus it passes smoothly, quietly.
Many such eves of gently whispering noise

> May we together pass, and calmly try
> What are this world's true joys – ere the great voice,
> From its fair face, shall bid our spirits fly.

John Keats

Keats's narrative poems

The second generation Romantic poets all wrote long narrative poems and Keats was no exception. *The Eve of Saint Agnes* is considered his best work of this type. It is an exploration of some of Keats's ideas about life, death and love rather than an example of pure storytelling. It is a tale that has parallels with Shakespeare's *Romeo and Juliet*. It concerns lovers, Madeline and Porphyro, who are kept apart by her family's hatred of him and includes a scene where he wakens her from sleep before they elope – without mishap, unlike Romeo and Juliet. Other significant members of the 'cast' are an old nurse, Angela, and an 'ancient Beadsman' or 'holy man'.

According to an old superstition, if on St Agnes' Eve a young woman fasts and goes straight to bed without speaking or looking around, her future husband may appear to her in a dream. Madeline tries this and is rewarded with a dream of her lover, Porphyro. Porphyro, meanwhile, has gained access to her chamber. She awakens to find her dream has become 'reality', and they run away to start a new life together. The 'romance' is set within a contrasting frame. The poem begins – and ends – with the elderly beadsman who prays in the bitter cold, and with thoughts of death. He passes the statues of knights and ladies of the past. It seems that no amount of praying can keep death at bay.

The Eve of St Agnes

I

> St Agnes' Eve – Ah, bitter chill it was!
> The owl, for all his feathers, was a-cold;
> The hare limped trembling through the frozen grass,
> And silent was the flock in woolly fold:
> Numb were the Beadsman's fingers, while he told
> His rosary, and while his frosted breath,
> Like pious incense from a censer old,
> Seemed taking flight for heaven, without a death,
> Past the sweet Virgin's picture, while his prayer he saith.

II

> His prayer he saith, this patient, holy man;
> Then takes his lamp, and riseth from his knees,
> And back returneth, meagre, barefoot, wan,
> Along the chapel aisle by slow degrees:
> The sculptured dead, on each side, seem to freeze,
> Emprisoned in black, purgatorial rails;
> Knights, ladies, praying in dumb orat'ries,

He passeth by; and his weak spirit fails
To think how they may ache in icy hoods and mails.

Inside the castle, meanwhile, the scene is entirely different. A celebration is in progress, although Madeline's mind is elsewhere:

V

At length burst in the argent revelry,
With plume, tiara, and all rich array,
Numerous as shadows haunting faerily
The brain, new stuffed, in youth, with triumphs gay
Of old romance. These let us wish away,
And turn sole-thoughted, to one Lady there,
Whose heart had brooded, all that wintry day,
On love, and winged St Agnes' saintly care,
As she had heard old dames full many times declare.

VI

They told her how, upon St Agnes' Eve,
Young virgins might have visions of delight,
And soft adorings from their loves receive
Upon the honeyed middle of the night,
If ceremonies due they did aright;
As supperless to bed they must retire,
And couch supine their beauties, lily white;
Nor look behind, nor sideways, but require
Of Heaven with upward eyes for all that they desire.

Activity

> **1** Compare the way Keats presents the 'outside world' in the two
>   opening stanzas with his language and imagery here, inside the castle.
> **2** Compare Madeline's 'prayers' with the beadsman's.

While she lingers half-heartedly at the ball, Porphyro arrives. He too is 'praying':

IX

So, purposing each moment to retire,
She lingered still. Meantime, across the moors,
Had come young Porphyro, with heart on fire
For Madeline. Beside the portal doors,
Buttressed from moonlight, stands he, and implores
All saints to give him sight of Madeline
But for one moment in the tedious hours,
That he might gaze and worship all unseen;
Perchance speak, kneel, touch, kiss – in sooth such things have been.

Porphyro risks his life to enter the castle of his 'Hyena foemen', where 'not one breast affords him any mercy' except an old woman, Angela. She takes some persuading, but eventually 'Angela gives promise she will do /Whatever he shall wish.'

XVI

Sudden a thought came like a full-blown rose,
Flushing his brow, and in his pained heart
Made purple riot; then doth he propose
A stratagem, that makes the beldame start:

...

XIX

Which was, to lead him, in close secrecy,
Even to Madeline's chamber, and there hide
Him in a closet, of such privacy
That he might see her beauty unespied,
And win perhaps that night a peerless bride,
While legioned faeries paced the coverlet,
And pale enchantment held her sleepy-eyed.

Activity | Look closely at the language Keats uses to describe Porphyro's feelings when his idea comes to him.

Having gained entrance to Madeline's chamber, Porphyro looks around. This is the stereotypical castle of Gothic romance and the moon lends further 'enchantment'. The description is incredibly rich and sumptuous. It is language like this that creates the atmosphere for which this poem is famous.

Activity | With a partner, read the following stanzas and discuss how Keats uses visual description, imagery and colour to create a sense of atmosphere.

XXIV

A casement high and triple-arched there was,
All garlanded with carven imag'ries
Of fruits, and flowers, and bunches of knot-grass,
And diamonded with panes of quaint device,
Innumerable of stains and splendid dyes,
As are the tiger-moth's deep-damasked wings;
And in the midsts, 'mong thousand heraldries,
And twilight saints, and dim emblazonings,
A shielded scutcheon blushed with blood of queens and kings.

XXV

Full on this casement shone the wintry moon,
And threw warm gules on Madeline's fair breast,
As down she knelt for heaven's grace and boon;
Rose-bloom fell on her hands, together pressed,
And on her silver cross soft amethyst,

And on her hair a glory, like a saint:
She seemed a splendid angel, newly dressed,
Save wings, for Heaven – Porphyro grew faint;
She knelt, so pure a thing, so free from mortal taint.

At the climax of the poem, Porphyro has watched Madeline sleep for some time, when, desperate for her to wake, he takes up her 'lute/Tumultuous, and in chords that tenderest be,' he plays an old song, *La belle dame sans mercy*. She does wake, but her reaction is interesting, and perhaps a little unexpected:

XXXIV

Her eyes were open, but she still beheld,
Now wide awake, the vision of her sleep –
There was a painful change, that nigh expelled
The blisses of her dream so pure and deep.
At which fair Madeline began to weep,
And moan forth witless words with many a sigh,
While still her gaze on Porphyro would keep;
Who knelt, with joined hands and piteous eye,
Fearing to move or speak, she looked so dreamingly.

XXXV

'Ah, Porphyro!' said she, 'but even now
Thy voice was a sweet tremble in mine ear,
Made tuneable with every sweetest vow,
And those sad eyes were spiritual and clear:
How changed thou art! How pallid, chill, and drear!
Give me that voice again, my Porphyro,
Those looks immortal, those complainings dear!
O leave me not in this eternal woe,
For if thou diest, my Love, I know not where to go.'

Activity

> 1 Madeline's dream has apparently come true. Why, then, do you think she begins to 'weep and moan'? What point might Keats be making here?
> 2 Now read the ending of the poem. In what ways does this ending fit the pattern of the conventional romance? Can you see any ways in which it is different or unexpected?

XXXVI

Beyond a mortal man impassioned far
At these voluptuous accents, he arose,
Ethereal, flushed, and like a throbbing star
Seen mid the sapphire heaven's deep repose;
Into her dream he melted, as the rose
Blended its odour with the violet –
Solution sweet. Meantime the frost-wind blows

Like Love's alarum pattering the sharp sleet
Against the window-panes; St Agnes' moon hath set.

...

XXXIX

   'Hark! 'tis an elfin-storm from faery land,
   Of haggard seeming, but a boon indeed:
   Arise – Arise! the morning is at hand.
   The bloated wassaillers will never heed –
   Let us away, my love, with happy speed –
   There are no ears to hear, or eyes to see,
   Drowned all in Rhenish and the sleepy mead;
   Awake! arise! my love, and fearless be,
For o'er the southern moors I have a home for thee.'

XL

   She hurried at his words, beset with fears,
   For there were sleeping dragons all around,
   At glaring watch, perhaps with ready spears –
   Down the wide stairs a darkling way they found.
   In all the house was heard no human sound.
   A chain-drooped lamp was flickering by each door;
   The arras, rich with horseman, hawk and hound,
   Fluttered in the besieging wind's uproar;
And the long carpets rose along the gusty floor.

XLI

   They glide, like phantoms, into the wide hall;
   Like phantoms, to the iron porch, they glide;
   Where lay the Porter, in uneasy sprawl,
   With a huge empty flaggon by his side:
   The wakeful bloodhound rose, and shook his hide,
   But his sagacious eye an inmate owns.
   By one, and one, the bolts full easy slide –
   The chains lie silent on the footworn stones –
The key turns, and the door upon its hinges groans.

XLII

   And they are gone – ay, ages long ago
   These lovers fled away into the storm.
   That night the Baron dreamt of many a woe,
   And all his warrior-guests, with shade and form
   Of witch, and demon, and large coffin-worm,
   Were long be-nightmared. Angela the old
   Died palsy-twitched, with meagre face deform;
   The Beadsman, after thousand aves told,
For aye unsought for slept among his ashes cold.

John Keats

Summary

• •

- In Madeline's dream, the Porphyro who came to her was not real, but an enchanted, perfect version of her lover, with eyes that were 'spiritual and clear' and whose voice was a 'sweet tremble'. When she wakes, the man before her cannot match this image. He is disappointingly 'pallid, chill, and drear', a physical, mortal, reality. She calls for the 'immortal' image which is everlasting, unlike the real man, who could die and leave her.

- In stanza XXXVI, the strength of his love seems to enable Porphyro to transcend – or go 'beyond' – the limits of 'mortal man', and he 'melts into her dream'. (This version of the poem leaves things vague. Though originally Keats made it clear that the lovers come together sexually at this point, the poem was censored by his publisher, who thought it 'unfit for Ladies'.) The lovers run off together, to a new life 'o'er the southern moors', escaping from the castle in a scene typical of Gothic romance, past the tapestries of 'horseman, hawk and hound' and with the long carpets rising off the floor in the draughty halls. However, Keats's ending is not quite the conventional happy one. The lovers are not seen heading out into the sunshine of an ideal future, but into a very real, wintry storm. Once the enchantment of St Agnes Eve has passed, and 'St Agnes' moon hath set', their 'romance', like Madeline's idealized image of Porphyro, must be replaced with 'reality'.

- What Keats seems to be saying is that it is all very well having high-flown, spiritual visions of love, but when it comes down to it, love can only have a reality if it is between real, flesh-and-blood people, who have to live in an imperfect, harsh world. By setting his 'romance' between images of age and death, he shows that Madeline and Porphyro have to go out of the enchanted castle and make the most of love and life here on earth, before death overtakes them, as it inevitably must.

Activity

> In what ways might *The Eve of St Agnes* be considered 'Romantic'? Discuss the poem and makes notes on how it relates to any of the ideas and characteristics we have encountered in this Feature.

13 Reading for Meaning

Variations on a theme

One of the major themes running of the

Tension grows in Vietnam Conflict
Further Unrest In Asia

prose, poetry drama, non-fiction

different representations of similar experiences in World War One.

Objectives
- To consider a theme-based approach to texts
- To explore some different types of non-fiction prose texts
- To practise writing about short texts linked by theme

Reading round a theme

Some English Literature specifications include a module that specifies a particular theme or period which you study in advance, familiarizing yourself with a variety of texts and their historical and literary context. The module is usually assessed in one of two ways:

1 You plan your own wide reading and then sit an examination paper in which you are presented with several extracts or short texts and asked to write about them in detail, comparing them and setting them within the framework of your knowledge of the period or theme. You are not necessarily expected to have read the particular texts given, although if you have read widely and prepared thoroughly, you may find that you recognize some of them. It is best, however, to be ready to encounter them as unprepared texts for close reading.

2 You may be provided with a 'pre-release' anthology of texts and extracts on a given theme to prepare in advance, and asked to write on several of them in detail in the examination. In this case, you are expected to be

very familiar with the material. When you are first issued with the anthology, you will need to subject it to close reading and analysis and to annotate it carefully, if you are permitted to do so. Check the regulations for your specification.

If you are preparing to encounter unfamiliar texts, you will find the strategies suggested in Unit 10 are a useful place to start, but there are some additional factors to consider.

- As well as analysing unseen texts in detail, questions will require you to place them in context in some of the ways we considered in Unit 12 and to compare them, as we did in Unit 11.

- You can improve your chances of success by carefully studying your set theme or period and reading widely, so that you become aware of recurring ideas and conventions and are familiar with the key authors and their works.

- The wider your reading around the topic, the more likely you are to be able to make interesting connections with other texts. You may find that you have already read the 'unprepared' texts, which can give you a real advantage.

- A word of warning is necessary too. You should still give most of your attention to *in-depth exploration of the texts in front of you*. Don't spend *more* of your time writing about your other reading than you spend on these, however much you think it may impress the examiner. If, for example, you are presented with an extract from a novel you have read, beware of showing off your command of the rest of the plot at the expense of analysing the extract in detail. Use your knowledge, but only when it is *relevant*! The point of this exercise is for you to demonstrate your skill at *close reading* as well as your *wider reading*.

Non-fiction prose

In the first section of this book, you were introduced to all the main literary genres which are usually set for A-level. However, there is one form of literature still to consider: non-fiction prose. 'Prose' means any form of continuous writing that is not poetry, although the distinction can sometimes be blurred. This includes novels and short stories, of course, but here we are concerned with prose writings other than fiction.

Prose writers can have many different purposes. These can include:

- describing or reporting events
- propounding new ideas or points of view
- teaching or explaining
- reflecting on or expressing opinions about people, events, or situations
- raising awareness of social issues or injustices

- persuading or influencing readers on political issues; for example, by presenting arguments from a particular point of view.
- entertaining or amusing by presenting topics in original or clever ways

It is unlikely that you will study non-fiction prose writing as a set text, but you may well read some if your are preparing for a theme-based paper. It can also be rewarding to study for coursework. A useful 'spin-off' from the study of such prose texts is that they can help us to build up our understanding of the historical, political, or cultural context in which the other forms of literature are produced.

When studying non-fiction prose texts, our approach is not necessarily any different from when we study novels or even poetry. We still need to ask the key questions: What is the text about? How has the author chosen to write about it? and we may also ask: Why is the author writing this? In more specific terms, we need to examine:

- the surface and deeper meanings presented
- the writer's purpose or aim
- the author's viewpoint. Is the text written in the first person or the third person? The effects of this choice in fiction texts are explored in Unit 2 (see pages 13–17), but in non-fiction prose, they can be even more important. Writing in the third person suggests a more objective viewpoint while writing in the first person tends to give a more opinionated or subjective view. Some texts will need careful thought to determine where the author stands in relation to the material and to the reader
- the structure of the text. In argumentative writing, for example, both sides of the issue may be presented in a measured way before making a judgement or the author may be concerned only with building up the evidence one-sidedly. In contrast, personal, reflective writing may be loose, informal, or even quite unconventional in the way it is structured
- the tone of the writing and the emotions behind the words
- use of imagery and vocabulary
- other stylistic features, such as length and construction of sentences

These aspects all need to be borne in mind as we go on to consider the main types of prose texts that you may encounter at A-level: essays, autobiography and diaries, documentary writing, and journalism. However, you may find that it is sometimes difficult to put texts into categories in this way: essays can be journalistic and a diary can 'document' events.

The essay

In its pure form, the published essay is relatively rare nowadays. However, it used to be a popular way for an author to explore a topic of interest or to convey opinions about current affairs. From the Seventeenth Century, essays were circulated in pamphlets or published in magazines. These remained very popular forms of mass communication until radio and television took over as more powerful vehicles for the expression of personal or political views.

Essays are written in many styles: they can be witty, angry, and satirical or gentle and thoughtful, but they usually present a personal or subjective view of a topic, and do not pretend to be objective. Earlier essay writers often paid great attention to the way they used language, balancing their sentences and weighing their words, so that their writing can be quite stylized and formal. There is an example of an essay from the Seventeenth Century in the short anthology later in this Unit.

Biography, autobiography and memoirs

These forms of writing provide fascinating insights into the lives of people, past and present. Biographies document or celebrate the lives of famous – or infamous – people. They may be the product of the author's friendship with his subject or the result of extensive research. For example, two biographies of Charlotte Brontë, one by her contemporary and friend, Elizabeth Gaskell which is personal and anecdotal, the other by the Twentieth-Century scholar Winifred Gerin which is scholarly and more objective, present very different insights into the life of this Victorian writer.

Autobiographical writing or memoirs might review a whole lifetime, or may focus on particular events or a significant period in the author's life as Brian Keenan does in his autobiography *An Evil Cradling*. This is his account of the years he spent as a hostage in Beirut.

Activity

1 Read the following extract in which Keenan invites us to share his experience of confinement and isolation, something which most of us would fear.
2 Discuss the text with a partner and make notes on how Keenan uses language:
 • to involve the reader in his experiences
 • to convey the monotony of life in the cell
 • to describe how he is affected by captivity and how he copes with the situation
In particular, consider:
 • the sentence patterns Keenan uses
 • the effect of his strong use of the first person

An Evil Cradling

Come now into the cell with me and stay here and feel if you can and if you will that time, whatever time it was, for however long, for time means nothing in this cell. Come, come in.
I am back from my daily ablutions. I hear the padlock slam behind me and I lift the towel which has draped my head from my face. I look at the food on the

floor. The round of Arab bread, a boiled egg, the jam I will not eat, the slice or two of processed cheese and perhaps some houmus. Every day I look to see if it will change, if there will be some new morsel of food that will make this day different from all the other days, but there is no change. This day is the same as all the days in the past and as all the days to come. It will always be the same food sitting on the floor in the same place.

I set down my plastic bottle of drinking water and the other empty bottle. From bottle to bottle, through me, this fluid will daily run. I set the urine bottle at the far corner away from the food. This I put in a plastic bag to keep it fresh. In this heat the bread rapidly turns stale and hard. It is like eating cardboard. I pace my four paces backwards and forwards, slowly feeling my mind empty, wondering where it will go today. Will I go with it or will I try to hold it back, like a father and an unruly child? There is a greasy patch on the wall where I lay my head. Like a dog I sniff it.

I begin as I have always begun these days to think of something, anything upon which I can concentrate. Something I can think about and so try to push away the crushing emptiness of this tiny, tiny cell and the day's long silence. I try with desperation to recall the dream of the night before or perhaps to push away the horror of it. The nights are filled with dreaming. The cinema of the mind, the reels flashing and flashing by and suddenly stopping at some point when with strange contortions it throws up some absurd drama that I cannot understand. I try to block it out. Strange how in the daytime the dreams that we do not wish to remember come flickering back into the conscious mind. Those dreams that we desperately want to have with us in the daylight will not come to us but have gone and cannot be enticed back. It is as if we are running down a long empty tunnel looking for something that we left behind but cannot see in the blackness. The guards are gone. I have not heard a noise for several hours now. It must be time to eat. I tear off a quarter of the unleavened bread and begin to peel the shell from the egg. The word 'albumen' intrigues me for a while and I wonder where the name came from. How someone decided once to call that part of the egg 'albumen'. The shape of an egg has lost its fascination for me. I have exhausted thinking about the form of an egg. A boiled egg with dry bread is doubly tasteless. I make this meaningless remark to myself every day and don't know why.

Brian Keenan

Letters and diaries

Reading letters or diaries can be a very direct and fascinating way of entering into a writer's experience. They are informal autobiography, not necessarily written for publication. We are an audience the writer may never have imagined, reading material that was intended to be private. There is often controversy when writers die, or even during their lifetimes, about whether their personal diaries or letters should be made available for other people to read. However, some writers (if they are sure of their own importance!) do expect that their 'private' papers will be made public.

The following brief extract is from another account of the experience of captivity, by Oscar Wilde, who was imprisoned in 1895 for homosexual 'offences'. He wrote at length about his experiences in a 'letter' explaining his actions and motives, and expressing his feelings of betrayal to his young friend Lord Alfred Douglas, who was planning to publish some of the intimate letters he had received from Wilde. It seems likely that he expected this letter to be published and it later became known as *De profundis*, which means 'Out of the depths', echoing Psalm 130, which is a prayer for forgiveness.

From *De Profundis*

All this took place in the early part of November of the year before last. A great river of life flows between me and a date so distant. Hardly, if at all, can you see across so wide a waste. But to me it seems to have occurred, I will not say yesterday, but to-day. Suffering is one very long moment. We cannot divide it by seasons. We can only record its moods, and chronicle their return. With us time itself does not progress, it revolves. It seems to circle round one centre of pain. The paralysing immobility of a life every circumstance of which is regulated after an unchangeable pattern, so that we eat and drink and lie down and pray, or kneel at least for prayer, according to the inflexible laws of an iron formula: this immobile quality, that makes each dreadful day in the very minutest detail like its brother, seems to communicate itself to those external forces, the very essence of whose existence is ceaseless change. Of seed-time or harvest, of the reapers bending over the corn, or the grape gatherers threading through the vines, of the grass in the orchard made white with broken blossoms or strewn with fallen fruit: of these we know nothing, and can know nothing.

For us there is only one season, the season of sorrow. The very sun and moon seem taken from us. Outside, the day may be blue and gold, but the light that creeps down through the thickly-muffled glass of the small iron-barred window beneath which one sits is grey and niggard. It is always twilight in one's cell, as it is always twilight in one's heart. And in the sphere of thought, no less than in the sphere of time, motion is no more. The thing that you personally have forgotten, or can easily forget, is happening to me now, and will happen to me again to-morrow. Remember this, and you will be able to understand a little of why I am writing, and in this manner writing ...

Oscar Wilde

Activity   Re-read the extracts by Brian Keenan and Oscar Wilde on the theme of imprisonment, making notes on the ways in which they can be connected or contrasted.

Documentary writing

Sometimes authors use recorded facts and figures and the words of writers, experts, or witnesses (i.e. 'documentation') to produce their own interpretation of events. The maker of a television documentary works in a similar way.

In *Hiroshima*, John Hersey traces the experiences of six survivors of the first atomic bomb. He introduces each person individually, describing everyday details of their lives very precisely so that we can picture them in the moments before the bomb fell. He then goes on to track each of them through the year that follows. He originally wrote the book in 1946, only one year after the destruction of the city. Forty years later, he returned to Hiroshima to find out how the same six people had coped with the aftermath of the catastrophe and added a further chapter to his book. This extract from the opening of the book begins the tale of Toshiko Sasaki.

Hiroshima

Miss Toshiko Sasaki, the East Asia Tin Works clerk … got up at three o'clock in the morning on the day the bomb fell. There was extra housework to do. Her eleven-month-old brother, Akio, had come down the day before with a serious stomach upset; her mother had taken him to the Tamura Paediatric Hospital and was staying there with him. Miss Sasaki, who was about twenty, had to cook breakfast for her father, a brother, a sister, and herself, and – since the hospital, because of the war, was unable to provide food – to prepare a whole day's meals for her mother and the baby, in time for her father, who worked in a factory making rubber earplugs for artillery crews, to take the food by on his way to the plant. When she had finished and had cleaned and put away the cooking things, it was nearly seven. The family lived in Koi, and she had a forty-five minute trip to the tin works, in the section of town called Kannonmachi. She was in charge of the personnel records in the factory …

Miss Sasaki … sat down at her desk. She was quite far from the windows, which were off to her left, and behind her were a couple of tall bookcases containing all the books of the factory library, which the personnel department had organized. She settled herself at her desk, put some things in a drawer, and shifted papers. She thought that before she began to make entries in her lists of new employees, discharges, and departures for the Army, she would chat for a moment with the girl at her right. Just as she turned her head away from the windows, the room was filled with a blinding light. She was paralyzed by fear, fixed still in her chair for a long moment (the plant was 1,600 yards from the centre [of the explosion]). Everything fell, and Miss Sasaki lost consciousness. The ceiling dropped suddenly and the wooden floor above collapsed in splinters and the people up there came down and the roof above them gave way; but principally and first of all, the bookcases right behind her swooped forward and the contents threw her down, with her left leg horribly twisted and breaking underneath her. There, in the tin factory, in the first moment of the atomic age, a human being was crushed by books.

John Hersey

Journalism

You may have noticed that several of the prose texts in this Unit deal with disturbing or disastrous events. This seems particularly true when we look at journalistic writing, because typically it focuses on 'bad news'. Indeed, the exposure of injustice or suffering seems to inspire journalists to produce their most powerful work. Journalism can, of course, be very humorous, satirical, or entertaining but it is often intended to alert us to some form of wrongdoing.

John Pilger, an Australian journalist, has written bitingly about injustices all over the world. He has a particular concern to expose the ways in which the media and propaganda are used to distort people's perception of events. In the extract below, he shows how the language used by those responsible for bombing campaigns in Vietnam and in the Gulf War blunted people's awareness of the human suffering involved.

Video Nasties

In 1972, I watched American B52s bombing southern Vietnam, near the ashes of a town called An Loc. From a distance of two miles, I could see three ladders of bombs curved in the sky; and, as each rung reached the ground, there was a plume of fire and a sound that welled and rippled, then quaked the ground beneath me.

This was Operation Arc Light, described by the Pentagon as 'high performance denial interdiction, with minimized collateral damage': jargon that echoes today. The B52s were unseen above the clouds; between them they dropped seventy tons of explosives in a 'long-box' pattern that extended several miles. Almost everything that moved inside the box was deemed 'redundant'.

On inspection, a road that connected two villages had been replaced by craters, one of them almost a quarter of a mile wide. Houses had vanished. There was no life; cooking pots lay strewn in a ditch, no doubt dropped in haste. People a hundred yards from the point of contact had not left even their scorched shadows, which the dead had left at Hiroshima. Visitors to Indo-China today are shocked by the moonscape of craters in Vietnam, Laos and Cambodia, where people lived.

The B52s now operating over Iraq are the same type of thirty-year-old aircraft. We are told they are bombing Saddam Hussein's Republican Guard, and the 'outskirts' of Baghdad. Before the introduction in Vietnam of military euphemisms designed to make palatable to Congress new hi-tech 'anti-people' weapons, the term used was carpet-bombing. This was vivid and accurate, for these aircraft lay carpets of death, killing and destroying comprehensively and indiscriminately. This is what they were built to do; and that is what they are no doubt doing in a country where most people neither have shelters nor are 'dug in'.

The other night, on television, a senior ex-RAF officer included the current B52 raids in his description of 'pinpoint strikes ... part of the extraordinary precision work of the Allies'. John Major and Tom King constantly refer to this 'remarkable precision' and, by clear implication, the equally remarkable humanitarian benefits this brings to the innocent people of Iraq, although further information about these benefits is curiously unforthcoming.

... The principal weapons used against Iraq, such as the Tomahawk cruise missile, have a 'circular error probability'. This means they are targeted to fall within a circle, like a dart landing anywhere on a dart board. They do not have to hit, or even damage, the bull's-eye to be considered 'effective' or 'successful'. Some have hit the bull's-eye – the Tomahawk that demolished the Ministry of Defence building in Baghdad is the most famous – but many, if not most, clearly have not. What else have they hit? What else is within the circle? People, maybe? The numerous autocues say nothing.

General Powell has also referred to 'minimized collateral damage'. Like 'circular error probability' this term was invented in Vietnam. It means dead civilians: men, women, and children. Their number is 'minimized', of course ...

John Pilger

Activity

1 Look at paragraphs 1 to 3. In what ways do Pilger's language, style, and attitude in the second paragraph differ from those of the first and third? What is his aim here? Find other examples of this in the text.

2 Pilger talks about 'military euphemisms'. A euphemism is a word or phrase which we use when stating the truth baldly would be too painful or embarrassing. Examine the words and phrases in quotation marks – the official jargon. What is their purpose and effect? Devise substitute phrases which would express the truth more graphically. Create some euphemisms of your own for the effects of warfare.

3 'The ... remarkable humanitarian benefits this brings to the innocent people of Iraq, although further information about these benefits is curiously unforthcoming.' How would you describe Pilger's tone in this extract? Find other examples in the text to support your views.

4 Make notes and then write a short essay in response to the question which follows:

John Pilger and John Hersey are both concerned about the civilian casualties of modern warfare, although they tackle the theme in very different ways. Write about the connections and contrasts between the two extracts, examining in detail the ways in which each writer treats the subject. Consider

- the writers' aims and attitudes
- their use of language
- the tone of the writing
- the 'focus' of each extract: are we seeing a 'close-up' or a 'distance-shot'? Why might this be significant?
- the effect each piece has on you as a reader – and why.

Texts on a theme: Gender, equality and education

The selection of texts that follows can be used as a sample of the kind of material you may find in a theme-based examination paper or a pre-release anthology. The texts, which come from a variety of genres and periods, are all concerned with gender stereotyping and in particular with the roles and education of women.

Activity

> 1 First, read through the selection of texts quite quickly, noting the ideas and arguments each writer puts forward.
> 2 Use any of the approaches from earlier units to make detailed notes on each text and on ways they can be linked, compared or contrasted. For example, you could apply the close reading strategy from Unit 10 to individual texts and then compare your findings as we suggested in Unit 11. Make as many connections and cross-references as you can and don't forget to examine the language.
> 3 Work on some of the questions and activities suggested for particular texts and then attempt the examination practice questions at the end.

Extract A

Bathsua Makin was born around 1612. She became highly accomplished in languages ('Tongues') and mathematics and was appointed to teach Princess Elizabeth, the daughter of King Charles I. She believed firmly in the value of good education for women at a time when it was very unusual. The text that follows is part of an essay that she published in pamphlet form. She uses various tactics here, such as pretending to be a man – in order to be taken seriously – and inventing an imaginary 'objector' around whose 'letter' the essay is structured.

An ESSAY To Revive the Antient Education OF Gentlewomen IN Religion, Manners, Arts & Tongues
WITH An Answer to the Objections against this Way of Education.

To all Ingenious and Vertuous Ladies, more especially to her Highness the Lady MARY, *Eldest Daughter to his Royal Highness the Duke of* YORK.

Custom, when it is inveterate, hath a mighty influence: it hath the force of Nature it self. The Barbarous custom to breed Women low, is grown general amongst us, and hath prevailed so far, that it is verily believed (especially amongst a sort of debauched Sots) that Women are not endued with such Reason, as Men; nor capable of improvement by Education, as they are. It is lookt upon as a monstrous thing, to pretend the contrary. A Learned Woman is thought to be a Comet, that bodes mischief, when ever it appears. To offer to the World the liberal Education of Women is to deface the Image of God in Man, it will make Women so high, and men so low, like Fire in the House-top, it will set the whole world in a Flame.

    These things and worse then these, are commonly talked of, and verily believed by many, who think themselves wise Men: to contradict these is a bold attempt; where the Attempter must expect to meet with much opposition. Therefore, Ladyes, I beg the candid Opinion of your sex, whose Interest I assert. More especially I implore the Favour of your Royal Highness, a Person most

Eminent amongst them, whose Patronage alone will be a sufficient Protection. What I have written is not out of humour to show how much may be said of a trivial thing to little purpose. I verily think, Women were formerly Educated in the knowledge of Arts and Tongues, and by their Education, many did rise to a great height in Learning. Were Women thus Educated now, I am confident the advantage would be very great: The Women would have Honour and Pleasure, their Relations Profit, and the whole Nation Advantage. ...

Were a competent number of Schools erected to Educate Ladyes ingenuously, methinks I see how asham'd Men would be of their Ignorance, and how industrious the next Generation would be to wipe off their Reproach.

I expect to meet with many Scoffes and Taunts from inconsiderate and illiterate Men, that prize their own Lusts and Pleasure more than your Profit and Content. I shall be the less concern'd at these, so long as I am in your favour, and this discourse may be a Weapon in your hands to defend your selves, whilst you endeavour to polish your Souls, that you may glorify God, and answer the end of your Creation, to be meet helps to your Husbands. Let not your Ladiships be offended, that I do not (as some have wittily done) plead for Female Preeminence. To ask too much is the way to be denied all. God hath made the Man the Head, if you be educated and instructed, as I propose, I am sure you will acknowledge it, and be satisfied that you are helps, that your Husbands do consult and advise with you (which if you be wife they will be glad of) and that your Husbands have the casting-Voice, in whose determinations you will acquiesce. That this may be the effect of this Education in all Ladyes that shall attempt it, is the desire of

Your Servant.

To the Reader

I hope I shall not need to beg the patience of Ladyes to peruse this Pamphlet: I have bespoken, and do expect your Patronage; because it is your Cause I plead against an ill custom, pre-judicial to you, which Men will not willingly suffer to be broken. I would desire Men not to prejudge and cast aside this Book upon the sight of the Title. If I have solidly proposed something that may be profitable to Man-kind, let it not be rejected. If this way of Educating ladies should (as its like, it never will) be generally practised, the greatest hurt, that I fore-see, can ensue, is, to put your Sons upon greater diligence to advance themselves in Arts and Languages, that they may be Superior to Women in Parts as well as in Place. This is the great thing I designe. I am a Man my Self, that would not suggest a thing prejudicial to our Sex. To propose Women rivals with us to Learning, will make us court Minerva more heartily, lest they should be more in her Favour. I do verily think this to be the best way to dispell the Clouds of Ignorance, and to stop the Flouds of Debauchery, that the next Generation may be more wise and vertuous than any of their Predecessours. It is an easie matter to quibble and droll upon a subject of this nature, to scoff at Women kept ignorant, on purpose to be made slaves. This savours not at all of a Manly Spirit, to trample upon those that are down. I forbid Scoffing and Scolding. Let any think themselves agrived, and come forth fairly into the Field against this feeble Sex, with solid Arguments to refute what I have asserted, I think I may promise to be their Champion.

SIR,

I have heard you discourse of the Education of Gentlewomen in Arts and Tongues. I wonder any should think of so vain a thing.

Women do not much desire Knowledge; they are of low parts, soft fickle natures, they have other things to do they will not mind if they be once Bookish; The end of Learning is to fit one for publick employment, which Women are not capable of. Women must not speak in the Church, its against custom. Solomon's good House-wife is not commended for Arts and Tongues, but for looking after her Servants; And that which is worst of all, they are of such ill natures, they will abuse their Education, and be so intolerably Proud, there will be no living with them: If all these things could be answered, they would not have leisure.

We send our Sons to School seven years, and yet not above one in five get so much of the Tongues only, so as to keep them, and nothing of Arts.

Girls cannot have more than half the time allotted them. If they were capable, and had time, I cannot imagine what good it would do them. If it would do them good, where should they be Instructed, their converse with Boyes would do them more hurt than all their Learning would do them good.

I have no prejudice against the Sex, but would gladly have a fair answer to these things, or else shall breed up my Daughters as our fore-fathers did.

Sir your Condescension herein will very much oblige,

        Your affectionate Friend.

May 19. 1673.

After this fictional 'letter', in which she presents some of the arguments against women's education that were commonplace at the time, Makin sets about answering them in the main part of her essay, from which the next passage is taken.

Care ought to be taken by us to Educate Women in Learning

... I do not deny but Women ought to be brought up to a comely and decent carriage, to their Needle, to Neatness, to understand all those things that do particularly belong to their Sex. But when these things are competently cared for, and where there are Endowments of Nature and leasure, then higher things ought to be endeavoured after. Meerly to teach Gentlewomen to Frisk and Dance, to paint their Faces, to curl their Hair, to put on a Whisk, to wear gay Clothes, is not truly to adorn, but to adulterate their Bodies; yea, (what is worse) to defile their Souls. This ... turns them to Beasts; whilst their Belly is their God, they become Swine; whilst Lust, they become Goats; and whilst Pride is their God, they become very Devils. Doubtless this under-breeding of Women began amongst Heathen and Barbarous People; it continues with the *Indians*, where they make their Women meer slaves, and wear them out in drudgery ...

Had God Intended Women onely as a finer sort of Cattle, he would not have made them reasonable. Bruits, a few degrees higher than Drils or Monkies, (which the *Indians* use to do many Offices) might have better fitted some mens Lust, Pride, and Pleasure; especially those that desire to keep them ignorant to be tyrranized over.

God intended Woman as a help-meet to Man, in his constant conversation, and in the concerns of his Family and Estate, when he should most need, in sickness, weakness, absence, death, etc. Whilst we neglect to fit them for these things, we renounce God's Blessing, he hath appointed Women for, are ungrateful to him, cruel to them, and injurious to our selves.

Bathsua Makin

Activity

Read through the essay again, making notes on the following:
- the effect of the opening sentences ('inveterate' means 'deep-rooted' or 'long-lasting')
- the tone Makin adopts in the different sections of the text. What response is she expecting from her readers in the opening address? Look particularly at the 'objector's letter'. Has she succeeded in making his a separate 'voice'? Does anything about it give away the fact that it is a fictional device?
- the arguments given on each side of the debate
- Makin's tactics and techniques of persuasion
- the language and imagery she uses to describe women and men

Extract B

The next piece is by the Romantic poet Anna Barbauld (1743–1825). Despite the title and opening lines of her poem, she was not really a campaigner for women's rights, as you will see.

The Rights of Woman

Yes, injured Woman! rise, assert thy right!
Woman! too long degraded, scorned, oppressed;
O born to rule in partial Law's despite,
Resume thy native empire o'er the breast!

Go forth arrayed in panoply divine,
That angel pureness which admits no stain;
Go, bid proud Man his boasted rule resign
And kiss the golden sceptre of thy reign.

Go, gird thyself with grace, collect thy store
Of bright artillery glancing from afar;
Soft melting tones thy thundering cannon's roar,
Blushes and fears thy magazine of war.

Thy rights are empire: urge no meaner claim, –
Felt, not defined, and if debated, lost;
Like sacred mysteries, which withheld from fame,
Shunning discussion, are revered the most.

Try all that wit and art suggest to bend
Of thy imperial foe the stubborn knee;

Make treacherous Man thy subject, not thy friend;
Thou mayst command, but never canst be free.

Awe the licentious and restrain the rude;
Soften the sullen, clear the cloudy brow:
Be, more than princes' gifts, thy favours sued; –
She hazards all, who will the least allow.

But hope not, courted idol of mankind,
On this proud eminence secure to stay;
Subduing and subdued, thou soon shalt find
Thy coldness soften, and thy pride give way.

Then, then, abandon each ambitious thought;
Conquest or rule thy heart shall feeble move,
In Nature's school, by her soft maxims taught
That separate rights are lost in mutual love.

Anna Barbauld

Activity

> Discuss this poem with a partner or small group. Make notes on the following points.
> - What expectations are built up in you by the first three lines of the poem?
> - What is the meaning and effect of line 4? What is the poem really about?
> - What roles does she call on women to play in order to win their 'rights'? What are these 'rights'? Look closely at the imagery used to describe women in relationship to men. List words and images of a Royalty **b** religion **c** war
> - What's love got to do with it ...? What happens in the last two stanzas?
> - What is your response to the poem?
> - How would you connect or contrast it with the previous extract?

Extract C

Most of Virginia Woolf's novels are 'serious', and in her essays she often tackles the issue of the inequality of the sexes. However, in *Orlando*, which she called 'a writer's holiday', she let her imagination run riot and created a character who lives for several centuries and changes sex half way through the book. At this point, not long after she has turned from a man into a woman, Orlando begins to think about 'the penalties and privileges of her position', in other words, to wonder which sex has the better deal. The novel was published in 1928.

Orlando

'Lord,' she thought, when she had recovered from her start, stretching herself out at length under her awning, 'this is a pleasant, lazy way of life, to be sure. But,' she thought, giving her legs a kick, 'these skirts are plaguey things to have about one's heels. Yet the stuff (flowered paduasoy[1]) is the loveliest in the world. Never have I seen my own skin (here she laid her hand on her knee) look to such advantage as now. Could I, however, leap overboard and swim in clothes like these? No! Therefore, I should have to trust to the protection of a blue-jacket.[2] Do I object to that? Now do I?' she wondered, here encountering the first knot in the smooth skein of her argument.

Dinner came before she had untied it, and then it was the Captain himself – Captain Nicholas Benedict Bartolus, a sea captain of distinguished aspect, who did it for her as he helped her to a slice of corned beef.

'A little of the fat, Ma'am?' he asked. 'Let me cut you just the tiniest little slice the size of your finger-nail.' At those words a delicious tremor ran through her frame. Birds sang; the torrents rushed. It recalled the feeling of indescribable pleasure with which she had first seen Sasha, hundreds of years ago. Then she had pursued, now she fled. Which is the greater ecstasy? The man's or the woman's? And are they not perhaps the same? No, she thought, this is the most delicious (thanking the Captain but refusing), to refuse and see him frown. Well, she would, if he wished it, have the very thinnest, smallest sliver in the world. This was the most delicious of all, to yield and see him smile. 'For nothing,' she thought, regaining her couch on deck, and continung the argument, 'is more heavenly, to resist and to yield; to yield and to resist. Surely it throws the spirit into such a rapture as nothing else can. So that I'm not sure,' she continued, 'that I won't throw myself overboard, for the mere pleasure of being rescued by a blue-jacket after all.'

(It must be remembered that she was like a child entering into possession of a pleasaunce or toy-cupboard; her arguments would not commend themselves to mature women, who have had the run of it all their lives.)

'But what used we young fellows in the cockpit of the *Marie Rose* to say about a woman who threw herself overboard for the pleasure of being rescued by a blue-jacket?' she said. 'We had a word for the. Ah! I have it. ...' (But we must omit that word; it was disrespectful in the extreme and passing strange on a lady's lips.) 'Lord! Lord!' she cried again at the conclusion of her thoughts, 'must I then begin to respect the opinion of the other sex, however monstrous I think it? If I wear skirts, if I can't swim, if I have to be rescued by a blue-jacket, by God!' she cried, 'I must!' Upon which a gloom fell over her. Candid by nature, and averse to all kinds of equivocation, to tell lies bored her. It seemed to her a roundabout way of going to work. Yet, she reflected, the flowered paduasoy – the pleasure of being rescued by a blue-jacket – if these were only to be obtained by roundabout ways, roundabout one must go, she supposed. She remembered how, as a young man, she had insisted that women must be obedient, chaste, scented, and exquisitely apparelled. 'Now I shall have to pay in my own person for those desires,' she reflected; 'for women are not (judging by my own short experience of the sex) obedient, chaste, scented, and exquisitely apparelled by nature. They can only attain these graces, without which they may enjoy none of the delights of life, by the most tedious discipline. There's the hairdressing,' she thought, 'that alone will take an hour of my morning; there's looking in the looking-glass another hour; there's staying and lacing; there's washing and powdering; there's changing from silk to lace and from lace to paduasoy; there's being chaste year in, year out....' Here she tossed her foot impatiently, and showed an inch or two of calf. A sailor on the mast, who happened to look down at the moment, started so violently that he missed his footing and only saved himself by the skin of his teeth. 'If the sight of my ankles means death to an honest fellow who, no doubt, has a wife and family to support, I must, in all humanity, keep them covered,' Orlando thought. Yet her legs were among her chiefest beauties. And she fell to thinking what an odd pass we have come to when all a woman's beauty has to be kept covered lest a sailor may fall from a masthead. 'A pox on them!' she said, realizing for the first time what, in other circumstances, she would have been taught as a child, that is to say, the sacred responsibilities of womanhood.

'And that's the last oath I shall ever be able to swear,' she thought; 'once I set foot on English soil. And I shall never be able to crack a man over the head, or tell him he lies in his teeth, or draw my sword and run him through the body, or sit among my peers, or wear a coronet, or walk in procession, or sentence a man to death, or lead an army, or prance down Whitehall on a charger, or wear seventy-two different medals on my breast. All I can do, once I set foot on English soil, is to pour out tea and ask my lords how they like it. "D'you take sugar? D'you take cream?"' And mincing out the words, she was horrified to perceive how low an opinion she was forming of the other sex, the manly, to which it had once been her pride to belong. 'To fall from a masthead,' she thought, 'because you see a woman's ankles; to dress up like a Guy Fawkes and parade the streets, so that women may praise you; to deny a woman teaching lest she may laugh at you; to be the slave of the frailest chit in petticoats, and yet to go about as if you were the Lords of creation – Heavens!' she thought, 'what fools they make of us – what fools we are!'

Virginia Woolf

1 *paduasoy*: silk from Padua, Italy.
2 *blue-jacket*: sailor

Activity

> 1 After reading the passage carefully, discuss and/or make notes on the way Woolf uses humour to make serious points about the respective roles and stereotypes of women and men, and the way relationships between them are traditionally supposed to operate.
> 2 How many ways can you find to connect this with the previous extracts? How does Woolf's approach differ from that of the earlier writers?
> 3 Working alone or with a partner, experiment with writing a parallel piece where a woman has just become a man. You could set this in any time or context that interests you.

Extract D

Fay Weldon's novel *Praxis* was written in the 1970s, when the women's movement was at its most militant and outspoken. It is what can be described as a 'women's world' novel, focusing on the daily lives of women and the issues that affect them most. Here, the heroine looks back to when she and her friends Irma and Colleen were students at Reading University. She has just become involved with Willy, an older student.

Praxis

Willy and Praxis went to bed together between lectures: that, at any rate, was how they described it. They seldom actually reached the bed. No sooner were they inside the door than he would bear down upon her, pressing her on to the floor, table, chair, anywhere, in his urgency ...

'Thank you', he would say: and he was fond of her and she of him: the nakedness of his need touched her: but neither he, nor she herself, seemed to expect a female response in the least equivalent to the male. She never cried out, or thought she should, or knew that women did, or why they would.

She typed Willy's essays though, and found books for him in the library, getting there early so as to be first in the queue when work was set. After Willy's essays were completed and typed, she would then begin on her own. She typed slowly, using only two fingers. It was assumed by both of them that this was the proper distribution of their joint energies. He got A's and she got C's.

'Well and truly snapped up,' said Irma, 'more fool you. It's war, you know. They lose and you win, or vice versa. It's vice versa for you. Mind you, they're all like that in the Humanities Department. They talk virtue and practice vice.'

Irma often got A's, but pretended she got C's. To look at her, as Colleen remarked, you wouldn't think she had a brain in her head, and that was the way Irma wanted it. Irma was looking for a husband. She'd tried to get into Oxford and had failed – there were few places available for women – and so had missed out, she felt, on her chances of marrying a future Prime Minister. She was, perforce, now prepared to settle for an embryo famous novelist, atomic scientist or Nobel prize winner, of the kind who could presumably be found at the lesser provincial universities. Provided, of course, one could spot a winner. Irma was certain she could.

Skirts were narrow and calf-length and split up the back. Irma wiggled her bottom, pouted her orangey-red lips and wriggled out of goodnight kisses and away from groping, futureless hands ...

One week Praxis got an A for her essay, on political establishments in the USA in the eighteenth century, and Willy got a C for his on the same theme. Praxis could not understand why he was so cross, or why he felt obliged to hurt her. But he certainly did ... Praxis, said Willy, was a neurotic, a bore, a rotten cook, and a slow typist.

Praxis reeled, at the sudden presentation of the malice which underlies love; the resentment which interleaves affection between the sexes, of which whe had until that moment no notion. She was shocked; she would not cry. ...

The next day, Willy came round and apologised, and even bought her a half of shandy and paid for it himself. She was vastly relieved. Her main fear had been that she would presently find Willy in the students' bar investing in the gin and lime which would buy him his next term's sex, comfort, company and secretarial services.

Praxis made sure that her next essay was poorly executed and badly presented, and she inserted a few good extra paragraphs of her own composition into Willy's essay while typing it out for him; this time he got a straight A and she a C minus and a sorrowful note from her tutor.

The earlier A had been a flash in the pan, her tutor could only suppose. One of the tantalising little flashes girls in higher education would occasionally display: for the most part flickering dimly and then going out, extinguished by the basic, domestic nature of the female sex, altogether quenched by desire to serve the male. Indeed, the consensus of the college authorities was, not surprisingly, that girls seldom lived up to early promise: were rarely capable of intellectual excellence; seemed to somehow go rotten and fall off before ripening, like plums in a bad season. The extension of equal educational facilities to girls had been a hopeful, and perhaps an inevitable undertaking, but was scarcely justifiable by results. He had hoped it was not true, but was beginning to believe it was.

For Praxis, Willy's A's and her own C's seemed a small price to pay for Willy's protection, Willy's interest, Willy's concern; for the status of having a steady boyfriend.

Fay Weldon

Activity

> **1** Make detailed notes on how Weldon presents her female and male characters.
> **2** In a small group, discuss this view of the relationship between the sexes. What is your response to it? Is it still valid at the beginning of the Twenty-First Century, or have things changed?
> **3** To what extent do we encounter the same issues in the Weldon extract as we did in the earlier texts? What differences are there in her perspective and the way she makes her points?

Sample examination questions

The question that follows illustrates how you might be expected to write about texts on a theme, whether you have studied a pre-release anthology or done your own wide reading.

Activity

> Choose three of the extracts A, B, C, and D. Compare the ways in which these writers treat their subject matter, paying attention to how this has changed over time. You need to consider:
> • language, form and structure
> • the ways writers use different genres to explore their ideas and feelings
> • their attitudes to women and men
> • the tone of the writing and attitude to the reader
> • the influence of the different times of writing

Special Feature: The First World War in Literature

●●●●●●●●●●●●●●●●●●●●●●●●●●●●●●●●●●●

The historical context

The 'Great War' of 1914–1918, one of the greatest catastrophes of modern times, cast a long shadow over Twentieth-Century Europe. This so-called 'war to end wars' did nothing of the kind, but it did bring about profound changes in society, culture and ways of thinking. It is said to have marked the true beginning of the 'modern age'.

You may already have some knowledge of the events of the First World War. If not, you will find it useful to read a straightforward account in an encyclopaedia or textbook, to get to know basic names and dates that are likely to be mentioned in the literary texts you read. Television documentaries or history programmes are also useful. To start you off, here is a helpful summary from Paul Fussell's introduction to *The Bloody Game*, a huge, fascinating anthology of the literature of modern war.

It had all begun in June 1914, when Archduke Francis Ferdinand, heir to the throne of Austria-Hungary, was assassinated in Sarajevo, Bosnia-Herzegovina, by a Serbian patriot fed up with Austrian domination of his country. Austria-Hungary used the occasion to pick a long-desired quarrel with Serbia and to issue an ultimatum that could only produce war. At this point the system of European alliances, negotiated over many decades, had to be honored: Russia came to the aid of Serbia, whereupon Germany jumped in on the side of Austria-Hungary. France then honored her treaty with Russia, Britain hers with France. By October 1914, Turkey had joined the side of Germany and Austria-Hungary (the 'Central Powers'). By the end of the year the notorious trench system was emplaced in Belgium and France, running 400 miles from its northern anchor at the North Sea to its southern end at the Swiss border, while in the east, another front developed along the Russian border with Austria-Hungary. Italy came in on the side of the Allies in 1915, opening a front against Austria. And in April 1917, the United States, exasperated by German sinking of its ships, joined the Allies, although it took many months for an American army to be assembled, supplied, trained, shipped to Europe and installed in the line. The Americans arrived so late in the war that although they fought impressively and were generally credited with supplying the needed weight to win the war, they suffered only about one-tenth the casualties of the British, and more American soldiers died from influenza than from gas and bullets and shells.

Certain features of the First World War made it different from anything that had gone before.

- The sheer **number of casualties**. Over 37 million people died or were wounded.

- War as a **mass activity**. All eligible (male) civilians were called up or conscripted to fight, where previously wars had been fought by professional armies at a distance from civilian life. The first ever air raids – from Zeppelin airships – also brought war much closer to home.

- **Technology.** Machine guns, tanks, barbed wire and poison gas were used for the first time. These new weapons killed indiscriminately, regardless of whether soldiers were 'brave' or not. Enemies did not have to see each other and the personal element of face-to-face combat was removed. It became easier, literally and psychologically, to kill.

- **Trench warfare.** Much of the war was fought in a system of deep, muddy ditches in which soldiers lived, in appalling conditions, for months on end, facing the 'enemy' across fifty yards of 'no man's land'.

- **Gender issues.** Women did not participate directly in the fighting – although some did experience the war at close quarters through serving as army nurses – but the war had a drastic effect on their lives. The loss of so many men left gaps in the workforce and caused an imbalance between the genders. Some women took on roles that had never been open to them before, while many more, who had lost husbands or lovers, had no choice but to remain single.

Writing the war: the literary context

The war occurred at a time when literature flourished and was highly respected, and it prompted a great outpouring of writing of all sorts. Its peculiar horrors have continued to inspire and fascinate authors to the present day.

As well as knowing the 'facts', it is vital that you develop some understanding of how people typically thought and felt about these events, both at the time and afterwards, so that you are able to recognize the recurring themes, ideas and 'motifs' of First World War literature. Here are some things to be aware of.

- The features of First World War combat, mentioned above, are reflected in an increasing sense of **depersonalization**. Soldiers became mere numbers, not individuals. Literary accounts of the **dehumanizing** experience of the trenches became more graphic as the war went on, while contemporary authors like Pat Barker and Sebastian Faulks continue the trend. Look out for language and imagery that reflect this.

- **Dichotomies**   First World War literature is full of starkly contrasted images. The war generated a tendency to see things in 'black and white', in terms of two-sided 'splits' or contrasts, between for example:
  – 'us' and 'them' (the 'enemy')
  – people who fought and people who stayed at home

– soldiers at the front and high-ranking officials who gave their orders from safe places

– men and women – men could not communicate the full horror of their experiences to women who had stayed at home, which caused misunderstanding and resentment

– the horror of war and the comfort of home; the smart restaurants and theatres of London were sometimes no more than seventy miles from the trenches

– the ugliness of the war-torn landscape and the beauty of nature

- **Loss of innocence** or **faith**   In 1914, people were filled with a patriotic fervour and idealism which, with hindsight, appears painfully naive. Young men, susceptible to propaganda, saw the war as a 'big picnic', and dying for their country was regarded as an honour, or a religious duty. By the time the war ended, those that were left felt resigned or cynical. Religion no longer offered consolation, and soldiers had little to rely on except the comradeship they shared. British poetry before and early in the war tended to be lyrical and pastoral, or 'Georgian', extolling nature and idealizing English country life. It is easy to see the contrast between the high-flown rhetoric and religious language used early in the war and the bitter realism, which doesn't mince words, of later writing.

- **Propaganda** and **censorship**   Away from the front, governments and the press – which was heavily censored – continued to present the war to the public in old-fashioned, idealized language. Soldiers were still 'gallant warriors' and horses were 'steeds'. Writers like Siegfried Sassoon and Wilfred Owen wanted to expose this dishonesty, and poetry was a 'safe' way of expressing protest. When Sassoon protested openly in a public statement, he was sent to a mental institution.

- **Language**   Trench warfare generated a language of its own. As well as vocabulary associated with the trenches themselves ('dugouts', 'funk-holes') and the technology of war ('whizz-bangs', 'five-nines'), soldiers had their own codes and euphemisms to describe their activities. Some who were stationed in France also developed a kind of 'pidgin' French.

Writers of the First World War

This is just a selection of those who have written significantly about the war and of the works you may wish to explore in your wider reading.

Writers who experienced the war

Rupert Brooke: Poetry; also letters.
Robert Graves: Memoir *Goodbye to All That*
R.C. Sherriff: Drama *Journey's End*
Wilfred Owen: Poetry; letters.
David Jones: Memoir *In Parenthesis*

Siegfried Sassoon: Poetry; memoirs, especially the semi fictional *Memoirs of an Infantry Officer* and *Sherston's Progress*; diaries.
Ivor Gurney: Poetry; letters.
Erich Maria Remarque: Memoir *All Quiet on the Western Front*
Charles Hamilton Sorley: Poetry
Julian Grenfell: Poetry
Vera Brittain: Memoir *Testament of Youth*; poetry; letters.

More poetry written by women during the war appears in an anthology, *Scars upon my heart* edited by Catherine Reilly.

Later writings

Virginia Woolf: Her novel *Mrs Dalloway* includes a portrait of a shell-shocked soldier attempting to come to terms with his experience and the lack of understanding of the people around him.
Sebastian Faulks: Novel *Birdsong*.
Pat Barker: Novels *Regeneration*, *The Eye in the Door*, *The Ghost Road*; also *Another World*.

Many other authors have written on the war, and their work is included in anthologies, which are a very useful way of seeing the variety of writing produced. The section on First World War literature in Paul Fussell's *The Bloody Game*, already mentioned, is invaluable. For background reading, his study of how the First World War drastically affected society, culture and ways of thinking in the Twentieth Century – *The First World War and Modern Memory* – is also well worth reading.

Activities

1 Create a time-line or diagram to show the main events of the First World War.
2 Do some research about the most significant writers of the First World War. Each member of your group could find out about the life and work of one author. Present your findings to the whole group.
3 Make a glossary or collection of First World War vocabulary. Here is some to get you started. Add to it as you continue to study the period:

Blighty	(slang) England; a minor wound, sufficiently serious to warrant being sent home – to 'Blighty' – but not to cause permanent damage
Bosche	German
duckboards	wooden walkways in the mud
dugout	officers' quarters or command posts in deep holes
five-nine	a type of shell
Huns	Germans (slang)
Jerry	German (slang)

The First World War: a sample anthology

The texts and extracts that follow have been selected to help you start your exploration of First World War literature, and to demonstrate a range of different genres, styles and points of view. You can approach the pieces in various ways.

- Read them as an introduction to the literature of the period.
- Make notes on any or all of them, using the close reading strategy outlined in Unit 10.
- Note the many ways in which the texts can be connected, compared and contrasted.
- Use the questions and activities to explore how these texts reflect the themes and ideas suggested above, and to practise writing about this kind of material.

1 The spirit of 1914

Laurence Binyon's famous poem *For the Fallen* was written very early in the war and is characteristic of the mood of religious, idealized, patriotic fervour.

For the Fallen
(September 1914)

With proud thanksgiving, a mother for her children,
England mourns for her dead across the sea.
Flesh of her flesh they were, spirit of her spirit.
Fallen in the cause of the free.

Solemn the drums thrill: Death august and royal
Sings sorrow up into immortal spheres.
There is music in the midst of desolation
And a glory that shines upon our tears.

They went with songs to the battle, they were young,
Straight of limb, true of eye, steady and aglow.
They were staunch to the end against odds uncounted,
They fell with their faces to the foe.

They shall grow not old, as we that are left grow old:
Age shall not weary them, nor the years condemn.
At the going down of the sun and in the morning
We will remember them.

They mingle not with their laughing comrades again;
They sit no more at familiar tables of home;
They have no lot in our labour of the day-time;
They sleep beyond England's foam.

But where our desires are and our hopes profound,
Felt as a well-spring that is hidden from sight,
To the innermost heart of their own land they are known
As the stars are known to the night.

As the stars that shall be bright when we are dust,
Moving in marches upon the heavenly plain,
As the stars that are starry in the time of our darkness,
To the end, to the end, they remain.

Laurence Binyon

1 Working on your own or with a partner, read the poem carefully and make notes. In particular, think about
  • how England and death are presented in the poem
  • how the soldiers are described in stanza 3
  • the effect of the form and rhythm of the poem
  • the imagery of stars in stanzas 6 and 7
  • how imagery, vocabulary, rhyme, rhythm and sound are used to create the atmosphere or tone of the poem, and to reinforce the message Binyon wishes to convey
  • Binyon's use of 'we' for the voice of the poem
  • whether the ideas in the poem are 'concrete' (real, down to earth) or 'abstract'
2 Use your notes to write a detailed account of the poem. Include your own response to Binyon's view of what it means to die for your country.

2 Letters home

These two letters, in which young officer poets relate some of their experiences to loved ones at home, illustrate the change in attitude that occurred between the excitement of the early months of the war and the disillusionment of the later years, as well as the different personalities of the writers. The first is from Rupert Brooke to his friend Katharine Cox, and was written from a transport ship in the Aegean Sea, between Greece and North Africa. At this stage, he can still describe the experience of war as 'romantic'. In the second letter, Wilfred Owen writes to his mother of the realities of 'Flanders'. Both letters show evidence of the censorship that prevented soldiers from giving away too much about their activities. Neither of these young men survived the war: Rupert Brooke died at sea and was buried on a small Greek island, and Owen was killed only days before the Armistice in 1918.

To KATHARINE COX   *19–24 March [1915]*

Somewhere
(some way from the front)
Dear Ka,
    Your letter of the 3rd of March has just reached me. Fairly quick. There are said to be 80 bags of mail still (parcels, if anything, I suspect) at headquarters

(here). But your letter is the only letter I've had since we sailed. It *is* fun getting letters. Tell people – Dudley and such – to write occasionally. I can't write much. There's very little I *could*, of interest. And that, as a rule, I *mayn't*. This letter is to be censored by the Brigade Chaplain. ... Here three quarters of the day is dullish – routine – and the society is unnatural – over a long period – all men. Anyway, it's nice to hear.

... Yes: this is romantic. (But I won't admit that Flanders isn't.) But I'm afraid I can't tell you most of the romantic things, at present.

My own lot have seen no fighting yet, and very likely won't for months. The only thing that seems almost certain is that one doesn't know from day to day what's to happen. The other day we – some of us – were told that we sailed next day to make a landing. A few thousand of us. Off we stole that night through the phosphorescent Aegean, scribbling farewell letters, and snatching periods of dream-broken, excited sleep. At four we rose, buckled on our panoply[1], hung ourselves with glasses compasses periscopes revolvers food and the rest, and had a stealthy large breakfast. *That* was a mistake. It is ruinous to load up one's belly four or five hours before it expects it: it throws the machinery out of gear for a week. I felt extremely ill the rest of that day.

We paraded in silence, under paling stars, along the sides of the ship. The darkness on the sea was full of scattered flashing lights, hinting at our fellow-transports and the rest. Slowly the day became wan and green and the sea opal. Everyone's face looked drawn and ghastly. *If* we landed, my company was to be the first to land... We made out that we were only a mile or two from a dim shore. I was seized with an agony of remorse that I hadn't taught my platoon a thousand things more energetically and competently. The light grew. The shore looked to be crammed with Fate, and most ominously silent. One man thought he saw a camel through his glasses ...

There were some hours of silence.

About seven someone said 'We're going home.' We dismissed the stokers, who said, quietly, 'When's the next battle?'; and disempanoplied, and had another breakfast. If we were a 'feint', or if it was too rough to land, or, in general, what little part we blindly played, we never knew, and shall not. Still, we did our bit; not ignobly, I trust. We did not see the enemy. We did not fire at them; nor they at us. It seemed improbable they saw us. One of B Company – she was rolling very slightly – was sick on parade. Otherwise no casualties. A notable battle.

All is well. Good-bye.

Rupert

1 *Panoply*: full suit of armour (old-fashioned word; suggests what knights would wear)

To Susan Owen

Friday, 19 January 1917   *2nd Manchester Regiment,*
                                              British Expeditionary Force.

We are now a long way back in a ruined village, all huddled together in a farm. We all sleep in the same room where we eat and try to live. My bed is a hammock of rabbit-wire stuck up beside a great shell hole in the wall. Snow is deep about, and melts through the gaping roof, on to my blanket. We are wretched beyond my previous imagination – but safe.

Last night indeed I had to 'go up' with a party. We got lost in the snow. I went on ahead to scout – foolishly – alone – and when half a mile away from the party, got overtaken by

GAS

It was only tear-gas from a shell, and I got safely back (to the party) in my helmet, with nothing worse than a severe fright! And a few tears, some natural, some unnatural.

Here is an Addition to my List of Wants:

Safety Razor (in my drawer) & Blades

Socks (2 pairs)

6 handkerchiefs

Celluloid Soap Box (Boots)

Cigarette Holder (Bone, 3d. or 6d.)

Paraffin for Hair.

(I can't wash hair and have taken to washing my face with snow.)

Coal, water, candles, accommodation, everything is scarce. We have not always air! When I took my helmet off last night – O Air it was a heavenly thing!

Please thank uncle for his letter, and send the Compass. I scattered abroad some 50 Field Post Cards from the Base, which should bring forth a good harvest of letters. But nothing but a daily one from you will keep me up.

I think Colin might try a weekly letter. And Father?

We have a Gramophone, and so musical does it seem now that I shall never more disparage one. Indeed I can never disparage anything in Blighty again for a long time except certain parvenus living in a street of the same name as you take to go to the Abbey. [*i.e. Westminster.*]

They want to call No Man's Land 'England' because we keep supremacy there.

It is like the eternal place of gnashing of teeth; the Slough of Despond could be contained in one of its crater-holes; the fires of Sodom and Gomorrah could not light a candle to it – to find the way to Babylon the Fallen.

It is pock-marked like a body of foulest disease and its odour is the breath of cancer.

I have not seen any dead. I have done worse. In the dank air I have <u>perceived</u> it, and in the darkness, <u>felt</u>. Those 'Somme Pictures' are the laughing stock of the army – like the trenches on exhibition in Kensington.

No Man's Land under snow is like the face of the moon, chaotic, crater-ridden, uninhabitable, awful, the abode of madness.

To call it 'England'!

... Now I have let myself tell you more facts than I should, in the exuberance of having already done '<u>a Bit</u>.' <u>It is done</u>, and we are all going still farther back for a long time. A long time. The people of England needn't hope. They must agitate. But they are not yet agitated even. Let them imagine 50 strong men trembling as with ague for 50 hours!

Dearer & stronger love than ever. W.E.O.

Activity

> 1 Read the letters carefully, thinking about the following questions:
>   - What are the main topics and concerns of each writer?
>   - In what ways are the letters alike? How do they differ?
>   - What is each writer's attitude to his experience of war?
>   - What are their attitudes to people at home – public figures and/or their family and friends?
>   - How is each letter influenced by the time at which it was written?
>   - How does each writer reveal that his words are subject to censorship?
>   - What evidence can you detect, from the ways they use language, that these two young soldiers are also poets?
> 2 Write as fully as you can about these two letters, examining the similarities and differences between the ways these young men portray their experience of war.

3 'Dulce et decorum est pro patria mori'?

Now look at two poems in which the same writers reveal contrasting attitudes to death in battle. Brooke's five patriotic *Sonnets 1914* won huge popularity early in the war. For Owen, however, exposing the horror and the pity of war is the main concern.

The Dead

Blow out, you bugles, over the rich Dead!
   There's none of these so lonely and poor of old.
   But, dying, has made us rarer gifts than gold.
These laid the world away; poured out the red
Sweet wine of youth; gave up the years to be
   Of work and joy, and that unhoped serene,
   That men call age; and those who would have been,
Their sons, they gave, their immortality.

Blow, Bugles, Blow! They brought us, for our dearth,
   Holiness, lacked so long, and Love, and Pain.
Honour has come back, as a king, to earth,
   And paid his subjects with a royal wage;
And Nobleness walks in our ways again;
   And we have come into our heritage.

Rupert Brooke

Futility

Move him into the sun –
Gently its touch awoke him once,
At home, whipering of fields unsown.
Always it woke him, even in France,
Until this morning and this snow.

If anything might rouse him now
The kind old sun will know.

Think how it wakes the seeds, –
Woke, once, the clays of cold star.
Are limbs, so dear-achieved, are sides,
Full-nerved – still warm – too hard to stir?
Was it for this the clay grew tall?
– O what made fatuous sunbeams toil
To break earth's sleep at all?

Wilfred Owen

Activity　Looking closely at the language and imagery of each poet, write a comparison of their attitudes to death and war.

4 Night in the trenches

Here, a less widely known author, who served as a private rather than an officer, describes the experience of being involved in night-time manoeuvres at the Front. Ivor Gurney was a promising musician and poet who left his studies at the Royal College of Music to serve in the Gloucester Regiment as a private. He had often enjoyed playing the music of Bach, and found it particularly uplifting. His love of the Cotswold scenery of his native county Gloucestershire permeates his work.

Near Vermand was written soon after the war. Gurney later succumbed to mental illness and lived his last fifteen years in an asylum.

Near Vermand

Lying flat on my belly shivering in clutch-frost,
There was time to watch the stars, we had dug in:
Looking eastward over the low ridge; March scurried its blast
At our senses, no use either dying or struggling.
Low woods to left – (Cotswold her spinnies if ever) –
Showed through snow flurries and the clearer star weather,
And nothing but chill and wonder lived in mind; nothing
But loathing and fine beauty, and wet loathed clothing.
Here were thoughts. Cold smothering and fire-desiring,
A day to follow like this or in the digging or wiring.
                              *
Worry in snow flurry and lying flat, flesh the earth loathing.
I was the forward sentry and would be relieved
In a quarter or so, but nothing more better than to crouch
Low in the scraped holes and to have frozen and rocky couch –
To be by desperate home thoughts clutched at, and heart-grieved.

Was I ever there – a lit warm room and Bach, to search out sacred
Meaning; and to find no luck; and to take love as believed?

Ivor Gurney

Activity

> **1** Discuss and make notes on the following points:
> - the way the poet presents the 'dichotomy' or contrast between the natural world – especially the night sky, moon and stars – and the landscape of war
> - the imagery employed
> - the atmosphere, 'feeling', or mood of the poem
>
> **2** Write as fully as you can about the poem and your response to it, exploring how Gurney evokes the experience of night manoevres at the Front.

5 'If you want to find the Sergeant Major ...'

The next two poems deal with the attitudes of soldiers at the Front to the senior officers who commanded them. Though they are very different, they both use irony and shock tactics to get their message across. To understand the impact of Owen's poem fully, you need to remind yourself of the Biblical story of Abraham and Isaac (Old Testament; Genesis, chapters 21 and 22).

The Parable of the Old Man and the Young

So Abram rose, and clave the wood, and went,
And took the fire with him, and a knife.
And as they sojourned both of them together,
Isaac the first-born spake and said, My Father,
Behold the preparations, fire and iron,
But where the lamb for this burnt-offering?
Then Abram bound the youth with belts and straps,
And builded parapets and trenches there,
And stretched forth the knife to slay his son.
When lo! an angel called him out of heaven,
Saying, Lay not thy hand upon the lad,
Neither do anything to him. Behold,
A ram, caught in a thicket by its horns;
Offer the Ram of Pride instead of him.
But the old man would not so, but slew his son,
And half the seed of Europe, one by one.

Wilfred Owen

Base Details

If I were fierce, and bald, and short of breath,
    I'd live with scarlet Majors at the Base,

And speed glum heroes up the line to death.
  You'd see me with my puffy petulant face,
Guzzling and gulping in the best hotel,
  Reading the Roll of Honour. 'Poor young chap,'
I'd say – 'I used to know his father well;
  Yes, we've lost heavily in this last scrap.'
And when the war is done and youth stone dead,
I'd toddle safely home and die – in bed.

Siegfried Sassoon

Activity

> **1** Read the two poems and make notes on
>   • how each is structured
>   • the tone or feeling behind each
>   • the use of irony, satire, and surprise in each
>   • the different styles and ways of using language
> **2** Write an account of how these texts convey the attitude of soldiers on active service towards those who commanded their activities.

6 'Keep the homefires burning?'

Unless they volunteered for active service as nurses or in the women's sections of the army and navy, women were unlikely to have any direct experience of the war. Even then, they could never share the horror of trench warfare. Early in the war, some women felt that the men were having 'adventures' that were denied to them, although this attitude died out as the slaughter progressed. Women who did serve often struggled to combine their new roles with meeting the stereotypical expectations of their families and friends. In this excerpt from her autobiography of the war years, *Testament of Youth*, Vera Brittain explores this feeling of dividing her loyalty between the army and the needs of her middle-class parents.

She had fought long and hard to gain a place at Oxford University, but when her fiance Roland, her brother Edward and their friends had all gone to the Front, Brittain left her studies to become a V.A.D. nurse in an army hospital in London. After Roland was killed on the very day he was due home for Christmas leave, she considered returning to college, but a visit to Oxford convinced her that she should continue nursing until after the war.

Testament of Youth

Back at Camberwell, I found a notice pinned to the board in the dining-hall asking for volunteers for foreign service. Now that Roland was irretrievably gone and my decision about Oxford had finally been made, there seemed to be no reason for withholding my name. It was the logical conclusion, I thought, of service in England, though quite a number of V.A.D.s refused to sign because their parents wouldn't like it, or they were too inexperienced, or had had pneumonia when they were five years old.

Their calm readiness to admit their fears amazed me. Not being composed in even the smallest measure of the stuff of which heroines are made, I was terrified of going abroad – so much publicity was now given to the German submarine campaign that the possibility of being torpedoed was a nightmare to me – but I was even more afraid of acknowledging my cowardice to myself, let alone to others. ... If once I allowed myself to recognise my fear of foreign service, and especially of submarines, all kinds of alarming things that I had survived quite tolerably – such as Zeppelin raids, and pitch-black slum streets, and being alone in a large hut on night-duty – would become impossible.

So I put down my name on the active service list, and never permitted my conscious self to hear the dastardly prayer of my unconscious that when my orders came they might be for anywhere but a hospital ship or the Mediterranean.

*   *   *

The final and worst stage of my refusal to be reconciled to my world after the loss of Roland was precipitated by quite a trivial event.

When the bitter Christmas weeks were over, my parents, for the sake of economy, had moved from the Grand Hotel to a smaller one, where the service was indifferent and the wartime cooking atrocious. As the result of its cold draughtiness, its bad food, and her anxiety over Edward, my mother, in the middle of March, was overcome by an acute species of chill. Believing herself, in sudden panic, to be worse than she was, she wrote begging me to get leave and come down to Brighton and nurse her.

After much difficulty and two or three interviews, I managed to obtain the grudging and sceptical leave of absence granted to V.A.D.s who had sick relatives – always regarded as a form of shirking, since the Army was supposed to be above all but the most vital domestic obligations. When I arrived at the hotel to find that my mother, in more stoical mood, had already struggled out of bed and was in no urgent need of me, I felt that I was perpetrating exactly the deceit of which I had been suspected. Forgetting that parents who had been brought up by their own forebears to regard young women as perpetually at the disposal of husbands or fathers, could hardly be expected to realise that Army discipline – so demonstrably implacable in the case of men – now operated with the same stern rigidity for daughters as for sons, I gave way to an outburst of inconsiderate fury that plunged me back into the depths of despondency from which I had been struggling to climb.

Wretched, remorseful, and still feeling horribly guilty of obtaining leave on false pretences, I stayed in Brighton for the two days that I had demanded. But the episode had pushed my misery to the point of mental crisis, and the first time that I was off duty after returning to Camberwell, I went up to Denmark Hill to try to think out in solitude all the implications of my spasmodic angers, my furious, uncontrolled resentments.

It was a bitter, grey afternoon, and an icy wind drove flurries of snow into my face as I got off the tram and hastened into the hostel. Huddling into a coat in my cheerless cubicle, I watched the snowflakes falling, and wondered how ever I was going to get through the weary remainder of life. I was only at the beginning of my twenties; I might have another forty, perhaps even fifty, years to live. The prospect seemed appalling, and I shuddered with cold and desolation as my numbed fingers wrote in my diary an abject, incoherent confession of self-hatred and despair.

Vera Brittain

Activity

> **1** After reading the passage, discuss these points with a partner or in a small group:
>   • what the passage reveals about the kinds of experiences women had and the roles they were expected to play during the war
>   • how Brittain describes her thoughts and feelings
>   • whether you think there is anything about the content and style of the passage, compared with the other texts you have read, which suggests that women and men write differently about their experiences.
> **2** Write about the extract, exploring how Brittain presents her experiences of loss and confusion.

Sample examination questions

1 'The war began in jubilation and innocence' which was followed by 'an ironic reversal to horror and disillusion.'

Use three or four texts, and any relevant wider reading you have done, as the basis for a discussion of the above quotation.

2 Would you agree that a 'sense of despair verging on the absurd became the dominant tone of the writing that emerged from the First World War'? Write with close reference to three texts and your own wider reading.

3 It has been said of First World War poems that:

'Collapsing so seldom into the hysteria one might think appropriate, they remain conventional in means, and their conventionality doubly emphasizes the awfulness of what they convey.'

Discuss this view with reference to any three poems you have read.

4 Choose three extracts, and by referring to any other material you have read, examine how typical these are, in content and style, of literature from the First World War. Consider:

• language, form and structure
• how the writers use their chosen genres to express their thoughts and feelings
• the writers' attitudes to war
• how the texts are affected by the time at which they were written
• the gender of the writers.

Section III
Approaching Revision and Assessment

14 Different Types of Response

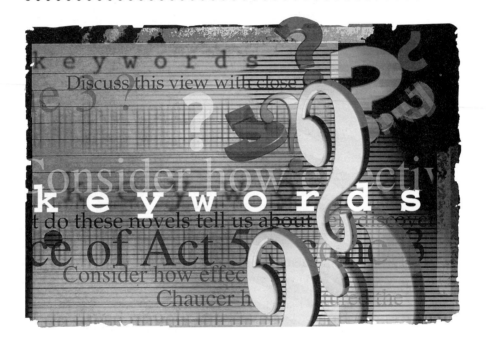

Objectives
- To understand the different question types to be found on AS and A-level English Literature examination papers
- To think about appropriate ways of responding to these question types

Range of question types

In AS and A-level English Literature exams various types of questions are used. These require different approaches and different kinds of responses but ultimately their objective is the same – to allow you to show to the best of your ability your knowledge, understanding, and personal response to the particular text in question.

One way in which you can prepare yourself for the exam is to be fully aware of the various kinds of questions you can be asked to respond to. Exactly what question types you will encounter on your course and in what combination will depend on the specification you are studying. Options do vary considerably from board to board. Here are the question types you will find on AS and A-level Literature papers.

- Texts in context question
- Shakespeare questions
- Comparison questions
- Thematic questions
- Synoptic questions
- 'Unseen' questions

Some examination modules will allow you to take texts into the examination with you, while others are 'closed book' examinations where you are not allowed access to the texts.

Remember that all exam questions are designed to test your ability to show an informed response to the literature in terms of the specific Assessment Objectives set and that a key element in your success will be developing the ability to read the question and understand what it is asking you to do. Whatever part of the exam you are preparing for, it is essential that you spend time looking at past or specimen papers to become completely familiar with the format and phrasing that are commonly used in the questions. Your teacher will probably be able to provide you with specimen and past-paper questions or you can obtain these from the examination board.

Approaching questions

When presented with any question that you have not seen before it is vital that you read it carefully and are totally clear what it is asking of you. One useful way of doing this, as mentioned in Unit 7 (pages 172–173), is to identify the key words and the focus of the question. Circle or underline the key words or phrases and then jot down in a few words what the question is asking you to focus on. For example:

Shakespeare: *Othello*
Remind yourself of the final scene of the play. Examine the ways in which Shakespeare uses language to create his effects in this scene and the ways in which this contributes to the overall impact of the ending of the play.

Keywords   final scene; language; create effects; contributes; overall impact; ending

Chaucer: *The Miller's Tale*
Lines 13–34 describe Nicholas; lines 35–47 describe the carpenter; lines 48–86 describe the carpenter's wife. How does Chaucer, through his descriptive devices in these lines, excite your anticipation for the story that is to follow?

Keywords   descriptive devices; excite; anticipation
Focus   Lines 13–86 leading to the rest of the poem

Activity

> Now practise this technique for yourself. Look at a selection of essay questions on the texts that you have studied. You could take these from past papers or use ones supplied by your teacher. Go through them identifying clearly the key words and the focus of each. It can be useful to work in pairs on this and discuss your ideas with a partner.

Now let us have closer look at some specific question types.

Texts in context

In this kind of question the emphasis is on the context of the reader and the writer and how interpretation of the text changes through time and according to circumstance (see Unit 12).

Here are some examples of the kinds of question that you might encounter on this examination paper.

> Sheridan: *The Rivals*
> What does Sheridan's presentation of character in *The Rivals* tell us about Eighteenth-Century attitudes towards love and marriage?

Or

> Larkin is often praised for his close observation of the human condition in post-war Britain. What have you found interesting about the ways in which this condition is presented in *A Whitsun Wedding*?

Activity

> Think about the text that you are studying for this paper and make up three questions, based on the two examples just given, that would require you to examine the context in which the text was written or the kind of society that it portrays. Now plan answers for these questions.

Shakespeare questions

If you choose an option that requires you to sit an examination on the Shakespeare text you have studied, it is worth noting that the aim of the unit is '... to introduce the candidate to a detailed study of **one** Shakespeare text by offering as much freedom as possible in choice of text and assignment.' This means that the question style on the Shakespeare text can be varied. However, as this is an open book paper, it allows the examiner to ask detailed questions that are focused on a particular part of the text. For example:

> Remind yourself of the opening of *The Taming of the Shrew* (Act I Scene 1 – The Induction). What do you think was Shakespeare's purpose here?

In your answer you should focus on:
- the significance of this 'Induction'
- Sly's words
- The Lord's words
- its relevance to the rest of the play

Alternatively you might get a more general type of question such as:

What is your view of Shakespeare's presentation of Petruchio?

In this kind of paper it is often the practice to offer students one question focusing on a detailed examination of one passage or scene, perhaps with reference to the rest of the play, and one more general question.

Activity

> Think about the Shakespeare text you have studied and create one exam-type question based on a specified passage, and one more general, wide-ranging question. Then plan how you would answer these questions.

Thematic and comparative questions

Some exam modules involve the study of two texts linked by theme. There are many themes to choose from, and this approach produces another style of exam question requiring the comparison of one text with another.

For example, one of the options for Unit 5 of AQA Specification A is 'Visions of the Future', which involves a study of Aldous Huxley's Brave New World and George Orwell's *Nineteen Eighty-four*. Here is one kind of question you might get on these texts:

> Remind yourself of the opening chapters of each novel. Compare and contrast the ways in which each writer creates the sense of a futuristic setting for his story and the success with which the authors establish a distinctive atmosphere in which to develop their ideas.

This kind of question focuses closely on particular parts of the texts, and asks you to undertake a quite specific task, and then to relate the ideas you have explored to the broader idea of the novels' themes.

Other questions can be much more general, as in this one:

> Do these novels have anything important to tell us about possible 'Visions of the Future'?

In this kind of question it is important to remember to give equal weight to both texts. It would be a bad idea to answer the last question by writing three sides on *Nineteen Eighty-four* without mentioning *Brave New World* except for a couple of brief references in the final paragraph. It would also be a poor answer, however, if it devoted a page to one text then a page to the other. A better answer would integrate comments on both texts together and give equal coverage to both.

Sometimes a different approach is adopted, where two texts are studied that are 'linked', perhaps by form, author, or period. Again the questions address both texts, as in this example using *The Duchess of Malfi* and *The Changeling*:

> 'Jacobean dramatists encourage their audience to be too fascinated by the gruesome.'
> How far does your reading of the two plays support this view?

or

Look again at the opening scenes of each play. Draw out at least three ways in which the scenes echo each other and provide the reader with clues about plot development.

Unit 11, Literary Connections, looks in detail at the skills involved in comparing texts.

Synoptic and 'unseen' questions

As part of what is called the 'synoptic' unit in any specification, you will be asked to demonstrate the skills, knowledge and understanding you have developed throughout the course and demonstrate understanding of the connections between the different elements of the subject. This will involve you in close detailed study of texts from a range of periods and genres. In AQA Specification A, the specific materials on which you will answer questions in the exam will not be available until you start the exam itself – in other words, they will be unseen. However, you will know what topic these pieces of writing will be based on. For example, the area of study for examination in 2002 is 'War in Literature' with special emphasis on literature written about and during the First World War. Without reproducing the actual texts it is difficult to give meaningful examples of exam questions involving 'unseen' texts, but perhaps the following will at least give a flavour of the type of thing to expect.

Basing your answer on extract A examine the ways in which Antony is presented by Shakespeare. Do you think Antony is a fool or a hero? Consider the evidence of each of these views in the construction of your own interpretation.

By comparing extracts B, C and D and referring to your own wider reading, examine how effectively these writings convey an impression of The First World War. In your answer you should consider:
- language, form and structure
- the ways in which the writers use the genre of choice to express their thoughts and feelings
- the writers' attitude to war and the society of the time
- the pressures of the time that could have influenced them
- the gender of the writers.

For more examples, see Unit 13, Reading for Meaning.

'Closed Text' and 'Open Book' questions

In your AS or A2 course you will find that some of the units allow you to take your texts into the examination with you while others do not. Very often you will detect a difference in question type depending on whether the exam is 'Closed Book' or 'Open Book'. The essential difference between the two hinges on the fact that the 'Closed Book' style of question does not refer you to a particular part of the text for the good reason that you do not have the text with you in the exam. Sometimes, however, in a 'Closed Book' exam you will find a lengthy passage from the text printed on the exam paper, to allow the examiner to set questions that require close reading and textual analysis. The 'Open Book' question, on the other hand, is very likely to refer you to a part of the text, or ask you to look again at a particular scene, chapter, and so on. But it is worth noting that sometimes 'traditional' question styles can still appear on 'Open Book' papers.

Becoming familiar with the phraseology and formats that are frequently used in such questions, will help you to handle different types in the exam.

'Open Book' type questions

One feature of an 'Open Book' exam is that it allows Chief Examiners to set a much wider range of question types. Very often questions will direct you to a specific section or passage and will ask you about some aspect or aspects of it. These might focus on elements such as use of language, what the chosen section reveals about character, what its dramatic significance or impact might be, etc. Sometimes this kind of question will then ask you to place the passage you have examined within a broader context, as in this question on Hamlet:

> Examine the speech of the Ghost in Act 1 Scene V which begins 'Ay, that incestuous, that adulterate beast,' and ends 'Adieu, adieu, adieu. Remember me.'

> What do you find of interest in the language used here? Go on to discuss the effect which this speech has on Hamlet, comparing his behaviour and language before his meeting with his father's ghost with the way he behaves and speaks immediately afterwards (up to the end of this scene). (AEB 1995)

You will notice that part of the focus of this question involves a detailed look at the kind of language used in the Ghost's speech but then students are asked to compare how Hamlet speaks and behaves before and after seeing his father's ghost.

This is how one second-year A-level English Literature student tackled the question. She produced her answer in one hour working under timed conditions.

Activity | Read this student's response through noting the annotations that draw attention to certain features of her work.

Sets the scene in context, perhaps a little over-long

Here the ghost of Hamlet's father has appeared for the third time on consecutive nights. Previous to this scene the ghost has not spoken, and only the guards and then Horatio have been present. However, Horatio told Hamlet of the appearance and on this third night Hamlet has accompanied the guards and Horatio. When the ghost appeared he beckoned Hamlet and this is where he speaks for the first time. The ghost reveals that since his death he has been suffering in purgatory during the day (because he did not receive absolution before his death) and that he wanders the earth at night.

He also reveals and confirms Hamlet's suspicion, that he has died
unnaturally. This marks a turning point in the plot and is also
crucial in the change we see in Hamlet's character. The ghost then
goes on to reveal that 'The serpent that did sting thy father's life
Now wears his crown'.

Aware of the importance of this speech for the plot...

...and the effect it will have on Hamlet

Focus on the question. Quickly begins to deal with issue of 'language'

The language used by the ghost in the passage reflects the ghost's
feelings towards Claudius and shows Hamlet the extreme villainy
and wickedness of Claudius. The ghost also refers to Claudius and
Gertrude's marriage as 'incestuous' which echoes Hamlet's first
soliloquy and feelings. To fully expose Claudius's wicked character
he tells Hamlet that Claudius 'with the witchcraft of his wit'
seduced Gertrude while she was married to him. Although Hamlet's
father recognizes Gertrude's guilt in the affair and is upset by her
betrayal, he sees Claudius as the ultimate guilty party saying he
used his witchcraft to put a spell over her and with his shameful
lust he seduced her. The ghost realizes that Gertrude will suffer
through her conscience for the affair 'Leave her to heaven, And to
those thorns that in her bosom lodge To prick and sting her'.

Aware of the linguistic link here to the way Hamlet felt even before the appearance of the Ghost

Picks up on a word that is of key significance

Focus on language and effects

The language the ghost uses in describing Gertrude and Claudius's
marriage reflects the disgust he feels about it. He speaks of it as
incestuous and that the royal bed of Denmark is now 'A couch for
Luxury and damned incest'. This echoes all of Hamlet's feelings
seen in the previous scenes and the ghost emphasizes this point by
talking about shameful lust, seduce and traitorous gifts'. The
ghost also is very upset by Gertrude's betrayal morally and also her
desertion of him, 'my most seeming virtuous Queen. What a falling
off was there.'

Maintains focus on language

A little repetitive

Good specific reference to language of the text

However, the ghost's language does imply that although
disappointed and hurt by Gertrude, he does not despise and hate
her, he blames Claudius for all the affair. His referral to Gertrude as
'a shape of heaven', 'a radiant angel' and his contrasting reference
to Claudius as garbage 'adulterate beast' and as a traitor reflects
his true feelings of hate for Claudius and his feelings of
disappointment in Gertrude for being vulnerable enough to be
seduced by the calculating Claudius.

Sustains focus on language

Good awareness of language reflecting attitude

Good point – this awareness of the contrasting attitude to Gertrude/ Claudius

Hamlet's father finally describes his death. In graphic detail he
describes how Claudius poured some poison in his ear while he
was asleep in the orchard and how 'The leprous distillment'
affected his body and 'Thus was (he) sleeping by a brother's hand'.
The ghost makes it perfectly clear that he wants Hamlet to revenge
his death on Claudius but not on Gertrude.

Briefly narrative

Now begins to address second part of question

This speech marks a crucial point where Hamlet's character changes considerably. Before this speech we see that Hamlet is deeply disturbed by his father's death. He is bitter and resentful at Claudius for taking over his father's position so quickly and at the people for accepting their new king so readily. Hamlet is also extremely grief stricken and distraught. This is shown in his first soliloquy by his fragmented language (O God, God', 'Fie on't ah fie', 'Must I remember') This language shows how much turmoil Hamlet feels and how distraught and alone he feels without his father. He also now looks unfavourably on his mother, and appears cynical of all women, (Frailty, thy name is woman', because of the short space of time she has spent grieving. Just like the ghost's speech he mentions (incestuous sheets') showing his irrational state of mind, as although closely related it is not incest, but Hamlet views it with complete disgust. As Hamlet at this point believes his father died by being poisoned by a snake, he seems more troubled by his mother's marriage and the circumstance of her marriage seems to be eating away at him more than his father's death. The isolation that Hamlet feels at this point is reflected in his soliloquy, he is very depressed and suicidal, 'Or that the Everlasting had not fixed His canon 'gainst self slaughter'. Hamlet expresses he wishes he could cease to exist. However, Hamlet's character changes after the ghost's revelations. Hamlet is more devastated and disturbed than before. His language is fragmented again, 'O all you host of heaven! O earth! What else', showing the deep distress and turmoil he feels. However, as well as this Hamlet displays extreme anger at Claudius and his mother (O most pernicious woman') 'damned villain' and he expresses his desire for revenge. Hamlet vows to wipe every other task from his mind and keep his mind on the ghost's 'commandment' for him to get revenge. Although Hamlet is in a more distressed and emotional state, it shows a crucial point where Hamlet forgets all thoughts of suicide and concentrates on the one thing he must obtain – revenge. Although he does not relish his task, it does give Hamlet some objective and motivation and rationalizes his state of mind so he can plan his revenge for his father's death.

The prospect of getting back at Claudius who he loathes appears to excite Hamlet as he cries 'Hillo, ho, ho, boy!'

The speech causes the turning point in Hamlet's character. Distressed, lonely and suicidal, thinking he has nothing left, because even his mother had deserted him, Hamlet is in turmoil, however, the revelations of the ghost and the task he gives him

Awareness of H's state of mind reflected in his language

Again aware of link between language and state of mind

Good assessment of Hamlet's state of mind here

Brief summary – to the point and reflecting on the key ideas

Addresses H's behaviour and language before meeting his father's ghost

Attitude to his mother and the 'incestuous' link

Perceptive points

Now addresses the final part of the question

Good focus on specific detail of language

Yes, H does exhibit a kind of 'excitement'. Interesting comment with textual support changes Hamlet's character drastically. Although still extremely upset and distressed, he becomes excited and appears anxious to start his 'commandment' – the revenge he has to exact on Claudius for his father's murder.

Louise   *Louise shows a great deal of insight here and a good textual grasp in her appreciation of the issues raised by the question. Her exploration of the ideas is confident and focuses well on the implications of language use and its effects using specific details to support her comments though in places these comments could be more clearly expressed. Nevertheless, she has a good overview and relates the speech effectively to what has gone before and what comes after. She rarely paraphrases and displays clear close reading skills.*

Activity

> 1 Choose a text that you have studied as part of your course and create a question based on that text. Your question should:
> - refer to a specific section or passage from the text
> - ask something quite specific which will involve looking in detail at the language used in your chosen passage
> - require a response that relates the selected passage to another part of the text or the text as a whole
>
> 2 When you have finished, exchange questions with a partner and plan an answer to each other's questions. Discuss the plans you make.

Often on an exam paper you will find two questions on a set text and you will have the choice of which one to answer. Usually, one of these questions requires a detailed examination of a section of the text, while the other presents a broader topic involving a consideration of an aspect of the whole play. For example, the question paired with the previous example was this:

> Why cannot Hamlet sweep to his revenge?
> (AEB 1995)

Clearly this question is much wider in range and does not involve the same detailed examination of a passage from the play. This question addresses broader ideas and a good answer would need to be supported by close reference to the text but with references ranging widely across the whole play.

Summary

Here are some examples of the more traditional question types.
- The quotation used as a springboard for the question as in:
  '*Wuthering Heights* remains a popular novel.' What particular aspects of the text make it so, in your view?
- The quotation for discussion as in:
  'Fundamentally, Marlowe is sympathetic to Faustus.' Discuss this view with close reference to the text.
- The 'Consider ...' type of question as in:
  Consider how effectively Chaucer uses descriptive detail in *The Franklin's Tale*.

- The 'comparison' question as in:
  Compare the characters of Nicholas and Absolon and consider the importance of this comparison to the total effect of *The Miller's Tale*. (Note that this also includes a 'consider' question too – really two questions in one and you would need to deal with both parts fully.)

There are many other common ways of phrasing questions: 'To what extent ...', 'Explore the ways ...', 'What impression do you gain ...', 'Do you think ...', etc. All occur frequently.

Although these question types come under the 'traditional' heading, they can also appear within an 'Open Book' type question. For example, the question might direct you to a passage and ask for some close analysis of it and then the second part of the question could be couched in one of the above formats.

Activity

> 1 Gather together as many questions as you can on the texts that you have studied and look carefully at the different ways in which they are worded. Draw up a table or a list to analyse the different forms that the questions take.
> 2 In note form, plan answers for as many questions as you can.

The use of quotation

The question of how much direct quotation to include in an answer is one which students often feel unsure about. In any kind of literature exam lengthy quotation is definitely not advisable. The two key points about quotation are that it should be short and it should be relevant. Only include a quotation when you use it to illustrate a comment or to act as a discussion point. It is important to choose your quotations very carefully – they should not appear to be just 'stuck in' without comment but woven in to the fabric of your writing so as to become an essential part of what you have to say.

When you have the books with you in the exam there is a danger or a temptation to over-quote to illustrate your points. Remember – time is too short to waste on simply copying out of the book. Sometimes students go into the exam having marked what they see as key quotations in their texts and seem determined to use them come what may.

Examiners also often complain that the same few quotations crop up in essay after essay from a particular centre as if students are parroting information from a common set of notes. Obviously, there will be certain quotations that are relevant to a question but it is not likely that there will only be the same three or four! Think for yourself and use the material that best suits the points that you want to make. Then you will be articulating those 'informed, independent opinions and judgements' that the objectives require.

In using quotation and textual support in the exam avoid giving the examiner some kind of instruction such as 'There is some evidence that Jane felt attracted to Rochester at this point (see page 276)' or 'You can see that this is true on page 178' or even worse 'Quote, page 71, lines 212–230'! This kind of blanket reference is of no use whatsoever and certainly will not send the examiner thumbing through the pages of the text to find the sentences you have indicated.

Very short quotations of three or four words are best worked in to the structure of your own sentence. For example:

In this soliloquy Hamlet appears deeply depressed as he considers whether it is better 'To be, or not to be ...' and his mind dwells on what death might hold.

Longer quotations need setting out on a separate line but they should still be worked into the fabric of your argument to form an integrated part of it. Avoid using quotation so that it seems to be just inserted into the text of your essay and detached from the structure of your own writing, as in this example:

> Hamlet thinks that people carry on even though life is painful for them because they are afraid of the unknown and what death might hold.
> 'But that the dread of something after death,
> The undiscovered country, from whose bourn
> No traveller returns, puzzles the will,
> And makes us rather bear those ills we have,
> Than fly to others that we know not of?'

This quotation would be more effective if it were integrated into the essay in a shortened form. As it is, it appears like a 'chunk' of text inserted with no real sense of unity with the student's own words. A more effective use of the material would be:

> Hamlet thinks that people carry on even though life is painful for them because of a
> '... dread of something after death,
> The undiscovered country, from whose bourn
> No traveller returns ...'
> It is this fear that '... makes us rather bear those ills we have' rather than willingly go to others that are unknown.

It is not always necessary to use direct quotation to support your ideas. 'With reference to the text' means just that and it is perfectly possible to refer to the text without quoting verbatim from it. You can explain the significance of a certain comment or draw examples from the text without using direct quotation at all. It is textual reference which supports your argument that matters, not quotation for its own sake. For example, this student makes the same point but without using direct quotation at all:

> Hamlet thinks that people carry on even though life is painful for them because of the fear of what might come after death. It is this fear that drives people to continue with life no matter how hard or painful rather than go into the unknown which might be even worse.

Remember that the whole point of using quotation or textual support is to reinforce a particular point or to support close analysis: in short to add to the overall meaning or relevance of your essay. For more on the effective use of quotation see Unit 8, page 180.

15 Revising Set Texts

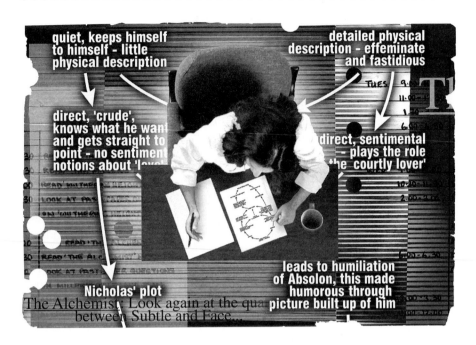

Objectives	• To plan the revision of your set texts
	• To consider approaches to essay planning and working under timed conditions

A key role

Set texts obviously play a key role in your final assessment for either the AS- or A-level course and it is essential that you revise them very carefully in readiness for the exam. Exactly how many texts you have studied will depend on the way the particular course that you are following has been designed by your teacher or lecturer but a total of eight is typical. Your grade will depend on the quality and effectiveness of this preparation and so it is well worth planning how you intend to revise your set texts in good time. This is not a matter that you should put off until the last minute; hasty, inadequate revision could well damage your chances of getting the grade that you want. Students who do well will show an independence of mind which reveals the ability to think for themselves and to think under the pressure of exam conditions. Revision is key to these skills.

Now let us have a look at some of the things that you can do to help revise your set texts and prepare yourself for the exam.

Reading, re-reading, and re-reading again

By this stage you will, no doubt, have read your texts a number of times. This reading and re-reading of the texts is essential to the development of your understanding and appreciation of them.

However, different kinds of reading are appropriate depending on why you are doing the reading. You may read the text quickly before you start to study it in detail. The next time you read it you will probably read it quite slowly and carefully so as to follow the plot carefully, to examine the ways in which the characters emerge, and to get used to the style and language used. Subsequent reads will be different again. You may skim through the text to quickly refresh your memory of the whole thing or you may scan the text looking for particular references to images or ideas. These various readings are extremely important for a number of reasons:

- They help you to become very familiar with the text, not just in terms of the plot (although some books do need to be read several times just to sort out what is happening) but also in terms of picking up on the details of the text. Most texts chosen for AS- and A-level are very complex and every time you read them you notice something new, something that you had not picked up the first, second, or even third time round.
- You tend to come to an understanding of a text over a period of time. You do not just read it, understand it, and that is that, you are ready for the exam. The kinds of texts that you will have encountered in your AS- and A-level studies need thinking about. You need to allow yourself this thinking time in order to reflect on what you have read, to absorb the material, and then return to it again.

Obviously this kind of reading is part of a developmental process which enhances your knowledge and understanding of your set texts and, therefore, it needs to be planned for over a period of time.

Time management

Time is a crucial factor in your revision programme. Building time into your programme for sufficient practice on a variety of tasks is vital. To make sure that you do this, it is advisable to draw up a revision programme to cover the build-up to the final exams. This can be quite loose in the initial stages but the closer you get to the exams, the tighter it needs to be. Make sure that you cover every aspect of assessment that you need to. Here are some basic principles to think about when drawing up your revision programme.

- Be realistic – do not overestimate how much you can get through in a given time. It is far better to start your revision programme earlier than to try to cram everything in at the last minute.
- Make sure that your programme gives the necessary attention to every text. Do not rely on the 'I know that one well enough so I needn't revise it' approach. Often, when you come to revise a text that you studied months before you remember things about it that you had forgotten or that had become hazy.

- Create a balance between revision activities which are reading based and those which involve writing tasks. For example, as well as the various reading activities mentioned on page 310 there are those involving written responses, such as practice on past papers, timed essays, essay planning etc. dealt with in the rest of this unit.
- Build in to your programme some 'time off' to relax. You will not work at your best if you spend all your time studying. Revision is best done with a fresh mind and in relatively short sessions with breaks. You can only take in so much at one sitting. One to two hours at a stretch is enough.

The form that your revision programme takes is up to you. This is part of the revision programme of a student who has already taken Units 1 and 2 of the AS examination on a Monday and has one week before sitting Unit 3. Her texts for Unit 3 are *The Rivals* and *Mean Time*. This revision programme covers the week between the two papers.

DAY	TIME	TASK
TUESDAY	9.00–10.30	Re-read The Rivals
	11.00–12.30	Review The Rivals notes.
	1.30–3.00	Read first five poems of Mean Time.
	6.00–6.30	Look at past-paper questions on The Rivals.
WEDNESDAY	9.00–10.00	Read notes on first five poems of Mean Time.
	10.30–11.30	Read five more poems.
	2.00–3.00	Look at past-paper questions on MT and plan answers.
	6.00–6.30	Look at some past-paper questions on The Rivals and classify into areas.
THURSDAY	2.00–3.30	Look at characters in The Rivals.
	6.00–7.00	Read five more poems from Mean Time.
FRIDAY	9.00–10.30	Study notes on poems read yesterday.
	11.00–12.00	Read notes on themes in The Rivals.
	2.00–3.00	Select suitable question and do timed essay on themes in The Rivals.
	3.30–4.30	Read five more poems from Mean Time.
SATURDAY	DAY OFF	
SUNDAY	2.00–2.30	Look at past questions on Mean Time and plan answers on one not already done.
	2.30–3.30	Watch video of The Rivals.
	4.00–5.00	Look over notes on Sheridan's stylistic technique.

You will have noticed that the student has arranged her time in manageable blocks (an hour-and-a-half at a stretch seems a reasonable maximum) and she has also worked into her programme 'time off' which is important too. She varies her activities so that her revision does not consist simply of reading but writing and watching too, and she allows time to think about questions and ideas.

It is important to keep a good balance between texts. Even if you feel you know a text really well, do not skimp on the revision of it. Remember, though, that a revision programme will need to be flexible in order to cater for the unexpected. Also, beware of wasting too much valuable revision time trying to create the 'perfect programme'.

Activity

> Try planning out a short revision programme for yourself lasting a week. If you are approaching your 'mock' or end-of-year examinations you could make the programme a little longer and actually use it to provide some structure to your revision.

Past-paper and specimen paper questions

As part of your revision programme, try to look at as many questions from past papers as you can. The value of this lies in giving you the flavour of the questions types that Chief Examiners set. Certainly, looking at past-paper questions on your texts will show you a range of topics that questions have focused on in the past and sometimes similar questions do appear again. However, do not learn 'model' answers and hope to be able to use these in the exam. If you come across specimen or model answers, regard them critically and as one possible way of answering but do not take them to be the definitive answer. Remember, in the exam you will be expected to respond using your own ideas and thoughts and examiners can spot immediately if you are parroting a 'model' answer you have learned.

Activity

> Gather as many questions as you can on the texts that you have studied. Draft out a rough essay plan for each of these questions. (Do not spend more than two or three minutes on each plan.)

As well as giving you ideas of the types of things that have been asked about before, looking at past-paper questions will also give you a clear idea of how questions can be worded and the style in which they are presented. (Refer back to Unit 14, pages 297–302 to remind yourself of some of the variations you could encounter.) The more you know in this respect, the less likely you are to be thrown by question phrasing or terminology. Looking at past papers can also show up gaps in your knowledge of a set text and allow you to remedy them.

Timed essays

As we have already mentioned, one of the main worries that students have in terms of answering on their set texts is how they are going to get all their ideas down in forty-five minutes. Certainly one of the most common problems students encounter in AS- and A-level English Literature exams is running out of time. Often this is due to too much time being spent on one question in particular (usually the first one) and so not allowing enough time to deal adequately with the rest of the questions. Sometimes the problem can be cumulative. For example, if you have three hours to answer four questions and you spend an hour on question one and fifty minutes on the next two that will leave you precisely twenty minutes to answer the final question. Running over by a few minutes on each question may not seem too bad but the cumulative effect can be disastrous.

For this reason it is extremely important that you get a good deal of practice writing under timed conditions. You will, no doubt, do some timed pieces in class but there is no reason why you should not practise them at home as well. All you need are some suitable questions, a quiet place, and some time. In one sense it does not even matter if the work is not marked (although obviously you will get even more benefit from it if it is) – what really matters with this is building up your experience of writing against the clock. One thing is certain – the more you practise, the quicker you will get. It really will help you to speed up and it will also show you how much information you can deal with in a specified time and how well you can plan your work under time pressures.

Essay planning

Practice in essay planning should form another key part in your revision process. The best essays are those where students have thought about what they want to say before they actually start to write. By planning essays you can ensure that your argument is coherent and that you are using your knowledge and evidence to best effect. Essays that are not planned can easily drift away from the main point of the question or become rambling and jumbled.

In the exam itself you will have little time to spend on planning; you will feel an in-built pressure to start writing as soon as possible. However, what you do in that first two or three minutes after reading the question can be vital to the success of your answer. Practice in the build-up to the exam will help you to develop the skills to plan quickly and effectively. There are a number of things you can do to help:

- Read the question very carefully and make sure that you understand all parts of it.
- Identify what aspect or aspects of the text the question is about – use the key words approach discussed in Unit 14, page 298 and Unit 7, pages 172–173.

- Analyse the question and note down the key topic areas it deals with.
- Briefly plan how you intend to deal with these areas – this may mean only three or four points each summed up in a few words. The main thing is that you will have a checklist of the points you are going to cover before you begin writing your essay.

Immediately after reading the question it is likely that ideas will whiz through your mind very quickly. If you do not get these down on paper in the form of a rough plan, there is a chance you might miss out an important point in the finished essay.

As well as doing your timed essays it will also be useful preparation if you can do essay plans for as many questions as you can. This will help to get you into the routine of planning but it will also give you the opportunity to think about a wide variety of issues related to your set texts.

There are many ways in which to create your essay plans. The following examples show the different ways in which students planned their response to this question on *The Miller's Tale*:

> Compare and contrast the characters of Nicholas and Absolon and examine their contribution to the overall effect of *The Miller's Tale*.

This is the spider diagram or 'pattern note' approach.

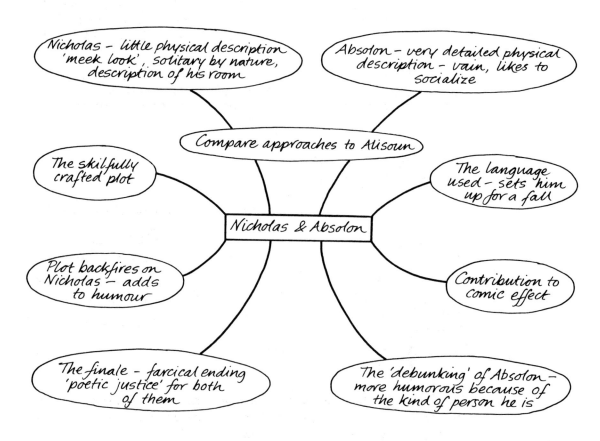

Another student preferred to use the 'flow-diagram' technique.

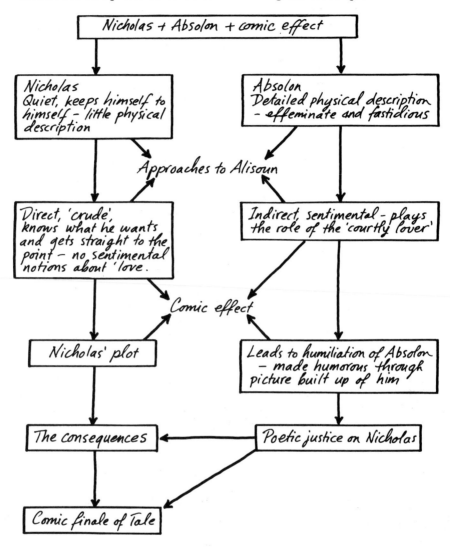

Other students find a straightforward list of points the most helpful, like this.

<u>Nicholas</u>	<u>Absolon</u>	<u>Comic effect</u>
Quiet	Detailed physical description	Through Nicholas' plot
Little physical description	Effeminate and fastidious	Humiliation of Absolon
'Described' through his possessions and interests	'Courtly Lover'	Poetic justice
Direct approach	Inflated opinion of himself	'Slapstick' ending
Clever		

You will need to find the method that suits your way of thinking best and which allows you to plan your work most effectively. For more methods of planning essays in detail see Unit 7, pages 172–178.

Writing your essay

Having completed your plan you are ready to write your essay. Here are some things to bear in mind.

Summary

- Always begin your essay by addressing the question directly. It can be a very useful technique to actually use some of the words of the question in your introduction. Your introduction should give a general indication of your response to the question or summarize the approach you intend to take, perhaps stating your viewpoint. The introduction might consist of your basic essay plan, expanded a little. However, keep the introduction brief and never include biographical information or plot summary.
- An alternative way to begin your essay, and one that can be very effective, is to respond to the question by starting with a strong, perhaps contentious idea that captures the reader's attention immediately. This will launch you straight into points that will support your argument.
- Develop your points clearly using evidence and references to the text to support your ideas.
- Assume that the examiner has read the text you are writing about and knows it extremely well so there is no need to explain the plot or who the characters are.
- Make sure that your essay deals with all parts of the question.
- If your answer is similar to an essay you have written before make sure that you are being relevant at all times and are not simply regurgitating a 'set' answer that is in your mind. Also, avoid rehashing your notes as an answer to a question.
- If you use quotation make sure that it is short and relevant. Do not copy out chunks of the text (see Unit 14, pages 306–308).
- Make sure that your essay has a conclusion in which you sum up your arguments and analysis. It is often through the conclusion that the relevance of certain points you have made is brought into focus and the essay is given a sense of unity and completeness.

Throughout your revision period bear in mind what you will be expected to show in the exam. Some factual knowledge will be required but not much. That you know the 'facts' about a text, the story-line, who the characters are, etc., will be taken as read. The emphasis will be much more on you showing judgement, analysis, sensitivity, and perception in your responses.

16 Coursework Assessment

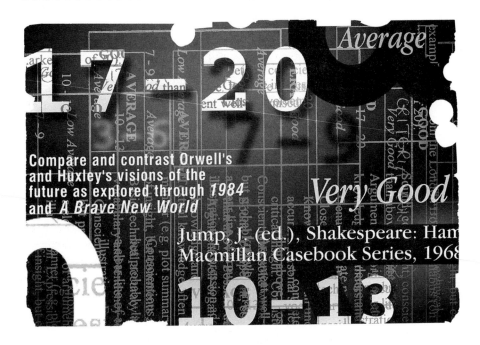

Objectives
- To think about the requirements of written coursework
- To consider the features of coursework titles
- To think about the use of secondary sources and a bibliography

What are the benefits of coursework?

The benefits that the coursework element can bring to a course and the breadth that it can give to your studies are well acknowledged.

Summary

In particular coursework can:
- offer you freedom in terms of choice of texts and more of a say in the nature of the work you undertake
- provide you with opportunities to set your own tasks and goals and pursue particular literary interests, so developing more independence in your learning
- allow you to produce work free of the constraints of exam conditions so that you can present more carefully planned and considered responses and employ the drafting process
- develop skills which will help you perform more effectively in the exams
- help you to gain experience in undertaking research and wider reading in preparation for studying English at degree level

Coursework requirements and assessment

AS and A2 specifications vary in their requirements for coursework. In AQA Specification A, you will have the option to do coursework for Unit 2 of the AS (Shakespeare) and for Unit 5 of the A2 (Literary Connections). For AS your coursework folder should consist of one essay on the Shakespeare play that you have studied and it should be approximately 2000 words in length. For A2 Unit 5 your coursework folder should consist of one essay which compares two texts and should be approximately 2500 words in length.

Coursework tasks

The type of coursework task that you face will depend on a number of factors. If your whole group is studying a particular coursework text, it is likely that you will have little input into the questions that you are set. You will probably be supplied with several appropriate titles and asked to choose one as the basis of your assignment. On the other hand, if you have chosen the text you are writing on, you will probably negotiate an essay title with your teacher. If so, you will need to identify aspects of the text about which you would like to write. Your teacher will discuss these ideas with you and will help you to formulate an essay title that is both suitable and phrased in the right way.

An essential difference between an exam essay and a coursework essay is reflected in the kinds of task set. Examination questions are specifically designed to be answered in forty-five minutes under exam conditions, whereas you might work on a coursework task for several weeks, using various research skills, reference to other writers, and critical works. For this reason, exam questions do not make the best titles for coursework assignments. For example:

How does Pip's childhood shape his adult life in *Great Expectations*?

might work well as an exam question but would be too tightly focused to allow the breadth of treatment that coursework would require you to apply to the text. On the other hand:

An examination of the characters in *Great Expectations*.

might be far too broad, lacking the necessary direction and focus to make a good coursework title. This kind of title could also become simply a catalogue of character studies. The wording and design of the question or essay title needs careful thought to allow you to show your knowledge and understanding of the text to their best effect.

Summary

Working out a suitable title is not easy. Here are some points to avoid.
- Do not mix genres unless you are quite specific in what you are aiming to achieve. For example:

  Hardy's vision of the world as expressed through his poetry and novels.

  This title not only mixes the genres of poetry and novel but does not present clear goals for this comparison. It is also far too broad in its scope.

A better alternative might be:
> An examination of Hardy's view of the world as expressed through three or four of his poems.

- Avoid being over-verbose in the wording of your title. For example:
  > An examination of the ways in which the linguistic fluctuations interrelate with the changing socio-economic position and psychological progression of Celie in *The Color Purple*.

Instead the title might be:
> How are Celie's changing fortunes reflected in the language of *The Color Purple*?

- Avoid titles that involve only description, or plot or character summary. For example:
  > An account of the main characters in Jane Austen's *Emma*.

A title that avoids this would be:
> What techniques does Jane Austen use to bring her characters to life?

- Avoid linking texts with only superficial features in common. For example:
  > Compare George Orwell's *Nineteen Eighty-four* with H. G. Wells' *The Time Machine*.

A better comparison might be:
> Compare and contrast Orwell's and Huxley's visions of the future as explored through *Nineteen Eighty-four* and *A Brave New World*.

Activity

> Devise a coursework essay title for a text or texts that you have studied. Think very carefully about the wording of your title. When you have written it, add a brief description (about 50 words or so) explaining how you would tackle the essay. Include the main ideas you put forward. In a small group, look at your titles individually and discuss their strengths and weaknesses, drawing up a master list of good and bad points.

Potential weaknesses

Overall, examiners report that a high standard of work is produced by students through coursework. However, here are some points that they have highlighted as weaknesses or problem areas in some of the work they have assessed:

- inappropriately framed or worded assignments
- tasks that focus on a general discussion of themes or 'character studies'. These tend to lack interest and focus
- titles that do not require close attention to text and critical judgement
- poor handling of non-fiction work. Often this is limited to a personal response to a newspaper or magazine article. A task based on non-fiction must still generate critical analysis of its literary quality

- too much biographical or historical background is given
- too much narrative retelling of the plot or events

The use of secondary sources

In producing coursework it is important that, if you use secondary sources, you learn how to use and acknowledge them correctly. Clearly, the primary source for the essay is the text that you are studying. The secondary sources are any other materials that help you in your work, such as study aids, critical works, or articles about the text. It can also be useful to 'read around the text' – to learn about the history, the art, and the music of the time. (The Chronology on pages 333–340 provides a starting point for this.)

Certainly use secondary sources if you wish. They can help to broaden your view of the text and show you other ways of looking at it. It does not matter whether you agree or disagree with the views and interpretations you read, because they will all help you to arrive at what you think. Remember that there are rarely right answers as far as literature is concerned – all texts are open to a variety of interpretations. Your view can be 'informed' by other sources but never let other views substitute for your own. Have confidence in your view, develop your own voice, and avoid plagiarism (even accidental) at all costs. If you use secondary source material make sure that you acknowledge every text you have used in the bibliography at the end of your assignment.

The bibliography

In order to acknowledge appropriately the books and other materials that you have read or consulted while writing your coursework essay, it is important to understand the conventions of bibliography writing.

Even if you have read only a part of a particular book or article it should be included in your bibliography. If you have used only the text itself you should still include a bibliography simply consisting of relevant details about the edition used. This will clearly show the examiner that you have used nothing other than the text itself and it will also give information about the particular edition that you have used.

Your bibliography should be arranged in the following format.

The surname of the author (authors listed alphabetically). The initials of the author. The title of the book (underlined) or article (inverted commas) and source. The publisher's name. The date of publication (usually the date when first published).

Here is the bibliography from a student's essay on *Hamlet*:

Bibliography
Baker, S., 'Hamlet's Bloody Thoughts and the Illusion of Inwardness' in
<u>Comparative Drama</u> (Vol. 21. No. 4) Winter, 1987-88
Bradley, A. C., <u>Shakespearean Tragedy</u> Macmillan, 1904
Brooks, J., <u>Hamlet</u> Macmillan Master Guides, 1986
Dover Wilson, J., <u>What Happens in Hamlet</u> Cambridge University Press, 1935
Holderness, G., <u>Hamlet Open Guides to Literature</u> The Open University Press,
1987
Jump, J. (ed.), <u>Shakespeare: Hamlet</u> Macmillan Casebook Series, 1968
Rossiter, A. C., <u>Angel With Horns</u> Longman, 1961

Activity

Using the library, find at least five books or articles on a particular topic, text, or author. Find the information that you would need for a bibliography, such as author, publisher, publication date, etc. and then, using the example above as a guide, order them in the way you would if you were creating a bibliography for a coursework essay.

17 The Examiner's View

Objectives
- To think about the things examiners look for in the work they mark
- To understand how examiners will mark your work

What the examiner looks for

An important person in the process of your assessment at AS or A-level is the examiner who will mark your work. 'Examiners' are not some special breed of people who spend their lives marking examination scripts. For the most part, they are practising teachers who spend their time working with students like yourself and helping them to prepare for exams. However, they can only mark the work that you present them with and the mark that is awarded depends *solely* on its quality. It is a fallacy that one examiner might be more generous with you than another. Careful procedures are followed to ensure that the mark you receive from one examiner is just the same as the mark that you would receive if another assessed your work. Indeed, it is not simply a case of one examiner looking at your work, giving a mark and that is the end of it. Exam scripts go through a number of processes which involve responses being looked at by several people before a final mark is awarded. How well you do is up to you, not the examiner.

It is also worth dispelling another misconception that some students have concerning the role of the examiner. They picture the examiner as some kind of merciless inquisitor who takes delight in catching them out. Examiners, so the thinking goes, look only for negative aspects in responses and ruthlessly dismantle every essay that they come across. Questions are their tools, designed to catch students out.

In fact, nothing could be further from the truth. Questions (as shown in Unit 14) are designed to let you to show your knowledge to the best of your ability. Obviously examiners will not reward qualities which are not present in your responses, but they will look for the positive features in your work. Examiners take far more pleasure and satisfaction in reading good quality material that they can reward than they do in poor work that achieves poor marks. Think of the examiner as an interested and positive audience for your writing, who will award marks fairly and look positively on responses wherever there are positive qualities to be found.

Bearing in mind the large number of students who sit exams in AS- and A-level Literature each year, it is very encouraging that examiners report that very few candidates reveal lack of knowledge, skills, or preparation and very weak answers are extremely uncommon. The vast majority of students show that they have prepared themselves to the best of their abilities for the papers. Having said that, there are aspects of the exam that examiners often comment on as areas that need more careful preparation. We will now go on to consider some of these.

The questions

- Questions are rarely prescriptive. They are 'open' so as to invite you to debate the issues and encourage you to develop informed judgements on the texts and the issues they raise. It is these judgements that the examiner is interested in seeing.
- Where the question contains some kind of proposition you are never expected to simply accept it. Acceptance or rejection needs to be supported with evidence and justification. One criticism frequently made by examiners is when the student simply agrees with or rejects the proposition and then goes on to write about something else entirely. This still happens with worrying regularity.
 The key thing in all this is to read the question and do what it says.

The unseen

- One fairly universal comment from examiners is that students need to improve their close reading skills. The best advice is to get as much practice as you can on this element (see Units 10 and 13 for more on this).
- As part of this practice, examiners recommend that you actively seek out meaning from the unseen texts and pay particular attention to organizing your responses.
 (Of course, these skills can also be applied to the set texts – see below.)

• In tackling the unseen, examiners recommend a detached perspective so that you focus on the text you have been given. It is better not to emphasize biographical or other background knowledge that you might have about the authors, or the complete text, for example.

Set texts

On Chaucer and Shakespeare, in particular, examiners often complain of students giving far too much paraphrase and too little focused commentary and detailed critical appraisal based on close reading (see pages 71–76 for Chaucer and Unit 5, pages 109–149 for Shakespeare).

Technical accuracy

Clearly the ideas that you express in your answers are of primary importance. However, these ideas will be not presented most effectively if your writing suffers from various technical inaccuracies. It is, therefore, crucial that your answers are as free from technical errors as you can make them.

Summary

....

There are several points that examiners draw attention to in this respect.

• **Punctuation**   Ensure that you use full stops, commas, quotation marks, etc. where appropriate. It is easy for these things to be forgotten in the heat of the exam but poor punctuation can mean that your ideas are communicated to the reader less effectively and this may affect your mark.

• **Sentences**   Make sure that you write in sentences and that you avoid long convoluted ones.

• **Paragraphing**   Few candidates fail to use paragraphs at all but examiners often point to the inappropriate use of paragraphs. For example, one-sentence paragraphs should be avoided and so should excessively long paragraphs.

• **Vocabulary**   Try to vary your vocabulary without becoming verbose simply to make your essay sound more 'impressive'.

• **Spelling**   Obviously you should try to make your work free of spelling errors. However, in the heat of writing under exam conditions some errors may well creep in. You should do your best to check each answer as you complete it to keep these to a minimum. If nothing else though, make sure that you are spelling the titles of the texts, the names of the characters, and the names of the authors correctly. It does not give a good impression if, after two years' study, you are still writing about 'Shakespear's play' or 'Jayne Austin's' novel.

• **Cliché, flattery, and slang**   Avoid the use of well-worn phrases such as 'Jane Eyre is a victim of male domination' or 'Lear acts like a man possessed'. Flattery towards authors, such as 'Shakespeare's portrayal of a man in emotional turmoil is second to none' or 'It is clear that Keats is one of the giants of English poetry' are equally to be avoided; so are slang expressions, such as 'Oskar Schindler is a bit of a Del-boy character' or 'Laertes goes ballistic when he hears about his father's death'.

- **Quotation**   If you are using quotation, make sure it is accurate. If you have the book with you in the exam there is really no excuse for misquoting (although it still happens).

   If you are relying on memory, it is very easy to misquote. Perhaps all that needs to be said is that it is better not to use a quotation than to misquote or worse still 'invent' a quote based on a rough idea of how it goes.

Model and prepared answers

Examiners report that they do not see model or prepared answers anywhere near as frequently as they used to in student responses. However, they do still crop up from time to time. There is nothing wrong with reading model answers as long as you use them wisely. They can be useful in presenting you with new ideas but be aware that they present just one way of answering a question. The examiner is interested in what *you* have to say on a particular topic or question, not what the writer of a prepared answer has to say.

Remember that the best responses are those in which your own voice can be heard. The whole point of the course that you are studying is to develop your ability to write confidently, relevantly, and thoughtfully about your ideas on the texts you have studied. Do not be afraid to use the pronoun 'I' occasionally in your essays and do not be afraid to respond genuinely to a question. Attempts to memorize prepared answers never work.

How the examiner will mark your work

Above all, examiners marking AS- or A-level English Literature scripts are trained to be positive and flexible.

The examiners (each of your exam papers is usually marked by a separate examiner) will look for the positive qualities in your work. They will not approach your response with a preconceived idea of an 'ideal answer' but will have an open mind. They will evaluate your efforts to provide an informed personal response to the question.

Answering the question

Examiners are always aware of students who do not read the questions carefully enough. You should make absolutely sure that you are well trained in studying carefully the exact wording of the question (see Unit 14, page 298). Remember that the question should be the whole basis and framework of your answer.

You will remember the Assessment Objectives that we looked at in Unit 1, and in particular Assessment Objectives 2 and 4, which referred to the importance of being able to respond to literary texts with 'knowledge and understanding' and to 'articulate independent opinions and judgements' about them. All the questions that you will encounter on A-level Literature papers have been specifically designed to give you the opportunity to do just this. Obviously your writing must be factually accurate, but the opinions and ideas you explore are up to you (providing you can support them through close reference and analysis of the text).

Length

Examiners do not award marks on the basis of the length of your essay but they will look for what you have achieved in your writing. An essay may appear brief but on closer inspection it may be a succinct and well-argued response and therefore worthy of a high mark. It is true to say, though, that essays that are very short often lack sufficient depth in the development of ideas. On the other hand, over-long essays can become repetitive, rambling and lacking in a coherent structure. Do your best to create a balanced answer.

Descriptors

In addition to the question-specific guidance that examiners are given, Exam Boards also provide them with descriptors to help them to place your essay in a particular mark band. Although these descriptors vary a little in content and format from board to board, all boards are testing the same Assessment Objectives, and in essence they are very similar. Here is an example of the kind of descriptors which examiners may use to help them arrive at an assessment of student responses.

Level 1 Work of the highest standard, showing thorough knowledge, insight, and understanding. The response is conceptualized, explores a wide range of ideas, using appropriate terminology and accurate written expression, focusing on the central elements of language and style. Quotations and references to the text are effectively woven into the fabric of the essay and are used to support close analysis. The response will show a clear mastery of the text and there will be signs of real perception and independent thought.

Level 2 Work displays a clear sense of critical response based on good textual understanding. There is evidence of close reading and awareness of the ways in which the writer's choices of form, structure, and language shape meanings. Analytical skills are used effectively and the response is well-structured and well-expressed.

Level 3 Work reveals knowledge of the text with sound understanding and relevance. Response may be generalized in places but comment is accurate and shows some awareness of implicit meaning. Some of the response may consist of paraphrase and quotation may be over-long but some analysis is apparent. The candidate is clearly aware of the task set and its implications. The expression is adequate to convey the ideas.

Level 4 Work that shows a basic response. It contains some relevant material but consists mainly or entirely of a narrative approach and presents some misreadings. The response does not focus on the question and may contain substantial irrelevant sections, although there could also be some implicit relevance to task. Expression is weak and quotation is over-long, possibly inappropriate, or poorly chosen, and is not commented on or analysed.

Level 5 Work may show some knowledge of the text but the response is thin and there may be frequent misreadings. The work is mainly narrative or descriptive. There are marked weaknesses of expression and any comments made are entirely unsupported. Overall the response fails to engage with the demands of the task.

In reading the descriptors you will see the key features that can bring you success in the exam, and to achieve them there are some basic things you can do. In fact if you are to achieve success there are certain things that you must do. You must make sure that:

- you have read your texts carefully several times
- you know your texts thoroughly
- you are fully aware of the issues, ideas, themes etc. they contain
- you are aware of the stylistic features of the texts you have studied
- you support your ideas and comments effectively

Remember: The secret of success is to be well prepared. Know your material and know what you think about it. If you can show through your responses that you possess '... independent opinions' and you can use these to express 'judgements' that show 'understanding', then you will have every chance of achieving the success that you seek in your studies.

Glossary

• •

Allegory: an allegory is a story or narrative, often told at some length, which has a deeper meaning below the surface. *The Pilgrim's Progress* by John Bunyan is a well-known allegory. A more modern example is George Orwell's *Animal Farm*, which on a surface level is about a group of animals who take over their farm but on a deeper level is an allegory of the Russian Revolution and the shortcomings of Communism.

Alliteration: the repetition of the same consonant sound, especially at the beginning of words. For example, 'Five miles meandering with a mazy motion'. (*Kubla Khan* by S. T. Coleridge)

Allusion: a reference to another event, person, place, or work of literature – the allusion is usually implied rather than explicit and often provides another layer of meaning to what is being said.

Ambiguity: use of language where the meaning is unclear or has two or more possible interpretations or meanings. It could be created through a weakness in the way the writer has expressed himself or herself but often it is used by writers quite deliberately to create layers of meaning in the mind of the reader.

Ambivalence: this indicates more than one possible attitude is being displayed by the writer towards a character, theme, or idea, etc.

Anachronism: something that is historically inaccurate, for example the reference to a clock chiming in Shakespeare's *Julius Caesar*.

Anthropomorphism: the endowment of something that is not human with human characteristics.

Antithesis: contrasting ideas or words that are balanced against each other.

Apostrophe: an interruption in a poem or narrative so that the speaker or writer can address a dead or absent person or particular audience directly.

Archaic: language that is old-fashioned – not completely obsolete but no longer in current modern use.

Assonance: the repetition of similar vowel sounds. For example: 'There must be Gods thrown down and trumpets blown' (*Hyperion* by John Keats). This shows the paired assonance of 'must', 'trum', 'thrown', 'blown'.

Atmosphere: the prevailing mood created by a piece of writing.

Ballad: a narrative poem that tells a story (traditional ballads were songs) usually in a straightforward way. The theme is often tragic or containing a whimsical, supernatural, or fantastical element.

Bathos: an anti-climax or sudden descent from the serious to the ridiculous – sometimes deliberate, sometimes unintentional on the part of the writer.

Blank verse: unrhymed poetry that adheres to a strict pattern in that each line is an iambic pentameter (a ten-syllable line with five stresses). It is close to the rhythm of speech or prose and is used a great deal by many writers including Shakespeare and Milton.

Caesura: a conscious break in a line of poetry (see Unit 3, page 62)

Caricature: a character often described through the exaggeration of a small number of features that he or she possesses.

Catharsis: a purging of the emotions which takes place at the end of a tragedy.

Cliché:	a phrase, idea, or image that has been used so much that is has lost much of its original meaning, impact, and freshness.
Colloquial:	ordinary, everyday speech and language.
Comedy:	originally simply a play or other work which ended happily. Now we use this term to describe something that is funny and which makes us laugh. In literature the comedy is not a necessarily a lightweight form. A play like Measure for Measure, for example, is, for the most part a serious and dark play but as it ends happily, it is described as a comedy.
Conceit:	an elaborate, extended, and sometimes surprising comparison between things that, at first sight, do not have much in common.
Connotation:	an implication or association attached to a word or phrase. A connotation is suggested or felt rather than being explicit.
Consonance:	the repetition of the same consonant sounds in two or more words in which the vowel sounds are different. For example: 'And by his smile, I knew that sullen hall, By his dead smile I knew we stood in Hell' (*Strange Meeting* by Wilfred Owen). Where consonance replaces the rhyme, as here, it is called half-rhyme.
Couplet:	two consecutive lines of verse that rhyme.
Dénouement:	the ending of a play, novel, or drama where 'all is revealed' and the plot is unravelled.
Diction:	the choice of words that a writer makes. Another term for 'vocabulary'.
Didactic:	a work that is intended to preach or teach, often containing a particular moral or political point.
Dramatic monologue:	a poem or prose piece in which a character addresses an audience. Often the monologue is complete in itself as in Alan Bennett's *Talking Heads*.
Elegy:	a meditative poem, usually sad and reflective in nature. Sometimes, though not always, it is concerned with the theme of death.
Empathy:	a feeling on the part of the reader of sharing the particular experience being described by the character or writer.
End stopping:	a verse line with a pause or a stop at the end of it.
Enjambement:	a line of verse that flows on into the next line without a pause.
Epic:	a long narrative poem, written in an elevated style and usually dealing with a heroic theme or story. Homer's *The Iliad* and Milton's *Paradise Lost* are examples of this.
Euphemism:	expressing an unpleasant or unsavoury idea in a less blunt and more pleasant way.
Euphony:	use of pleasant or melodious sounds.
Exemplum:	a story that contains or illustrates a moral point put forward as an 'example'.
Fabilau:	a short comic tale with a bawdy element, akin to the 'dirty story'. Chaucer's *The Miller's Tale* contains strong elements of the fabilau.
Fable:	a short story that presents a clear moral lesson.
Farce:	a play that aims to entertain the audience through absurd and ridiculous characters and action.
Feminine ending:	an extra unstressed syllable at the end of a line of poetry. (Contrast with a stressed syllable, a masculine ending.)
Figurative language:	language that is symbolic or metaphorical and not meant to be taken literally.

Foot:	a group of syllables forming a unit of verse – the basic unit of 'metre'. (See Unit 3, pages 62–64.)
Free verse:	verse written without any fixed structure (either in metre or rhyme).
Genre:	a particular type of writing, e.g. prose, poetry, drama.
Heptameter:	a verse line containing seven feet.
Hexameter:	a verse line containing six feet.
Hyperbole:	deliberate and extravagant exaggeration.
Iamb:	the most common metrical foot in English poetry, consisting of an unstressed syllable followed by a stressed syllable.
Idyll:	a story, often written in verse, usually concerning innocent and rustic characters in rural, idealized surroundings. This form can also deal with more heroic subjects, as in Tennyson's *Idylls of the King*. (See **Pastoral**.)
Imagery:	the use of words to create a picture or 'image' in the mind of the reader. Images can relate to any of the senses, not just sight, but also hearing, taste, touch, and smell. It is often used to refer to the use of descriptive language, particularly to the use of metaphors and similes.
Internal rhyme:	rhyming words within a line rather than at the end of lines.
Inter-textual:	having clear links with other texts through the themes, ideas, or issues which are explored.
Irony:	at its simplest level it means saying one thing while meaning another. It occurs where a word or phrase has one surface meaning but another contradictory, possibly opposite meaning is implied. Irony is frequently confused with sarcasm. Sarcasm is spoken, often relying on tone of voice and is much more blunt than irony.
Lament:	a poem expressing intense grief.
Lyric:	was originally a song performed to the accompaniment of a lyre (an early harp-like instrument) but now it can mean a song-like poem or a short poem expressing personal feeling.
Metaphor:	a comparison of one thing to another in order to make description more vivid. The metaphor actually states that one thing is the other. For example, the simile would be: 'The huge knight stood like an impregnable tower in the ranks of the enemy', whereas the metaphor would be: 'The huge knight was an impregnable tower in the ranks of the enemy'. (See **Simile** and **Personification**.)
Metre:	the regular use of stressed and unstressed syllables in poetry. (See **Foot** and Unit 3, pages 61–64.)
Mock heroic:	a poem that treats trivial subject matter in the grand and elevated style of epic poetry. The effect produced is often satirical, as in Pope's *The Rape of the Lock*.
Monometer:	a verse line consisting of only one metrical foot.
Motif:	a dominant theme, subject or idea which runs through a piece of literature. Often a 'motif' can assume a symbolic importance.
Narrative:	a piece of writing that tells a story.
Octameter:	a verse line consisting of eight feet.
Octave:	the first eight lines of a sonnet.
Ode:	a verse form similar to a lyric but often more lengthy and containing more serious and elevated thoughts.

Onomatopoeia:	the use of words whose sound copies the sound of the thing or process that they describe. On a simple level, words like 'bang', 'hiss', and 'splash' are onomatopoeic but it also has more subtle uses.
Oxymoron:	a figure of speech which joins together words of opposite meanings, e.g. 'the living dead', 'bitter sweet', etc.
Paradox:	a statement that appears contradictory, but when considered more closely is seen to contain a good deal of truth.
Parody:	a work that is written in imitation of another work, very often with the intention of making fun of the original.
Pastoral:	generally literature concerning rural life with idealized settings and rustic characters. Often pastorals are concerned with the lives of shepherds and shepherdesses presented in idyllic and unrealistic ways. (See **Idyll**.)
Pathos:	the effect in literature which makes the reader feel sadness or pity.
Pentameter:	a line of verse containing five feet.
Periphrasis:	a round-about or long-winded way of expressing something.
Personification:	the attribution of human feelings, emotions, or sensations to an inanimate object. Personification is a kind of metaphor where human qualities are given to things or abstract ideas.
Plot:	the sequence of events in a poem, play, novel, or short story that make up the main storyline.
Prose:	any kind of writing which is not verse – usually divided into fiction and non-fiction.
Protagonist:	the main character or speaker in a poem, monologue, play, or story.
Pun:	a play on words that have similar sounds but quite different meanings.
Quatrain:	a stanza of four lines which can have various rhyme schemes.
Refrain:	repetition throughout a poem of a phrase, line, or series of lines as in the 'chorus' of a song.
Rhetoric:	originally the art of speaking and writing in such a way as to persuade an audience to a particular point of view. Now it is often used to imply grand words that have no substance to them. There are a variety of rhetorical devices such as the rhetorical question – a question which does not require an answer as the answer is either obvious or implied in the question itself. (See **Apostrophe**, **Exemplum**.)
Rhyme:	corresponding sounds in words, usually at the end of each line but not always. (See **Internal Rhyme**.)
Rhyme scheme:	the pattern of the rhymes in a poem.
Rhythm:	the 'movement' of the poem as created through the metre and the way that language is stressed within the poem.
Satire:	the highlighting or exposing of human failings or foolishness within a society through ridiculing them. Satire can range from being gentle and light to being extremely biting and bitter in tone, e.g. Swift's *Gulliver's Travels* or *A Modest Proposal* and George Orwell's *Animal Farm*.
Scansion:	the analysis of metrical patterns in poetry. (See Unit 3, pages 61–64.)
Septet:	a seven-line stanza.
Sestet:	the last six lines of a sonnet.
Simile:	a comparison of one thing to another in order to make description more vivid. Similes use the words 'like' or 'as' in this comparison. (See **Metaphor**.)

Soliloquy: a speech in which a character, alone on stage, expresses his or her thoughts and feelings aloud for the benefit of the audience, often in a revealing way.

Sonnet: a fourteen-line poem, usually with ten syllables in each line. There are several ways in which the lines can be organized, but often they consist of an octave and a sestet.

Stanza: the blocks of lines into which a poem is divided. (Sometimes these are, less precisely, referred to as verses, which can lead to confusion as poetry is sometimes called 'verse'.)

Stream of consciousness: a technique in which the writer writes down thoughts and emotions in a 'stream' as they come to mind, without giving order or structure.

Structure: the way that a poem or play or other piece of writing has been put together. This can include the metre pattern, stanza arrangement, and the way the ideas are developed, etc.

Style: the individual way in which a writer has used language to express his or her ideas.

Sub-plot: a secondary storyline in a story or play. Often, as in some Shakespeare plays, the sub-plot can provide some comic relief from the main action, but sub-plots can also relate in quite complex ways to the main plot of a text.

Sub-text: ideas, themes, or issues that are not dealt with overtly by a text but which exist below the surface meaning of it.

Symbol: like images, symbols represent something else. In very simple terms a red rose is often used to symbolize love; distant thunder is often symbolic of approaching trouble. Symbols can be very subtle and multi-layered in their significance.

Syntax: the way in which sentences are structured. Sentences can be structured in different ways to achieve different effects.

Tetrameter: a verse line of four feet.

Theme: the central idea or ideas that the writer explores through a text.

Tone: the tone of a text is created through the combined effects of a number of features, such as diction, syntax, rhythm, etc. The tone is a major factor in establishing the overall impression of the piece of writing.

Trimeter: a verse line consisting of three feet.

Zeugma: a device that joins together two apparently incongruous things by applying a verb or adjective to them which only really applies to one of them, 'Kill the boys and the luggage' (Shakespeare's Henry V).

Chronology

• •

This chronology features texts that are often set for study at A- and AS-level English Literature. Some publication dates given, where no definitive date is known (as in the works of Shakespeare), should be taken as approximate. This is not an exhaustive list of literary works but, along with the social and political landmarks, it is intended to give the flavour of the times.

Significant social and political events		Significant literary events	
1327	Accession of Edward III.		
1337	Beginning of the Hundred Years' War.		
		c.1340	Chaucer born.
1348	First occurrence of Black Death in England.		
		c.1369	Chaucer, *The Book of the Duchess*.
1377	Death of Edward III. Accession of Richard II.	1377	Langland, *Piers Plowman*.
1381	Peasants' Revolt.	c.1381	Chaucer, *House of Fame*.
		c.1385	Chaucer, *The Parlement of Fowles* and *Troilus and Criseyde*.
		1387–1400	Chaucer, *The Canterbury Tales*.
1399	Death of Richard II. Accession of Henry IV (Earl of Bolingbroke).		
		1400	Chaucer dies.
1413	Death of Henry IV. Accession of Henry V.		
1415	Battle of Agincourt.		
1422	Henry dies of fever. Accession of Henry VI.		
1455	First battle in The Wars of the Roses.		
1461	Henry VI put to death. Accession of Edward IV.		
		1474	William Caxton prints first book in English.
1483	Death of Edward. Richard of Gloucester appointed as Protector. Murder of the Princes in the Tower. Accession of Richard of Gloucester as Richard III.		
1485	Richard III defeated at Battle of Bosworth. Succeeded by Henry VII.	1485	Mallory, *Morte D'Arthur*.
		1501	English poet, Thomas Wyatt born.
1503	Da Vinci, the *Mona Lisa*		
1509	Death of Henry VII. Accession of Henry VIII.		
		1510	*Everyman* – English morality play.
1512	Michelangelo finishes work on Sistine Chapel.		
1513	Battle of Flodden.		
		1516	Thomas More, *Utopia*.
1533–5	Henry VIII excommunicated: Acts of Succession and Supremacy. Henry makes himself Head of the Church of England. Thomas More executed.		
1540	Thomas Cromwell executed.		
1547	Death of Henry VIII. Accession of Edward VI.		
1549	The Book of Common Prayer.		
1553	Edward VI dies. Accession of Mary I.		
1558	Death of Mary I. Accession of Elizabeth I.		
1570	Elizabeth excommunicated by Pope Pius V.		
		1572	Ben Jonson and John Donne born.
		1575	Cyril Tourneur born.
1576	London's first playhouse 'The Theatre' opens.		
1577	Drake begins voyage round the world. London's second playhouse, 'The Curtain' opens.	1577	Raphael Holinshed, *Chronicles of England, Scotland and Ireland, a history in 2 volumes* published.
		1579	Edmund Spenser, *The Shepherd's Calender*

Significant social and political events		Significant literary events	
		1581	Sir Philip Sidney, *Astrophil and Stella.*
		1585	Shakespeare leaves Stratford for London.
1588	Spanish Armada defeated.	1588–92	Shakespeare's early plays, including *Henry VI (pts. 1,2 and 3), Richard III, A Comedy of Errors, The Taming of the Shrew, Love's Labour's Lost.*
		1588-92	Marlowe, *Doctor Faustus.*
		1590	Marlowe, *The Jew of Malta.* Spenser, *The Fairie Queene (Books 1–3)*
1592	Plague closes the London theatres.	1592	Thomas Kyd, *The Spanish Tragedy.*
		1593	Marlowe killed in tavern brawl.
		1593–1600	Shakespeare, *Titus Andronicus, Two Gentlemen of Verona, Romeo and Juliet, Henry IV (pts 1 and 2), Richard II, A Midsummer Night's Dream, The Merchant of Venice, Henry V, Much Ado About Nothing.*
1594	Theatres reopen.		
		1596	Spenser, *The Fairie Queene (Books 4–6)*
		1597	Francis Bacon, *Essays.*
		1598	Ben Jonson, *Every Man in His Humour.*
1599	Globe theatre built at Southwark. Shakespeare's plays performed here.		
		1601–4	Shakespeare, *Hamlet, Twelfth Night, All's Well That Ends Well, Measure for Measure, The Merry Wives of Windsor, Troilus and Cressida.*
		1602	Thomas Campion, *Observations in the Art of English Poesie.*
1603	Death of Elizabeth I. Accession of James I.		
1605	The Gunpowder Plot.	1604–8	Shakespeare, *Othello, King Lear, Macbeth, Antony and Cleopatra, Coriolanus.*
		1605	Bacon, *Advancement of Learning.*
1606	Rembrandt born.	1606	Jonson, *Volpone.*
		1608–13	Shakespeare, *Cymbeline, The Winter's Tale, The Tempest.*
		1610	Jonson, *The Alchemist.*
		1611	John Donne, *An Anatomy of the World.*
		1612	John Webster, *The White Devil.*
1613	Globe Theatre burns down.		
1614	Globe re-built.	1614	Webster, *The Duchess of Malfi.*
		1616	Shakespeare dies.
1618	Raleigh executed. The Thirty Years' War begins.		
1624	Frans Hals, *The Laughing Cavalier*		
1625	James I dies. Accession of Charles I.	1625	Drayton, *Nimphidia.*
1629	Dissolution of Parliament.	1629	John Ford, The Lover's Melancholy.
		1633	Donne, *Poems* (posth.) Ford, *'Tis Pity She's a Whore.*
		1634	Milton's *Comus* performed.
		1637	Jonson dies. Milton, *Lycidas.*
1640	Long Parliament summoned.		
1642	Civil War begins. All theatres in England closed by order of the Puritans.		
1649	Trial and execution of Charles I.		
1653	Oliver Cromwell becomes Lord Protector.		
1658	Cromwell dies. Succeeded by his son Richard.	1658	John Dryden, *Heroic Stanzas on Cromwell's Death.*
1660	Charles II restored to throne. Theatres re-open.	1660	Samuel Pepys begins his diary.
1663	Theatre Royal, Drury Lane opens.		

Significant social and political events	Significant literary events
	1664 Dryden, *The Rival Ladies.*
1665 Great Plague of London.	
1666 Great Fire of London.	
	1667 Milton, *Paradise Lost.*
	1669 Last entry in Pepys' diary.
	1670 Dryden appointed historiographer royal and Poet Laureate.
	1671 Aphra Benn, *The Forced Marriage.* Milton, *Paradise Regained.*
	1672 William Wycherley, *Love in a Wood.*
	1674 Milton dies.
1675 Wren begins rebuilding St Paul's Cathedral.	1675 Wycherley, *The Country Wife.*
	1678 Dryden, *All For Love.* John Bunyan, *Pilgrim's Progress. (pt.1)*
	1684 Bunyan, *Pilgrim's Progress (pt.2)*
1685 Charles II dies. Accession of James II. Monmouth invades and is defeated.	
1688 'The Glorious Revolution'. James II flees and William III and Mary succeed.	
	1700 William Congreve, *The Way of the World.*
1701 War of Spanish Succession begins. Act of Settlement provides for Protestant succession of House of Hanover.	
1702 William III dies. Accession of Queen Anne.	
1704 Battle of Blenheim. J. S. Bach writes first cantata.	
	1706 George Farquhar, *The Recruiting Officer.*
1707 Union of England and Scotland.	1707 Farquhar, *The Beaux' Stratagem.*
	1711 *The Spectator* begun by Addison and Steele. Alexander Pope, *Essay on Criticism.*
	1712 Pope, *The Rape of the Lock.*
1713 Peace of Utrecht ends War of Spanish Succession.	
1714 Queen Anne dies and is succeeded by George I.	
1715 Jacobite Rebellion in support of James Edward Stuart, the 'Old Pretender'. Jacobites defeated.	
	1719 Daniel Defoe, *Robinson Crusoe.*
	1722 Defoe, *Moll Flanders, Journal of the Plague Year.*
	1726 Jonathan Swift, *Gulliver's Travels.*
1727 George I dies. George II succeeds.	
	1728 Pope, *The Dunciad.*
	1740 Samuel Richardson, *Pamela.*
	1742 Henry Fielding, *Joseph Andrews.*
1745 Second Jacobite Rebellion led by Charles Edward Stuart, the 'Young Pretender' or 'Bonnie Prince Charlie'.	
1746 After initial success the rebellion is crushed at Battle of Culloden. Charles flees to France.	
	1748 Samuel Richardson, *Clarissa.*
	1749 Fielding, *The History of Tom Jones, a Foundling.*
	1750 Thomas Gray, *Elegy Written in an English Country Church Yard.*
1754 Anglo-French War in North America.	
	1755–73 Dr Samuel Johnson, *Dictionary of the English Language.*
1756 Britain declares war on France. 120 Britons die in 'Black Hole of Calcutta'.	
1760 George II dies. Accession of his grandson, George III.	
	1763 Boswell meets Johnson for first time.
1764 Mozart (age 8) writes his first symphony.	1764 The Literary Club founded in London by Dr Johnson, Burke, Gibbon, Goldsmith, Reynolds, and others.

Significant social and political events		**Significant literary events**	
		1766	Oliver Goldsmith, *The Vicar of Wakefield*.
		1767	Laurence Sterne, *Tristram Shandy*.
		1773	Oliver Goldsmith, *She Stoops to Conquer*.
1775	American Revolution begins. J. M. W. Turner born.	1775	Dr Johnson, *A Journey to the Western Isles of Scotland*. Richard Sheridan, *The Rivals*.
1776	American Declaration of Independence.		
		1777	Sheridan, *The School for Scandal*.
1781	British defeated at Yorktown.		
1783	Britain and America proclaim cessation of hostilities. Peace of Versailles – Britain recognizes independence of the United States.	1783	William Blake, *Poetical Sketches*. George Crabbe, *The Village*.
1784	Invention of steam engine by James Watt.		
		1785	William Cowper, *The Task, John Gilpin*.
1789	The French Revolution. The Bastille falls (14 July), the Declaration of the Rights of Man (4 August).	1789	William Blake, *Songs of Innocence*.
		1790	Robert Burns, *Tam O'Shanter*.
1791	Louis XVI tries to leave France with his family but is caught and returned to Paris.		
1792	Louis is tried. The first guillotine execution in Paris. Massacres take place.		
1793	Louis is executed. 'The Terror' begins. Britain joins war against France. Queen Marie Antoinette executed.		
1794	Habeas Corpus Act suspended in Britain.	1794	Blake, *Songs of Experience*.
		1795	Robert Southey, *Poems*.
1797	Napoleon appointed to command forces for invasion of Britain.	1797	Samuel Taylor Coleridge, *Kubla Khan* (pub. 1816).
1798	French defeated by Nelson at the Battle of the Nile.	1798	Wordsworth and Coleridge, *The Lyrical Ballads*.
1804	Spain declares war on Britain. Napoleon becomes Emperor Napoleon I.		
1805	Combined French and Spanish fleet destroyed by Nelson at Trafalgar.	1805	Scott, *The Lay of the Last Minstrel*.
1807	Abolition of the slave trade in the British Empire.	1807	Lord Byron, *Hours of Idleness*. Charles and Mary Lamb, *Tales From Shakespeare*.
1808	Beethoven's symphonies 5 and 6.	1808	Walter Scott, *Marmion*.
1811	Luddite riots.	1811	Jane Austen, *Sense and Sensibility*.
1812	French retreat from Moscow.	1812	Byron, *Childe Harold's Pilgrimage*.
		1813	Jane Austen, *Pride and Prejudice*.
1814	Napoleon abdicates and is banished to Elba.	1814	Jane Austen, *Mansfield Park*. Walter Scott, *Waverley*. Wordsworth, *The Excursion*.
1815	Napoleon leaves Elba and is defeated by Wellington at Waterloo. Corn Laws are passed.		
		1816	Jane Austen, *Emma*.
		1817	Jane Austen dies.
		1818	Jane Austen, *Northanger Abbey and Persuasion* (posth.).
1819	'Peterloo' massacre in Manchester.	1819	John Keats, *Hyperion* (pub. 1856).
1820	Death of George III. Succeeded by the Prince Regent, George IV.	1820	Keats, *Ode to a Nightingale*. Walter Scott, *Ivanhoe*. P. B. Shelley, *Prometheus Unbound*.
		1821	William Hazlitt, *Table Talk*. P. B. Shelley, *Adonais*. Keats dies.
		1822	P. B. Shelley drowns.
1824	The National Gallery opens.	1824	Byron dies at Missolonghi, in Turko-Greek war.

Significant social and political events	**Significant literary events**
	1824 Walter Scott, *Redgauntlet.*
1825 The Stockton to Darlington railway opens – the first passenger carrying line.	1825 William Hazlitt, *The Spirit of the Age.* *The Diaries of Samuel Pepys* (1633–1703) published.
1829 New Act of Parliament establishes an effective police force in London.	
1830 George IV dies. Succeeded by William IV. Agitation for reform.	1830 Alfred Lord Tennyson, *Poems, Chiefly Lyrical.*
	1836-7 Charles Dickens, *Pickwick Papers* serialized.
1837 Death of William IV. Accession of Queen Victoria.	
1838 Anti-Corn Law League established in Manchester.	1838 Elizabeth Barratt Browning, *The Seraphim and Other Poems.*
1840 Queen Victoria marries Prince Albert. Afghan War ends. Penny postage established.	
1842 Chartist Riots – riots and strikes in industrial areas in North of England.	
	1843 Robert Browning, *A Blot in the Scutcheon.* Dickens, *A Christmas Carol* and *Martin Chuzzlewit.* Tennyson, *Morte d'Arthur, Locksley Hall.*
1844 Turner's 'Rain, Steam and Speed'.	1844 Elizabeth Barratt Browning, *Poems.* W. M. Thackeray, *Barry Lyndon.*
1846 Repeal of Corn Laws. Famine in Ireland.	
1847 Factory Act restricts working day for women and children to ten hours.	1847 Charlotte Brontë, *Jane Eyre.* Emily Brontë, *Wuthering Heights.* Anne Brontë, *Agnes Grey.* W. M. Thackeray, *Vanity Fair.*
	1848 Elizabeth Gaskell, *Mary Barton.*
	1849 Dickens, *David Copperfield.*
	1850 Wordsworth dies.
1851 The Great Exhibition.	1853 Matthew Arnold, *The Scholar Gypsy.* Charlotte Brontë, *Villette*
1854 Crimean War begins. Battles of Alma, Inkerman, and Balaclava.	1854 Charles Kingsley, *Westward Ho!* Tennyson, *The Charge of the Light Brigade.*
1856 Peace of Paris ends Crimean War.	
1857 Indian Mutiny. Siege of Delhi.	1857 Anthony Trollope, *Barchester Towers.*
1858 Peace proclaimed in India.	
	1859 Dickens, *A Tale of Two Cities.* George Eliot, *Adam Bede.* Tennyson, *Idylls of the King.*
	1860 Wilkie Collins, *The Woman in White.* George Eliot, *The Mill on the Floss.*
1861 Prince Albert dies. Start of American Civil War.	1861 Dickens, *Great Expectations.* George Eliot, *Silas Marner.*
1864 Geneva Convention established.	
1865 President Lincoln assassinated. American Civil War ends.	
1867 The Second Reform Act. North America Act establishes dominion of Canada.	
	1868 Wilkie Collins, *The Moonstone.*
1870 Forster's Education Act. Franco-Prussian War.	1870 Dickens dies.
	1871 George Eliot, *Middlemarch.*
	1872 Thomas Hardy, *Under the Greenwood Tree.*
1874 First Impressionist exhibition.	1874 Hardy, *Far From the Madding Crowd.*
	1878 Hardy, *The Return of the Native.* Walter Swinburne, *Poems and Ballads.*
1879 Zulu War. British massacred at Isandhlwana. Public granted unrestricted admission to British Museum.	

Significant social and political events		Significant literary events	
1885	The Mahdi takes Khartoum, General Gordon killed. Benz builds first internal combustion engine for motor car. Radio waves discovered.		
1886	Seurat, *Sunday Afternoon on the Grande Jatte*.	1886	R. L. Stevenson, *Dr Jekyll and Mr Hyde, Kidnapped*.
		1890	Oscar Wilde, *The Picture of Dorian Gray*.
		1891	Hardy, *Tess of the D'Urbervilles*.
		1894	Rudyard Kipling, *The Jungle Book*. George Bernard Shaw, *Arms and the Man*.
1895	X-rays discovered. Marconi invents radio telegraphy. Tchaikovsky, *Swan Lake*.	1895	H. G. Wells, *The Time Machine*. Thomas Hardy, *Jude the Obscure*.
		1896	A. E. Housman, *A Shropshire Lad*.
1897	Victoria's Diamond Jubilee.	1897	H. G. Wells, *The Invisible Man*. W. B. Yeats, *Adoration of the Magi*.
1898	Kitchener wins Battle of Omdurman. Zeppelin builds his airship.	1898	H. G. Wells, *The War of the Worlds*. Hardy, *Wessex Poems*. Oscar Wilde, *The Ballad of Reading Gaol*.
1899–1902	Boer War.	1899	Wilde, *The Importance of Being Ernest*. Rudyard Kipling, *Stalkey and Co.*
1900	Edward Elgar, *Dream of Gerontius*, Puccini, Tosca.		
1901	Queen Victoria dies. Succeeded by her son Edward VII.		
1903	First aeroplane flight.	1902	Joseph Conrad, *Youth*.
		1904	Conrad, *Nostromo*. J. M. Synge, *Riders to the Sea*.
		1906	John Galsworthy, *Man of Property, The Silver Box*.
		1908	E. M. Forster, *A Room With a View*.
1909	Louis Bleriot flies across English Channel.		
1910	Edward VII dies. Accession of George V.	1910	Arnold Bennett, *Clayhanger*. E. M. Forster, *Howards End*. H. G. Wells, *The History of Mr Polly*.
1912	Sinking of Titanic.	1912	J. M. Synge, *Playboy of the Western World*.
		1913	D. H. Lawrence, *Son and Lovers*.
1914–18	The First World War.	1914	James Joyce, *Dubliners*.
		1915	D. H. Lawrence, *The Rainbow*. W. Somerset Maugham, *Of Human Bondage*.
1916	The Easter Rising in Dublin. Battle of the Somme.	1916	Joyce, *Portrait of the Artist as a Young Man*.
1917	Russian Revolution.	1917	T. S. Eliot, *Prufrock and Other Observations*.
1918	Germany surrenders and Armistice signed to end First World War.	1918	Lytton Strachey, *Eminent Victorians*.
1919	First flight across Atlantic by Alcock and Brown.	1919	Hardy, *Collected Poems*.
1921	Irish Free State established.	1921	D. H. Lawrence, *Women in Love*. Shaw, *Heartbreak House*.
		1922	T. S. Eliot, *The Waste Land*. Joyce, *Ulysses*. Katherine Mansfield, *The Garden Party*.
1924	First Labour government elected.	1924	E. M. Forster, *A Passage to India*. Sean O'Casey, *Juno and the Paycock*.
1926	General Strike.	1926	T. E. Lawrence, *Seven Pillars of Wisdom*.
		1927	Virginia Woolf, *To the Lighthouse*.
1929	Salvador Dali joins surrealist group.	1929	Robert Graves, *Goodbye to All That*. Ernest Hemingway, *A Farewell to Arms*.

	Significant social and political events		**Significant literary events**
			J. B. Priestley, *The Good Companions.*
			Erich Maria Remarque, *All Quiet on the Western Front.*
			R. C. Sherriff, *Journey's End.*
1930	World economic depression.	1930	W. H. Auden, *Poems.*
			Noel Coward, *Private Lives.*
			T. S. Eliot, *Ash Wednesday.*
1932	Shakespeare Memorial Theatre opens in Stratford-upon-Avon.		
		1932	Aldous Huxley, *Brave New World.*
1933	Hitler becomes Chancellor of Germany. The first concentration camps erected by Nazis.		
		1934	Graves, *I Claudius,* and *Claudius the God.*
		1935	T. S. Eliot, *Murder in the Cathedral.*
1936	Spanish Civil War. George V dies. Succeeded by his son Edward VIII. Edward abdicates and is succeeded by his brother, George VI.		
1937	Picasso, *Guernica.*		
1938	Germany mobilizes forces and occupies Sudetenland. Munich Agreement.		
1939	Spanish Civil War ends. Germany invades Poland and Britain and France declare war. Second World War begins.	1939	Joyce, *Finnegan's Wake.* John Steinbeck, *Grapes of Wrath.*
1940	British Army retreats from Dunkirk. Battle of Britain.	1940	Graham Greene, *The Power and the Glory.* Hemingway, *For Whom the Bell Tolls.*
1941	Japanese bomb Pearl Harbour. US enters war.	1941	Noel Coward, *Blithe Spirit.*
1944	D-Day landings in Normandy.	1944	H. E. Bates, *Fair Stood the Wind for France.* T. S. Eliot, *Four Quartets.*
1945	Germany surrenders, ending war in Europe. Japan surrenders, Second World War ends.	1945	Evelyn Waugh, *Brideshead Revisited.* John Betjeman, *New Bats in Old Belfries.* George Orwell, *Animal Farm.*
1946	Coal industry nationalized. The National Health Service founded.	1946	Arthur Miller, *All My Sons.* Eugene O'Neill, *The Iceman Cometh.* Terence Rattigan, *The Winslow Boy.* J. B. Priestley, *An Inspector Calls.*
1947	Independence of India and Pakistan.	1947	Tennessee Williams, *A Streetcar Named Desire.*
		1949	T. S. Eliot, *The Cocktail Party.* Miller, *Death of a Salesman.* Orwell, *Nineteen Eighty-four.*
1950	Britain recognizes Israel. North Korea invades South Korea.	1950	Christopher Fry, *The Lady's Not For Burning.*
		1951	J. D. Salinger, *The Catcher in the Rye.* John Wyndham, *The Day of the Triffids.*
1952	Churchill announces that Britain has produced an atomic bomb. King George VI dies and is succeeded by his daughter Queen Elizabeth II.	1952	Dylan Thomas, *Collected Poems.* Samuel Beckett, *Waiting for Godot.*
1953	Korean War ends.	1953	Miller, *The Crucible.*
		1954	Kingsley Amis, *Lucky Jim.* William Golding, *Lord of the Flies.* Dylan Thomas, *Under Milk Wood.*
		1955	Philip Larkin, *The Less Deceived.*
1956	Egypt nationalizes Suez Canal. Attempted intervention by Britain, France, and Israel.	1956	John Osborne, *Look Back in Anger.* Angus Wilson, *Anglo-Saxon Attitudes.*

Significant social and political events		Significant literary events	
		1957	Ted Hughes, *The Hawk in the Rain.* Jack Kerouac, *On the Road.* Beckett, *Endgame.* Osborne, *The Entertainer.*
		1958	Truman Capote, *Breakfast at Tiffany's.* Harold Pinter, *The Birthday Party.* Iris Murdoch, *The Bell.*
		1959	Colin MacInnes, *Absolute Beginners.*
		1960	Robert Bolt, *A Man For All Seasons.* Harper Lee, *To Kill a Mockingbird.* Pinter, *The Caretaker.*
1961	Attempted invasion of Cuba – 'Bay of Pigs' fiasco.	1961	Joseph Heller, *Catch 22.* Greene, *A Burnt-Out Case.*
1962	Cuban Missile Crisis.	1962	Edward Albee, *Who's Afraid of Virginia Woolf?*
1963	President Kennedy assassinated.	1963	Sylvia Plath, *The Bell Jar.* Margaret Drabble, *A Summer Birdcage.* Iris Murdoch, *The Unicorn.*
1964	US aircraft attack North Vietnamese bases.	1964	Peter Schaffer, *The Royal Hunt of the Sun.* Larkin, *The Whitsun Weddings.*
1965	Churchill dies.		
		1966	Jean Rhys, *Wide Sargasso Sea.*
1967	Homosexuality and abortion legalized.	1967	Angela Carter, *The Magic Toyshop.*
1969	'Troubles' in Northern Ireland. British troops sent in. Abolition of capital punishment.	1969	Margaret Atwood, *The Edible Woman.*
			John Fowles, *The French Lieutenant's Woman.*
1970	'Voting age' reduced from 21 to 18.	1970	Hughes, *Crow.*
1973	Britain joins European Economic Community.	1973	Schaffer, *Equus.* Martin Amis, *The Rachel Papers.*
		1974	Larkin, *High Windows.* W. H. Auden, *Thank You Fog: Last Poems.*
1975	South Vietnam surrenders to North Vietnam. US withdrawal and end of Vietnam War.	1975	Malcolm Bradbury, *The History Man.*
1979	First direct election to European Parliament.	1977	Paul Scott, *Staying On.*
		1980	Golding, *Rites of Passage.*
1981	Wedding of HRH the Prince of Wales and Lady Diana Spencer.		
1982	The Falklands War.	1982	Thomas Keneally, *Schindler's Ark.* Paul Theroux, *The Mosquito Coast.*
		1983	Susan Hill, *The Woman in Black.*
1984	Worldwide reaction to famine in Ethiopia – 'Band Aid'.	1984	J. G. Ballard, *Empire of the Sun.* Anita Brookner, *Hotel du Lac.* Angela Carter, *Nights at the Circus.* Iain Banks, *The Wasp Factory.*
		1987	Alan Bennett, *Talking Heads.* Toni Morrison, *The Beloved.*
		1989	Kazuo Ishiguro, *The Remains of the Day.* Martin Amis, *London Fields.*
1990	Reunification of Germany. Iraq invades Kuwait.	1990	A. S. Byatt, *Possession.* Anita Brookner, *Brief Lives.*
		1991	Susan Hill, *Air and Angels.*
		1992	Michael Ondaatje, *The English Patient.* Adam Thorpe, *Ulverton.* Banks, *The Crow Road.*
		1993	John Banville, *Ghosts.* A. N. Wilson, *The Vicar of Sorrows.*
1994	Opening of Channel Tunnel.	1994	Margaret Atwood, *The Robber Bride.* Bennett, *Writing Home.* Anita Brookner, *A Private View.*

Index